Cases on Cross-Cultural Counseling Strategies

Bonnie C. King
Midwestern State University, USA

Tiffany A. Stewart
Midwestern State University, USA

A volume in the Advances in Human Services and Public Health (AHSPH) Book Series

IGI Global
DISSEMINATOR OF KNOWLEDGE

Published in the United States of America by
IGI Global
Medical Information Science Reference (an imprint of IGI Global)
701 E. Chocolate Avenue
Hershey PA, USA 17033
Tel: 717-533-8845
Fax: 717-533-8661
E-mail: cust@igi-global.com
Web site: http://www.igi-global.com

Library of Congress Cataloging-in-Publication Data

Names: King, Bonnie C., 1984- editor. | Stewart, Tiffany A., 1974- editor.
Title: Cases on cross-cultural counseling strategies / Bonnie C. King and Tiffany A. Stewart, editors.
Description: Hershey PA : Medical Information Science Reference, [2020] | Includes bibliographical references.
Identifiers: LCCN 2019015424| ISBN 9781799800224 (hardcover) | ISBN 9781799800248 (ebook)
Subjects: | MESH: Counseling--methods | Culturally Competent Care | Social Justice | Cultural Diversity | Case Reports
Classification: LCC RC466 | NLM WM 40 | DDC 362.1/04256--dc23 LC record available at https://lccn.loc.gov/2019015424

This book is published in the IGI Global book series Advances in Human Services and Public Health (AHSPH) (ISSN: 2475-6571; eISSN: 2475-658X)

British Cataloguing in Publication Data
A Cataloguing in Publication record for this book is available from the British Library.

All work contributed to this book is new, previously-unpublished material.
The views expressed in this book are those of the authors, but not necessarily of the publisher.

For electronic access to this publication, please contact: eresources@igi-global.com.

Advances in Human Services and Public Health (AHSPH) Book Series

ISSN:2475-6571
EISSN:2475-658X

Editor-in-Chief: Jennifer Martin, RMIT University, Australia

MISSION

The well-being of the general public should be a primary concern for any modern civilization. Ongoing research in the field of human services and public healthcare is necessary to evaluate, manage, and respond to the health and social needs of the global population.

The **Advances in Human Services and Public Health (AHSPH)** book series aims to publish high-quality reference publications focused on the latest methodologies, tools, issues, and strategies for managing the health and social welfare of the public. The AHSPH book series will be especially relevant for healthcare professionals, policy makers, government officials, and students seeking the latest research in this field.

COVERAGE

- Public Funding
- Assistance Programs
- Medicare and Medicaid
- Youth Development
- Social Work
- Public Welfare
- Social Welfare Policy
- Domestic Violence
- Healthcare Reform
- Health policy

IGI Global is currently accepting manuscripts for publication within this series. To submit a proposal for a volume in this series, please contact our Acquisition Editors at Acquisitions@igi-global.com or visit: http://www.igi-global.com/publish/.

The Advances in Human Services and Public Health (AHSPH) Book Series (ISSN 2475-6571) is published by IGI Global, 701 E. Chocolate Avenue, Hershey, PA 17033-1240, USA, www.igi-global.com. This series is composed of titles available for purchase individually; each title is edited to be contextually exclusive from any other title within the series. For pricing and ordering information please visit http://www.igi-global.com/book-series/advances-human-services-public-health/102256. Postmaster: Send all address changes to above address.

Titles in this Series

For a list of additional titles in this series, please visit:
https://www.igi-global.com/book-series/advances-human-services-public-health/102256

Environmental Exposures and Human Health Challenges
Paraskevi Papadopoulou (Deree – The American College of Greece, Greece) Christina Marouli (Deree – The American College of Greece, Greece) and Anastasia Misseyanni (Deree – The American College of Greec, Greece)
Medical Information Science Reference • ©2019 • 449pp • H/C (ISBN: 9781522576358) • US $255.00

Forecasting and Managing Risk in the Health and Safety Sectors
Luisa Dall'Acqua (Scientific Lyceum TCO, Italy & University of Bologa, Italy)
Medical Information Science Reference • ©2019 • 304pp • H/C (ISBN: 9781522579038) • US $245.00

Psycho-Socio-Physical Dimensions of Adolescent Health Management Emerging Research and Opportunities
Sapna Nanda (Panjab University, India)
Medical Information Science Reference • ©2019 • 202pp • H/C (ISBN: 9781522573845) • US $195.00

Mental Health Policy, Practice, and Service Accessibility in Contemporary Society
Jennifer M. Martin (Swinburne University, Australia)
Medical Information Science Reference • ©2019 • 323pp • H/C (ISBN: 9781522574026) • US $245.00

Socio-Cultural Influences on Teenage Pregnancy and Contemporary Prevention Measures
Devi Akella (Albany State University, USA)
Information Science Reference • ©2019 • 349pp • H/C (ISBN: 9781522561088) • US $195.00

For an entire list of titles in this series, please visit:
https://www.igi-global.com/book-series/advances-human-services-public-health/102256

IGI Global
DISSEMINATOR OF KNOWLEDGE

701 East Chocolate Avenue, Hershey, PA 17033, USA
Tel: 717-533-8845 x100 • Fax: 717-533-8661
E-Mail: cust@igi-global.com • www.igi-global.com

Table of Contents

Detailed Table of Contents

This case study examines the life of Rose, a 17-year-old junior attending a public high school in a southeastern city. In the state where Rose resides, the year of "aging-out" of the foster care system is 18-years-old. With the age of 18 being such a pivotal year, Rose must not only think about her potential post-secondary options, but her ability to achieve adult self-sufficiency at such a young age as well. With no supports, this proves to be a daunting task for Rose. It becomes Rose's thorn. This chapter will explore the career and college readiness self-efficacy of Rose as she navigates her post-secondary options, builds her support networks, and discovers resources for adolescents aging out of the foster care system via her work with Dr. Williams, creator and counselor of the Students That Are Reaching Success (S.T.A.R.S.) program. Results from Rose's participation in the program will be shared and implications for counselors working with adolescents aging out of the foster care system will be reviewed.

Lucia is a Latina first-generation college student (FGCS) attending a predominantly white institution, a state university in her hometown, located in a large metropolitan city in the Southern United States. While in her sophomore year, Lucia accessed counseling services on her campus to discuss having difficultly balancing school, work, and home responsibilities. In this chapter, the author discussed the challenges experienced by Latinx FGCS along with the strengths they bring to college settings. In addition, the author utilized the case study of Lucia to discuss her counseling approach for helping Latinx FGCS navigate the terrains of higher education.

This chapter will focus on an underrepresented student in STEM Charlotte and the utility of Acceptance and Commitment Therapy (ACT) and how African-American college students' access to STEM careers remains low with representation of eight percent in varied STEM fields by Georgetown University Center on Education and Workforce Analysis. This chapter highlights psychological flexibility in ACT in connection with counseling an African-American female, and first-generation college student in STEM who has academic, financial, emotional, and familial stressors. A multicultural and social justice perspective (MSJCC) addresses some of the unique challenges this student faces while focusing on her holistic growth in the counseling process. Recommendations for higher education, counseling, and STEM are discussed.

The purpose of this chapter is to examine the integration of the existentialist counseling approach and MSJCC as it relates to the case study of Aaron. Authors review the case of Aaron, a college student, who identifies within the LDS faith, struggling with symptoms of depression and anxiety. The authors include a review of the foundation and history of the LDS church, as well as the modern structure and implications for counseling. The authors also describe their own cultural backgrounds and counseling approaches when working with Aaron. Following this review is a case conceptualization through an existential theoretical lens with the inclusion of short-term and long-term goals alongside a treatment plan.

The authors will utilize the case of Harper to delineate how to counsel clients to remain true to one's personal identity, while still developing a culturally competent identity in empathetic relationship with others. Harper is coming to counseling because she is facing a move from her homogeneous cultural community in Western North Carolina to the diversity of Washington, DC. Harper states she is fearful and anxious about (1) having to set her values aside, (2) being offensive because she lacks awareness of other cultures, and (3) the unknown of what living around different religions, ethnicities, and cultures may entail. The authors will explore practical ways in which the MSJCC can be implemented in the clinical setting for the sake of counseling clients toward cultural competency. Counselors will examine the importance of counselor self-awareness, regarding marginalization and privilege, within the therapeutic relationship. The authors will provide examples of experiential, solutions focused, and group therapy interventions to help clients move toward cultural competency.

This chapter seeks to bring awareness to the multiple identities that international (graduate/doctoral counseling) students bring to college and university campuses. The multiple identities are examined through the intersectionality paradigm and the RESPECTFUL model, and apply the Multicultural and Social Justice Counseling Competencies (MSJCC). It is intended to help counselors-in-training, counselor educators, supervisors, and administrators examine current intrapersonal, interpersonal, institutional, community, public, international/global views, and potential roles related to working with clients/students/peers who comprise our growing international student population.

The following chapter describes the experience of counseling a woman named Heidi (name and identifying details changed to protect confidentiality) using Ecotherapy and the Multicultural Counseling Competencies. The chapter describes Heidi and her presenting problems, an introduction of the author, and the author's unique approach to counseling, the application of theory to her work with Heidi using existential and systems theories, as well as practicing in nature. The goals and progress that was made in their journey together through the counseling relationship is described. Throughout their journey together, Heidi utilized her strengths, which empowered her to make changes in her life that were beneficial for her growth, health, and happiness by implementing changes in her life that fully honored the complexity of her humanity.

Over 2.4 million American service men and women were deployed overseas between 2001 to 2011. Families of these service members include over one million spouses and two million children under the age of 18. There is a growing need for counselors to understand the mental health needs of military service men and woman, and the unique aspects of military culture. This chapter will demonstrate how to practically apply the Multicultural and Social Justice Counseling Competencies (MSJCC) to counseling work with the military population through a case study.

Preface

OVERVIEW

The book *Cases on Cross-Cultural Counseling* includes counseling case studies of multicultural clients and counselors in a variety of settings. Spanning the client lifespan from childhood to older adulthood, diverse counselors address intersectional aspects of human development: race and ethnicity, religion, socioeconomic status, sexual orientation, gender, and other important components of client identity that impact the client intra-personally and within the larger context in which they live. As counselors, the clinicians in this book describe their cultural identity in relation to the client, client goals, their personal approaches to counseling, and the process by which they engage in relationship with their client, which influences the process and outcomes that result from the counseling process.

The authors themselves have complex and diverse intersectional identities, and they share with the reader their own personal varied aspects of identity, their approach to counseling, and how their cultural identity and self-awareness surrounding their identity, which is an important aspect of cultural counseling competence. All of the authors have in common a professional counselor identity, and dedication to utilizing culturally competent counseling strategies.

Over the past thirty-plus years, counselors have worked to shift the counseling profession to embrace diversity and create guidelines of best practice to serve diverse populations, especially populations that experience marginalization in society. Counselors are expected to respect the cultures of their clients while avoiding imparting their own personal values (ACA, A4.b., 2014). This requires self-examination as well as a curiosity and awareness of the values of the client. In order to accomplish this task, counselors must be trained, and culturally competent. Multicultural competence has traditionally focused on working with diverse clients with regard to ethnicity and race. Sue, Arredondo and McDavis, (1992) recognized the cross-cultural nature of counseling, and applied aspirational competencies to the practice of counseling.

MULTICULTURAL COUNSELING TODAY

Since 1992, the scope of multicultural counseling has expanded to include other diverse and marginalized groups whose membership is based on factors such as religious affiliation, ability status, sexual orientation, and gender variance (Bidell, 2012). The ACA has officially endorsed the Multicultural and Social Justice Competencies (MSJCC) (Ratts et al., 2016), which builds upon the work of Sue, Arrendondo and McDavis. Counselors' understanding of multicultural competence has evolved to include recognition of intersectionality of various aspects of identity (Ratts et al., 2016). The MSJCC reflects this shift, and outlines the need for counselors to recognize power, privilege and oppression, and its impact on clients and the counseling relationship. The MSJCC includes developmental domains such as (1) counselor self-awareness, (2) client worldview, (3) counseling relationship, and (4) counseling and advocacy interventions (Ratts et al, 2016) and aspirational competencies, which include within the domains, attitudes, knowledge, skills and actions (AKSA). The culturally-competent counselor strives to apply the developmental domains and aspirational competencies to their practice with all clients.

The MSJCC is a guideline of standards for use in best practices for multicultural counseling competence. Counselors acknowledge, and understand their own varied identities in addition to seeking understanding of the complex and rich intersectionality of identities that are present in the individuals they serve. Counselors are bound by the American Counseling Association's Code of Ethics (2014) to achieve multicultural competence in counseling. This means that counselors respect and value the diverse identities of the clients they serve, and seek to understand the client's worldview, and intersectionality of various aspects of identity such as geographical location, ethnicity and race, religion, sexual orientation, gender identity, socio-economic status, education, culture and history, celebrations, holidays, and the various aspects of the client that defines their culture.

Counselors respect and honor the beliefs of clients, and what makes them feel whole and well. In addition to seeking understanding of the worldview of the client, counselors seek self-awareness to understand how their biases could potentially impact the counseling process. In addition, counselors are also aware of the counseling relationship, and cultural factors of both the counselor and the client that can influence the counseling relationship. Finally, counselors are expected to advocate for clients in a variety of appropriate ways both with, and "on-behalf" of clients. The goal of Cases on Cross-Cultural Counseling Strategies, is for counselors to share their multicultural approaches to working with clients.

TARGET AUDIENCE

This book is an appropriate resource for counselor educators who would like their students to understand "real world" counseling applications of the MSJCC. Students and counseling practitioners are exposed to the worldview of the clients in the cases presented in this book, through rich descriptions of demographic and interpersonal aspects of identity that are considered by the counselor in the therapeutic relationship. This resource would be an excellent addition to multicultural counseling coursework in masters of counseling programs across the nation to provide application of the Multicultural and Social Justice Competencies (MSJCC) that were officially endorsed by the American Counseling Association in 2016. This book is appropriate for students in a multicultural counseling class, as well as for practitioners who are already practicing in the field of counseling.

The editors' goal is to "shed light" on the creative approaches used by counselors working with diverse clients in a variety of geographical locations, developmental levels, and complex and varied identities. The book highlights how the identities and approaches of the counselors co-mingle with the rich and varied lives of clients, each case describes how counselors help clients heal and grow. The case studies provide application of the MSJCC to counseling work with clients. This book benefits students and practitioners attempting to gain a deeper understanding of counseling approaches with specific populations, and ideas for advocacy with a wide variety of clients. This book will help counselors gain a deeper understanding of how to apply the MSJCC to current work with clients, as well as exposing readers to effective approaches to counseling with a diverse array of clients. The theme of this book can impact the counseling profession by providing practical tools and approaches for working with diverse clientele. Counselors will feel empowered after reading this book to apply the Multicultural and Social Justice Competencies to work with current clients. They will gain a deeper understanding of themselves and the counseling process. They will feel excited to work with diverse populations in counseling. By helping others learn, it is the goal of the editors to improve counseling practice for many, thereby serving more people effectively through the counseling profession.

OVERVIEW OF CHAPTERS

Part one of *Cases on Cross-Cultural Counseling Strategies* starts at the beginning stages of human development with children and family case studies. The first chapter of the book is entitled "Healing Alex's Wound: Application of MSJCC in Adlerian Play Therapy." The author in this chapter acknowledges the importance of working from a multiculturally competent counseling perspective through the use of the MSJCC. The author provides an overview of the effects of adverse childhood experiences (ACES) and the impacts ACES can have on individuals, in particular, Hispanic children. Adlerian Play Therapy with a multicultural approach, is used with to help Alex, a Hispanic child thrive in a healthy way, despite the many ACES he has experienced in his life.

Chapter two, "Just Eat! The Case of the Martinez Family" applies the MSJCC with an eclectic family systems approach to counseling a Latin@ family. The Martinez family started family counseling due to the concerns of a school counselor regarding the disordered eating of 15 year-old Javier. The case study includes a rich description of the first session with the Mexican-American Martinez family, and examines family dynamics around the identified client, Javier. A discussion of the author's cultural background, counseling approach, and use of the MSJCC lens when working with the Martinez family is also included. Initial goals and prognosis for treatment are considered.

The third chapter involves counseling an Islamic family experiencing Islamaphobia in the United States. In "Counseling with a Muslim American Family: Beyond Islamaphobia," the authors explore the unfounded fear of Islam and resulting hostility that Muslims experience as a religious minority in the U.S. Experiencing islamaphobia increases the risk for poor mental health outcomes and compounds stigma around help-seeking behaviors. In this case study, a family unit presented for counseling due to stress resulting from life cycle stressors. However, the intersectionality of their religious identity affected how the individuals experienced transitions as well as microaggressions. This case study includes a counselor's application of the Multicultural and Social Justice Counseling Competencies, treatment interventions, and extensions for further professional development.

The fourth chapter "Case Study for Counseling Same Sex Couples Through the Fertility Process: Jane and Kelsey," explores the topic of same sex couples navigating the process of fertility treatment. Fertility and reproductive technologies are increasingly important topics for counseling LGBT+ individuals. As legislation has changed to support same sex couples in the U.S., lesbian couples have more opportunities to expand their families. This chapter describes the unique barriers a lesbian couple faces when experiencing the fertility process in a heteronormative society. A description of the counseling relationship with the couple is provided and the MSJCC and Relational-Cultural Theory, a feminist theory, is used to help Jane and Kelsey set goals consistent with the theory and their personal concerns.

Part two of *Cases on Cross-Cultural Counseling* focuses on the counseling concerns of older adolescents and young adults, with case studies taking place in high school and college years for clients. Chapter five, which starts part two of the book is entitled "Rose's Thorn: Navigating Career and College Readiness Self-

Efficacy While Aging-Out of the Foster Care System." This chapter explores a counseling relationship centered around seventeen year-old Rose, who is aging out of the foster care system and managing a variety of concerns related to occupation and education. Rose is struggling with impending life after high school with a very limited support system, which is a situation faced by many who are aging out of the foster care system. This chapter describes the career and college readiness of Rose as she navigates her post-secondary options, builds her support networks, and discovers resources for adolescents aging out of the foster care system via her work with Dr. Williams, creator and counselor of the Students That Are Reaching Success (S.T.A.R.S.) program. Rose's participation in the program is described, and implications are provided for counselors working with adolescents aging out of the foster care system.

Chapter six, "Lucia's Journey of Bridging Two Worlds: Counseling Latinx First-Generation College Students," Describes Lucia's journey in counseling and higher education as a first generation college student (FGCS). Lucia attended counseling during her sophomore year of college to manage concerns related to balancing school, work, and home responsibilities. In this chapter, the author addresses the strengths and the challenges that Latinx FGCS experience in higher education settings. In addition, the author outlines her counseling approach to working with Latinx FGCS who are navigating higher education systems.

Chapter seven, "Utilization of Acceptance and Commitment Therapy (ACT) with Charlotte Underrepresented on Campus," describes another first generation college student (FGCS) named Charlotte. The case study focuses on an African American, female, nineteen-year-old undergraduate premedical student majoring in chemistry, to highlight an underrepresented student in science, engineering, and mathematics (STEM) The author describes using Acceptance and Commitment Therapy (ACT) with Charlotte, and outlines concerns related to underrepresentation in a STEM field on her campus, as an African-American female. This chapter highlights psychological flexibility in ACT (Hayes et al., 1999) and. The presenting concerns of Charlotte including stressors related to academic achievement, emotional regulation, financial concerns, and stress related to family. A multicultural and social justice perspective (MSJCC) addresses some of the unique challenges this student faces while focusing on her holistic growth in the counseling process. Recommendations for higher education, counseling and STEM are discussed.

The eighth chapter, "Aaron: Exploring the Intersection of Religion and Identity With an LDS Client," introduces the readers to Aaron, a college student who identifies with the LDS faith who is struggling with symptoms of anxiety and depression. The chapter utilizes the MSJCC and an existentialist approach to counseling. The authors include a review of the foundation and history of the LDS church, as well as the modern structure and implications for counseling. A case conceptualization and treatment plan utilizing the MSJCC and an existential theoretical approach addressed Aaron's short- and long-term goals.

Chapter nine addresses a client who attends counseling to become more open to different cultures and experiences. In "The Case of Harper, Courageous Cultural Conversations in the Counseling Room: Overcoming Complacency with Competence and Confidence," the authors utilized the case of Harper to describe how to help clients remain true to their personal identity, while developing a culturally competent identity in empathetic relationship with others. The counselor helped Harper manage anxiety around a geographical move, and her fear and anxiety about the unknown on her journey to becoming more connected with people who are culturally different. The authors explored practical ways to implement the MSJCC in the clinical setting to help clients when they have a goal to become more culturally aware. The authors examine the importance of counselor self-awareness, regarding marginalization and privilege, within the therapeutic relationship. They provide examples of experiential, solution focused, and group therapy interventions to help clients move toward cultural awareness and tolerance.

Part three of *Cases on Cross-Cultural Counseling* focuses on counseling adults and older adult populations. In Chapter ten, "Deepa's Discovery – An Examination of Intersectionality When Multiple Identities Collide: Managing Family Roles, Doctoral Work, and Clashing Eurocentric Worldviews," the reader learns about multiple identities that international (graduate/doctoral counseling) students bring to college and university campuses. The multiple identities are examined through the intersectionality paradigm (Collins & Bilge, 2016; Crenshaw, 1991) and the RESPECTFUL model (D'Andrae & Daniels, 2001). The authors also apply the Multicultural and Social Justice Counseling Competencies (Ratts, et al., 2016) to Deepa's case. It is intended to help counselors-in-training, counselor educators, supervisors, and administrators examine current intrapersonal, interpersonal, institutional, community, public, international/global views and potential roles related to working with clients/students/peers who comprise our growing international student population.

Chapter 11, "Hiking With Heidi: A Multicultural Approach to Ecotherapy," describes the experience of counseling a woman named Heidi using Ecotherapy and the Multicultural Counseling Competencies (MSJCC) of Ratts et al., 2016. The chapter applies the MSJCC and existential and systems theories to Heidi, a mid-thirties, middle class woman struggling with major depressive disorder. Throughout the counseling process, Heidi utilized her personal strengths, which empowered her to make changes in her life that were beneficial for her growth, health and happiness. Heidi utilized the benefits of spending time in nature and implemented changes in her life that fully honored the complexity of her humanity.

Chapter 12, "Flying With Eddie: Complicated Grief in the Military." Describes the growing need for counselors to understand the mental health needs of military service men and woman, and the unique aspects of military culture. The chapter demonstrates how to practically apply the Multicultural and Social Justice Counseling Competencies (MSJCC) to counseling work with the military population through the case of Eddie who is struggling with complicated grief. The counselor utilizes the MSJCC and a solution focused approach to helping Eddie.

Chapter 13, "Navigating Toxic Masculinity in Clients as a Beginning Therapist" provides counselors with a framework that will allow them to broach gender with male clients and to navigate conversations that may elicit anxiety for beginning counselors. The case is of Whitney, a graduate student who just started internship. Her client is Rick, a client in his 50's, who is coming to services because of receiving a DUI and needing to complete counseling for his diversion mandate. Whitney is younger than Rick and has the experience of having some uncomfortable exchanges with him, such as remarks on how "bright" she is and a passing comment her outfit. The strategies proposed in this case study are grounded in the Multicultural and Social Justice Counseling Competencies (Ratts et al., 2016) and in Relational Cultural Theory (Miller, 1976) and will give students a framework for understanding clients who may respond like Rick.

The purpose of Chapter 14, "Mondays with Mac: An Interpersonal Journey of Cultural Humility," is to "paint a picture of the counseling process" through rich description of how the Multicultural and Social Justice Counseling Competencies (Ratts, Singh, Nassar-McMillan, Butler, & McCullough, 2015) can be applied through a model and attitude of cultural humility (Hook, Davis, Owen, Worthington Jr., & Utsey, 2013; Tervalon & Murray-Garcia, 1998), rather than a blanket state of achieving "cultural competence" in cross-cultural counseling. The mission of this chapter was to convey the critical nature of accounting for the first author's ("counselor") positions of privilege, including positions of racial, age, socioeconomic status, and legal status privileges, over the client ("Mac"), and recognized how cultural humility needs to be evoked within the counselor in order to apply tenants of the MSJCC as well as the counselor's interpersonal and relational-cultural approach (Comstock et al., 2008; Newhill et al., 2000; Miller, 1976) to counseling and facilitating client growth and healing.

In Chapter 15, we meet Lucille in "Lucille: Cross Cultural Counseling with Older Adult Populations." The percentage of the population in the United States comprised of older adults (65+), sometimes referred to as Baby Boomers (birth year 1946 – 1964) and the Silent Generation (birth year 1925 – 1945) is steadily on the rise (U.S. Department of Health and Human Services, 2015). This population is often overlooked and has a unique subset of issues when it comes to counseling competencies. Layered multicultural competencies affecting these individuals include race, gender, sexual orientation, religion, and ageism. Counseling concerns related to age include but are not limited to loss of autonomy, loss of physical ability, loss of loved ones, and a changing definition of self. From an existential therapeutic background blended with Cognitive Behavioral Therapy (CBT) interventions, the author reviews the case study of Lucille with a focus on therapeutic intervention and Multicultural and Social Justice Counseling Competencies (MSJCC's).

CONCLUSION

The cases in this book help "paint a picture" of what culturally competent counseling looks like in the real world. The diversity of the counselors is provided with a description of who they are, and how their complex identities interact in the counseling room with complex client identity. The authors provide robust case studies that show the complexity of all aspects of identity in the room, presenting problems, specific treatment approaches with goals, a plan, and progress. Authors also acknowledging the important aspects of the MSJCC in their work with clients, such as the four developmental domains: (1) counselor self-awareness, (2) client worldview, (3) counseling relationship, and (4) counseling and advocacy interventions and aspirational competencies, and the aspirational competencies of, attitudes, knowledge, skills and actions (AKSA) (Ratts et al, 2016). Authors directly apply these competencies to their work with the counseling clients in the book, providing the reader with examples of how these competencies are embedded into the counseling practices of licensed professionals in the field.

This book is a fantastic resource for counselor educators and counselors who desire to understand real-world application of the MSJCC, various theoretical approaches and models, and for work with specific types of clients and populations. The cases in the book are incredibly diverse, spanning the life-span from working with young children, to the elderly adult population. Diverse socio-economic, racial and ethnic, sexual orientations and genders, counseling goals and concerns, religion, and experiences within the broader society are identified and explored. The counselors sharing their cases in this book are also diverse in a variety of ways. They all demonstrate cultural competence and approaches to clients that serve the complex identities in the room. Readers will enjoy connecting with clients and counselors alike as they experience the counseling journey of the clients depicted in *Cases on Cross-Cultural Counseling*.

REFERENCES

American Counseling Association. (2014). *ACA code of ethics*. Alexandria, VA: Author. Retrieved from http://www.counseling.org/

Bidell, M. P. (2012). Examining school counseling students' multicultural and sexual orientation competencies through a cross-specialization comparison. *Journal of Counseling and Development*, *90*(2), 200–207. doi:10.1111/j.1556-6676.2012.00025.x

Collins, P. H., & Bilge, S. (2016). *Intersectionality*. Malden, MA: Polity Press.

Comstock, D. L., Hammer, T. R., Strentzsch, J., Cannon, K., Parsons, J., & Salazar, I. I. G. (2008). Relational-cultural theory: A framework for bridging relational, multicultural, and social justice competencies. *Journal of Counseling and Development*, *86*(3), 279–287. doi:10.1002/j.1556-6678.2008.tb00510.x

Crenshaw, K. (1991). Mapping the margins: Intersectionality, identity politics, and violence against women of color. *Stanford Law Review*, *43*(6), 1241–1299. doi:10.2307/1229039

D'Andrea, M., & Daniels, J. (2001). RESPECTFUL counseling: An integrative model for counselors. In D. Pope-Davis & H. Coleman (Eds.), *The Interface of Class, Culture and Gender in Counseling* (pp. 417–466). Thousand Oaks, CA: Sage. doi:10.4135/9781452231846.n17

Hook, J. N., Davis, D. E., Owen, J., Worthington, E. L., & Utsey, S. O. (2013). Cultural humility: Measuring openness to culturally diverse clients. *Journal of Counseling Psychology*, *60*(3), 353–366. doi:10.1037/a0032595 PMID:23647387

Miller, J. B. (1976). *Toward a new psychology of women*. Boston, MA: Beacon Press.

Newhill, C. E., Safran, J. D., & Muran, J. C. (2000). *Negotiating the therapeutic alliance: A relational treatment guide*. New York, NY: Guilford Press.

Ratts, M. J., Singh, A. A., Nassar-McMillan, S., Butler, S. K., & McCullough, J. R. (2015). *Multicultural and Social Justice Counseling Competencies*. Retrieved from https://www.counseling.org/docs/default-source/competencies/multicultural- and-social-justice-counseling-competencies.pdf?sfvrsn=20

Ratts, M. J., Singh, A. A., Nassar-McMillan, S., Butler, S. K., & McCullough, J. R. (2016). Multicultural and Social Justice Counseling Competencies: Guidelines for the Counseling Profession. *Journal of Multicultural Counseling and Development*, *44*(1), 28–48. doi:10.1002/jmcd.12035

Sue, D. W., Arredondo, P., & McDavis, R. J. (1992). Multicultural Counseling Competencies and Standards: A Call to the Profession. *Journal of Counseling and Development*, *70*(4), 477–486. doi:10.1002/j.1556-6676.1992.tb01642.x

Tervalon, M., & Murray-Garcia, J. (1998). Cultural humility versus cultural competence: A critical distinction in in defining physician training outcomes in multicultural education. *Journal of Health Care for the Poor and Underserved*, *9*(2), 117–125. doi:10.1353/hpu.2010.0233 PMID:10073197

U.S. Department of Health and Human Services. (2015). *Administration on aging: Aging statistics*. Retrieved from: http://www.aoa.acl.gov/Aging_Statistics/index.aspx

Acknowledgment

The editors of Cases on Cross-Cultural Counseling Strategies would like to acknowledge IGI Global for the opportunity to publish this book, and for support throughout the publication process. We would also like to thank the chapter authors for their insight, creativity, clinical conceptualization skills; in addition to their empathy and thoughtfulness in crafting the stories of their clients. Finally we would like to thank the clients who shared their stories with the chapter authors. Your brave contributions will provide insight for counselors who read this book.

Thank you to my family, partner, friends, and colleagues. Without a supportive system in which to create, this goal could not be accomplished. Thank you for your support and friendship throughout the writing and editing process.

Bonnie C. King
Midwestern State University, USA

Deepest gratitude goes to my daughter, Tori, family, mentors, colleagues, and students for both intentional and unintentional support and encouragement in making this project possible.

Tiffany A. Stewart
Midwestern State University, USA

Chapter 1
Healing Alex's Wound: Application of MSJCC in Adlerian Play Therapy

Szu-Yu Chen
Palo Alto University, USA

EXECUTIVE SUMMARY

Multicultural and Social Justice Counseling Competencies (MSJCC) has emphasized the need to consider multicultural and social justice factors into all aspects of the counseling profession. Consistent with the MSJCC guideline, it is essential that counselors provide developmentally and culturally responsive interventions when working with children from diverse backgrounds. Adlerian play therapy is a unique approach in which counselors incorporate basic tenets of individual psychology and premise of play therapy to help children work through different types of emotional or behavioral issues. This chapter provides an overview of the effects of adverse childhood experiences (ACEs) on children's mental health, particularly the multitude of effects on Hispanic children. The author then illustrates the application of Adlerian play therapy from MSJCC's perspective to work with a Hispanic boy exposed to a high level of ACEs.

DOI: 10.4018/978-1-7998-0022-4.ch001

INTRODUCTION TO THE CASE

In this case study, to protect the child and his families' confidentiality and anonymity, pseudonyms are used. Alex was a 6-year-old Hispanic boy living with his grandparents, Mr. and Mrs. Garcia, two uncles, and a younger sister, Abby. Mr. and Mrs. Garcia were first generation immigrants in the United States and their children and grandchildren were born and raised in the United States. Mr. and Mrs. Garcia brought Alex to play therapy services because of Alex's increasingly aggressive behavior. Mr. and Mrs. Garcia reported that Alex's biological mother left the family when Alex was three years old due to the abusive relationship with Alex's father. Before living with Mr. and Mrs. Garcia, Alex and Abby had moved a lot with the father and his girlfriend, and Alex was asked to call the father's girlfriend "Mom".

Mr. and Mrs. Garcia reported that they called Child Protective Service (CPS) after finding out their grandchildren were victims of domestic violence by the father. They shared it was a hard decision for them to contact CPS because he was their son and they felt shame to reveal this incident to everyone. However, they wanted to protect their grandchildren and they think it was better for their grandchildren to leave their father. They noted that Alex's father was physically and emotionally abusive toward Alex and Abby when the father was angry or drunk. After CPS had been involved, they had removed Alex and Abby from the father's house. Alex and Abby had lived with their grandparents for about a half year since the removal. Although the father would visit the children once a week, Mr. and Mrs. Garcia reported that Alex would feel confused about why his father would come and go every week. They further reported that the father recently gave up the guardianship, so they had become legal guardian of their grandchildren. However, recently, the children's biological mother re-entered their lives and wanted guardianship of her children. Mr. and Mrs. Garcia were worried about losing their grandchildren. They shared the mother was not likely to get the guardianship back because she had not contacted the family since she left. Yet, it would be an ongoing issue in the family.

Mr. and Mrs. Garcia described that Alex would behave like his father when he got angry. For example, Alex would show anger outbursts, such as kicking, hitting, yelling, and threatening towards his grandparents and sister. However, his behavioral issues seemed to only occur at home. Alex's kindergarten teacher reported that Alex did not show any behavioral problems in the classroom and described Alex as a cooperative and polite child in the school setting. He seemed to get along with his peers well. However, the teacher commented that when Alex felt sad, he tended to hold his tears back from teachers and peers.

The grandparents reported feeling stressed and helpless about Alex's behavioral issues because they have tried different ways to discipline him, such as telling him not to hit people when angry, using timeout, or taking his toys or TV time away.

However, their parenting methods did not seem to work. They were worried about Alex's aggressive behavior and their families' safety. They shared their hopes to decrease Alex's aggression and improve his relationships with his families.

ADVERSE CHILDHOOD EXPERIENCES IN HISPANIC CHILDREN

Adverse childhood experiences (ACEs) are chronic and traumatic experiences and events, ranging from abuse and neglect to parental separation or divorce, and may have negative, lasting effects on well-being in childhood or later in life (Sacks, Murphey, & Moore, 2014). A growing body of research has shown that ACEs are becoming a critical mental health issue (Sacks & Murphey, 2018). Adverse childhood experiences study was first conducted by Kaiser Permanente, a health insurance company in collaboration with the Center for Disease Control and Prevention (CDC) from 1995 to 1997. Over 17,000 middle-class adult participants completed the survey exploring their current physical health status, social functioning, and behavior along with questions related to their childhood maltreatment and family dysfunction. The questionnaire used in this study categorized ACEs into three groups: abuse, neglect, and family/household challenges. There are 10 ACE factors, including emotional, sexual, and physical abuse, emotional and physical neglect, substance abuse and mental illness within household, mother treated violently, parental separation or divorce, and incarcerated household member. Each factor weighs one point and the total score of the different categories of ACEs reported by participants was added up to assess cumulative childhood stress ranging from 0 to 10 points in which higher ACE scores indicate higher exposure to adversity events. The results indicated that almost two-thirds of study participants reported at least one ACE and more than one in five reported three or more ACEs (Centers for Disease Control and Prevention [CDC], 2016). The findings further revealed the greater exposure to ACEs is positively associated to the greater risk of behavioral and physical health across the lifespan (CDC, 2016). Numerous research studies have shown that children exposed to ACEs are more likely to develop physical, mental, behavioral, psychosocial, and/or cognitive issues into adolescence and adulthood, such as substance abuse, depression, poor academic and work performance, and risk for intimate partner and sexual violence (Burke, Hellman, Scott, Weems, & Carrion, 2011; Flaherty et al., 2013; Jimenez, Wade, Schwartz-Soicher, Lin, & Reichman, 2017; Kerker et al., 2015; Mersky, Topitzes, & Reynolds, 2013).

Hispanic children currently account for one-fourth of U.S. children and are projected to remain the largest ethnic minority group among children (Passel & Cohn, 2008). Hispanic children who are US-born or in the immigrant families (foreign-born children with at least one foreign-born parent, or US-born children with at least one foreign-born parent) are at high risk for mental health disorders stemming from poverty, exposure to trauma, acculturative stressors, and discrimination (Caballero et al., 2017). Sacks and Murphey (2018) examined the prevalence of ACEs among children using nationally representative data from the 2016 National Survey of Children's Health (NSCH). They found that 51 percent of Hispanic children have experienced at least one ACE, compared with 40 percent of white non-Hispanic children. Caballero, Johnson, Muñoz Buchanan, and DeCamp (2017) surveyed adverse childhood experiences among more than 12,000 Hispanic children from immigrant and U.S.-native families. The results indicated that about 30 percent of Hispanic children in U.S.-native families and 16 percent of children in immigrant families are in high ACE exposures (≥2 ACEs), including poverty, abuse, neglect, household dysfunction (e.g., parents' divorce, violence, and substance abuse, etc.). Specifically, economic hardship, the divorce or separation of a parent or guardian, living with an adult with a substance use problem, and parental incarceration are the most common ACEs reported for Hispanic children (Sacks & Murphey, 2018).

Childhood trauma exposure have been linked to an array of mental health issues, including externalizing and internalizing problems (Martinez, Gudiño, & Lau, 2013). Thus, children who have experienced ACEs often need mental health counseling services. Martinez et al. (2013) investigated the use of mental health services by children (N=1,600; 19.3% Hispanic) who had experienced some form of maltreatment and found that neither internalizing nor externalizing problems predicted the use of mental health service for the Hispanic children population. However, they indicated that cultural and family issues might discourage Hispanic parents to seek mental health services after their child's exposure to maltreatment. As a result, many mental health professionals have addressed a need to identify the predictors of mental health services among Hispanic children and enhance competencies to work with children using developmentally appropriate and culturally responsive interventions due to an increased concern about mental health for at-risk Hispanic children.

Play therapy has been identified as a developmentally appropriate approach to counseling children from age 3 to 10 because play is children's natural way to communicate and express their feelings and thoughts (Landreth, 2012; Ray, 2011). In play therapy, counselors utilize selected toys, art materials, and other play media, and build a safe and trusting relationship in which children can explore their world and express themselves more fully through the form of symbolic play (Landreth, 2012; Kottman & Meany-Walen, 2016). Meta-analytic results for play therapy outcome research have shown play therapy to be an effective intervention for children with a variety of presenting problems (LeBlanc & Ritchie, 1999; Bratton, Ray, Rhine, & Jones, 2005). There are different theoretical approaches to play therapy resulting in unique ways of counseling children and conceptualizing children's presenting issues.

Adlerian play therapy developed by Terry Kottman (1995) is a play therapy model based on the theoretical constructs of individual psychology (Adler, 1964) and is adapted to meet children's development level. Kottman and Meany-Walen (2016) indicated that therapists use Adlerian play therapy in clinics and school setting and the interventions are effective when working with children who exhibit a variety of presenting concerns. This approach has shown especially appropriate with children who have issues related to power and control, poor self-concepts, inadequate social skills, strained families relationships, and traumatic experiences (e.g., Kottman, 1999; Kottman, 2001; Kottman & Warlick, 1989; Meany-Walen, Bratton, & Kottman, 2014; Meany-Walen, Kottman, Bullis, & Dillman Taylor, 2015; Morrison, 2009; Rotter, Horak Jr., & Heidt, 1999; Snow, Buckley, & Williams, 1999).

To work effectively with diverse populations, the Multicultural Counseling Competencies Revisions Committee (2015) has developed the Multicultural and Social Justice Counseling Competencies (MSJCC) that serve as a conceptual framework for competent multicultural counseling practice. This framework signifies the need to focus on multiculturalism and social justice as the center of all aspects of the counseling profession. The core belief of MSJCC is that counselors and clients both bring to the therapeutic relationship various cultural values, beliefs, biases, and complex identities consisting of different race, ethnicity, gender, sexual orientation, socioeconomic status, religious/spirituality, and disability. Counselors, therefore, need to address how the interactions of power, privilege, and oppression influence the counseling relationship. Adlerians focus on an individual's subjective perspective and interpretation of an individual's world. By understanding an individual's experience, counselors can begin to understand the impact of culture may have on clients' values and perceptions. Thus, Adlerian play therapy may also work well with children from diverse cultures and ethnic groups (Kottman, Bryant, Alexander, & Kroger, 2009). In this chapter, the author shares her cultural identity and approach to counseling children. The author further illustrates the application of the MSJCC in Adlerian play therapy process with Alex and his families.

COUNSELOR BACKGROUND

Counselor's Cultural Background

I was born and raised in Taipei, Taiwan and immigrated to the United States approximately 12 years ago to pursue higher educations and trainings in clinical mental health counseling and play therapy and now being a counselor educator in a university setting. When I lived in Taiwan, I was aware of my power and privilege status, as I was raised in an upper-middle class family and in a capital city. I was able to receive many resources, such as education opportunities and financial supports to achieve my personal and professional goals and development. However, moving to the states, I become part of an ethnic minority for the first time in my life and have to think about my identity in a new way. In the U.S., I identity myself as an East Asian immigrant. Specifically, I am a heterosexual female counselor and counselor educator of color. I became aware of my transition to the marginalized group and the impact of my social status on my worldview, values, beliefs, and biases.

I have experienced various challenges during this acculturative process, including culture shocks, immigration status, acculturative stress, language barriers, limited support system, low self-efficacy, career concerns, discriminations, and oppression. Among these challenges, I reflected how my cultural values have interfaced with the western culture and how my cultural background and acculturative process have impacted my identity as a counselor and a counselor educator.

Confucianism, Buddhism, and Taoism are the main cultural values that have profoundly influenced my view of myself, others, the world, and counseling relationships with clients. Confucianism defines family and society as hierarchical and authoritative where relationships are based upon moral principles, which reflect love, integrity, loyalty, sincerity, and benevolence (Jung, 1998). Buddhism indicates human beings are leading their own lives with guiding rules, refraining from evil and purifying own mind (Jung, 1998). Discovering harmony with the natural order of things as well as stressing themes of passivity, asceticism, and the search for immortality are the major tenets in Taoism (Jung, 1998). I believe that these philosophies, including collectivism, hierarchical structure in the family and society, well-defined social roles and norms, repression of the expression of emotions and problems, harmony, and indirect forms of communication (Sheu & Fukuyama, 2007) and my upbringing have shaped my worldview, interpersonal relationships, expectations of self and others, and communication styles.

Counselor's Counseling Approach

My counseling approach is based on Alfred Adler's individual psychology. Adlerian theory serves as my guiding theory because its underpinning philosophy is the most congruent with my beliefs about people and their personalities. I believe that people are socially embedded and striving for a sense of belonging and significance. I believe that people's behavior and beliefs are purposeful and they have the capacity and power to pursue a successful life. I also believe that people's family history and life experiences have influenced their personality and perception of the world. It is my fundamental belief that our experiences are not the cause of who we become but, rather, it is our personal understanding of our experiences that gives meaning to our lives. This personal understanding is essential to the way in which we develop relationships, pursue our life goals, and how we respond to adversity and challenges. Therefore, I endeavor to understand each client as a whole and unique individual with distinct attributes, personal values and strengths, and life purpose.

I view the therapeutic relationship as an imperative factor for growth and positive change to occur in the counseling process. Hence, I work with clients to identify their goals of counseling and I help clients recognize thoughts and behaviors that keep them from reaching their goals. Moreover, I support clients in recognizing solutions to their concerns. I expect through our collaborative effort that clients will grow and find new ways of seeing the world around them and create a more meaningful way of being in the world.

MSJCC IN ADLERIAN PLAY THERAPY

Historically, Adlerians have worked with children in the context of family and school in the form of family therapy, parent education and teacher consultation (Dreikurs, 1967). In Adler's view, children's play provides rich information about children's present situation as well as their future (Dreikurs). Adler considered children's play as an opportunity for counselors to view children's characteristic ways of behaving; hence, counselors may confirm their hypotheses of children's lifestyle by observing children's play behavior (Dreikurs). One of Adler's major assumptions was that an individual is guided by one's lifestyle that can be presented in every expression of the personality. Thus, counselors may observe and interpret children's lifestyle through their verbal and nonverbal behavior (Adler, 1956). Adler also believed people are socially embedded and considered social interest as a criterion for mental health (Mosak, 1989). Thus, Adler indicated that therapists could determine children's social feelings by observing children's group play and further provide an opportunity for children to develop their social interest as needed. It is obvious that play can give counselors clues to understand children's lifestyle, goals of behaviors, private logic, and interpersonal relationships.

Based on Adler's view of children, Terry Kottman (1995) integrated Adlerian theory with play therapy and developed Adlerian play therapy for working with children, parents, and teachers from a systematic approach. Kottman and Warlick (1989) posited that the concepts of individual psychology and various Adlerian therapy techniques could be incorporated with the premise of play therapy to create a model for helping children who exhibit various types of emotional or behavioral problems.

Theoretical Foundation of Adlerian Play Therapy

Adlerian play therapy exemplifies the tenets of individual psychology and applies them within a framework of how children view themselves, others, and the world. Adlerian play therapy may foster collaboration and purposeful movement, and help children master life tasks (Even & Armstrong, 2011; Kottman, 2003; Kottman & Warlick, 1989). Kottman (2003) defined play therapy as "an approach to communicating therapeutically with clients using toys, art materials, games, and other play media, giving clients a safe and nurturing relationship in which they can explore and express feelings, gain insight into their own motivation and into their interaction with others, and learn and practice socially appropriate behaviors" (p.1). Some primary theoretical tenets and constructs that Adlerian play therapy rests on are described below.

People are Socially Embedded

Adlerian play therapists work with children based on the beliefs that people are socially embedded, goal-directed, subjective, and creative human beings (Ansbacher & Ansbacher, 1956; Carlson & Slavik, 1997). One of the basic tenets of individual psychology is social interest and this is considered a criteria for mental health. Adler believed that people are born with an innate desire to develop social interests and connections with others, and strive for belongings and significance in their families, classrooms, communities, and other social groups (Ansbacher & Ansbacher, 1956; Carlson, Watts, & Maniacci, 2006).

As part of the development, children must form a secure attachment with their primary caretakers who are able to help them flourish their connections to the community at large (Kottman & Meany-Walen, 2016). Hence, Adlerian play therapists must investigate and understand how children build relationships and make connections with others. They accomplish this by observing their play in the playroom and discussing with parents and teachers the child's ways of interacting with others and seeking significance and belonging outside the playroom, such as schools and neighbors (Kottman & Meany-Walen). In addition, Adlerian play therapists want to assess children's level of social interest and try to increase children's social interest by modeling healthy ways to connect with others and maintain relationships, and fostering these abilities in children through encouragement (Kottman & Meany-Walen).

People Behavior is Goal-Directed

Another tenet in Adlerian play therapy is that children's behavior is purposeful and goal-directed. As children interpret their environment, they make early decisions regarding the predictable way that they will behave to achieve that goal (Ansbacher & Ansbacher, 1956; Carlson et al., 2006). Kottman and Meany-Walen (2016) stated that Adlerian play therapists must help children recognize their goals of behavior and support them to strive toward constructive goals. Play therapists particularly focus on children's goals of misbehavior (Dreikurs & Soltz, 1964) and four crucial Cs: count, connect, capable, and courage (Bettner & Lew, 2005).

Lew and Bettner (1996) postulated that children strive toward these four crucial Cs and believed that children needed to perceive themselves as possessing attributes of the crucial Cs in order to grow and mature successfully in society. Adlerian play therapists make hypotheses about children's assets and limitations and the ways in which they approach life by assessing the crucial Cs (Kottman & Meany-Walen, 2016). Adlerian play therapists consider the crucial Cs on a continuum to observe how children connect with others, believe they are significant, believe they are capable of success, and they demonstrate courage to be imperfect and try new tasks (Kottman & Meany-Walen).

Dreikurs and Soltz (1964) posited four goals of children's misbehavior: attention, power, revenge, and proving inadequacy, and believed that children use these behaviors to meet their needs. Adlerians believe that when children feel discouraged and lack feelings of belonging and connecting with others, they may unconsciously use goals of misbehavior to meet their needs (Dreikurs, 1964). Hence, Adlerian play therapists aim to understand how children behave to meet their goals by observing children's play, consulting parents and teachers about children's behavior that upset them, examining reactions of adults, and observing children's reactions to corrections (Kottman & Meany-Walen, 2016). Once play therapists understand children's goals of misbehavior, they can help children strive for more positive goals, such as the crucial Cs.

In order to gain a better understanding of children and their dynamics, play therapists can use goals of misbehavior and crucial Cs as tools to conceptualize children's lifestyle and potential personality priorities, including superiority, control, pleasing, and comfort. Play therapists assess children's lifestyle by looking for patterns of behaviors, thoughts, attitudes, and relationships that help children navigate their life. Moreover, play therapists can apply these concepts to enhance their understanding of children's parents and teachers as well (Kottman & Meany-Walen).

Play therapists use play techniques to investigate children's lifestyle, help children examine their faulty assumptions, and help them draw more positive perceptions about self, others, and the world. When observing children exhibiting more socially appropriate goals, play therapists can encourage children's behavior to help them move toward the positive goals of behavior (Kottman & Meany-Walen).

People's Perspective is Subjective

Another central construct in individual psychology is that people view their life subjectively. They filter the reality through their subjective interpretation of facts based on their convictions in their lifestyle and perception of how they believe about self, others, and the world (Ansbacher & Ansbacher, 1956; Carlson et al., 2006). Children usually develop their lifestyle and perceptions about self, others, and the world before the age of eight by observing interactions and reactions, examining self-worth, and exploring best ways to gain belonging and significance (Kottman & Meany-Walen, 2016).

Some of these perceptions and conclusions about life and relationships are not accurate because children lack experiences and perception to accurately evaluate and interpret the situations and relationships, leading them to develop mistaken beliefs and private logic. Hence, Adlerian play therapists must be aware of each child's subjective interpretation of various issues. When play therapists gather information from parents or teachers, they also need to remind themselves that parents and teachers may have different views of the relationships and situations.

Striving for Superiority

Adlerians believe that children are born inferior and not yet having a place of belonging and significance in their social environment; thus, they are motivated to move from feelings of inferior to superiority in which they feel competent and significant (Ansbacher & Ansbacher, 1956; Carlson et al., 2006). A sense of inferior can result in discouragement. Adlerian play therapists believe that children who feel discouraged may feel overwhelmed and worthless, and thereby may experience maladjustment because of their mistaken beliefs about self, others, and the world (Kottman & Meany-Walen, 2016).

Encouragement is a distinguish feature of Adlerian play therapy and is a significant intervention strategy throughout the play therapy process (Kottman, 2003). Encouragement is essential for children to learn and feel significant in their social environment. Encouragement also fosters a sense of significance and responsibility for children (Kottman). Adlerian play therapists focus on children's assets, effort, and improvement of children, parents, and teachers to enhance everyone's self-efficacy and encouraged feelings. Therefore, play therapists encourage children, parents, and teachers by providing unconditional acceptance, showing faiths in their abilities, recognizing their efforts, focusing on their strengths and assets, focusing on the positive, modeling the courage to be imperfect, helping them learn from mistakes, and developing positive ways to gain a sense of belonging (Kottman).

ADLERIAN PLAY THERAPY PROCESS

Adlerian play therapists work with the children and primary caregivers through four phases: (a) building an egalitarian relationship, (b) exploring the child's lifestyle, (c) helping the child gain insight, and (d) reorienting and reeducating the child (Kottman & Meany-Walen, 2016). In the first stage, Adlerian play therapists establish an egalitarian relationship with the children through tracking children's play behavior, reflection of feelings and content, questioning strategies, encouragement, active interaction with the children, cleaning playroom collaboratively, and limit settings (Kottman & Meany-Walen).

During the phase of exploring the child's lifestyle, play therapists not only observe children's play behavior and actively interact with children, but also use other strategies, such as questioning techniques and art assessments to gather information about children's goals of behavior, the Crucial Cs, personality priorities, the family constellation, family atmosphere, early recollections, assets, and private logic (Kottman & Meany-Walen, 2016). Play therapists conceptualize children based on the information obtained from the play sessions and parent consultations and further develop treatment plans, including goals and strategies for children and parents (Kottman & Meany-Walen).

In the third stage of Adlerian play therapy, play therapists' goal is to help the children better understand the goals of their behavior, their convictions about self, others, and the world, and the behavior they uses to get a sense of significance and belonging. Play therapists make interpretations of the children's play in the form of hypothesis about the goals of their behavior and lifestyles, and use role playing, metaphor, art techniques, confrontation, immediacy, and humor to help the children reexamine their thoughts, feelings, perceptions, attitudes, and behavior (Kottman & Meany-Walen, 2016). When children gain insight into their lifestyles and clarify about the purposes of their behavior, they may decide which of these behaviors or attitudes they want to continue or they want to make some changes in their life (Kottman & Meany-Walen).

In the reorientation/reeducation phase, play therapists help children learn and practice new ways of viewing self, others, and the world, behaving in different situations, and connecting to others. Play therapists use brainstorming and problem-solving strategies to help children learn new constructive manners and interactional patterns while helping parents enhance their parenting skills (Kottman & Meany-Walen, 2016). Importantly, Kottman and Meany-Walen noted that these phases are not discrete. It is essential that play therapists continue to build relationships with children throughout the process. Play therapists also can flexibly combine the techniques to help the children gain insights into their private logic or mistaken beliefs during the investigation phase or choose to teach some new skills during the insight phase. In order to have effective outcomes, it is crucial to go through the four phases.

ROLE OF ADLERIAN PLAY THERAPIST

In Adlerian play therapy, counselors conceptualize children and their social environment from an Adlerian perspective (Kottman, 2003). Traditionally, Adlerian counselors are more active and directive to facilitate client's insight and encourage client's reorientation and growth. Adlerian play therapists generally follow the four phases of Adlerian therapy; however, the role of the therapist is rather fluid throughout the course of play therapy (Kottman, 2003).

Kottman and Meany-Walen (2016) indicated that in the first phase, Adlerian play therapists use a relatively non-directive approach to allow children to explore the playroom freely. In the second phase, play therapists tend to be more active and directive to gather children's and parents' lifestyle information, including attitude, perceptions, thoughts, feelings, and interpersonal relationships (Kottman & Meany-Walen). During the third phase, play therapists play a partner role to communicate essential information, including children's lifestyle, goals of misbehavior, and mistaken beliefs to children and parents (Kottman & Meany-Walen). Play therapists may challenge children's mistaken beliefs about self, others, and the world, support their decision making to changes and crucial Cs, and encourage increased social interest. In the final phase, play therapists actively educate and encourage children and their parents and possibly teachers to make necessary changes in attitudes, behaviors, and beliefs with the goal of reorienting the insight gained in the therapy. Play therapists provide opportunities to allow children and parents to practice various skills, such as communication skills, social skills, and parenting skills to enhance interactions and cope with situations (Kottman & Meany-Walen).

CONSULTING PRIMARY CAREGIVERS AND TEACHERS

Watts (2006) stated that effective counselors needed to be capable of providing consultation and educational services. Kottman (2003) indicated that consulting with children's primary caregivers and teachers is a critical component in Adlerian play therapy because these adults play significant roles in children's life and bring important impact on children's lifestyle. In addition, primary caregivers and teachers can provide valuable information about children's developmental history, learning style, or interactional patterns. Importantly, they can provide support and encouragement for children's change throughout the therapy process. As children learn new ways to view themselves, others, and the world and develop new skills to practice socially appropriate behavior, primary caregivers and teachers can help children apply their new learning outside the playroom (Kottman).

Usually, primary caregivers and teachers also need play therapists' education to help them move in positive ways to interact with children (Kottman, 2003). Hence, having primary caregivers and teachers involvement is an imperative component of Adlerian play therapy. Alderian play therapists use basic counseling skills and teaching strategies to engage primary caregivers and teachers and tailor the consultations to meet individual needs of families and teachers (Kottman).

Caregiver Consultation

Caregiver consultations follow the same phases as Adlerian play therapy with a focus on investigating lifestyles of primary caregivers and children. The goals for consultations depend on the phase of play therapy (Kottman, 2003). During the first phase, play therapists work to build egalitarian relationships with parents. In the parent consultation, play therapists aim to explore parents' views about themselves as parents, their parenting styles, marital issues, and personal issues that may inhibit their ability to interact in a healthy manner with children. In the second phase, play therapists discuss the treatment plans with parents and outline strategies for working with parents based on their understanding of their children's needs (Kottman). In the third phase, play therapists simultaneously work with parents on helping them gain an understanding of lifestyles of parents and children with a goal of helping parents change their views and attitudes toward themselves and children (Kottman). In the reorientation/ reeducation phase, play therapists facilitate various strategies, such as modeling, brainstorming, problem solving, and teaching to help parents practice new strategies in their interactions with children (Kottman). Additionally, it is recommended that play therapists conduct a parenting training based on Adlerian principals, such as *Systematic Training for Effective Parenting (STEP)* program (Dinkmeyer & McKay, 1989) and *Positive Discipline* (Nelsen, 2006). Play therapists can also use a filial therapy model (Guerney, 1997) to train parents as therapeutic agents to enhance their relationships with children.

Teacher Consultation

Dinkmeyer (1987) indicated that during the therapeutic process, counselors needed to focus on their relationships with teachers as well. Kottman (2003) recommended that play therapists build relationships with teachers with a professional and collaborative manner. In order to get a holistic view of children's lifestyle, it is important for play therapists to gather information about children's interpersonal relationships at schools and children's view of self, others, and schools (Kottman, 2003). It is also helpful to investigate teachers' lifestyles, teaching styles, and their views toward children. Play therapists are encouraged to observe children at schools if permitted because play therapists can observe children's interactions with others and feel the atmosphere in the classrooms (Kottman, 2003). Some goals for teacher consultation are to share play therapists' information and insights about children's interactions with teachers and to help teachers gain a better understanding of the children's goals of behaviors and attitudes (Kottman, 2003). During the teacher consultation, play therapists provide some important information on Adlerian principals, including crucial Cs, goals of misbehavior, logical consequences, encouragement, and techniques that are applicable in the classrooms (Dinkmeyer, Dinkmeyer, & Sperry, 1987; Kottman, 2003). Similarly, several resources are available for teachers to incorporate Adlerian principals in the classrooms, including *Positive Discipline in the Classroom: Developing Mutual Respect, Cooperation, and Responsibility in Your Classroom* (Nelson, Lott, & Glenn, 2013), and *Systematic Training for Effective Teaching (STET)* (Dinkmeyer, McKay, & Dinkmeyer, 1980). Kinder Training (White, Flynt, & Draper, 1997) is another teacher training model that can be helpful for teachers to apply basic play therapy skills and Adlerian constructs in the classrooms.

APPLICATION OF THE MSJCC IN ADLERIAN PLAY THERAPY PROCESS

The Adlerian play therapy process is consistent with the MSJCC's emphasis of seeing clients' issues from a culturally contextual framework and its recommendations for working with clients from individual and systems levels. The MSJCC expect counselors to understand the sociocultural system that influences clients' well-being and to address corresponding issues appropriately through counseling and advocacy interventions. Specifically, counselors are suggested to provide interventions and strategies at the interpersonal, intrapersonal, institutional, community, policy, and global levels (Ratts, Singh, Butler, Nassar-McMillan, & McCullough, 2015). Adlerians believe that people must be understood within their cultural or social experiences. Adler postulated that an individual's culture, climate in which an individual live, and perception of his or her community and society at large play a role in an individual's creation of lifestyle and beliefs of self, others, and the world (Oberst & Stewart, 2003).

The MSJCC note privileged and marginalized counselors must develop self-awareness by exploring their attitudes and beliefs, develop knowledge, skills, and action relative to their self-awareness and worldview. Kottman and Meany-Walen (2016) stressed the importance of examining one's beliefs and held biases about other cultures when working with diverse children and their families. For example, Adlerian play therapists are recommended to ask self "What are your beliefs about the work ethic or intelligence of low-income families?", "What are your beliefs about parenting and discipline styles of different ethnic families?", "What is your internal reaction when you learn that a child is being raised by grandparents, same-sex parents, or single parent?", and "What resources do you provide to families who speak different language than yours?" (Kottman & Meany-Walen, p.32).

Multicultural and social justice competent counselors take initiative to explore clients' relationships with families, friends, and their communities so that counselors are able to identify clients' obstacles to progress and help them develop their support systems (Ratts et al., 2015). Adlerian play therapists observe children's interactions with families inside and outside of the therapy, attend to children's play behavior in the playroom to explore children's subjective view of self, others, and the world, and conduct classroom observations to identify children's classroom behavior and relationships with peers and teachers.

Counselors are also recommended to facilitate open and genuine conversations with clients to discuss their own cultures and identities, gather information about their clients' experiences with microaggression, discrimination, and oppression, and explore how privileged and marginalized identities might enhance or impede the counseling relationship (Ratts et al., 2015). Counselors also want to explore clients' issues through societal lenses by considering the impact of cultural norms and values on clients' well-being. In the Adlerian play therapy process, it is important that counselors bring this discussion into parent and teacher consultations by exploring how cultural backgrounds and experiences affect their relationships with child clients and counselors. Counselors also focus on discussing if children and their families think that society holds negative stereotypes or attitudes about their membership in a privileged or marginalized group. Counselors may utilize toys, art materials, games, and other play media to establish a trusting and working relationship so that children can explore and express their feelings and thoughts about their world. By using play media, children are able to gain awareness of their experiences and interaction with families and communities resulting in their interpersonal relationships and lifestyle.

In addition to focusing on individual changes, multicultural and social justice competent counselors also make efforts into community and institutional change (Ratts et al., 2015). Adlerian play therapists advocate for children by collaborating with children's families and school personnel to improve home and school environments that might inhibit children's well-being and growth. For example, Adlerian play therapists might advocate for children's emotional and behavioral needs by attending a school meeting to discuss inequity issues that are affecting children's learning environment. Counselors also provide teacher consultations and professional development trainings to help teachers gain a better understanding of children's needs and learn new ways of interacting with children.

CASE CONCEPTUALIZATION AND TREATMENT PROCESS

Lifestyle Conceptualization

From an Adlerian perspective, counselors can develop a picture of how children's lifestyles are reflected in their patterns of misbehaviors, thoughts, attitudes and relationships by considering the crucial Cs, the goals of misbehavior, and personality priorities (Kottman, 2003). Kottman indicated that in order to survive and flourish, children must master each of the crucial Cs, which are courage, connect, capable, and count. Based on my observation of Alex's play behavior and his report, Alex seemed to struggle with connect and count. Children who do not have the skills necessary to connect will feel isolated and insecure, where those who do not feel as though they count will feel insignificant (Kottman). In the playroom, Alex showed a play theme of relationship building as evidenced by his frequently saying "look, I did it" or "look what I got" and bringing all the toys in front of me and inviting me to join his play, indicating his desire to get attention from me. Alex also shared the need to protect his sister from bad people and he would play out wishing to have his own bedroom in the family dollhouse, indicating Alex's challenge of feeling counted in the family.

Given that Alex had been exposed to various ACEs, he appeared to seek connections with his family and me in order to feel that he has a sense of belonging in the playroom and with his family. Alex also seemed to possess low self-esteem and caution to answer the questions about his family when I explored his family atmosphere and relationships. He would look down or change play behavior when

I reflected his emotions and thoughts about the family issues. Additionally, Alex seemed to feel no power or control in his life and to believe that he only counts if he protects his sister and takes care of his family.

In terms of personality priority, Dinkmeyer and Sperry (2000) described it is a pattern of behaviors and reactions that are based on a person's convictions about how he or she acquires belonging, significance, and a sense of mastery. Alex seemed to have developed control as his personality priority as evidenced by his attempt to control my reflections and behavior in the playroom. He was eager to get more attention from his grandparents and uncles through goals of misbehavior.

Alex's family atmosphere appears to be chaotic-conflictual, hopelessness, and inharmonious. Parents in this type of family atmosphere often discipline their children in an inconsistent manner and structure, depending on their mood and status of their marital conflict (Kottman & Meany-Walen, 2016). Having witnessed verbal or physical abuse between their parents, children from chaotic-conflictual families often develop an idea that having power and control is the only way interacting with others (Kottman & Meany-Walen). Therefore, Alex seemed to develop mistaken beliefs that by acting angry, he can control others, connect with them, and receive more attention. He also seemed to believe the need to protect his family, which is a typical characteristic of a first-born child in the family constellation. Mr. Garcia further shared that he told Alex to be brave and to protect his family because in Latino culture men are supposed to be strong and protect their families. Consequently, Alex's lifestyle is a method of expressing anger, frustration, and power in order to obtain a sense of significance, belonging, and to engage with others.

Due to the childhood trauma of abuse, domestic violence, and mother's absence, Alex had experienced fear, worry, insecurity, and sadness in his life. Impacted by his father, Alex seemed to tend to express his anger with physical aggressions toward his family and he often had bad dreams about monster's coming at night. Alex seemed to strive for a sense of belonging in the family as evidenced by his report that he did not have a room in grandparent's house and grandparent's report that Alex had moved from one house to another house with his father.

Treatment Goals and Therapy Process

Over the course of Adlerian play therapy, I conducted 22 weekly individual play therapy sessions with Alex and five caregiver consultation sessions to support Mr. and Mrs. Garcia. My overall treatment goals included (a) increasing Alex's positive goals of behavior and self-regulation skills, (b) helping Alex substitute positive convictions from mistaken beliefs, (c) enhancing Alex's grandparent's compassion toward Alex's behavior and needs by teaching Alex's grandparents basic play therapy skills and language, and (d) improving caregiver-child attachment. The following illustrates how I worked with Alex and his grandparents through Adlerian play therapy four phases using the MSJCC framework.

Prior to the first play session, I conducted a caregiver consultation session with Mr. and Mrs. Garcia and one of Alex's uncle to gather more information about Alex's background, presenting issues, and his family's goals of counseling. I was aware that Mr. and Mrs. Garcia's preferred language is Spanish, but they tried their best to communicate with me in English given that I am not a Spanish-speaking counselor. Alex's uncle would sometimes translate his parents' disclosure in the session. I observed Mr. and Mrs. Garcia's uncertainty of the counseling process and their tendency to see me as an expert. Therefore, I made efforts to foster an egalitarian relationship with them by sharing my professional background, clinical experiences, explaining my role in the play therapy process, and my expectations for their involvement in the treatment. I also shared how my cultural background may be very different from their values and beliefs and thus, I appreciate their sharing to help me gain a better understanding of Alex's and their needs. They all seemed appreciative of my genuineness and care about Alex's situation.

In the first play session, I observed Alex's interactions with his sister and grandparents in the waiting area. Alex looked cautious and nervous about going to the playroom when I met him in the waiting area. Being aware of his young age and his history of ACEs, I began the play therapy process by building a collaborative and egalitarian relationship with Alex. I communicated respect, unconditional acceptance, and trust in Alex's abilities in the playroom by means of tracking his play, reflecting feeling and content, consistent limits setting, and encouragement. After the first session, Alex seemed happier and less anxious walking to the playroom. During the first several sessions, Alex looked hesitant to initiate the play and he did more exploratory play by looking around the room and playing briefly with different categories of toys. Gradually, Alex appeared to play more freely and had more interactions with me as evidenced by his increased verbal communication and invitation to his play after four play therapy sessions.

In the phase of exploring the child's life, I made efforts to gain a deeper understanding of Alex's lifestyle, personality priority, goals of behavior, and crucial Cs through his verbalization and play behavior in the playroom as well as consultation with Mr. and Mrs. Garcia. During one self-directed puppet show, Alex created a scene where an alligator puppet was fighting for a rabbit puppet. I observed that Alex was not completely comfortable sharing his feelings yet; therefore, I used metaphoric techniques to reflect my observation of the puppet's goals and emotions. Alex then reported that the rabbit is his sister and he had to protect his sister because he is always her brother and he had to protect grandparents, too. After the session of the puppet show, Alex's play themes of dominance, control, and need to take care of others became apparent. Alex had shown control as his personality priority as evidenced by his attempt to control my reflections and behavior. For example, he frequently told me what to do and say. He was also eager to show me his power through some aggressive play behavior and would feel upset or frustrated when things did not go the way he wanted to in the playroom. I reflected his need to correct my responses, feel powerful by maintaining a sense of control, and seek attention from me through metacommunications.

Based on my observation of Alex's play behavior and reports, he seemed to feel challenged with the crucial C's of connect and count causing Alex feelings of isolation, insecurity, and insignificance. Alex had developed a mistaken belief that he only counts if he shows others his power to protect his sister and taking care of his grandparents. Alex also constantly sought attention from his family and me in order to feel that he belongs in the playroom and to his family. In addition, Alex's exposure to adverse events caused his perception of the family atmosphere as a skewed dynamic of chaos and powerless. Consequently, Alex had also developed a conviction that only by acting out angrily and aggressively, he could build relationships with others and receive attentions from others. I concluded that Alex's lifestyle is a method of expressing anger and frustration in order to obtain power, control, and attachment. Due to the trauma of physical and emotional abuse and abandonment, Alex had experienced fear, worry, insecurity, and sadness in his life. Lacking a secure attachment and role model, Alex tended to express his emotions with aggressions toward his family as well.

In the insight phase, in order to help Alex gain awareness of his lifestyle and mistaken beliefs, I elected to use puppets, mutual storytelling, and other creative arts to communicate the value of building relationships, empathize Alex's feelings and beliefs about connecting, and teach him new ways of connecting with others. I conveyed my tentative hypothesis about his mistaken beliefs about himself, others, and the world. I also facilitated encouragement to help him know that he is significant and counts. Moreover, I reflected the purpose of his attention seeking behavior to facilitate his insight into his goal of misbehavior and to help him understand that he does not need to be the center of attention to gain a sense of belonging. Furthermore, I continuously provided a safe environment where he can be a child and enjoy playing and having fun. I aimed to convey the idea that he can feel safe without showing aggression and even when he cannot control situations.

Alex's play behavior in the final phase was considerably different from his play at the beginning of our counseling relationship. His play became more spontaneous and relaxed with a sense of pleasure. He no longer exhibited a need to control my behavior or responses and did not seek attention from me to approve his abilities or significance. Instead, he connected with me in positive ways and showed play themes of mastery and resiliency. For example, during one session, he created a challenging situation where toy soldiers were in a battle. He was able to use different strategies to end the war and he was proud that no one was injured. In the earlier stage of therapy, I would sense his frustration and disturbance whenever he was in a chaotic and deconstructive play. This change indicated that Alex made improvements in increasing his self-regulation skills, healing his traumatic experiences, and overcoming his faulty assumptions of his perceived world. Mr. and Mrs. Garcia also reported observing significant improvements in Alex's aggressive behavior at home. He interacted and communicated better with his family.

Throughout the course of play therapy, I regularly conducted caregiver consultations. I began with assessing Mr. and Mrs. Garcia's lifestyle and supported their parenting roles in Alex's transition. I helped them understand Alex's lifestyle, mistaken beliefs, and goals of misbehavior. I discussed Alex's need for gaining a sense of control and belonging. I showed my respect toward their cultural value of patriarchal structure. However, I shared with them that Alex's childhood trauma influenced his sense of value and potentially affected Alex's perception of himself, others, and the world. They seemed to get a better understanding of Alex's underlying purpose of behavior. I collaborated with them to come up some ideas to help Alex feel safe, decrease his fear of abandonment, and seek healthy ways to seek power. Additionally, I taught them some basic play therapy skills, such as reflection of feelings, encouragement, limits setting, and choice giving to help them develop better relationships with Alex, feel capable of parenting, and help Alex feel significant and count. Mr. and Mrs. Garcia were very cooperative and willing to adapt new ways to interact with Alex. Alex's uncles were also supportive and understanding of Alex's situation. His uncles would take turns to attend the caregiver consultations with Mr. and Mrs. Garcia as well. Knowing that Alex missed a father figure in his life, the two uncles both wanted to show him a good role model.

In addition to conducting caregiver consultation, with caregivers' permission, I contacted Alex's schoolteacher over the phone to address the teacher's concerns. Although Alex's behavioral issues mostly were presented at home, I aimed to advocate for Alex's needs systematically. Thus, I encouraged the teacher to be aware of Alex's withdrawing behavior in the classroom and showed the teacher ways, such as active listening, to reflect Alex's behavioral and emotional needs. I also helped the teacher find creative ways to help Alex feel significant in the classroom, such as assigning him a special task to help peers so that he would increase his self-esteem and feel counted. The teacher shared her appreciation for me reaching out and helping her feel more prepared to address Alex's needs if necessary.

CONCLUSION

Research has indicated that adverse childhood experiences (ACEs) can cause negative outcomes on physical and mental health issues, including asthma, obesity, attention-deficit hyperactivity disorder, depression, and substance use over the lifespan (Caballero et al., 2017; Loria & Caughy, 2017). Hispanic immigrant children are the fastest-growing child population in the U.S. (Passel & Cohn, 2008). Hispanic children, including US-born and foreign-born children have shown a higher prevalence of ACEs exposures in the U.S. (Loria & Caughy, 2018). Children who have experienced ACEs are more likely to have emotional and behavioral challenges (Sacks & Murphey, 2018). Consequently, they may benefit from counseling services.

Adlerian play therapy developed by Terry Kottman (1995) is a play therapy model based on the theoretical constructs of individual psychology (Adler, 1964). It is a developmentally appropriate approach where counselors use play as a modality to work with children exhibiting a wide spectrum of social-emotional and behavioral issues (Kottman & Meany-Walen, 2016). Adlerian play therapy is also a culturally responsive intervention. It has shown its effectiveness to work with children from diverse cultures and ethnic groups (Kottman & Meany-Walen). Moreover, given Adlerian's focus on clients' subjective perception of self, others, and the world, counselors are able to understand how clients' views lead to their responses to ethnic values and perceptions.

Multicultural and social justice competencies have been considered as core values to work effectively with clients from diverse backgrounds. The Multicultural and Social Justice Counseling Competencies (MSJCC) developed by Ratts et al. (2015) has served as a conceptual framework for competent multicultural counseling practice. The central concern of MSJCC is that counselors and clients both bring to the counseling relationship a constellation of identities, social locations, cultural values, beliefs, and biases. It is important that counselors address how the interactions of power, privilege, and oppression influence the client in all aspects of the counseling profession.

The process of Adlerian play therapy is congruent with MSJCC framework. It addresses the complex of identities that counselors and clients bring to the therapeutic relationship. The ultimate goal in Adlerian play therapy is for counselors to use the therapeutic relationship with children and their families to help the family enhance their understanding of interpersonal and intrapersonal dynamics and to allow the family to use these insights to make necessary changes in their thoughts, feelings, behavior, and attitude (Kottman & Meany-Walen, 2016). To accomplish this goal, it is crucial that Adlerian play therapists develop self-awareness, knowledge, skills, and action related to their self-awareness and worldview. Adlerian play therapists are recommended to examine their beliefs and biases or prejudice about other cultures when working with diverse children and their families. Adlerian play therapists conceptualize children's presenting issues from a cultural and social context and work with them from individual and systems levels (Oberst & Stewart, 2003). Adlerian play therapists discuss children's experiences with power, privilege, and oppression during parent and teacher consultations by exploring how cultural backgrounds and experiences affect their relationships with child clients and counselors. During play therapy sessions, counselors utilize toys, art materials, games, and other play media to establish a trusting and working relationship with children and allow children to explore and express their feelings and thoughts about their world.

To help children develop their support system, Adlerian play therapists take initiative to observe children's interactions with families both inside and outside of the therapy, attend to children's play behavior in the playroom to explore children's subjective view of self, others, and the world, and conduct classroom observations to better understand children's school behavior and interpersonal relationships. Notably, Adlerian play therapists advocate for children's mental health by collaborating with children's families and school personnel to improve the social environment that might impede children's well-being and growth. The presented case example of Alex and his families illustrates how I, a marginalized counselor, worked with a marginalized child who has experienced ACEs. Utilizing MSJCC as a framework, I was aware of my power and privilege that may bring in our counseling relationship. Thus, I was mindful of my approach to involving Alex and his families in the therapy by understanding their needs in a cultural context. I was able to address barriers and create opportunities for advocacy when helping Alex heal his wound.

REFERENCES

Adler, A. (1964). *The individual psychology of Alfred Adler: A systematic presentation in selections from his writings* (H. L. Ansbacher & R. R. Ansbacher, Eds.). New York, NY: Harper Perennial. (Original work published 1956)

Ansbacher, H., & Ansbacher, R. (Eds.). (1956). *The individual psychology of Alfred Adler: A system presentation in selection from his writings*. San Francisco, CA: Harper & Row.

Bettner, B. L., & Lew, A. (2005). *Raising kids who can.* Connexions.

Bratton, S., Ray, D., Rhine, T., & Jones, L. (2005). The efficacy of play therapy with children: A Meta-analytic review of the outcome research. *Professional Psychology, Research and Practice*, *36*(4), 376–390. doi:10.1037/0735-7028.36.4.376

Burke, N. J., Hellman, J. L., Scott, B. G., Weems, C. F., & Carrion, V. G. (2011). The impact of adverse childhood experiences on an urban pediatric population. *Child Abuse & Neglect, 35*(6), 408–413. doi:10.1016/j.chiabu.2011.02.006 PMID:21652073

Caballero, T. M., Johnson, S. B., Muñoz Buchanan, C. R., & DeCamp, L. R. (2017). Adverse childhood experiences among Hispanic children in immigrant families versus US-native families. *Pediatrics, 140*(5), e20170297. doi:10.1542/peds.2017-0297 PMID:28993445

Carlson, J., & Slavik, S. (Eds.). (1997). *Techniques in Adlerian psychology*. Washington, DC: Accelerated Development.

Carlson, J., Watts, R. E., & Maniacci, M. (2006). *Adlerian therapy: Theory and practice*. Washington, DC: American Psychological Association. doi:10.1037/11363-000

Centers for Disease Control and Prevention. (2016). *Adverse childhood experiences (ACEs)*. Retrieved from https://www.cdc.gov/ violenceprevention/acestudy/index.html

Dinkmeyer, D. C., Dinkmeyer, D. C. Jr, & Sperry, L. (1987). *Adlerian counseling and psychotherapy* (2nd ed.). Columbus, OH: Merrill.

Dinkmeyer, D. C., McKay, G., & Dinkmeyer, D. Jr. (1980). *Systematic training for effective teaching (STET)*. Circle Pines, MN: American Guidance Service.

Dinkmeyer, D. C., & McKay, G. D. (1989). *The parent's handbook: Systematic training for effective parenting* (3rd ed.). Circle Pines, MN: American Guidance Service.

Dreikurs, R., & Soltz, V. (1964). *Children: The challenge. New York, NY.* Hawthorn: Dutton.

Flaherty, E. G., Thompson, R., Dubowitz, H., Harvey, E. M., English, D. J., Proctor, L. J., & Runyan, D. K. (2013). Adverse childhood experiences and child health in early adolescence. *JAMA Pediatrics, 167*(7), 622–629. doi:10.1001/jamapediatrics.2013.22 PMID:23645114

Guerney, L. F. (1997). *Filial therapy*. Hoboken, NJ: John Wiley & Sons.

Jimenez, M. E., Wade, R. Jr, Schwartz-Soicher, O., Lin, Y., & Reichman, N. E. (2017). Adverse childhood experiences and ADHD diagnosis at age 9 years in a national urban sample. *Journal of the American Academy of Pediatrics, 17*(4), 356–361. doi:10.1016/j.acap.2016.12.009 PMID:28003143

Jung, M. (1998). *Chinese American family therapy: A new model for clinicians.* San Francisco, CA: Jossey-Bass.

Kerker, B. D., Zhang, J., Nadeem, E., Stein, R. E., Hurlburt, M. S., Heneghan, A., ... McCue Horwitz, S. (2015). Adverse childhood experiences and mental health, chronic medical conditions, and development in young children. *Journal of the American Academy of Pediatrics*, *15*(5), 510–517. doi:10.1016/j.acap.2015.05.005 PMID:26183001

Kottman, T. (1995). *Partners in play: An Adlerian approach to play therapy.* Alexandra, VA: American Counseling Association.

Kottman, T. (1999). Integrating the crucial Cs into Adlerian play therapy. *Journal of Individual Psychology*, *55*(3), 288–297.

Kottman, T. (2001). Adlerian play therapy. *International Journal of Play Therapy*, *10*(2), 1–12. doi:10.1037/h0089476

Kottman, T. (2003). *Partners in play: An Adlerian approach to play therapy* (2nd ed.). Alexandra, VA: American Counseling Association.

Kottman, T., Bryant, J., Alexander, J., & Kroger, S. (2009). Partners in the schools: Adlerian school counseling. In A. Vernon & T. Kottman (Eds.), *Counseling theories: Practical applications with children and adolescents in school settings* (pp. 47–83). Denver, CO: Love.

Kottman, T., & Meany-Walen, K. (2016). *Partners in play: An Adlerian approach to play therapy* (3rd ed.). Alexandra, VA: American Counseling Association.

Kottman, T., & Warlick, J. (1989). Adlerian play therapy: Practical considerations. *Journal of Individual Psychology*, *45*(4), 433–446.

Landreth, G. (2012). *Play therapy: The art of the relationship* (3rd ed.). New York, NY: Routledge. doi:10.4324/9780203835159

LeBlanc, M., & Ritchie, M. (1999). Predictors of play therapy outcomes. *International Journal of Play Therapy*, *8*(2), 19–34. doi:10.1037/h0089429

Lew, A., & Bettner, B. L. (1996). *A parent's guide to understanding and motivating children.* Connexions Press.

Loria, H., & Caughy, M. (2018). Prevalence of adverse childhood experiences in low-income Latino immigrant and nonimmigrant children. *The Journal of Pediatrics*, *192*, 209–216. doi:10.1016/j.jpeds.2017.09.056 PMID:29246345

Martinez, J. I., Gudiño, O. G., & Lau, A. S. (2013). Problem-specific racial/ethnic disparities in pathways from maltreatment exposure to specialty mental health service use for youth in child welfare. *Child Maltreatment*, *18*(2), 98–107. doi:10.1177/1077559513483549 PMID:23630401

Meany-Walen, K. K., Bratton, S., & Kottman, T. (2014). Effects of Adlerian play therapy on reducing students' disruptive behaviors. *Journal of Counseling and Development*, *92*(1), 47–56. doi:10.1002/j.1556-6676.2014.00129.x

Meany-Walen, K. K., Kottman, T., Bullis, Q., & Dillman Taylor, D. (2015). Adlerian play therapy with children with externalizing behaviors: Single case design. *Journal of Counseling and Development*, *93*, 294–428. doi:10.1002/jcad.12040

Mersky, J. P., Topitzes, J., & Reynolds, A. J. (2013). Impacts of adverse childhood experiences on health, mental health, and substance use in early adulthood: A cohort study of an urban, minority sample in the U.S. *Child Abuse & Neglect*, *37*(11), 917–925. doi:10.1016/j.chiabu.2013.07.011 PMID:23978575

Morrison, M. O. (2009). Adlerian play therapy with a traumatized boy. *Journal of Individual Psychology*, *65*, 57–68.

Nelsen, J. (2006). *Positive discipline* (Rev. ed.). New York: Ballantine Books.

Nelsen, J., Lott, L., & Glenn, S. (2013). *Positive discipline in the classroom: Developing mutual respect, cooperation, and responsibility in your classroom* (4th ed.). New York, NY: Three Rivers Press.

Oberst, U., & Stewart, A. (2003). *Adlerian psychotherapy: An advanced approach to individual psychology*. New York, NY: Brunner-Routledge.

Passel, J. S., & Cohn, D. (2008). U.S. population projections: 2005-2050. *Pew Research Center*. Retrieved from www.pewhispanic.org/2008/02/11/us-population-projections-2005-2050

Ratts, M. J., Singh, A. A., Nassar-McMillan, S., Butler, S. K., & McCullough, J. R. (2015). *Multicultural and social justice competencies*. Retrieved from https://www.counseling.org/docs/default-source/competencies/multicultural-and-social-justice-counseling-competencies.pdf?sfvrsn=20

Ray, D. (2011). *Advanced play therapy: Essential conditions, knowledge, and skills for child practice*. New York, NY: Routledge. doi:10.4324/9780203837269

Rotter, J. C., Horak, R. A. Jr, & Heidt, H. M. (1999). Incorporating children's drawings as early recollections in Adlerian psychotherapy. *Journal of Individual Psychology*, *55*, 316–327.

Sacks, V., & Murphey, D. (2018). *The prevalence of adverse childhood experiences, nationally, by state, and by race or ethnicity*. Retrieved from https://www.childtrends.org/publications/prevalence-adverse-childhood-experiences-nationally-state-race-ethnicity

Sacks, V., Murphey, D., & Moore, K. (2014). *Adverse childhood experiences: National and state level prevalence* (Research Brief No. 2014-28). Retrieved from https://childtrends-ciw49tixgw5lbab.stackpathdns.com/wp-content/uploads/2014/07/Brief-adverse-childhood-experiences_FINAL.pdf

Sheu, H., & Fukuyama, M. A. (2007). Counseling international students from East Asia. In H. D. Singaravelu & M. Pope (Eds.), *A handbook for counseling international students in the United States* (pp. 173–193). Alexandria, VA: American Counseling Association.

Snow, M. S., Buckley, M. R., & Williams, S. C. (1999). Case study using Adlerian play therapy. *Journal of Individual Psychology*, *55*(3), 288–297.

White, J., Flynt, M., & Draper, K. (1997). Kinder Therapy: Teachers as therapeutic agents. *International Journal of Play Therapy*, *6*(2), 33–49. doi:10.1037/h0089407

Chapter 2
Just Eat!
The Case of the Martinez Family

Kristen N. Dickens
Georgia Southern University, USA

EXECUTIVE SUMMARY

This chapter explores the application of the 2015 Multicultural and Social Justice Counseling Competencies (MSJCC) in conjunction with an eclectic family systems when counseling a Latin@ family. The Martinez family was referred to family counseling due to concerns of one of the children's school counselors, regarding a possible eating disorder diagnosis. The case study includes a rich description of the first session with the Mexican-American Martinez family, and examines family dynamics around the identified client, Javier. The Martinez family includes the following members: (1) Mañuel, Javier's 41 year-old father who owns his own construction business; (2) Camila, Javier's 38 year-old stay-at-home mother; (3) Alejandro, Javier's 17-year-old brother; and (4) Isabella, Javier's 12 year-old sister. A discussion of the author's cultural background, counseling approach, and use of the MSJCC lens when working with the Martinez family is also included. Initial goals and prognosis for treatment are considered.

DOI: 10.4018/978-1-7998-0022-4.ch002

INTRODUCTION TO THE CASE

This chapter explores the application of the Multicultural and Social Justice Counseling Competencies (MSJCC; Ratts, Singh, Nassar-McMillan, Butler, & McCullough, 2015) in conjunction with an integrative family systems approach when counseling a Latin@ family. The Martinez family was referred to family counseling due to concerns of one of the children's school counselors, regarding depressive symptoms and a possible eating disorder diagnosis. The case study includes a rich description of the first session with the Mexican-American Martinez family, and examines family dynamics around the identified client, 15-year-old Javier. The Martinez family includes the additional following members: (a) Mañuel, Javier's 41-year-old father; (b) Camila, Javier's 38-year-old mother; (c) Alejandro, Javier's 17-year-old brother; and (d) Isabella, Javier's 12-year-old sister. Mañuel and Camila were both born and raised in the United States. Mañuel's parents were born in Mexico and are currently deceased; Camila's parents were born in Mexico and immigrated to the United States before Camila was born. A discussion of the author's cultural background, counseling approach, and use of the MSJCC lens when working with the Martinez family is also included. Initial goals and prognosis for treatment are also considered.

Use of the Term "Latin@s"

Latina/o and *Hispanic* are two terms historically used to describe individuals living in the United States with ancestral ties to Central and South American Spanish and non-Spanish speaking countries (Sue, Sue, Neville, & Smith, 2019). Furthermore, some individuals prefer specific ethnic descriptors that speak to the certain countries (e.g., *Puerto Rican, Cuban, Chicano*), despite the U.S. Census usage of the term *Hispanic*. In recent years scholars advocated for gender neutral ethnic identifiers such as *Latinx* and *Latin@/@s* rather than the gendered terms *Latina* and *Latino* (Ratts and Pedersen, 2014; Sue et al., 2019). In this chapter the term *Latin@/@s* will be used as the ethic descriptor for the client.

Counseling Latin@s

The literature on counseling Latin@s is vast; however, in this chapter I will share brief information on this client population, including cultural values and characteristics and implications for counseling. The African diaspora, the immigration of individuals from Asian and European countries, combined with the blending of indigenous people in Latin America led to a broad continuum of physical traits and phenotypes, and influenced which ethnic labels individuals use as self-descriptors (U.S. Census

Bureau, 2017). In 2018, Latin@s represented approximately 18.1% of the population, and continue to be the minority group with the largest population in the United States (Sue et al., 2019; U.S. Census Bureau, 2019). The origins of Latin ancestry include Puerto Rico, Central America (Nicaragua, Costa Rica, Honduras, El Salvador, Panama, Guatemala), Spain, Mexico, Cuba, and South America (Venezuela, Argentina, Ecuador, Bolivia, Peru, Chile, Uruguay, Colombia, Paraguay) (U.S. Census Bureau, 2017). The three largest Latin@ groups in the United States are Cubans, Mexicans, and Puerto Ricans (Ratts & Pedersen, 2014). In the United States, Spanish is the second most common language after English (Ratts & Pedersen, 2014).

For individuals to conceptualize the experiences of Latin@s in present day, they must also acknowledge the transgenerational effects of colonization within the Latin@ community. European and North American white settlers used manifest destiny to justify the removal, rape, and genocide of Latin@s from their homelands over time, including parts of North America. The colonizers' belief in "manifest destiny" or "divine intervention from God" promoted a false narrative that dehumanized and delegitimized the rights of indigenous people to their native lands (Ratts & Pedersen, 2014, p. 180). The early relations and history of aggressive displacement laid the groundwork of long-standing mistrust between Latin@s and Anglo-Americans.

Cultural stereotypes and prejudices towards Latin@s persisted over time, and significantly impacted the way Latin@ individuals are viewed in the present day (Ratts & Pedersen, 2014; Sue et al., 2019). For example, despite the long history of Latin@s living in the United States, many Americans view them as having immigrated to North America (Ratts & Pedersen, 2014). Almost one-fourth of the 37% of Latin@ adult immigrants are undocumented, though approximately half of all Latin@ Americans adults report fears that they, or a friend or family member will be deported (Lopez, Taylor, Funk, & Gonzalez-Barrera, 2013). It is imperative for counselors to be aware of the history of racism and discrimination that Latin@s historically—and currently—face in the United States. For example, a Latin@ client referred to a white counselor may be apprehensive to disclose information about their family, especially if a family member is undocumented (Lopez et al., 2013). If the counselor is unaware of the history and current political climate affecting Latin@ individuals, there will likely be some difficulty establishing rapport and building trust with the client. Important considerations for counselors working with Latin@ clients is carefully explaining the nature and limits of confidentiality and how information is kept. These practices can help dispel myths that client information will be shared with immigration authorities such as Border Patrol officers (Velasquez, Gonzales, Butcher, Castillo-Canez, Apodaca, & Chavira, 1997).

Latin@ Cultural Values

One important cultural value of Latin@s is *familisimo*, which relates to family connectedness and interdependence (Baumann, Kuhlberg, & Zayas, 2010). The role of family, including extended family members is widely recognized in Latin@ culture, and includes many positive aspects. Implication for counseling includes the counselor's consideration of how family members' opinions of presenting issues affect the main individual client, or in family counseling, the individual(s) whose behavior prompted the family to seek counseling.

Gender roles and expectations are additional cultural values counselors should consider when working with Latin@s. Hierarchical gender roles are common in Latin@ families, including a male family member as the authority (e.g., father), while children are expected to respectful and follow parental orders (Sue et al., 2019). Counselors should be aware of an individual's role within their family system, including gender stereotypes and hierarchies, and how family norms and rules impact the individual's ability to function in the world (including outside of the family). When working with families, counselors assist members into exploring family values and unspoken messages that shaped their understanding of gender roles and stereotypes. For example, men are expected to be providers for the family and exude *machismo*, conveying strength, dominance, and toughness (Sue et al, 2019). Conversely, women are socialized to be selfless, nurturing, and passive; children are expected to obey parents. Conflict can arise Latin@ individuals struggle with the gender role expectations put upon them.

Stigma around mental health and illness is a significant cultural challenge for Latin@ clients (Sue et al., 2019). Counselors must take time to build rapport and establish trust with clients in an effort to form a collaborative relationship. Counselor should also consider incorporating psychoeducation about the nature of counseling into sessions. When clients employ different therapeutic techniques or assessments, it is wise to discuss them with clients ahead of time (Sue et al., 2019). Acculturation conflicts are another challenge to consider for counselors working with Latin@ clients. The concept of "acculturation" is broadly defined "as the process by which individuals adapt to a new living environment and potentially adopt the norms, values, and practices of their new host society" (Abraído-Lanza, Echeverría, & Flórez, 2016, p. 220). Differences in societal values, including those between a non-Latin@ counselor and a Latin@ client, are critical for multiculturally competent counselors to consider. Counselors should be prepared to discuss acculturation conflicts with clients, in an effort to be sensitive to their cultural value clashes (Sue et al., 2019).

INTRODUCTION TO THE COUNSELOR

Cultural Background

I identify as an English-European, white, cisgender, heterosexual, nondisabled, middle-class, educated, female counselor educator. I grew up in the southern United States, specifically Texas and North Carolina, had two parents (in a heterosexual egalitarian marriage) who both earned higher education master's degrees in helping professions (e.g., Pastoral Counseling and Speech Pathology). I have always lived in the middle-class socioeconomic status bracket and had close relationships with both parents. I teach at a rural university in the southeastern United States. I regularly teach the Multicultural Counseling course my counselor education program, during which time I work with students to identity and unpack their various levels of power, privilege, and oppressed statuses. I teach students about the importance of deciphering who they are as multicultural beings, and how this impacts their relationships with future clients. One tool that assists clients with this process is Johnson's (2018) chapter on "privilege, oppression, and difference," in which he presented Loden and Rosener's (1991) "Diversity Wheel." Loden and Rosener's (1991) wheel includes an internal ring of social characteristics (e.g., sexual orientation, race, age, gender, sex, physical abilities, qualities like height) and an outer ring that includes other categories (e.g., marital status, religion, parental status, social class, education, occupation, and income) (as cited in Johnson, 2018). Johnson (2018) discussed the concept of mapping our individual differences, in order to take inventory of our status in different privileged and marginalized groups. Students are tasked with completing the wheel, and then contemplating how their lives would be different if one of their privileged statuses were taken away (e.g., going from being nondisabled to having a physical disability). We also discuss the ways in which clients may judge us based on our noticeable levels of privilege, especially if they belong to marginalized groups that are diametrically in conflict with the counselor's privilege. For example, as a white able-bodied woman with a doctorate, some clients my initially be vary of my racial, ability, and educational privileges before we even discuss their reasons for coming to counseling. Conversely, I lack some gender privilege when it comes to working with male clients due to the pervasive sexist and patriarchal messages that exist in the United States. There have been some male clients who challenged my ability to counsel them solely based on my female gender (also intersected with my age). When clients voice a concern about my competency as a counselor as tied to one of my privileged or marginalized statuses, I explore their interpretation of how it could impact our therapeutic alliance.

Counseling Approach

My identity as a clinical mental health counselor stems from my initial master's-level training in the marriage and family concentration coursework. During my master's program, I learned about the various types of systems that exist within society, ranging from partnerships to families-of-origin and families-of-choice. My foundation as a counselor is rooted in my beliefs that everything exists within a system and that individuals are often influenced to think, feel, and act by the various systems in which they live. Due to my training in couples and family work, my counseling philosophy and approach is best described as systemic, with roots in Adlerian, Feminist, and Social Constructionist theories (e.g., Narrative Therapy). Narrative Therapy resonates with me, particularly the tenet that people are not the problems; problems are the problem (White, 2007). I believe it is vital to never assume and label the client's problem, but rather rely on the client to identify problem that they want to work through. The same is true for family counseling.

Through my clinical experiences, I observed a multitude of ways in which individuals sought to interpret their surroundings and find meaning in them. I listened to clients' narratives that often derived from the larger systems and social contexts in which dominant culture stories reign. When working as an in-home counselor in the field, I gained firsthand experience observing the ways in which family systems affect early childhood and adolescent development. Additional clinical experience working with hospitalized women and men struggling with disordered eating added to my foundational knowledge of systems, specifically the medical-model based hospital system. As a clinical mental health counselor, I advocate for the wellness model in lieu of the medical model. I view pathology as a limiting and potentially destructive method of classification that objectifies and labels people as the problem, rather than observing the client as someone experiencing a problem. I am trained in clinical diagnosing and developing corresponding treatment plans; however, I work to empower clients to separate them from their diagnoses. I also discuss with clients the importance of knowing how to unpack diagnoses and recognize the implications of diagnoses.

Clients come to counseling with a variety of expectations, goals, and values stemming from their individual experiences and diverse backgrounds. It is important for me to consider how clients' gender, race, culture, ability, sexual and affectional orientations, religion, age, and ethnicity factor into their readiness and openness for change. I view the client(s) as the expert and invite them to take leadership of their sessions and of their treatment, as part of my combined systems and Feminist theoretical approach to counseling (Bitter, 2014; Brown, 2010).

My counseling approach rooted in systems and social-constructionist theories align with family counseling, because dominant culture stories exist within the microcosm of any system. Families adopt narratives from the dominant culture about what a family should be, or how a partner should treat the other. There are stories that delineate the role of each person in the system. Working with families is similar to working with individuals, because each member is seeking to make meaning out of their experiences (Bitter, 2014). For example, each member of a family contributes their own (constantly changing) story to the dominant story about the family. Families attend counseling when the stories are in conflict with each other and/or when problems arise on both an individual and family or couple levels. I typically begin sessions by asking each family member to describe their perception of why they came to family counseling. This first step allows me to explore with the family how the problem has disrupted the family system, during which I make sure to hear from all individuals within the family. I emphasize to the family that the family unit is the main client, and it is vital to address overall family goals. I also provide space for individual family members to express their personal goals and explores how their goals align with (or do not) the family unit's goal(s). Once goals are established, my goal is to collaborate with clients on how to re-author a new story, one in which they feel empowered and supported to thrive (White, 2007). In subsequent sessions, I incorporate aspects of Adlerian Family Therapy, in which the family completes an Adlerian Lifestyle Assessment that provides detailed information about family history, as well as information regarding mental health diagnoses, health problems, familial relationships (e.g., enmeshed, strained, cohesive), addictions, births, deaths, and other major family milestones. Using a teleological lens, when completing the assessment, I'm considering potential reasons for why family members are acting and interacting in certain ways (Bitter, 2014). In other words, having a framework for understanding the family dynamics provides deeper context for the purpose of individual members' behaviors. Once I have developed hypotheses about family members' behavior, I share them with the family, and discuss what new stories they want to create for the family unit looking forward. We then discuss ways to weave the potential new narratives into the family and individual goals for treatment.

MSJCC Lens

As a counselor and counselor educator, I am required by the American Counseling Association to integrate the MSJCC (Ratts et al., 2015) into my work with clients by integrating it into my theoretical counseling framework. The MSJCC's also serve as a lens through which I view the client and take into account the levels of privileged and marginalized statuses in the counseling relationship. The dimensions of the competencies require me to evaluate my self-awareness, the client's worldview, the dynamics of the counseling relationship, and counseling and advocacy initiatives. In each dimension, there is a repeated order for counselors to consider: awareness, knowledge, skills, and action (Ratts et al., 2015). The verbs in each of the four sub-dimensions hold special meaning for me: "acknowledge" (e.g., levels of awareness), "develop" (e.g., knowledge), "acquire" (e.g., various skills), and "take action" (e.g., seek out immersive cultural experiences) (Ratts et al., 2015). These words speak to my role as a counselor and provide direction for how I can increase my ongoing multicultural competence and infuse my knowledge into work with clients. Early in my development as a counselor-in-training, I struggled to understand the levels of power and privilege I held. When reading seminal works by McIntosh (1989) and Tatum (1997), I realized my skin color allowed me access to spaces and places to which people of color historically did not have access. I learned that even if I do not see my whiteness that others do, and it can impact our interactions. I started taking inventory of my privilege (e.g., race, education, ability) and recognized times when I am in the minority group lacking privilege (e.g., gender). Multicultural competence is a lifelong journey, not a destination; thus, I am continuously self-reflecting on my biases, attitudes, and beliefs, as well as educating myself on various clients, cultures, and issues that are unfamiliar to me.

When I meet with clients, I take a quick inventory of the varying levels of power and privilege in the counseling relationship and remember that they may be doing the same in regards to me. In an effort to be transparent with clients, I will often acknowledge obvious differences in the room, such as age, race, and gender. I broach this conversation differently depending on the client, but typically build it into the discussion of what counseling is and sharing a little about who I am. I also ask the client to consider factors about the counseling relationship they perceive will help them engage in the counseling process, especially if relates to observed differences between us (e.g., race, gender, age). Engaging in this conversation takes additional time depending on the type of counseling, such as individual, couples, or family counseling. If a client expresses concerns about differences between us being potential barriers to counseling, we spend time unpacking those concerns and consider ways to overcome them.

Case Conceptualization

The Martinez family was referred to me by Javier's individual counselor. Javier is a 15-year-old Latin@ male client who is engaging in restricting behaviors, consistent with eating disorder-related diagnoses, and recently reported feeling depressed and overwhelmed. Javier's homeroom teacher observed Javier's behavioral decline from the beginning of the school year in August, when he was very engaged in his social relationships with peers and was excelling in his school work. Two months later, Javier's teacher reported a decrease in academic performance in class, and his isolation from peers. The teacher referred Javier to the school counselor, who subsequently referred Javier to an outpatient individual counselor. After meeting with Javier for three sessions, the counselor recommended family counseling as part of his treatment plan.

When the Martinez family arrived, Javier sat away from his parents and siblings in a chair. On an oversized couch, Isabella sat next to Camila, and Alejandro sat next to Mañuel. After everyone settled in their seats and briefly identified themselves by name, the following dialogue ensued:

Counselor: "I'm wondering who would like to share first why you are here."

All family members looked to Mañuel, except for Javier, who looked down and began playing with his shoe laces.

Mañuel: "Javier is the reason we're here, and I think he should be the one to tell you why."

Javier (without making eye contact): "I don't have a problem; my school counselor is making me talk to strangers for nothing…I'm fine."

Mañuel (looking directly at Javier while other family members looked away): (sternly) "Mijo, you tell the counselor why we're here, otherwise you are wasting time and money and we will leave."

I noticed Javier's eyes filling with tears, but he quickly wiped them away. Isabella left the couch to sit next to Javier, who turned away from her.

Isabella (looking at me): "Javi is sad because he thinks no one understands him. He used to play games with me, but now all he does is stay in his room."

Alejandro (rolling his eyes): "Yeah, I don't get what his problem is. He's in his room all the time."

Mañuel: "His two counselors said he's depressed and may have an eating disorder since he's not eating much anymore…I only thought girls and ballerinas had those! All I know is once he didn't make the soccer team, he started disrespecting us (pointing to Camila) by not eating the dinner that I work hard to pay for, and his mamá works hard to make. I don't know what his problem is, but he better figure it out soon, because he's making me take time away from my job to be here!"

Camila (looking at me): "I'm worried about Javi. I know he's been sad, but he won't talk about it. We've all tried to talk to him many times, but he won't be honest. He says he's not hungry at mealtimes, and then sits at the table in silence. He used to play soccer with this brother and sister, but now he says he will study in his room instead. He can't be studying because his grades are bad. I don't know what to do any more. It's like he's a ghost."

Continuing to talk with the family, I learned that Mañuel and Alejandro are very close, as are Camila and Isabella. Camila and Mañuel claimed they were all very close, but admitted that it's hard to spend time with Javier since he isolates himself.

Camila: "We've learned to leave him alone if he wants to be alone."

Mañuel: "No offense, but we don't really see the need for family counseling since this is Javier's issue. We're only here so his other counselor will keep seeing him." (Turns to Javier) "Javi, if you don't want to talk to strangers anymore, just eat and get over it. It will save us all a lot of time."

Theoretical Approach

When I meet with families for counseling, I address the "identified client" in the family last. The reason the Martinez family came to see me was due to Javier's behavior, as indicated by family members. The reasoning for this approach is to model that even if one family member required they all attend counseling, that member is not the root of the family distress. After everyone shared their brief opinions about the presenting problem, it was appropriate for me to check in directly with Javier. Javier continued to struggle to make eye contact with me when speaking, instead looking down and playing with his shoe laces. I first clarified his preference on being called "Javi" or "Javier." He responded that "Javi" was his preferred name, and said it was okay for me to use it when addressing him. This was important to me, as I hoped it would strengthen the therapeutic alliance between us. My plan after the aforementioned conversation with the Martinez family was to gain clarification from Javier about his view of the "problem." My initial clinical impressions were that he was struggling from low self-esteem, potentially stemming from: (a) not making the soccer team; (b) being a middle child who feels "lost" in the family due to poor familial bonds/connections; (c) a lack of established identity. Speaking directly to Javi, I acknowledged that everyone in the room seemed to have an opinion about what was going on with him, but I was curious to know what he thought. Javi was hesitant to respond, so I asked if he preferred I check in with his siblings and parents first, and then come back to hear his opinions. Javi nodded "yes" silently.

Having each family member clarify their opinions on why they came to counseling is vital to the family therapy process, as it allows members to communicate their thoughts openly with each other and sets the stage for establishing shared family goals (Bitter, 2014). Within family counseling, tension can arise if individual goals are in conflict with overarching goals for the family unit. Recognizing that the Latin@ family structure can include the father as the leader, I first invited Mañuel to expand his perspective on the problem (Sue et al., 2019). I do this while also considering the cultural values of *familisimo* and *machismo* I previously observed Mañuel taking the lead at the beginning of the session. Mañuel stated again that he felt like Javi's problem was not eating, and that because of his disrespectful behavior, the family was forced by his counselor to attend family counseling. I asked Mañuel to share about himself; he owns and operates a construction company, so he is often working long hours and is not home very much during the day. He stated that he found it disrespectful that Javi stopped listening to his parents and preferred to spend all his time in his room, now that he didn't make the soccer team. Mañuel further explained that he played soccer in high school, and taught Alejandro and Javi to play when they were small children. Mañuel said he was disappointed Javi didn't make the soccer team, because he wanted him to follow in his footsteps. Camila explained that she is a stay-at-home mom who loves spending time with her children and wants to know what they are doing at all times. She described herself as being firm, but loving, and stated her belief that mothers should always know what is going on with their children. She understood that they needed to come to family counseling because Javi "won't tell anyone what's going on so they can help fix it." Alejandro shrugged when it was his turn and told me he was annoyed with Javi and his "acting like an emotional girl." Isabella chose not to add more when prompted, and just said "Javi's sad, so we are all sad." When I returned back to Javi for his opinion, he shared that all his friends made the soccer team but him, so now he feels alone at school. He also mentioned that Isabella and Alejandro sometimes kick around the soccer ball at home, but he no longer has interest in playing.

After hearing from all parties, I explained the nature of family counseling, being sure to emphasize that the family members are the experts of their own lives, not me as the counselor. As previously mentioned, I inquired about any potential barriers they see to family counseling, including any concerns they had about my role as the counselor. Mañuel inquired how much expertise I would bring to the session, and if I was going to tell them how to be different. I assured him that I recognized and respected each individual's autonomy to make choices, and the family's autonomy to make decisions. Mañuel then corrected me and stated that he makes the family decisions, with some consultation from Camila.

Operating from my previously described family systems theoretical stance, I began hypothesizing possible reasons for Javi's distress resulting from stress within the family unit. Problems can emerge when family members are in conflict, such as dyads or triads, against other family members (Bitter, 2014), and when members argue about whose opinion is "correct." Within the Martinez family, three dyads were apparent: Mañuel and Alejandro, Isabella and Camila, and Mañuel and Camila. Javi appeared as a disconnected middle child, despite Isabella coming to sit by him earlier. It was evident that there were allies within the family; but who was Javi's ally? I also considered Javi's lack of social connections post not making the soccer team. It was clear that soccer was a beloved sport within the family, and something Mañuel hoped to pass down to his children. If Javi's main connection to his father was soccer, how would they connect now? Camila seemed unsure how to connect with Javi due to his intentional disconnection, yet her way of addressing it seemed to push Javi further away.

Next, I wanted to obtain discuss individual members' perspectives about the family, specifically the ways they interact, family rules and norms, and ways they think things could be "better." During this conversation I was mindful not to attribute problems to Javier, as he is already the "identified problem" in the family. The main vehicle through which we explored these concepts was through the Adlerian Lifestyle Assessment. Before using the assessment, I discussed its purpose and how it is meant to be used as a way to gain contextual information about the family. Because the assessment can feel deeply personal, I printed copies for Mañuel and Camila for their review. We discussed their questions and concerns prior to starting the assessment. Over the course of two sessions the Martinez family and I worked to address questions about their family system, including cultural values and influences, familial relationships, social relationships, family rules, family patterns of interacting, gender roles and expectations, and the influence of religion and spirituality. For the first part of the assessment, I met privately with Mañuel and Camila, as I wanted to recognize them as the heads of the family and receive their input first. We then completed the assessment with the opinions and feedback from all three children. When the assessment was completed, we discussed the stories that were told during the assessment and considered the current story of the family. We discussed what, if any, new stories family members wanted to tell, and how that could relate to setting family and individual goals in subsequent sessions.

Other Applicable Theories or Models

Historically, eating disorders and patterns of disordered eating have largely been attributed to females, despite evidence in the 17th century of men being diagnosed with symptoms similar to anorexia nervosa (Reyes-Rodriguez et al., 2011). Though evidence-based research points to the prevalence of eating disorders for boys and men, much stigma still remains due to lingering stereotypes associated with girls and women (Reyes-Rodriguez et al., 2011). Eating disorder risk factors for boys and men include, but are not limited to, those are athletes, survivors of childhood sexual abuse, and gay men (Reyes-Rodriguez et al., 2011). Research remains limited for Latino males, though this should not be perceived as an indicator that disordered eating is less of an issue for this client population.

Family counseling is one of the major components of evidenced-based eating disorder treatment, as it allows families to consider the impact of interpersonal dynamics on the individual with the alleged diagnosis (Fairburn, Cooper, & Shafran, 2003). Family counseling also requires that all members of the immediate family consider their role in the development of the eating disorder for the individual in question, oftentimes with the counselor highlighting breakdowns in communication and boundaries within the family unit. In the paperwork I received from Javi's referring counselor, there was evidence of disordered eating behaviors; however, there was not an official eating disorder-related diagnosis. Though Javi did not meet diagnostic criteria for an eating-related disorder, his weight loss and decreased appetite was still a significant clinical concern. I requested his parents take him to his pediatrician to have a wellness checkup and have his weight recorded. Additionally, I shared contact information for different nutritionists with whom the Martinez's could consult about Javi's eating habits. Mr. and Mrs. Martinez verbally contracted with me that they would not micromanage Javi's weight and eating habits, but rather save their concerns for a family counseling session. Javi is hypervigilant about his parents' observations of him, which could lead him to seeking ways to rebel by further isolating himself and disordered eating patterns (Fairburn, Cooper, & Shafran, 2003). As I continued to work with the family, Javi's individual counselor and primary care physician and I consulted about his depression symptoms and his eating patterns. Fortunately, Javi did not continue to lose weight, and slowly started to eat more regularly at home and school.

TREATMENT

Goals

Within the following two to four sessions, each family member was able to agree upon an overarching familial goal, as well as set at least one individual goal. The overarching goals for the family were to re-establish family cohesion and set appropriate boundaries. All members were able to articulate their vision of these goals and how they would know if they reached them. Camila stated that a cohesive family unit would include Mañuel being home for family dinner with her and the children. Javi said it would include him spending more time with Mañuel, instead of Mañuel and Alejandro spending time together away from Javi. He also mentioned that his parents and siblings would respect when he needed time alone to himself. Isabella said a cohesive family would include everyone eating and laughing together. Mañuel stated that his ideal cohesive family unit would include the children listening and obeying him and Camila, and that he would be able to dedicate individual time to each of his children while also setting aside time for just Camila. He also mentioned that he wasn't sure how to honor the boundary requests of his children, but he would try to listen to them more. Alejandro said that his siblings and parents would give him space when he asked for it, and that he would try to spend more time with Javi. Each member spent time considering what their role would be in helping reach the family goals, and intentionally set their personal goal(s) to align with the family goal. For example, Javi recognized that if he wanted his parents to respect his boundaries, he needed to take a proactive stance in honoring family rules instead of lashing out with anger and locking himself in his room for hours at a time. Mañuel realized that he needed to start talking less and listening more to his children (especially Javi) when they conveyed they were upset about something. Camila's goal was to try to be less intrusive with her children, and instead give them freedom to emote without her trying to problem-solve. Isabella said she would ask to spend time with her brothers, instead of barging into their rooms and tattle-telling on them to Camila. Lastly, Alejandro stated how he wanted his independence to be with his friends, but that he would make more of an effort to spend time with his family during the week and weekends. He noted that he would also stop making fun of Javi, and instead would try and be a supportive older brother.

Progress

Over the course of several sessions, the Martinez family was able to make progress toward their overarching family goals. One thing we discussed early on in our work together was the nonlinear process of change. I shared how oftentimes one family member will start working on their individual goals and forget to prioritize the family goals above their own. Conflict can emerge when individual goals take precedent, and members lose sight of the importance of family goals. I normalized this process and reminded the Martinez' that even when conflict arose, it indicated that members were still striving for change. Initially I observed family members struggling to uphold the family goal of setting boundaries, particularly when Camila and Mañuel were frustrated with Javi's low performance in school. After some coaxing, they were able to recognize that when they felt disappointed in Javi, they behaved in ways that unintentionally communicated anger toward Javi, who responded by isolating himself. By discussing these missed connection opportunities, we were able to explore how Javi preferred his parents communicate with him, and vice-versa. At times different family members would role play scenarios that happened in between counseling sessions and act out alternative endings that depicted what would happen if everyone was trying to meet the overall family goals.

I observed that as less of the focus was on Javi's behaviors, he seemed to open up more in session, and speak directly to his family members instead of to me about his family members. His initial trepidation and shyness from the first session soon dissipated as he became more comfortable with the family counseling format. If at times his parents or siblings wanted to focus on just Javi, I reminded them that family counseling is about everyone, so we would explore everyone's behavior and goals.

Despite Mañuel and Alejandro's initial discomfort and disengagement, I observed them to increase their participation in session and practice active listening skills. Mañuel also appeared to open up more with me as time went on, and I remained congruent in my stance from week to week. Before we utilized certain techniques (such as role plays) in session, I presented it as an option to the family, and allowed all members to weigh in. The agreement was that all members had to vote "yes" or "no" before a decision was made. It was rare that a technique was discarded by an individual, but nevertheless, my goal was to empower them to make decisions as a family unit.

A major focus was on open communication and boundaries within the family unit. Though I did not assume gender and hierarchical family roles for Latin@ families would automatically apply to the Martinez family, I did observe traditional gender roles and expectations as playing a role in the family conflict. For example, I observed Mañuel's frustration with Javi (and at times Alejandro) when they could not articulate their thoughts, and then when Javi tried to explain his feelings of loneliness. When Javi or Alejandro expressed any emotion other than "happy," Mañuel reacted strongly. This was a reaction I noticed early on in our work; however, I waited until Mañuel and I had built rapport before I specifically addressed his behavioral pattern. Eventually Mañuel shared that his father and grandfather never talked about their feelings, and he thought that women were the only ones who should express their emotions. Additionally, Javi shared that he did not know how to talk about his feelings, so he kept them bottled up and stayed to himself when he was upset. Camila acknowledged her desire to rescue Javi from being upset; however, this led to her pushing him further away. Overall, specific dyad relationships had to be examined and explored in order for members to discover new and effective ways of communicating with each other. When the Martinez family and I finally terminated the relationship, Javi had identified multiple adaptive coping skills he could use when he was upset, as had all other members of the family. Mañuel reported recognizing the value of expressing emotions, and even though he still did not feel entirely comfortable emoting, he was able to respect and honor when his children and wife needed to express their feelings. Camila was able to recognize boundaries set by her children (and vice-versa) and found meaningful ways to connect with them instead of being intrusive. Alejandro and Javi found ways to reconnect as brothers, and also find ways to spend time with their little sister. Though Javi was still sad about not making the soccer team, he was able reconnect with some of his peers at school and discovered new activities he enjoyed. As a family, the Martinez's made weeknight dinners a priority, and considered it sacred time where they meaningful tried to connect with each other, without problem-solving or judgment.

CONCLUSION

The MSJCC's serve as pertinent guidelines to counselors when working with all client populations and issues, even those with which we are familiar (Ratts et al., 2015). It is vital to our work as counselors to continuously check in on our potential biases, beliefs, and attitudes, and evaluate levels of privilege and marginalization within the counseling relationship. Part of being a multiculturally competent counselor is educating yourself on client populations with which you are unfamiliar. The MSJCC's can be used in conjunction with counseling theoretical approaches and techniques and assist counselors in building rapport with clients as they seek to acknowledge (and perhaps even celebrate) their differences. In times when counselors recognize a perceived bias or value-conflict they hold toward a client, it is vital that they seek their own counsel, supervision, and/or peer consultation, so as they do not unintentionally inflict harm on the client (American Counseling Association, 2014).

REFERENCES

Abraído-Lanza, A. F., Echeverría, S. E., & Flórez, K. R. (2016). Latino immigrants, acculturation, and health: Promising new directions in research. *Annual Review of Public Health*, *37*(1), 219–236. doi:10.1146/annurev-publhealth-032315-021545 PMID:26735431

American Counseling Association. (2014). *ACA Code of Ethics*. Alexandria, VA: Author.

Baumann, A. A., Kuhlberg, J. A., & Zayas, L. H. (2010). Familism, mother-daughter mutuality and suicide attempts of adolescent Latinas. *Journal of Family Psychology*, *24*(5), 616–624. doi:10.1037/a0020584 PMID:20954772

Bitter, J. R. (2014). *Theory and practice of family therapy and counseling* (2nd ed.). Belmont, CA: Brooks/Cole, Cengage Learning.

Brown, L. (2010). *Feminist therapy*. Washington, DC: American Psychological Association.

Fairburn, C. G., Cooper, Z., & Shafran, R. (2003). Cognitive behavior therapy for eating disorders: A "transdiagnostic" theory and treatment. *Behaviour Research and Therapy*, *41*(5), 509–528. doi:10.1016/S0005-7967(02)00088-8 PMID:12711261

Johnson, A. G. (2018). *Privilege, power, and difference* (3rd ed.). Boston, MA: McGraw-Hill. doi:10.4324/9780429494802-12

Loden, M., & Rosener, J. B. (1991). *Workforce America: Managing employee diversity as a vital resource*. New York, NY: McGraw-Hill Education.

Lopez, M. H., Taylor, P., Funk, C., & Gonzalez-Barrera, A. (2013). *On immigration policy, deportation relief seen as more important than citizenship*. Retrieved from http://www.pewhispanic.org/2013/12/19/on-immigration-policy-deportation-relief-seen-as-more-important-than-citizenship/

McIntosh, P. (1989, July/August). White privilege: Unpacking the invisible knapsack. *Peace and Freedom,* 8-10.

Ratts, M. J., & Pedersen, P. B. (2014). *Counseling for multiculturalism and social justice: Integration, theory, and application* (4th ed.). Alexandria, VA: American Counseling Association.

Ratts, M. J., Singh, A. A., Nassar-McMillan, S., Butler, S. K., & McCullough, J. R. (2015). Multicultural and social justice counseling competencies: Guidelines for the counseling profession. *Journal of Multicultural Counseling and Development, 44*(1), 28–48. doi:10.1002/jmcd.12035

Reyes-Rodriguez, M. L., Sala, M., Von Holle, A., Unikel, C., Bulik, C. M., Camara-Fuentes, L., & Suarez-Torres, A. (2011). A description of disordered eating behaviors in Latino males. *Journal of American College Health, 59*(4), 266–272. doi:10.1080/07448481.2010.502205 PMID:21308586

Sue, D. W., Sue, D., Neville, H. A., & Smith, L. (2019). *Counseling the culturally diverse: Theory and practice* (8th ed.). Hoboken, NJ, US: John Wiley & Sons Inc.

Tatum, B. D. (1997). *Why are all the black kids sitting together in the cafeteria?* New York, NY: Basic Books.

U.S. Census Bureau. (2017). *Income and poverty in the United States; 2016*. Report No. P60-259. Retrieved from https://www.census.gov/content/dam/Census/library/publications/2017/demo/P60-259.pdf

U.S. Census Bureau. (2019). *Quick facts*. Retrieved from https://www.census.gov/quickfacts/fact/table/US/RHI725217#RHI725217

Velasquez, R. J., Gonzales, M., Butcher, J. N., Castillo-Canez, I., Apodaca, J. X., & Chavira, D. (1997). Use of the MMPI-2 with Chicanos: Strategies for counselors. *Journal of Multicultural Counseling and Development, 25*(2), 107–120. doi:10.1002/j.2161-1912.1997.tb00321.x

White, M. (2007). *Maps of narrative practice*. New York, NY: Norton.

Chapter 3
Counseling With a Muslim-American Family:
Beyond Islamaphobia

Margaux Hanes Brown
Augusta University, USA

Ari-Elle R. West
Augusta University, USA

EXECUTIVE SUMMARY

Islamophobia is the unfounded fear of Islam and resulting hostility that Muslims experience as a religious minority in the U.S. For a marginalized community in the U.S., this increases the risk for poor mental health outcomes and further compounds stigma around help-seeking behaviors. In this case study, a family unit presented for counseling with stress resulting from life cycle stressors. However, the intersectionality of their religious identity affected how the individuals experienced transitions as well as microaggressions. This case study includes a counselor's application of the Multicultural and Social Justice Counseling Competencies, treatment interventions, and extensions for further professional development.

DOI: 10.4018/978-1-7998-0022-4.ch003

INTRODUCTION

Since the September 11th attacks on the United States, Muslims around the world have experienced increased discrimination and bigotry. In 2004, Kofi Annan, the then-Secretary General of the United Nations, held a conference on confronting Islamophobia. There he stated, "it is a sad and troubling development" when "the world coins a new term." He continued, "Too many people see Islam as a monolith and as intrinsically opposed to the West... [The] caricature remains widespread and the gulf of ignorance is dangerously deep" (Esposito & Mogahed, 2007, pp. 135-136). While the 2001 attacks did not ignite a new discourse an Islamic identity in the U.S, they were a catalyst for revising Muslim identity in America (Abdo, 2005). Unfortunately, Gallup poll results indicated that nearly a quarter of Americans who were surveyed would not want a Muslim neighbor, and less than half believed that Muslim Americans are loyal to the U.S. (Esposito & Mogahed, 2007). There are numerous implications for counselors that can be explored within the intersectionality of the marginalized and oppressed identity statuses of Muslim Americans. In this chapter, we describe a family unit who presents for counseling with concerns as a unit, issues among subsystems, and individual issues. We select and describe specific issues about faith that are salient in family counseling. We introduce a family counselor and provide a conceptual framework for counseling that includes systems theory, acculturation, and the Multicultural and Social Justice Counseling Competencies (MSJCC; Ratts, Singh, Nassar-McMillan, Butler, & McCullough, 2016). We describe a course of treatment with counseling outcomes and conclude with extensions and resources for professional development.

CASE DESCRIPTION

Muhammad, immigrated to the U.S. in college and is an engineer. He volunteers at the weekend school at the local mosque. Nadia, his wife, is U.S.-born to immigrant parents and is a pharmacist. They have an arranged marriage, and both identity as the same nationality and Muslim denomination. Omar is their 16-year old son in 10th grade. He performs well academically and competes year-round in a local swim league. His parents expect him to pursue a career in the medical field. Fatima is an 11-year-old girl in the 6th grade. The family resides in a suburban area where the persons of color make up 40% of the population, a vast majority of the population identifies as Christian, and less than 5% are foreign-born.

The family sought counseling after Omar was involved in an underage drinking incident where law enforcement intervened. On the night of the incident, Omar was supposed to be studying with a group of peers; instead decided to attend a party with friends on the swim team. Though Omar was not legally intoxicated and was not in possession of any substances, like some of his peers, he was the last youth to be released by the authorities to his parents. A fallout of the incident was that his parents discovered that he has had a girlfriend for over a year and had consumed alcohol. Omar has begun to rebel against his parents at home too. He began to resist going to the mosque with the family for prayer and community events. He did not end his romantic relationship. He argued with his parents about their prohibiting him from dating at all and especially girls who are not Muslim. Fatima began sixth grade at the local school after having four years of homeschooling. She has been victimized for wearing her hijab in her new school. She reports feeling pressure at school to dress and act like her peers, including socializing with boys, in ways that are incongruent with ways she has been taught to act in her family and faith community. Nadia has recently returned to work part-time, and the family seems to be in continual conflict. Nadia called to initiate counseling. She stated that her husband was reluctant to attend but agreed to come to the first session. Muhammad and Nadia have been looking to relocate closer to both of their places of work; however, they have been unsuccessful in securing a contract on a home in a more conveniently located affluent neighborhood despite offering a substantial down payment.

Specific Issues

We acknowledge that the specific issues we have selected here are informed by our own experiences and perceptions and may contain unintended bias. We also recognize that our judgments informed how to select information for the case and also conform to the space limitations. Therefore, we encourage readers to go beyond what we have summarized and refer to current and comprehensive reference books on Islam by current experts, *Handbook of Arab American Psychology* (Amer & Awad, 2016) and *Islam: The Straight Path, 5th ed.* (Esposito, 2016).

Religion

Islam means “a strong commitment to God” (Esposito & Mogaded, 2007, p. 7). The primary tenet of Islam is that there is one God, Allah, which is a genderless word in Arabic used to refer to God (Daneshpour, 2017). Muslims also believe that Muhammad was the last messenger or prophet, and they believe that other historically influential religious individuals are prophets including Abraham, Moses, and Jesus (S. Syed, Personal Communication, March 2, 2019). The Quran is the word of God, the traditional practices known as the Sunnah and the recorded sayings of the prophet Muhammad called the Hadith contain guidance on how to live in interpret the Quran (Daneshpour, 2017). There are two major denominations in Islam: Sunni and Shia. There are the core spiritual practices called the Five Pillars that touch every aspect of Muslim life.

Islam is a way of life (Nassar-McMillan, Al-Qimlass, & Gonzales, 2018). Self-responsibility is essential as it holds the individual accountable for their actions and awareness of God, which motivates Muslims to lead ethical lives (V. Clare, Personal Communication, April 12, 2018). Islamic law is written to help believers lead ethical lives that respect others different than them and promotes peace (Nassar-McMillan et al., 2018). Gender roles in Islam are also important and often misunderstood (Douglass & Dunn, 2002). Males and females are equal in status, property ownership, decision-making, while sociopolitical influences may inform local customs that limit women's rights (Nassar-McMillan, 2010; Nassar-McMillan et al., 2018). Mothers hold a higher status with God than fathers, are considered partners with God and should be honored (Abdul-Rauf, 2007).

Religiosity, or the degree to which an individual ascribes to religious beliefs and practices, varies among Muslims, which is similar to members of other religious groups (Amri, Nassar-McMillan, Amen-Bryan, & Misenhimer, 2013). Religiosity among a sample of Muslim college students was found to predict meaning and purpose in life and buffer stress (Abu-Hilal, Al-Bahrani, & Al-Zedjali, 2017). Gulamhussein and Eaton (2015) reported that, consistent with previous research, Muslim women who self-reported higher levels of religiosity and wore loose-fitting clothing also experienced lower levels of depressive and anxious symptoms.

In contrast, degree of religiosity impacts an individual's feelings surrounding religion. It is important that individuals with lower levels of religiosity feel safe and encouraged to talk about religion and spirituality aids in the exploration of issues related to uncertainties and guilt that surrounds religion (Eltaiba, 2014). Additionally, counselors will need to consider the client and their own privileged and marginalized statuses related to membership in a faith group in order to foster a positive therapeutic relationship (Ibrahim & Dykeman, 2011; Ratts et al., 2016).

Islamophobia

Muslim Americans have become increasingly stereotyped as hostile and misunderstood as antithetical to "the West" since September 11, 2001 (Haque, Tubbs, Kahumoku-Fessler, & Brown, 2019). Bleich (2011) defined Islamophobia as "indiscriminate negative attitudes or emotions directed at Islam or Muslims" (p. 1582). Muslim Americans share the unique experience of Islamophobia. Islamophobia has evolved from a political concept to a vague, widely used term in studies in social sciences with no accepted uniform definition (Bleich, 2011). Muslim Americans encounter multiple forms of discriminatory practices, a byproduct of racism, at the macrosystem level and individually, including marginalization and microaggressions, and these experiences pose mental health risks (Haque et al., 2019; Phillips & Lauterback, 2017). Muslim American mental health is emerging in the larger conversation in counseling; however, research is still limited (Ciftci, Jones, & Corrigan, 2013). In a future section, we will discuss mental health stigma.

Country of Origin and Colonialism

Currently, the majority (62%) of the world's population of Muslims live in the Pacific-Asia region (62%), followed by the Middle East-North African region (20%) and Sub-Saharan Africa (15%), Europe (3%), and the Americas (less than 0.5%) (Pew Forum on Religious and Public Life, 2011). Some countries within these regions are Islamic states, meaning that the government is based on Islamic law or favors Islam in general (Pew Research Center, 2017b). In the U.S., the current number of Muslims, about 3.45 million, is expected to continue growing, and by 2040, the number of persons ascribing to Islam is expected to surpass those who identify as Jewish (Pew Research Center, 2017a). While the majority (58%) of Muslims in the U.S. are foreign-born, many Muslims (42%) are U.S.-born, characterizing themselves descendants of Muslims and converts (Pew Research Center, 2017a). In other words, Muslims in America are a growing population with diverse ethnic origins. It is important for counselors to explore countries of origin and the histories of those countries.

Daneshpour (2017) devoted a chapter to colonialism in her text on providing mental health services to Muslim families. We have not encountered another author who comparably explicated the history of colonial rule, a chronosystem of power and oppression, and implications for family counseling. She highlighted that colonial rule existed through the mid-1970s in Muslim territories from Southeast Asia to Sub-saharan Africa, and the legacy of colonialism reverberates in these regions (Daneshpour, 2017). Adaptation post-colonialism is marked by corrupt leaders, military rule, and authoritarian dictatorships (Daneshpour, 2017). This history is essential for counselors to understand and recognize that dominant forces have reduced generations of Muslim families' values, beliefs, and customs, and Daneshpour (2017) posited that globalization perpetuated by the West is a "fancier and more sophisticated title that fools many into thinking this new arrangement is more democratic and egalitarian than the previous one" (p. 59). We believe that counselors will have an increased awareness and understanding of Muslim clients with this contextual understanding. In the counseling process, counselors need to attend to how families perceive their marital relationship, parenting styles, and other areas where power and Western models of operating may influence relationships (Daneshpour, 2017).

Therefore, when working with Muslim Americans, and specifically immigrants as in our case study, it is essential for counselors to establish the client's level of identification with their country of origin or nationality. Exploring cultural issues in counseling is widely understood as best practice, and it is also necessary for people who ascribe to the Muslim faith who vary nationally, politically, culturally, and religiously (Ibrahim & Dykeman, 2011; Sue & Sue, 2016). The client is a family unit with U.S.-born children to parents who immigrated to the U.S. Cultural characteristics like collectivism, religion, and faith and migration-specific experiences like identity development and acculturation will be explored. In this case study, however, country of origin is omitted intentionally to avoid perpetuating a stereotype that all Muslims are Arab and that all Arabs ascribe to Islam (Hamada, 2001; Haque et al., 2019). While the implications of nationality on identity, sect, language, and culture are complex and beyond the scope of this chapter, it is important to note that Arab Muslim immigrants may encounter discrimination attributed to Islamophobia compared to other Muslims based on their assumed religious affiliation and ethnicity (Al-Waqfi & Forstenlechner, 2010; Bozorgmehr, Ong, & Tosh, 2016; Haque et al., 2019).

Additionally, Muslim immigrants from Arab countries struggle to acculturate due to cultural and religious differences, perceptions of Arabs in media, and gender stereotypes (Wekhian, 2016). Nassar-McMillan and colleagues (2018) explicated heterogeneity of Arab Americans, and Daneshpour (2017) described intraethnic differences and family dynamics among predominantly Muslim countries. In sum, in this case study, we focus on the intersection of being Muslim and immigrant, which implies not only a different religion but also a different native culture from country of residence (Wekhian, 2016).

Stigma and Mental Health

Stigma is best defined as situations that exclude certain individuals from receiving full acceptance in society (Goffman, 1963). There are two experiences of stigma that impact minority groups to include label avoidance and public stigma. When minority groups avoid mental health services, they are exhibiting label avoidance due to them not wanting to be associated with a psychiatric diagnosis. Public stigma is when one discriminates against minority groups, which is associated with lack of access to services and opportunities that majority groups tend to have access to due to negative stereotypes (Ciftci et al., 2013). As practitioners, we need to understand the implications that label avoidance and public stigma have on minority groups seeking mental health care services.

The stigma associated with mental health is a salient issue for persons with mental illness (Abdullah & Brown, 2011). However, individuals who face cultural adversities such as negative stereotypes, prejudice, and discrimination are at increased risk for stigma (Soheilian & Inmam, 2009). Previous research has suggested that minority groups have higher levels of mental health stigma compared to majority groups. This is known as double stigma. Double stigma is defined as stigma that results from prejudice and discrimination based on an individual's racial identity and mental health disorder (Ciftci et al., 2013). The intersection of these minority statuses, or intersectionality exhibit significant implications in which clinicians should be aware of the effects that multiple identities have on minority groups.

Sexuality and Coming of Age

According to Abbott, Springer, and Hollist (2012), talking about sexuality or sexual encounters is forbidden in the Muslim culture, especially discussing such topics with 'strangers' such as mental health professionals. However, it is important to note that sex is considered a healthy practice within a Muslim marriage as it is approved by Allah (Abbott et al., 2012). Sexual practices also vary depending on country of origin and sect (Abbott et al., 2012).

When Muslim youth reach the age of puberty, they can engage in self-responsibility and begin to choose how strongly they identify with their religion. Identity could be expressed outwardly, such as young girls wearing a hijab. Bakali (2016) suggested that young Muslim females may begin to wear their hijab because they want to strongly identify with their religion, which could buffer against acculturative stress (Abu-Hilal et al., 2017). Gulamhussein and Eaton (2015) reported that consistent with previous research, women who self-reported high levels of religiosity also experienced low levels of depressive and anxiety symptoms.

INTRODUCTION TO THE COUNSELOR

Cultural Background

Regarding my professional identity, I am a licensed professional counselor, counselor educator, and supervisor. I identify as a white heterosexual cisgender female. I am U.S.-born, identify as being "Southern," and do not identify myself as an immigrant. I also identify as a wife, mother, and child. These identities position me to identify as being both privileged and oppressed, and these affect my perspectives as a counselor and are complexities to navigate in practice and supervision.

Counseling Approach

Humanistic and family systems theories inform my approach to counseling. My optimistic worldview is influenced by my faith which fuels my purpose and social justice orientation to counseling with marginalized populations. As a counselor, I believe in the dignity of every human being, that every individual has the proclivity for growth and wellness, and that self-actualization includes integration of all parts of self through critical self-reflection. In counseling, I strongly draw from the humanistic and systems theories, particularly the emphasis that change requires an authentic, positive therapeutic relationship characterized by safety and openness in expression. I have presented and published on advocacy and educational policy, marginalized persons, and counselor development. I have conducted group counseling and workshops at the local mosque, co-presented with members of the mosque, and partnered with mosque leadership in creating opportunities for counselors-in-training at the mosque. These relationships have been instrumental to my development as a human being, a practitioner, and a scholar.

CASE CONCEPTUALIZATION

Family Systems Theory: Experiential Family Therapy

Experiential family therapy is based on humanistic models of Maslow and Rogers and family system and communication theories of Satir, Whitaker and Bateson. It is centered around working with the whole family, not pathology in an individual, and complements the collectivist cultural values of Muslim families (Daneshpour, 2017). It is congruent with Islamic teachings that stress a holistic, interconnectedness view of illness (Carter & Rashidi, 2004). This theoretical orientation also fits well with family issues related acculturation and acculturative stress because symptoms are conceptualized as coming from rigid, inflexible rules or patterns; treatment entails exploring how the family needs to change and adapt to new circumstances (Daneshpour, 2017). What makes this therapy "experiential" is the assumption that change occurs as a result of authentic, here-and-now, genuine self-expression and empathy experienced by the clients and the counselor in the therapeutic relationship (Greenberg, Watson, & Lietaer, 1998).

While the counselor directs the family, experiences of all persons during the session are of equal value in the therapeutic process. It is important that the counselor explain and seek ongoing feedback from the family to negotiate in-session dynamics of power and authority, congruence, and fullness of expression in order to avoid replicating oppression or inadvertently contradicting a patriarchal family structure in session. This typifies Roger's philosophy of working collaboratively, listening to understand, and then seeking to be understood (Carter & Rashidi, 2004). The family and counselor get to know one another in casual conversation, exchange of ideas, and seek to understand each other's' experiences in the moment (Daneshpour, 2017). The intervention is the intimate relationship characterized by trust and regard for one another experienced in session (Daneshpour, 2017).

Self-actualization among the individual family members and the counselor is a critical element of this approach. Self-actualization is a self-enhancing process of differentiating that requires self-awareness and is possible under the conditions positive regard from others (Rogers, 1977). This therapy requires a counselor who is self-actualized in order to create a nonjudgmental, congruent relationship through which change occurs (Daneshpour, 2017). The self-actualized counselor embodies the following qualities themself and then facilitates the development of these in the family members: an accurate perception of reality, non-defensiveness, creativity, compassion, and has and desires intimacy (Chang & Page, 1991).

The patriarchal family structure that is typical among Muslim families may be challenging for Western counselors to navigate, not pathologize, and try to change. Rather than advocating for shared roles among a husband and wife, for example, invite the clients to express to one another their emotional needs and process how they show one another love (Abbott et al., 2012). This would reveal unhealthy interactions, internalized rules from their families of origin, and expectations that impede development; these interactions would then be the focus of treatment (Abbott et al., 2012; Daneshpour, 2017). Self-actualization is the goal of individuals, and openness or rigidity in the family affect the process (Walsh & McGraw, 2002). The experiential family counselor may need to pay more attention to developing a trusting relationship in order to navigate resistance to sharing emotions and difficulties (Cook-Masaud & Wiggins, 2011). The focus on the counselor self-awareness, authentic therapeutic relationship, and individual responsibility to disclose and communicate emotional experiences make experiential family therapy a congruent approach to working with Muslim American families.

Identity Development and Acculturation

Phinney, Horenczyk, Lievkind, and Vedder (2001) proposed an interactional model for ethnic identity in which the interplay among an immigrant's characteristics and attitudes and the responses of the society in which they exist are moderated by the conditions of the immigrant group in that particular context. Ethnic identity development is also a critical task in adolescence, which is relevant to the case (Phinney et al., 2001). However, rather than considering identities and identity development in silos and linear in development, intersectionality theory addresses multiple cultural identities from an ecological perspective (e.g., race, gender, spirituality), and is a framework for considering cultural identities in relationship with each other in identity development (Chan, Core, & Band, 2018; Cole, 2009). Intersectionality encourages the exploration of interconnectedness among the development of cultural identities, including how political context affects individuals as marginalized from the privileged groups (Warner, 2008). In the family case here, the counselor will conceptualize identity development of the family unit and of individuals and examine the intersectionality of identities. These may include religion, religiosity, and family factors.

Acculturation is the change process that occurs when encountering a dominant culture, and stressor associated with the process is acculturative stress (Nassar-McMillan et al., 2018). Acculturative stress may include but not be limited to learning a new culture and a new language; it includes navigating structures such as education, politics, societal norms, and employment (Nassar-McMillan et al., 2018). Acculturative stress is an individual and family experience and occurs among recent and previous generations of immigrants (Nassar-McMillan et al., 2018).

In a large international study of over 5,000 immigrant youth, Berry, Phinney, Sam, and Vedder (2006) found distinct acculturation profiles and that adaptation occurs both psychologically and socioculturally. They concluded that immigrant youth should be encouraged to preserve a sense of identity linked to their ethnic heritage and also construct bonds within the larger society (Berry et al., 2006). Kabir (2015) discovered that young Muslim immigrants in Western countries identified themselves as having dual or multiple identities while others endorsed primarily a Muslim identity. Stuart and Ward (2011) employed mixed-method approach to examine identity development among Muslim youth in New Zealand. Results indicated that youth used three specific strategies (alternating orientations, blending orientations, and minimizing differences) in "achieving a balance" managing multiple roles, identities, and orientations (Stuart & Ward, 2011, p. 263). We cautiously interpret the generalizability of these findings to our case study. First, like the adolescents in our case study, Muslim youth in New Zealand are predominantly first generation (Stuart & Ward, 2011). However, unlike in New Zealand, a society widely known to be one of the most tolerant globally, the adolescents in our case study are situated in a context known to be less socially tolerant, and therefore, the youth may struggle more than the research participants to balance multiple cultural identities during the acculturative process (Legatum Institute, 2018).

Existing research on the relationship between acculturation and acculturative stress in the Muslim American population is limited with inconsistent findings. For example, Goforth, Pham, Chun, Castro-Olivo, and Yosai (2016) and Goforth, Oka, Leong, and Denis (2014) both concluded that acculturative stress among Arab youth was related to psychological symptoms. In contrast, Aprahamian, Kaplan, Windham,

Sutter, and Visser (2011) found that acculturation was not related to mental health in a sample of Arab American adults. Goforth, Pham, and Oka (2015) examined the relationship among parent-child acculturation gap, acculturative stress, and child behavior problems in Arab American parent-child pairs. The only confirmed hypothesis was that acculturation gap predicted child behavior problems. More research is needed to understand acculturation and acculturative stress among Muslim American immigrant youth and families. Taken together, the counselor conceptualized the family and members using intersectionality and acculturation theories.

Multicultural and Social Justice Counseling Competency

Multicultural and social justice concepts have been explicated throughout the chapter. Here we will follow the framework of the counseling competencies to conceptualize the case systematically (Ratts et al., 2015). Counselor self-awareness here means that the counselor would focus on the client's ethnic identity, the counselor's identities, and intersectionality of identities in the counseling process, particularly as they relate to privilege and oppression (Matthews, Barden, & Sherrell, 2018). The counselor may need to take action steps to increase knowledge (Amari et al., 2013), explore their own and client values (Cook-Masaud & Wiggins, 2011), and develop competencies to discuss race and racism (Murray-Garcia, Harrell, Garcia, Gizzi, & Simms-Mackey, 2014). The counselor may need to increase their knowledge about counseling Muslims, Muslim marriage, and counseling Muslim couples specifically (Abbott et al., 2012, Rassool, 2016). Developing a positive counseling relationship by applying the MSJCC is an essential mechanism through which change can occur (Daneshpour, 2017; Ibrahim & Huer, 2016b; Ratts et al., 2016). It is essential, as a non-Muslim counselor, to set aside cultural assumptions and take a genuine and curious stance towards the culture of your Muslim client (Springer, Abbott, & Reisbig, 2009). Counselor authenticity is one way to develop a genuine relationship with the unit and individuals and this works best through a not-knowing perspective (Ibrahim & Huer, 2016a). The counselor may enhance the therapeutic relationship and demonstrate MSJCC by building relationships with other persons in the extended family and organizations in the Muslim community (Ali, Milstein, & Marzuk, 2005; Nassar-McMillan et al., 2018). However, the counselor should process with the client whether this enhances the relationship and the counselor's ability to understand clients as well as matters of confidentiality (Nassar-McMillan et al., 2018). The counseling process should include an exploration of world views, conducting cultural assessments, and completing a genogram (Daneshpour, 2017; Ibrahim & Huer, 2016a). A critical intervention is focusing on the client strengths, especially strengths about Muslim faith and religiosity (Abu-Hilal et al., 2017). The culturally competent counselor would also incorporate religious beliefs and practices if desired by the client (Rassool, 2016). The counselor could embody the role of an advocate by helping clients gain insight into microaggressions they have experienced in the community and incorporate self-advocacy goals into the counseling work (Haque et al., 2019; Lee & Zalkane, 2018). Within the counseling process and outside of the counseling work, the counselor may work as an advocate to illuminate and reduce mental health stigma in the Muslim community (Ciftci et al., 2013).

TREATMENT

When working with the presenting case, I worked on several aspects of the families' presenting problems including promoting disclosure and understanding among family members, fostering openness in communication, discourse about cultural influences on parenting styles, processing acculturation and acculturative stressors, and interacting in ways that built trust and genuine relationships.

Preparation, Intake, and Establishing the Presenting Issue

I prepared for the initial session by planning goals and questions and inviting all the family members to join in the counseling. I had not worked with a Muslim American family before, so it was essential that I prepare. I located mental health resources for Muslims using websites for large, reputable organizations. I consulted via Skype with a counselor who lives in a Muslim country and provides online counseling. I studied how to greet family members, how to interact with each individual in terms of gender and age, and guidelines for physical contact and attire (Amri et al., 2013; Springer et al., 2009).

As the initial intake session began, I first started by building rapport with the family. I explained the limits of confidentiality, emphasized consent to participate, and clarified the purpose and any misconceptions about therapy (Daneshpour, 2017). I contracted with them to evaluate using assessments, including interviewing, cultural inventories, and a genogram during the intake process (Daneshpour, 2017; Ibrahim & Heuer, 2016). I observed Muhammad's authority in the family unit; I practiced balancing operating within the family's hierarchy and simultaneously structuring the session. The family members took turns sharing what they believe the problem to be, whom it is affecting and how, what is contributing to it, what has been done to try to resolve it, and new ideas (Daneshpour, 2017). Religion, faith behaviors, acculturation, and existing strengths were topics explored in the initial phases of counseling (Hamdan, 2007). It was then that I took time to process the emotional experiences of the evaluations and initial sessions paying close attention to the role of power in the developing counseling relationship (Chan et al., 2018). I focused on building a strong working alliance with each family member. I intertwined psychoeducation about the process of therapy and explored the process dimension in the here-and-now. Muslim families may expect the counselor to be an expert and want to receive information (S. Sumer, personal communication, February 5, 2019). Simultaneously, I was sensitive to not rush the process and clients quickly deferring to me for advice motivated by underlying feelings of inferiority (Springer et al., 2009). The presenting issues became more evident and defined collectively by the family members. I reframed some issues from multiple perspectives to increase flexibility in thinking and empathy.

I self-disclosed how I felt in the moment interacting with the family. For example, when Nadia tried to change the subject from herself to Fatima, I shared that I felt distracted by the diversion and wanted to learn more about Nadia. The family members became increasingly at ease disclosing to the counselor. Family members accepted new perspectives about normal reactions to feeling blamed or judged (Daneshpour, 2017). Aligning the with patriarchal culture of most Muslim families, I made certain to show the father respect and gained his trust and support in order to treat other members of the family (Springer et al., 2009). I was sensitive to the couple's marital roles considering that Nadia is returning to work because her changing role could be a significant contributor to marital problems (Al-Krenawi & Graham, 2005).

Goals

The counselor and family co-constructed a treatment plan with realistic goals and measurable steps to attain the goals; goals were congruent with their readiness for change. The counselor negotiated different priorities among the family members by asking each person about potential gains and losses if they reached their goals (Daneshpour, 2017). The first long-term goal was to increase communication and understanding among family members. The first short-term objective to reach the long-term goal was to have more joy and harmony in the home by reducing the tension in family interactions. I stated ways that I identified with each family member's experience and tried to create a safe environment for each person to express a full range of emotions, including anger, sadness, and guilt. They all agreed that Nadia was the emotional center and grounding force in the family and that her return to work impacted her energy level; they explored the pros and cons of her working and discussed new behaviors they could all do to increase harmony. The second short-term objective was to increase healthy communication and understanding of lived experiences between parents and children. The counselor provided psychoeducation on parenting styles and the family processed how each person experienced authority and power in the family. The family practiced "I"-messages to express feelings and desires. Omar and Fatima gained insight into their parents' well-intended protections and fears. Muhammad and Nadia began to understand that their children are in a context where there is liberality of thought, that it is acceptable to seek understanding, and why the children are questioning their practices that are different from the majority culture.

The second long-term goal was to increase disclosure and insight about the acculturative process and stressors. The first short-term goal was understanding and processing Omar having a girlfriend and negotiating dual identities. The counselor helped Muhammad and Nadia express their feelings of disappointment and loss productively, and the counselor helped Omar feel a sense of universality and normalcy in his balancing two worlds. The family members disclosed how they felt about Omar's recent behavior problems, and Omar expressed feeling misunderstood. For example, I identified that Omar was the scapegoat, or the target of the negative feelings (Daneshpour, 2017). I asked, "Do you think that if you continue to rebel against your parents' wishes that they will grow closer through their concern for you?" (Whitaker & Keith, 1982). I also posited the productivity in Omar's behavior. "Perhaps his breaking away from family expectations socially is his testing ground to see how Muhammad and Nadia would react if he decided not to pursue medicine." I modeled openness, non-defensiveness, and a desire to understand each person's feelings. I helped the family identify behaviors and communication patterns to increase understanding of each person's lived experiences.

The second short-term objective was to gain insight into and express feelings about experiences of oppression, racism (e.g., Islamophobia), and microaggressions. Microaggressions are normalized and an expected part of the experience among Muslim Americans (S. Sumar, personal communication, February 5, 2019), and I explored the stress experienced by each individual and the unit. For example, Fatima experiencing discrimination due to wearing a hijab. I helped the family identity her hijab-wearing as a protective factor as well as a strength because it allows her to more strongly identify with her faith (Abu-Hilal et al., 2017). I self-disclosed that I could identify with her parents' worries for her safety, as she could be threatened or harassed by displaying her Muslim identity in such a marked way when it was not necessary. Finally, I focused on client advocacy. I normalized challenges and helped the family foster resiliency to navigate microaggressions and marginalization (Haque et al., 2019). I explored microaggressions with the clients related to ignorance about diversity among Muslims, equality of women in Islam, and prevalent media images relaying stereotypes (Haque et al., 2019). The family members and I explored opportunities to educate "one-on-one conversations, participating in interfaith dialogues and gatherings, remaining friendly and approachable,... actively live the teachings of Islam through their character and mannerisms to dispel misconceptions" (Haque at al, 2019, p. 11).

Progress

I was an active agent in the process. I increased her self-awareness of identities in privileged and oppressed groups and recognized the intersections of these identities. I also maintained a not-knowing stance to learning about culture and the clients' contexts. I continued to promote self-actualization of the individuals, interconnectedness among the family members, and the illumination of the experiences within the therapy sessions. I sought supervision to process feelings of guilt, anxiety, and shame related to White privilege (Chan et al., 2018).

The couple experienced decreased marital tension and increased effective communication around Nadia's return to work and all the family member's contribution to creating a harmonious home. Muhammad and Nadia increased their sense of parenting self-efficacy and incorporated aspects of an authoritative parenting style. They increased understanding and disclosure about Omar's dual identity, which is a part of his acculturative process. Overall the family unit had an increased openness to emotional expression and had even begun to laugh and appear comfortable in session (Whitaker & Keith, 1982). Both the family unit and individuals continued to gain insight into microaggressions and have processed self-advocacy goals in counseling. Applications of self-advocacy were not realized during the course of treatment. However, the family shared among close friends at the local mosque that they were in counseling and referred another family to counseling. Termination was abrupt, and Nadia cancelled a scheduled session stating that they did not need to come anymore. I considered this a successful termination from the experiential family therapy perspective (Whitaker & Keith, 1982).

CONCLUSION

Summary

We wanted to illuminate the challenges that Muslim Americans face and the implications for counselors and counselor educators. In our case study, we highlighted several presenting concerns that a Muslim family may struggle with when acculturating into the United States. We focused our research on understanding Islam, the implications of discrimination experiences and Islamophobia, considerations for immigration and country of origin, mental health stigma, and sexuality within Muslim culture. This case study includes a counselor's application of the Multicultural and Social Justice Counseling Competencies, treatment interventions, and extensions for further professional development.

The authors' portrayal of the family and counselor's experience in therapy was informed by scholarship and the authors' relationships with numerous Muslim American families. The authors sought to authentically represent the events and perspectives that were shared them (e.g., S. Sumar, personal communication, February 5, 2019) and to integrate these with evidence from literature. The authors acknowledge the inherent limits of generalizable knowledge in a single case study and that this does not represent a comprehensive spectrum of cultural issues pertaining to counseling with Muslim American families. For example, the relative lack of resistance to counseling in this case may be incongruent with evidence suggesting that Muslim Americans may be reluctant to seeking therapy, particularly outside of religious leaders (Springer et al., 2009). Additionally, this case does not illustrate using religious beliefs in counseling, navigating the clients' submission to the authority of the counselor, or conflicts pertaining to gender differences (Carter & Rashidi, 2004; Springer et al., 2009). The authors encourage counselors to prepare for these potential experiences in counseling with Muslim American families.

Extensions for Professional Development

Discourse

We encourage counselors and counselor educators to continue to develop their competencies to counseling Muslim Americans and to facilitate development among others. These extensions, including reflection and discussion questions, activities, multimedia resources, and suggested readings, can be used in counselor preparation, continuing education workshops, or peer supervision settings. Counselor educators, supervisors, and other persons with power and privilege need to remain grounded in MSJCC as a framework for counselor development, and we suggest using intersectionality as a way to navigate these complex dynamics (Chan et al., 2018). Questions for reflection and discussion include: (1) consider and describe the family in terms of a family life cycle perspective; (2) give examples of process comments that you (the counselor) anticipate using to promote increased openness in communication among the parents and children; (3) discuss a possible homework activity for the family including objectives, potential resistance, and processing the completed activity; (4) identify issues of clinical concern in the case and explain how the client and counselor attitudes, knowledge, skills, and beliefs impact counseling interventions; (5) reflect and consider your (the counselor) identities that you share with the client(s), and discuss how self-disclosure may expand your power and privilege in the relationship (Chan et al., 2018).

Activities

An example of an extension activity is a directive to explore local, regional, or national Muslim organizations and have a conversation with one of the members about the organization and their role. Another activity is to write a reflective journal focusing on increased self-awareness of power, privilege, marginalization, and oppression after watching one of the films in the following resources section. An advocacy-focused activity is to create and deliver a presentation on Islam to a group that may not otherwise seek information on the topic.

Media

Resources include movies (e.g., *Eshtebak*, *Syriana*), organization websites (e.g., Islamic Society of North America, Islamic Networks Group), and documentaries (e.g., *Breaking Silence,* The *Rise of ISIS*). Suggested non-fiction texts include *How Does It Feel to Be a Problem? Being Young and Arab in America* by Bayoumi (2009) and *Burqas, Baseball, and Apple Pie: Being Muslim in America* by Idliby (2014).

REFERENCES

Abbott, D. A., Springer, P. R., & Hollist, C. S. (2012). Therapy with immigrant Muslim couples: Applying culturally appropriate interventions and strategies. *Journal of Couple & Relationship Therapy*, *11*(3), 254–266. doi:10.1080/15332691.2012.692946

Abdo, G. (2005). Islam in America: Separate but unequal. *The Washington Quarterly*, *28*(4), 7–17. doi:10.1162/0163660054798717

Abdul-Rauf, M. (2007). *The Islamic view of women and the family*. Alexandria, VA: Al-Saadawi Publications.

Abdullah, T., & Brown, T. L. (2011). Mental illness stigma and ethnocultural beliefs, values, and norms: An integrative review. *Clinical Psychology Review*, *31*(6), 934–948. doi:10.1016/j.cpr.2011.05.003 PMID:21683671

Abu-Hilal, M., Al-Bahrani, M., & Al-Zedjali, M. (2017). Can religiosity boost meaning in life and suppress stress for Muslim college students? *Mental Health, Religion & Culture*, *20*(3), 203–216. doi:10.1080/13674676.2017.1324835

Al-Krenawi, A., & Graham, J. (2005). Marital therapy for Arab Muslim Palestinian couples in the context of reacculturation. *The Family Journal (Alexandria, Va.)*, *13*(3), 300–310. doi:10.1177/1066480704273640

Al-Waqfi, M., & Forstenlechner, I. (2010). Stereotyping of citizens in an expatriate-dominated labour market: Implications for workforce localisation policy. *Employee Relations*, *32*(4), 364–381. doi:10.1108/01425451011051596

Ali, O. M., Milstein, G., & Marzuk, P. M. (2005). The Imam's role in meeting the counseling needs of Muslim communities in the United States. *Psychiatric Services (Washington, D.C.)*, *56*(2), 202–205. doi:10.1176/appi.ps.56.2.202 PMID:15703349

Amari, S., Nassar-McMillan, S., Amen-Bryan, S., & Misenhimer, M. M. (2013). Counseling Arab Americans. In C. C. Lee (Ed.), *Multicultural issues in counseling: New approaches to diversity* (4th ed.; pp. 87–104). Alexandria, VA: American Counseling Association.

Amer, M. M., & Awad, G. H. (2016). *Handbook of Arab American psychology* (1st ed.). New York, NY: Routledge.

Aprahamian, M., Kaplan, D. M., Windham, A. M., Sutter, J. A., & Visser, J. (2011). The relationship between acculturation and mental health of Arab Americans. *Journal of Mental Health Counseling*, *33*(1), 80–92. doi:10.17744/mehc.33.1.0356488305383630

Bakali, N. (2016). *Islamophobia: Understanding Anti-Muslim Racism Through the Lived Experiences of Muslim Youth*. Rotterdam: Sense Publishers. Retrieved from http://ezproxy.augusta.edu/login?url=http://search.ebscohost.com/login.aspx?direct=true&db=nlebk&AN=1429086&site=eds-live&scope=site

Berry, J. W., Phinney, J. S., Sam, D. L., & Vedder, P. (2006). Immigrant youth: Acculturation, identity, and adaptation. *Applied Psychology*, *55*(3), 303–332. doi:10.1111/j.1464-0597.2006.00256.x

Bleich, E. (2011). What is Islamophobia and how much is there? Theorizing and measuring an emerging comparative concept. *The American Behavioral Scientist*, *55*(12), 1581–1600. doi:10.1177/0002764211409387

Bozorgmehr, M., Ong, P., & Tosh, S. (2016). Panethnicity revisited: Contested group boundaries in the post-9/11 era. *Ethnic and Racial Studies*, *39*(5), 727–745. doi:10.1080/01419870.2015.1081959 PMID:27182093

Carter, D. J., & Rashidi, A. (2004). East meets West: Integrating psychotherapy approaches for Muslim women. *Holistic Nursing Practice*, *18*(3), 152–159. doi:10.1097/00004650-200405000-00007 PMID:15222603

Chan, C. D., Core, D. N., & Band, M. P. (2018). Privilege and oppression in counselor education: An intersectionality framework. *Journal of Multicultural Counseling and Development*, *46*(1), 58–73. doi:10.1002/jmcd.12092

Chang, R., & Page, R. C. (1991). Characteristics of the self-actualized person: Visions from the East and West. *Counseling and Values*, *36*(1), 2–10. doi:10.1002/j.2161-007X.1991.tb00772.x

Ciftci, A., Jones, N., & Corrigan, P. W. (2013). Mental health stigma in the Muslim community. *The Journal of Muslim Mental Health*, *7*(1), 17–32. doi:10.3998/jmmh.10381607.0007.102

Cole, E. R. (2009). Intersectionality and research in psychology. *The American Psychologist*, *64*(3), 170–180. doi:10.1037/a0014564 PMID:19348518

Cook-Masaud, C., & Wiggins, M. I. (2011). Counseling Muslim women: Navigating cultural and religious challenges. *Counseling and Values*, *55*(2), 247–246. doi:10.1002/j.2161-007X.2011.tb00035.x

Daneshpour, M. (2017). *Family therapy with Muslims*. New York, NY: Routledge/Taylor Francis Group.

Douglass, S. C., & Dunn, R. E. (2002). Interpreting Islam in American schools. In H. Donnan (Ed.), *Interpreting Islam* (pp. 76–98). Thousand Oaks, CA: Sage. doi:10.4135/9781446217467.n5

Eltaiba, N. (2014). Counseling with Muslim refugees: Building rapport. *Journal of Social Work Practice*, *28*(4), 397–403. doi:10.1080/02650533.2013.875523

Esposito, J. L. (2010). *The future of Islam*. New York, NY: Oxford University Press.

Esposito, J. L. (2016). *Islam: The straight path* (5th ed.). New York, NY: Oxford University Press.

Esposito, J. L., & Mogahed, D. (2007). *Who really speaks for Islam? What a billion Muslims really think*. New York, NY: Gallup Press.

Goffman, F. (1963). *Stigma: Notes on the management of spoiled identity*. New York, NY: Simon and Schuster.

Goforth, A. N., Oka, E. R., Leong, F. T. L., & Denis, D. J. (2014). Acculturation, acculturative stress, religiosity and psychological adjustment among Muslim Arab American adolescents. *The Journal of Muslim Mental Health*, *8*(2), 3–19. doi:10.3998/jmmh.10381607.0008.202

Goforth, A. N., Pham, A. V., & Oka, E. R. (2015). Parent-child conflict, acculturation gap, acculturative stress, and behavior problems in Arab American adolescents. *Journal of Cross-Cultural Psychology*, *46*(6), 821–836. doi:10.1177/0022022115585140

Gofoth, A. N., Pham, A. V., Chun, H., Castro-Olivo, S. M., & Yosai, E. R. (2016). Association of acculturative stress, Islamic practices, and internalizing symptoms among Arab American adolescents. *School Psychology Quarterly*, *31*(2), 198–212. doi:10.1037pq0000135 PMID:27243243

Greenberg, L. S., Watson, J. C., & Lietaer, G. (Eds.). (1998). *Handbook of experiential psychotherapy*. New York, NY: Guilford Press.

Gulamhussein, Q., & Eaton, N. R. (2015). Hijab, religiosity, and psychological wellbeing of Muslim women in the United States. *The Journal of Muslim Mental Health*, *9*(2), 25–40. doi:10.3998/jmmh.10381607.0009.202

Hamada, B. I. (2001). The Arab image in the minds of western image-makers. *The Journal of International Communication*, *7*(1), 7–35. doi:10.1080/13216597.2001.9751897

Haque, A., Tubbs, C. Y., Kahomodu-Fessler, E. P., & Brown, M. D. (2019). Microaggressions and Islamophobia: Experiences of Muslims across the United States and clinical implications. *Journal of Marital and Family Therapy*, *45*(1), 76–91. doi:10.1111/jmft.12339 PMID:29855055

Ibrahim, F., & Heuer, J. (2016a). Application of social justice and cultural responsiveness strategies: Using cultural assessments in counseling and psychotherapy. In *Social justice counseling: Client-specific interventions* (pp. 169–237). New York, NY: Springer. doi:10.1007/978-3-319-18057-1_8

Ibrahim, F., & Heuer, J. (2016b). Worldview: Implications for culturally responsive and ethical practice. In *Social justice counseling: Client-specific interventions* (pp. 51–75). New York, NY: Springer. doi:10.1007/978-3-319-18057-1_3

Ibrahim, F. A., & Dykeman, C. (2011). Counseling Muslim Americans: Cultural and spiritual assessments. *Journal of Counseling and Development*, *89*(4), 387–396. doi:10.1002/j.1556-6676.2011.tb02835.x

Kabir, N. A. (2015). Muslim identity formation in the West: The case of Australian, British, and American Muslims. In D. Iner & S. Yucel (Eds.), *Muslim identity formation in religiously diverse societies* (pp. 105–126). Tyne, UK: Cambridge Scholars Publishing.

Lee, C. C., & Zalkalne, E. (2018). The culturally competent counselor as an agent of social justice. In C. C. Lee (Ed.), *Multicultural issues in counseling: New approaches to diversity* (5th ed.). Alexandria, VA: American Counseling Association.

Legatum Institute. (2018). *The Legatum prosperity index 2018*. Retrieved from https://prosperitysite.s3-accelerate.amazonaws.com/2515/4321/8072/2018_Prosperity_Index.pdf

Matthews, J. J., Barden, S. M., & Sherrell, R. S. (2018). Examining the relationships between multicultural counseling competence, multicultural self-efficacy, and ethnic identity development of practicing counselors. *Journal of Mental Health Counseling*, *40*(2), 129–141. doi:10.17744/mehc.40.2.03

Murray-Garcia, J. L., Harrell, S., Garcia, J. A., Gizzi, E., & Simms-Mackey, P. (2014). Dialogue as a skill: Training a health professions workforce that can talk about race and racism. *The American Journal of Orthopsychiatry*, *84*(5), 590–596. doi:10.1037/ort0000026 PMID:25265221

Nassar-McMillan, S. C. (2010). Counseling Arab Americans. Boston, MA: Brooks-Cole: Cengage.

Nassar-McMillan, S. C., Al-Qimlass, A., & Gonzalez, L. M. (2018). Individuals and families of Arab descent. In D. G. Hays & B. T. Erford (Eds.), *Developing multicultural counseling competence: A systems approach* (pp. 87–104). New York, NY: Pearson.

Pew Forum on Religious and Public Life. (2011, January 27). *The future of the global Muslim population: Projections for 2010-2030*. Retrieved from https://web.archive.org/web/20110202043556/http://pewforum.org/The-Future-of-the-Global-Muslim-Population.aspx

Pew Research Center. (2017a, July 26). *U.S. Muslims concerned about their place in society but continue to believe in the American dream*. Retrieved from http://www.pewforum.org/2017/07/26/findings-from-pew-research-centers-2017-survey-of-us-muslims/

Pew Research Center. (2017b, October 3). *Many countries favor specific religions, officially or unofficially*. Retrieved from http://www.pewforum.org/2017/10/03/many-countries-favor-specific-religions-officially-or-unofficially/

Phillips, D., & Lauterbach, D. (2017). American Muslim immigrant mental health: The role of racism and mental health stigma. *The Journal of Muslim Mental Health, 11*(1), 39–56. doi:10.3998/jmmh.10381607.0011.103

Phinney, J. S., Horenczyk, G., Liebkind, K., & Vedder, P. (2001). Ethnic identity, immigration, and well-being: An interactional perspective. *The Journal of Social Issues, 57*(3), 493–510. doi:10.1111/0022-4537.00225

Rassool, H. G. (2016). *Islamic counselling: An introduction to theory and practice*. New York, NY: Routledge.

Ratts, M. H., Singh, A. A., Nassar-McMillan, S., Butler, S. K., & McCullough, J. R. (2016). Multicultural and social justice counseling competencies: Guidelines for the counseling profession. *Journal of Multicultural Counseling and Development, 44*(1), 28. doi:10.1002/jmcd.12035

Rogers, C. R. (1977). *Carl Rogers on personal power*. New York, NY: Delacorte Press.

Soheilian, S., & Inman, A. G. (2009). Middle Eastern Americans: The effects of stigma on attitudes toward counseling. *The Journal of Muslim Mental Health, 4*(2), 139–158. doi:10.1080/15564900903245766

Springer, P. R., Abbott, D. A., & Reisbig, A. M. (2009). Therapy with Muslim couples and families: Basic guidelines for effective practices. *The Family Journal, 17*(3), 229–235. doi:10.1177/1066480709337798

Stuart, J., & Ward, C. (2011). A question of balance: Exploring the acculturation and adaptation of Muslim immigrant youth. *Psychological Intervention, 20*(3), 255–267. doi:10.5093/in2011v20n3a3

Sue, D. W., & Sue, D. (2016). *Counseling the culturally diverse: Theory and Practice* (7th ed.). Hoboken, NJ: Wiley.

Walsh, W. M., & McGraw, J. A. (2002). *Essentials of family therapy: A structured summary of approaches* (2nd ed.). Denver, CO: Love Publishing.

Warner, L. R. (2008). A best practices guide to intersectional approaches in psychological research. *Sex Roles, 59*(5-6), 454–463. doi:10.100711199-008-9504-5

Wekhian, J. A. (2016). Acculturation process of Arab-Muslim immigrants in the United States. *Asian Culture and History, 8*(1), 88–99. doi:10.5539/ach.v8n1p89

Whitaker, C., & Keith, D. V. (1982). Symbolic-experiential family therapy. In J. R. Neill & D. P. Kniskern (Eds.), *From psyche to system: The evolving Therapy of Carl Whitaker* (pp. 330–378). New York, NY: Guilford.

Chapter 4
Case Study for Counseling Same Sex Couples Through the Fertility Process:
Jane and Kelsey

Meredith A. Rausch
Augusta University, USA

Haley D. Wikoff
Western Illinois University, USA

EXECUTIVE SUMMARY

Fertility and reproductive technologies are increasingly important topics for counseling LGBT+ individuals. As legislation improves, lesbian couples have additional opportunities to expand their families. Professional counselors may be aware of the various fertility methods (e.g., artificial insemination, in vitro fertilization), but may lack understanding of the specific differences inherent in the process for two females. Lesbians also face barriers present in a heteronormative society. This chapter describes a counseling relationship with a lesbian couple who are working through the fertility process. When performing counseling work, using the multicultural and social justice competencies allows the counselor to provide ethical practice. The counselors use Relational-Cultural Theory, a feminist theory, to help Jane and Kelsey set goals consistent with the tenets of the theory. Additionally, the counseling team and couple work through the unique barriers a lesbian couple faces when experiencing the fertility process in a heteronormative society.

DOI: 10.4018/978-1-7998-0022-4.ch004

BACKGROUND

In 2008, the California Supreme Court ruled that the Freedom of Religion does not allow the denial of fertility treatment for lesbian couples by fertility doctors (North Coast Women's Care Medical Group, Inc. v. San Diego County Superior Court, 2008). This step is a victory for women seeking reproductive technology in order to create options for childbearing for those previously denied access to fertility treatments ("First Amendment California Supreme Court," 2008). Similarly, in 2015 the legislature in Maryland passed two bills that would include same-sex couples in the insurance mandate for in vitro fertilization treatments (Adashi, 2015). Although California and Maryland have changed legislation to address the unique needs of gay and lesbian couples, not all states have laws that offer the same protections. As such, it is essential for counselors who are assisting lesbian couples, who are embarking on the fertility treatment process, recognize the myriad differences in the way fertility treatment is experienced for lesbian couples, as compared to heterosexual couples. Areas include, but are not limited to, legal differences, health insurance benefits, medical document language, familial levels of support, costs for procedures, multicultural awareness of doctors and staff, and treatment of the spouse or partner (Rausch & Wikoff, 2018).

The emotional and financial impact of fertility treatment is increasing in research, as an estimated 4.3 million individuals or their partners experience issues related to fertility (Chandra, Martinez, Mosher, Abma, & Jones, 2005). Topics such as stress associated with fertility treatment (Borneskog, Lampic, Sydsjö, Bladh, & Skoog Svanberg, 2017), cultural considerations within fertility counseling (Burnett, 2009), decision making during donor insemination (Chabot, & Ames, 2004), counseling lesbians opting into motherhood (Dunne, 2000; Erwin, 2007), transitioning from infertility to adoption choices (Goldberg, Downing, & Richardson, 2009), and consequences for non-genetic parenthood (Golombok, Murray, Jadva, Lycett, Maccullum, & Rust, 2006) have been studied within the lesbian population. While the use of reproductive technology increases across the globe, research focusing on heterosexual couples remains prevalent; however, this research may be helpful when examining the needs of lesbian couples.

More recent research focusing on heterosexual participants includes the impact of a partnership support program for couples who choose to engage in the fertility process (Asazawa, 2015), and the psychological impact of fertility treatment on a male partner (Dooley, Dineen, Sarma, & Nolan, 2014). Studies focusing on the impact of fertility on women examine mental and emotional health (e.g., anxiety, stress, depression, emotional regulation, life satisfaction) during fertility processes and treatment (Galhardo, Cunha, Pinto-Gouveia, & Matos, 2013; Grant & Cochrane, 2014; Kahaki, Nazari, & Khosravi, 2014; Van Der Merwe, & Greeff, 2015). Research results depict the relational hardships endured when facing challenges associated with fertility treatment. As counseling professionals, acknowledging these potential challenges and grounding our work in theory, multicultural competence, and social justice are all a part of ethical practice. This case study will examine the counseling work with Jane and Kelsey, a married couple who chose to undergo fertility treatment in order to add biological children to their family. We have grounded our work in Relational-Cultural Theory, a feminist theory which views the couple through a lens of multicultural competence and social justice. We will share this work, providing theoretical interventions with a specific focus on the Multicultural and Social Justice Counseling Competencies, finishing up with questions and answers to increase awareness and knowledge.

CASE DESCRIPTION

Jane is a 34-year old cisgender woman, married for four years to Kelsey, a 37-year old cisgender woman. They reside in the state of Iowa and have come to counseling to work through their experiences with the fertility process. After dating for three years, they knew they would begin trying to have a child with the help of some fertility process, but never expected they would struggle to maintain a successful pregnancy, resulting in a child. Although neither individual had undergone fertility testing before trying (health insurance would not cover fertility expenses until they had experienced a series of issues relating to getting or maintaining a pregnancy), they felt they had double the chances because they are two cisgender women.

Kelsey initially tried to become pregnant first, due to her age (better chances before the age of 35 with her eggs). They focused as a couple on selecting a sperm donor from the California Cryobank. Although not an easy process in which to engage, they both agreed on a sperm donor and purchased five vials, and the cost for storage of, sperm. They hoped to have two children, one with each egg and the same sperm donor; however, after the third unsuccessful attempt with Kelsey, they reported feeling anxious and hopeless regarding the process. Initially, the couple attempted the ICI process at home to make this step feel more comfortable than having it performed in an office setting; unfortunately, they were unsuccessful at achieving pregnancy with this method. They discovered their health insurance would not pay for fertility treatments unless they are at a medical facility and they have at least six months of unsuccessful pregnancy.

Kelsey and Jane looked for a fertility clinic online, with hopes of finding one supportive of same-sex parents. At their first appointment, they found some of the language on the paperwork to be confusing because it was heteronormative, but the staff helped answer questions and alter the forms to meet their needs. The fertility clinic required them to engage in one session of individual counseling and one session of couples' counseling as part of a routine process. After testing, Kelsey received a prescription for Clomid (oral medicine utilized for stimulating ovulation). After two weeks of taking Clomid, Kelsey began to feel very emotional, and the couple was arguing more often. Kelsey felt she was unable to control her emotions, and found herself crying every day. She feels like a failure for being a woman who cannot conceive. Kelsey feels torn between continuing with the process and stopping the medication. Kelsey's mother is deceased and her father "does not recognize" her marriage to Jane. Kelsey was very close to her mother and wished very intensely to become a mother herself, through the process of pregnancy.

Jane's family is very supportive, even lending them money to help purchase the sperm. While Jane has attended every appointment with Kelsey, she does not feel she can genuinely empathize with her situation and fears their relationship is suffering due to the two unsuccessful attempts at pregnancy and one miscarriage. She works to be patient with Kelsey and the emotionality caused by Clomid, but feels she has lost the person she married. Both Jane and Kelsey feel they are mourning the loss of a child, yet do not have the time or the funds to "take a break" from the fertility process. They fear their attempt to add to their family will result in breaking their marriage apart completely.

LITERATURE REVIEW

In Western culture, motherhood has long been synonymous with womanhood and femininity (Dunne, 2000; Rogalin & Brooks, 2018). There is a societal expectation that women will embrace the motherhood mandate and become mothers (Rogalin & Brooks, 2018). At one time due to their "social location" (Rogalin & Brooks, 2018, p. 2), lesbians were thought to be excluded from the social pressures of entering into motherhood (Dunne, 2000). Since the 1960s, societal and medical developments have allowed lesbian couples to embark on the journey toward parenthood (Ben-Ari & Livni, 2006); however, this process is unique and has its own set of challenges and hurdles. When "opting into motherhood" (Dunne, 2000, p. 32), unlike heterosexual couples, lesbian couples must be prepared to navigate systems that based on heteronormative practices (Rogalin & Brooks, 2018). The definition of heteronormativity involves a set of ordeals and norms that privilege heterosexual individuals while also excluding or oppressing those considered outside this ideal (Hopkins, Sorenson, & Taylor, 2013). Although same-sex female couples make up the third largest group of United States households (Rausch & Wikoff, 2017; United States Census, 2015), heteronormative worldviews surround their experiences with medical practices as they seek to achieve pregnancy.

As lesbian couples begin the road to parenthood, the first decision they encounter is whether either partner or which partner will be the biological carrier of the child. This conscious choice also calls for lesbians to consider "coming out" to their medical providers, who may have been previously unaware of their orientation (Markus, Weingarten, Duplessi, & Jones, 2010; Rausch & Wikoff, 2017). This unique stressor requires these couples to consider how coming out might affect their experience with the provider(s) during the "preconception, pregnancy, birth, and the postpartum process" (Markus et al., 2010, p.124). If couples choose to be open with their sexual orientation, fears of negative stigma and worry about provider detachment, quality of care, or even a refusal to work cooperatively with the couple surround the experience (Markus et al., 2010; Rausch & Wikoff, 2017). Alternatively, if couples choose to keep their sexual orientation and relationship status private, the non-biological partner may become an unseen or excluded part of the process, which carries its own pressures and potential strain on the relationship (Hayman & Wilkes, 2017; Markus et al., 2010; Rausch & Wikoff, 2017).

Choosing a method of conception is an essential part of the process for lesbian couples because traditional methods of conception are not viable means to achieve pregnancy (DeDiego, 2016). Lesbian couples face the complex decision of exploring assistive measures to conceive, which include: donor insemination (DI), In-vitro fertilization (IVF), surrogacy, and adoption (DeDiego, 2016; Markus et al., 2010). Regardless of the method, planning to conceive or intentionally create a family is a significant decision, socially, emotionally, and financially.

One of the most common forms of conception for lesbian couples is donor insemination (DI). Using DI is often a preferred method for lesbians because not only does it allow for a genetic connection, it is more easily accessible and affordable than other assistive measures (Chabot & Ames, 2004; Markus et al., 2010). There are three main ways for lesbian couples to inseminate using donor sperm: "fresh sperm from a known donor, frozen sperm from a known donor, or frozen sperm from an unknown donor" (Markus et al., 2010, p. 129). Couples can choose to inseminate at home through intracervical insemination (the use of a plastic syringe to insert sperm into the vagina) (ICI) or in a medical facility with assistance from a professional through ICI or intrauterine insemination (IUI). Although this is the most common method of conception, not all couples can achieve pregnancy through DI, so they must choose another mechanism to conceive (Rausch & Wikoff, 2017).

Lesbian couples may experience challenges in achieving pregnancy through less medically-invasive methods. These challenges require couples to consider other assistive reproductive technologies such as IVF (Getrajdman, Lee, & Copperman, 2017; McNair, Dempsey, Wise, & Perlesz, 2002). IVF is a risky, unpredictable, and emotional procedure (Zeiler & Malmquist, 2014), yet some lesbian couples choose this route because it is considered a final option for conceiving a biological child (Rausch & Wikoff, 2017). Other couples may engage in co-IVF because they are seeking a process that allows both partners to be biologically involved in the pregnancy. Co-IVF is a process where a doctor retrieves eggs from one partner and the other partner "receives the developed embryo and carries out the pregnancy" (Getrajdman et al., 2017, p. 416). Although IVF and co-IVF may be the last option for a genetic connection to a child, it is one of the most expensive options available and is described as a high-tech process that has been reported as a source of high stress for couples (Boivin, Griffiths, & Venetis, 2011; Rogalin & Brooks, 2018).

In addition to the medical procedures described above, lesbian couples may choose to achieve motherhood through other methods. If neither partner can (infertility, illness, advanced medical age) or chooses to be a biological carrier, surrogacy may be a viable option (DeDiego, 2016; Rausch & Wikoff, 2017). Other couples may look to foster care or adoption as a means of entering into parenthood. Although a federal judge ruled that same-sex couples can legally adopt in all 50 states, these couples may still face discrimination, additional challenges, and obstacles, as they navigate the systems when choosing options (DiDiego, 2016).

As part of a unique population, lesbians may endure additional barriers during the fertility process, which a heterosexual couple may not experience. These additional barriers may add to the stress that lesbians already experience due to the issues and strains placed on a couple by the fertility process itself. In order to maintain positive well-being both individually and as a couple, an examination of outside supports and stressors is warranted.

Feelings of positive well-being align with perceptions of support from families, friends, and partners (Uchino, 2004). Research on the impact of family support which surrounds same-sex relationships is scant; however, Graham and Barnow (2013) found that 14% of the well-being between couples includes perceptions of family support in both heterosexual and same-sex relationships. Graham and Barnow (2013) also discovered that higher levels of support from friends associate with higher levels of well-being. Support was perhaps most impactful between partners--with 15% of the well-being between couples associated with the perception of a supportive partner (Graham & Barnow, 2013). Sumontha, Farr, and Patterson (2016) studied sources of social support among a sample of lesbian, gay and heterosexual adoptive parents, and found same-sex couples reported similar levels of social support from their families. Lesbian couples who perceived higher levels of support from family also reported having stronger alliances as parents (Sumontha et al., 2016). Becoming parents together involves, at a minimum, a discussion of the fertility and reproductive process as a couple; more often, lesbian couples need to seek fertility services from healthcare professionals.

Even though lesbian couples seeking fertility services are increasing in number, fertility professionals may continue using forms and language representative of heteronormativity (Engström, Häggström-Nordin, Borneskog, & Almqvist, 2018). Engström et al. (2018) found that participants were aware of the heterosexual couples' images and heteronormative language used in marketing and informative materials. Signage around the facility used terms such as "Mom and Dad," rather than "Parents" (Engström et al., 2018). In order to provide ethical care, healthcare professionals should be aware of these types of barriers to feel supported and understood during the difficult processes experienced through fertility treatment (Engström et al., 2018). Asking for support in the healthcare, and other systems may prove difficult due to fear of rejection or unsupportive responses from those from whom a lesbian couple seeks support (Williams, Laduke, Klik, & Hutsell, 2016).

Societal acceptance of individuals identifying as lesbian increases as heterosexual individuals socially interact with gay individuals (Vonofakou, Hewstone, & Voci, 2007); however, those choosing to interact with lesbians socially likely do not belong to groups with strong negative opinions regarding sexuality--those who may demonstrate or carry out violent acts against lesbians. The perception of a lesbian couple within a heteronormative society may yield negative interactions (Camara, Katznelson, Hildebrandt-Sterling, & Parker, 2012) from the workplace, family, counselor, and medical staff working with a lesbian couple. These negative interactions will occur as long as lesbians are a part of a marginalized group.

Lesbian couples remain marginalized, even with increased acceptance of sexuality from members of the heterosexual population (Rostosky, Riggle, Horne, & Miller, 2009). Therefore, lesbian couples may endure more discrimination and stereotypes, while struggling with having less power than other individuals (Camara et al., 2012; Rostosky et al., 2009). This discrimination can occur across systems, impacting a lesbian couple in myriad ways. Due to their position as sexual minorities, lesbians may internalize sexual stigma, otherwise known as internalized homophobia (Herek, Gillis, & Cogan, 2009; Szymanski, Kashubeck-West, & Meyer, 2008). Research demonstrates rates of internalized homophobia can lead to poor health, anxiety, and depression (Newcomb & Mustanski, 2010; Szymanski et al., 2008), and impacts the way individuals interact with others (Mereish & Poteat, 2015).

Lesbian individuals may experience discrimination in the workplace, should they choose to identify as a lesbian to their coworkers. Additionally, the provision of health insurance benefits may not be the same as their heterosexual counterparts, particularly involving fertility treatments. Discrimination against lesbians is systemic beyond the workplace, reaching across government, media, schools, religion, and social history (Camara et al. 2012; Nadal, Wong, Issa, Meterko, Leon, & Wideman,

2011). Counselors will best serve their lesbian clients by attending to and advocating across these systems. Also, they must assist their clients in learning ways to advocate for themselves in the face of discrimination. Advocacy for lesbian clients begins with a counselor self-analysis, to better understand ways in which we individually may impact the counseling relationship and the systems-at-large.

INTRODUCTION TO THE COUNSELORS

I (Meredith) came from ancestors who resided in the northwestern portion of Europe (mainly Ireland and Norway). The majority of my life I spent with a Midwestern upbringing, and I am now engaging in the Southeastern United States culture. As a child, I enjoyed traveling to other countries to expand my awareness and perspective of the world--though I did not know that was the purpose at that time! My research has focused on three main areas: the military, where I engaged in training to receive an honorary rank with the United States Army; the LGBT+ population; and the female population. I focus on the areas of fertility, and counseling, as well as mentorship. My own experiences as a female and issues with fertility have led to a desire to further my awareness and worldview, as well as the awareness and worldview of other individuals working through similar issues and experiences. I believe in helping a client look at each context and set of systems which influence their phenomenology, including their childhood experiences. Each person is a whole being, functioning best when life feels balanced and well. I hope that my perspective continues to broaden as I add to my knowledge, then using that knowledge to develop skills which help others through the counseling profession.

I (Haley) came from ancestors that resided in Europe, mainly Germany and Ireland. Raised with a Midwestern upbringing, I am rooted in both Catholic and Protestant traditions. I continue to live in the Midwest, but I engage primarily in liberal circles, which form my viewpoint and perspective. My research has focused mainly on how counselors can engage with, and work to, create safe and inclusive environments for LGBTQ families and youth. My own experiences as a lesbian and a parent who experienced the fertility process with my wife have shaped my worldview and helped to generate a passion for helping others who share similar identities. In order to help clients, I believe in assisting them by navigating systems and working to advocate on their behalf. I believe that people and experiences shape individuals within the ecological systems around them. I hope to use my personal experiences and the knowledge I gain from the lived experiences of others, to develop best practices for the counseling professionals and the profession at large.

CASE CONCEPTUALIZATION

Relational Cultural Theory

Relational-Cultural Theory (RCT) posits that interpersonal relationships are essential to obtain healthy psychological growth and well-being (Olshansky, 2003). The theory, which falls under the feminist umbrella, was developed based on the work of Gilligan (1982) and Miller (1976), as well as several others (Coll, Surrey, & Weingarten, 1998; Gilligan, Rogers, & Tolman, 1991; Jordan, 1997; Miller & Stiver, 1997). This theory focuses on the psychological development of women (Olshansky, 2003). RCT recognizes the development of a strong sense of self as existing within the context of mutually healthy relationships with others (Olshansky, 2003), using a strengths-based approach (Jordan, 2010). For a lesbian couple, the use of RCT focuses not only on their psychological development based on their gender but also their relationship with another woman. In order for each woman to engage in, or maintain healthy psychological growth, their relationship must also be healthy.

Healthy or growth-fostering relationships include the maintenance of a healthy relationship amidst stressful experiences, which requires individuals in the relationship to have factors associated with resilience (Mereish & Poteat, 2015). RCT emphasizes connection, resilience, and empowerment within a cultural framework (Mereish & Poteat, 2015); with lesbian clients perhaps most benefiting from the use of the following tenets: cultural complexity, condemned isolation, shame, growth-fostering relationships, mutual empathy, authenticity, and "power-over relationships" (Singh & Moss, 2016, p. 401). The idea of connectedness incorporates a connection in all relationships--including the counseling relationship. Healthy relationships experience periods where they are highly connected and periods of disconnect. These are inevitable, according to RCT (Comstock, Hammer, Strentzsch, Cannon, Parsons, and Salazar, 2008). Mutual empathy is an expansion of Carl Rogers' concept of empathy, moving from individual empathy to a process of empathy between two individuals (Comstock et al., 2008). Goals for counseling clients should incorporate these tenets, examining ways the impact on the individual for each area. Through this examination, RCT posits that individuals will grow in their authenticity as they increase factors of resilience and authenticity (Mereish & Poteat, 2015). Recognizing instances of expressing empathy, increasing authenticity, and describing examples of shame are all methods for achieving the goals of RCT.

Heterosexism privileges those with heterosexual identities, subsequently oppressing lesbian individuals systemically (Singh & Moss, 2016). Internalized homophobia relates to the RCT idea which suggests that negative relational images negatively impact how lesbians interact with each other (Mereish & Poteat, 2015). Additionally, higher levels of internalized homophobia may impact the likelihood that a lesbian would disclose her sexual orientation (Szymanski et al., 2008). Other implications for higher levels of internalized homophobia include poorer health (Jordan, 2009), and a lower likelihood of demonstrating empathy to heterosexual friends (Mereish & Poteat, 2015). RCT includes a focus on the implications of privilege and oppression on individuals, particularly for individuals who find themselves in multiple non-majority groups (e.g., woman, lesbian; Jordan, 2010). Counselors using RCT initiate discussions with clients regarding specific ways they experience power, privilege, and oppression (Walker, 2008); this discussion provides a path towards awareness and healing (Jordan, 2010).

The fertility process may be a stressful experience for all types of couples; the financial and emotional expenses can lead to relational rifts or breaks. Working to help a lesbian couple maintain a healthy relationship during the fertility process may reduce these rifts and breaks. Healthy relationships, as defined by RCT, incorporate mutuality, empathy, and reciprocity (Olshansky, 2003). When individuals can engage in growth-fostering relationships, research finds increased levels of self-esteem, with decreased levels of loneliness, depression, and psychological distress (Frey, Beesley, & Miller, 2006; Frey, Tobin, & Beesley, 2004). Assisting lesbian clients in developing and increasing these positive aspects in their relationship may help reduce negative impacts of the fertility process, while also helping clients become increasingly authentic as they better understand the impact of heterosexism in their surrounding systems and ways to grow at a sociocultural level (Jordan & Hartling, 2002; Singh & Moss, 2016).

Assigning weekly homework provides an opportunity for the couple to continue to hold the strength of their relationship as a priority during the stressful times which accompany a focus on fertility. Creating homework assignments which focus on the key constructs of RCT (i.e., connectedness, empathy, mutuality, reciprocity, and authenticity) may strengthen the bond within the relationship (Rausch & Wikoff, 2017). Counselors working from an RCT perspective help clients recognize internalized homophobia, obstacles, and disconnection impact individuals due to societal oppression (Miller, 1976). Therefore, a focus on multiculturalism and social justice are integral to practicing RCT (Frey, 2013).

Many attributes have been found to rank as significant factors for resilience among LGBTQ individuals, including social support, community connectedness, high levels of being "out" in the community, and being involved in a relationship (Frost & Meyer, 2009; Meyer, 2010). These factors mirror the constructs of RCT and can serve as a focus for goal-setting during counseling sessions (Rausch & Wikoff, 2017).

Multicultural and Social Justice Counseling Competencies

Beginning with our counseling education, we both knew the importance of working to examine our attitudes and beliefs about same-sex relationships, same-sex parents, and the fertility process. This process of increasing self-awareness and expanding our perspectives is an ongoing journey for both of us and something we value for personal growth. Besides, it is ethical practice to focus on the multicultural and social justice competencies, viewing them as a necessary practice for all counseling relationships. Individuals grow and develop, and our awareness and worldview should continue to expand with our development of self.

Counselor Self-Awareness

I (Meredith) knew to be careful of my privilege as an individual in a heterosexual relationship. Although we are all women in this counseling relationship, my experiences with the fertility process differ significantly from those of Jane and Kelsey because I identify in the privileged group, which provides me with advantages. My experiences with medical forms and language match my sexual identity as a member of the culture with privilege. I did not have to make the same choices as Jane and Kelsey, as I had at my convenience items which they have to both make choices surrounding, and financially consider (e.g., sperm). My assumptions about the process will likely not align with their experience, and I will have to work to empathize with each additional stressor and barrier they encounter due to the negative consequences inherent in a heteronormative society.

I (Meredith) consulted with Haley, before my work with Jane and Kelsey, to help me recognize when my assumptions, privilege, power, values, or experiences enter into the counseling relationship. I value taking action to increase my multicultural awareness as necessary, understanding the potential for harm to Jane and Kelsey if I do not prioritize my competencies in our counseling work with this couple.

Counseling relationship. Throughout the counseling process, I valued working with Jane and Kelsey's experiences, individually, as a couple, and as partners navigating the fertility process. As a counselor focusing on multicultural and social justice competencies, I use the strengths and limitations of each person to work through the personal experiences each has during the fertility process and use it to help strengthen the relationship and bond between the two. When Jane and Kelsey exhibited vulnerability as it relates to expressing feelings of shame; for example, I encouraged this vulnerability, suggesting it helps each of them increase their expression of authenticity.

All three of us need to examine the impact their social identity, status, oppression, limitations, assumptions, attitudes, values, and beliefs have on the counseling relationship. It is essential to recognize the shared areas of marginalization, with ways each of us have used self-advocacy to overcome, or try to overcome, these barriers. Jane and Kelsey expressed areas of concern using humor to diffuse the message. I used this as an opportunity to have them examine how they have created diffusing messages when working to confront areas of discomfort. We set a goal of feeling comfortable expressing negative feelings regarding discrimination and marginalization authentically. I want them both to practice advocating for themselves and fighting against marginalization and oppression in a safe environment. I know this could lead to periods of disconnect in the relationship, but I trust that it will deepen the counseling relationship and work for everyone involved. As a privileged counselor with marginalized clients, this is imperative to growth and social justice counseling. This discussion and acknowledgment provide us with a strength-based groundwork.

Client Worldview

I know that the impact of the fertility process is not just an emotional impact on Jane and Kelsey. As women, and also as women identifying as lesbians, they will encounter barriers, assumptions, limitations, and discrimination across systems (e.g., family, neighborhood, health insurance, medical doctors/staff, state laws). It is vital that I stay abreast of the systemic impact at each level, helping Jane and Kelsey recognize their attitudes, beliefs, and knowledge of the impact. Discussing the impact of sex-role socialization for both of them as individuals, as well as the impact on them as a couple, was imperative, as it directly relates to their goal of becoming mothers. Both Jane and Kelsey experience oppression due to their identity as lesbians. The impact of this marginalization on their mental health may be something they resist fighting because they may feel as if there is no benefit to exerting this type of energy. This resistance may leave them feeling shame, exhaustion, and distress, reducing their factors of resilience and authenticity, reducing their relational development (Comstock et al., 2008); with relational health as the core of RCT, this could be a detrimental outcome.

Counseling and Advocacy Interventions

It is my responsibility to assist them in developing ways to navigate these feelings and barriers, advocate as they desire, and show them my advocacy efforts. Counselor efforts to advocate for lesbian couples can focus on various areas. Workplace benefits, including insurance and maternity leave, may vary based on the organization.

Counselors can advocate for organizations including same-sex couple benefits. Joining and becoming an active member of social justice organizations provides me with the current issues, allowing me to write to politicians to express my views and advocate for individuals like Jane and Kelsey. Our initial discussions may incorporate ways they currently experience oppression in their family, extended family, neighborhood, and city. We then can expand this awareness to the ways that government and historical context impact create systemic oppression. I knew it was essential to include intentional discussion and homework to provide a deeper understanding and development of each as an individual and couple, as well as within a set of complex systems.

TREATMENT

My long-term goal for Kelsey and Jane was to increase their relational competence through the development of their growth-fostering relationship. Beneath the umbrella of our long-term goal, I sought to achieve three short-term goals initially, including consistent reevaluation of the goals according to our progress and ever-changing context.

The first short-term goal involved increasing the connectedness between Kelsey and Jane. Part of my work included focusing on feelings of isolation for both Kelsey and Jane as individuals, as well as when faced with heterosexist barriers within a heteronormative society (Comstock et al., 2008). One area which was of particular importance, was the recognition of Jane as a co-mother, as this is particularly important for psychological health (Dahl & Malterud, 2015).

The second short-term goal worked on feelings of shame within the relationship (Singh & Moss, 2016). This shame comes with the cultural complexity inherent in identifying as a woman and as a lesbian within a male-driven, heteronormative context (Sing & Moss, 2016). As we work to identify the shame each of us faces, we chose to focus on creating feelings of mutual empathy as well as authenticity for both us as counselors and Jane and Kelsey. We recognize that counselors have an underlying power-over relationship which is something we need to discuss within the counseling relationship (Singh & Moss, 2016), in order for growth to occur (Duffey, Haberstroh, & Trepal, 2009).

My final short-term goal focused on social and relational support for Kelsey and Jane. The perception of support from family and friends correlates to higher levels of well-being (Graham & Barnow, 2013), which may be particularly helpful for a process which is described as "mentally demanding", accompanied by "great anticipation and fear of miscarriage" (Engström et al., 2018, p. 1447).

Progress

My long-term goal for Kelsey and Jane was to increase their relational competence through the development of their growth-fostering relationship. This goal includes increasing feelings of connectedness, mutual empathy, and empowerment. Upon beginning my counseling work with the couple, I described the tenets of RCT and how the tenets would be applied in our work together. Although Kelsey was hesitant, stating, "I do not think we need all of the systemic advocacy stuff...I don't think it is what we're into," our invitation to "trust the process" was accepted, and we set forth examining and collaborating on a few short-term goals which would lead us, hopefully, to complete our long-term aim.

The first short-term goal I set was to increase the connectedness between Kelsey and Jane. After taking the fertility medication, Clomid, Jane had mentioned a fear that she was "losing" her wife due to Kelsey's emotionality as a side effect of the prescription. Kelsey mentioned feeling lonely in her marriage, with no one in her family to turn to, as her mother is deceased and her father does not acknowledge her same-sex marriage. In RCT, we refer to this as condemned isolation--a feeling of isolation and aloneness (Miller, 1976) as a result of living in a heteronormative society (Katz, Joiner, & Kwon, 2002).

In essence, both Kelsey and Jane felt isolated in the fertility process--from each other, and parts of society. "I know I'm a beast on this Clomid! I wouldn't want to be around me either," Kelsey explained in our first session. I asked Jane, "what does it feel like to hear that?" and Jane explained, "it's not that I don't want to be around you, I just don't know what you're going through, and at least if I'm not around, I'm not bugging you!" Hearing this, Kelsey began crying, covering her face with her hands. Jane leaned over to hug her, but Kelsey drew back. This reaction visibly hurt Jane. I worked to empathize, "I cannot imagine feeling isolated in your marriage, when you experience isolation from the fertility process, from your father...from this medication…" After this statement, Jane's face grew serious, and she asked, "Kelsey, is that how you feel? Like everyone is isolating you?" Kelsey nodded, "and I don't blame them for doing it!" As the two embraced, I worked to uncover the ways both Kelsey and Jane felt isolated, starting with the fertility doctors and staff, followed by their careers, their families, and from each other. For homework, I gave them The Gottman Institute Love Map Exercise card deck to take home. I asked them to practice asking each other questions from the deck each day before bedtime, until their next appointment. I hoped this would begin to build connectedness and reduce feelings of condemned isolation.

At our next session, we discussed ways in which advertisements, brochures, and forms at the fertility clinic may be isolating, due to the heteronormative language and pictures presented. We discussed isolation from a financial standpoint--lesbian couples have to purchase, ship, and store sperm, which are financial burdens not necessarily present for a heterosexual couple. Other ways the couple may have felt isolated, which I addressed, included the need to disclose their sexual orientation and the need to advocate for including Jane as a co-mother. Ideas for advocacy included Jane choosing which terminology she felt "fit" her future experience, should the pregnancy result in a live birth. Jane chose "co-mother" over "non-birth mother" with the couple choosing to purchase bracelets with a "mom" charm attached to represent their journey as a team through the fertility process.

My second short-term goal examined feelings of shame within the relationship (Singh & Moss, 2016). Kelsey reported feeling shame that she was not successful this far along in the fertility process and that this made her feel "like less of a woman," particularly because her mother did not have any fertility issues. Jane also mentioned feeling shame, particularly in the fertility office, because she did not feel as if her decisions "counted." She said, "I'm going to be the mom too! Our child will have Mom 1 and Mom 2. That's it. No Dad. Why don't they get it?" It was essential for me to listen purely to the voices of Kelsey and Jane, hearing them until they were done speaking. I focused on clarifying both content and feeling, asking questions and making summarizing statements. I asked about shame across systems, both internal feelings and external expressions of shame. It took an entire counseling session. I sent them home with the task to practice genuinely listening to each other every time they had a conversation. I challenged them to not speak about themselves until they had asked one question reflecting content and one reflecting feeling. I normalized that this would feel awkward initially, but should grow easier prior with practice.

At our next appointment, I focused on ways that women and members of a same-sex relationship may experience additional feelings of shame. Kelsey's feelings of failure after not becoming pregnant from fertility treatment began with the societal belief that a woman is not successful unless she can bear children. Jane's shame arising from the heteronormative language at the fertility clinic comes from a heteronormative society, socialized to treat lesbians as outsiders. We traced these feelings back to their initial feelings of condemned isolation, which led to feelings of shame. These feelings of shame lead to feelings of disconnection within oneself, as well as with each other, and other systems which could help them through the fertility process (Marzullo & Libman, 2009). When I delivered this psychoeducational piece to Kelsey and Jane, their bodies relaxed with relief, with Jane responding, "Seriously? I have never thought of all of this as some ripple effect. Hearing it said in this way makes me feel more like a teammate with Kelsey and less like an outsider playing defense to her emotional pain." I sent Jane and Kelsey home with an open-ended questions card deck to help them better understand themselves and each other--a tenet of RCT.

The final short-term goal was to focus on social and relational support for Kelsey and Jane. Jane revealed a sense of frustration as a non-birth mother, looking for answers regarding the process. She stated that she wanted to be able to "be there" for Kelsey, but struggled to empathize because she did not fully understand all of the processes. In looking for fertility counseling groups, she found some online but felt uncomfortable as the only non-birth mother in a group of mothers and fathers. "I even tried going into a chat with other women experiencing fertility issues, to better understand what they were feeling, but it wasn't what I needed. I think I need another co-mother to say, 'yeah, me too!'" I thanked Jane for her authenticity and vulnerability in the retelling of her experience.

I continued to counsel Jane and Kelsey for another seven sessions, focusing on the central tenets of RCT, to encourage a growth-fostering relationship. During that time, Kelsey became pregnant. Our counseling goals changed a bit to include ways to continue to advocate for themselves with hospital doctors and staff, as well as making sure we all knew the laws in Iowa for co-mothers in regards to items such as the parents listed on the birth certificate. Jane and Kelsey have taken a break from counseling, with the hopes to return once the baby was born to continue to grow in their relationship during another stressful season of life.

CONCLUSION

Kelsey and Jane are just one couple out of many lesbian couples who will choose a reproductive option in order to add to their family. As rates of LGBT+ couples seeking reproductive and other fertility methods increase, it is imperative for counselors to increase their awareness and perspective in these areas. In order to serve our clients ethically and effectively, we must incorporate the MSJCC in our practice. In my work with Kelsey and Jane, we had to examine several areas which may impact the counseling relationship and progress in our work: privilege, discrimination, our own experiences with fertility and reproductive practice, and areas for improvement in our advocacy for this population.

Kelsey and Jane were open to the counseling relationship, demonstrating growth as individuals and as a couple. This growth aligns with the goals of RCT. I, as their counselor, also grew as individuals through this process. As a result of this work, I recognize new ways to advocate for lesbian couples and understand the experience of another couple engaging in tough counseling work, which broadens our perspective and changes our worldview. I have learned, among many other things, that intertwining the theoretical perspective of the counselor with the multicultural and social justice counseling competencies provides the opportunity to counsel while addressing barriers and creating avenues for advocacy in our work.

REFERENCES

Adashi, E. Y. (2015). A same-sex infertility health insurance mandate in Maryland? *Journal of the American Medical Association*, *314*(1), 15. doi:10.1001/jama.2015.6562 PMID:26151251

Asazawa, K. (2015). Effects of a partnership support program for couples undergoing Fertility treatment. *Japan Journal of Nursing Science*, *12*(4), 354–366. doi:10.1111/jjns.12074 PMID:25780939

Ben-Ari, A., & Livni, T. (2006). Motherhood is not a given thing: Experiences and constructed meanings of biological and nonbiological lesbian mothers. *Sex Roles*, *54*(7-8), 521–531. doi:10.100711199-006-9016-0

Boivin, J., Griffiths, E., & Venetis, C. A. (2011). Emotional distress in infertile women and failure of assisted reproductive technologies: Meta-analysis of prospective Psychosocial studies. *BMJ (Clinical Research Ed.)*, *342*(feb23 1), d223. doi:10.1136/bmj.d223 PMID:21345903

Borneskog, C., Lampic, C., Sydsjö, G., Bladh, M., & Skoog Svanberg, A. (2014). How do lesbian couples compare with heterosexual *in vitro* fertilization and spontaneously pregnant couples when it comes to parenting stress? *Acta Paediatrica (Oslo, Norway)*, *103*(5), 537–545. doi:10.1111/apa.12568 PMID:24456297

Burnett, J. A. (2009). Cultural considerations in counseling couples who experience fertility. *Journal of Multicultural Counseling and Development*, *37*(3), 166–177. doi:10.1002/j.2161-1912.2009.tb00100.x

Camara, S. K., Katznelson, A., Hildebrandt-Sterling, J., & Parker, T. (2012). Heterosexism in context: Qualitative interaction effects of co-cultural responses. *The Howard Journal of Communications*, *23*(4), 312–331. doi:10.1080/10646175.2012.722836

Chabot, J. M., & Ames, B. D. (2004). "It wasn't 'let's get pregnant and go do it':" Decision making in lesbian couples planning motherhood via donor insemination. *Family Relations*, *53*(4), 348–356. doi:10.1111/j.0197-6664.2004.00041.x

Chandra, A., Martinez, G. M., Mosher, W. D., Abma, J. C., & Jones, J. (2005). Fertility, Family planning, and reproductive health of U.S. women: Data from the 2002 National Survey of Family Growth. *Vital and Health Statistics*, *23*, 22–31. PMID:16532609

Coll, C. G., Surrey, J., & Weingarten, K. (1998). *Mothering against the odds: Diverse Voices of contemporary mothers*. New York, NY: The Guilford Press.

Comstock, D. L., Hammer, T. R., Strentzsch, J., Cannon, K., Parsons, J., & Ii, G. S.II. (2008). Relational-cultural theory: A framework for bridging relational, multicultural and social justice competencies. *Journal of Counseling and Development*, *86*(3), 279–287. doi:10.1002/j.1556-6678.2008.tb00510.x

Dahl, B., & Malterud, K. (2015). Neither father nor biological mother. A qualitative study about lesbian co-mothers' maternity care experiences. *Sexual & Reproductive Healthcare: Official Journal of the Swedish Association of Midwives*, *6*(3), 169–173. doi:10.1016/j.srhc.2015.02.002 PMID:26842641

DeDiego, A. C. (2016). A systemic perspective for working with same-sex parents. *Counseling Today*, *59*(4), 40–44.

Dooley, M., Dineen, T., Sarma, K., & Nolan, A. (2014). The psychological impact of infertility and fertility treatment on the male partner. *Human Fertility*, *17*(3), 203–209. doi:10.3109/14647273.2014.942390 PMID:25116275

Duffey, T., Haberstroh, S., & Trepal, H. (2009). A grounded theory of relational competencies and creativity in counseling. *Journal of Creativity in Mental Health*, *4*(2), 89–112. doi:10.1080/15401380902951911

Dunne, G. A. (2000). Opting into motherhood: Lesbians blurring the boundaries and transforming the meaning of parenthood and kinship. *Gender & Society*, *14*(1), 11–35. doi:10.1177/089124300014001003

Engström, H. A., Häggström-Nordin, E., Borneskog, C., & Almqvist, A. (2018). Mothers in same-sex relationships describe the process of forming a family as a stressful journey in a heteronormative world: A Swedish grounded theory study. *Maternal and Child Health Journal*, *22*(10), 1444–1450. doi:10.100710995-018-2525-y PMID:29740747

Erwin, T. (2007). Two moms and a baby: Counseling lesbian couples choosing motherhood. *Women & Therapy*, *30*(1/2), 99–149. doi:10.1300/J015v30n01_06

First Amendment California Supreme Court Holds that Free Exercise of Religion does not Give Fertility Doctors Right to Deny Treatment to Lesbians. North Coast Women's Care Medical Group, Inc. v. San Diego County Superior Court, 189 P.3d 959 (Cal. 2008). (2008). *Harvard Law Review*, *122*(2), 787–794. Retrieved from http://ezproxy.augusta.edu/login?url=https://search.ebscohost.com/login.aspx?direct=true&db=a9h&AN=35650955&site=ehost-live&scope=site

Frey, L. (2013). Relational-cultural therapy: Theory, research, adn application to counseling competencies. *Professional Psychology, Research and Practice*, *44*(3), 177–185. doi:10.1037/a0033121

Frey, L. L., Beesley, D., & Miller, M. (2006). Relational health, attachment, and psychological distress in college women and men. *Psychology of Women Quarterly*, *30*(3), 303–311. doi:10.1111/j.1471-6402.2006.00298.x

Frey, L. L., Tobin, J., & Beesley, D. (2004). Relational predictors of psychological distress in women and men presenting for university counseling center services. *Journal of College Counseling*, *7*(2), 129–139. doi:10.1002/j.2161-1882.2004.tb00244.x

Frost, D. M., & Meyer, I. H. (2009). Internalized homophobia and relationship quality among lesbians, gay men, and bisexuals. *Journal of Counseling Psychology*, *56*(1), 97–109. doi:10.1037/a0012844 PMID:20047016

Galhardo, A., Cunha, M., Pinto-Gouveia, J., & Matos, M. (2013). The mediator role of emotional regulation processes on infertility-related stress. *Journal of Clinical Psychology in Medical Settings*, *20*(4), 497–507. doi:10.100710880-013-9370-3 PMID:23821009

Genero, P., Baker Miller, J., Surrey, J., & Baldwin, L. M. (1992). Measuring perceived mutuality in close relationships: Validation of the Mutual Psychological Development Questionnaire. *Journal of Family Psychology*, *6*(1), 36–48. doi:10.1037/0893-3200.6.1.36

Getrajdman, C., Lee, J. A., & Copperman, A. B. (2017). Co-IVF for same-sex female couples. *Seminars in Reproductive Medicine*, *35*(5), 415–419. doi:10.1055-0037-1605380 PMID:29073679

Gilligan, C. (1982). *In a different voice: Psychological theory and women's development*. Cambridge, MA: Harvard University Press.

Gilligan, C., Rogers, A., & Tolman, D. (1991). *Women, girls, and psychotherapy: Reframing resistance*. Binghamton, NY: Haworth.

Goldberg, A. B., Downing, J. B., & Richardson, H. B. (2009). The transition from infertility to adoption: Perceptions of lesbian and heterosexual couples. *Journal of Social and Personal Relationships*, *26*(6-7), 938–963. doi:10.1177/0265407509345652

Golombok, S., & Murray, C. (2006). Non-genetic and non-gestational parenthood: Consequences for parent-child relationships and the psychological well-being of mothers, fathers and children at age 3. *Human Reproduction (Oxford, England)*, *21*(7), 1918–1924. doi:10.1093/humrep/del039 PMID:16517564

Graham, J. M., & Barnow, Z. B. (2013). Stress and social support in gay, lesbian, and heterosexual couples: Direct effects and buffering models. *Journal of Family Psychology*, *27*(4), 569–578. doi:10.1037/a0033420 PMID:23795604

Grant, L. E., & Cochrane, S. (2014). Acupuncture for the mental and emotional health of Women undergoing IVF treatment: A comprehensive review. *Australian Journal of Acupuncture & Chinese Medicine*, *9*(1), 5–12.

Hayman, B., & Wilkes, L. (2017). *De novo* families: Lesbian motherhood. *Journal of Homosexuality*, *64*(5), 577–591. doi:10.1080/00918369.2016.1194119 PMID:27228787

Herek, G. M., Gillis, J. R., & Cogan, J. C. (2009). Internalized stigma among sexual minority adults: Insights from a social psychological perspective. *Journal of Counseling Psychology*, *56*(1), 32–43. doi:10.1037/a0014672

Hopkins, J. J., Sorenson, A., & Taylor, V. (2013). Same-sex couples, families, and Marriage: Embracing and resisting heteronormativity. *Sociology Compass*, *7*(2), 97–110. doi:10.1111oc4.12016

Jordan, J. V. (1997). *Women's growth in diversity*. New York: Guilford.

Jordan, J. V. (2009). *Relational-cultural therapy*. Washington, DC: American Psychological Association.

Jordan, J. V. (2010). *The power of connection: Recent developments in relational-cultural theory*. New York, NY: Routledge.

Jordan, J. V., & Hartling, L. M. (2002). New developments in relational cultural theory. In M. Ballou & L. S. Brown (Eds.), *Rethinking mental health and disorder* (pp. 48–70). New York, NY: Guilford Press.

Kahaki, F., & Khosravi, M. (2014). A survey of the relationship between anxiety, stress, depression, and life satisfaction in fertile and infertile women. *Journal of Jahrom University of Medical Sciences*, *11*, 160–160.

Katz, J., Joiner, T. E. Jr, & Kwon, P. (2002). Membership in a devalued social group and emotional well-being: Developing a model of personal self-esteem, collective self-esteem, and group socialization. *Sex Roles*, *4*(9/10), 419–443. doi:10.1023/A:1021644225878

Liang, B., Tracy, A., Taylor, C. A., Williams, L. M., Jordan, J. V., & Baker Miller, J. (2002). The Relational Health Indices: A study of women's relationships. *Psychology of Women Quarterly*, *26*(1), 25–35. doi:10.1111/1471-6402.00040

Markus, E., Weingarten, A., Duplessi, Y., & Jones, J. (2010). Lesbian couples seeking pregnancy with donor insemination. *Journal of Midwifery & Women's Health*, *55*(2), 124–132. doi:10.1016/j.jmwh.2009.09.014 PMID:20189131

Marzullo, A., & Libman, A. J. (2009). *Research overview: HAte crimes and violence against lesbian, gay, bisexual and transgender people*. Washington, DC: Human Rights Campaign Foundation. Retrieved from http://www.hrc.org/resources/entry/hate-crimes-and-violence-against-lgbt-people

McNair, R., Dempsey, D., Wise, S., & Perlesz, A. (2002). Lesbian parenting: Issues, strengths,and challenges. *Family Matters (Melbourne, Vic.)*, *63*, 40–49.

Mereish, E. H., & Poteat, V. P. (2015). The conditions under which growth-fostering relationships promote resilience and alleviate psychological distress among sexual minorities: Applications of relational cultural theory. *Psychology of Sexual Orientation and Gender Diversity*, *2*(3), 339–344. doi:10.1037gd0000121 PMID:26380836

Meyer, I. (2010). Identity, stress, and resilience in lesbians, gay men, and bisexuals of color. *The Counseling Psychologist*, *38*(3), 442–454. doi:10.1177/0011000009351601 PMID:24347674

Miller, J. B. (1976). *Toward a new psychology of women*. Boston: Beacon.

Miller, J. B., & Stiver, I. P. (1997). *The healing connection: How women form relationships in therapy and in life*. Boston: Beacon Press.

Nadal, K. L., Wong, Y., Issa, M., Meterko, V., Leon, J., & Wideman, M. (2011). Sexual orientation microaggressions: Processes and coping mechanisms for lesbian, gay, and bisexual individuals. *Journal of LGBT Issues in Counseling*, *5*(1), 21–46. doi:10.1080/15538605.2011.554606

Newcomb, M. E., & Mustanski, B. (2010). Internalized homophobia and internalizing mental health problems: A meta-analytic review. *Clinical Psychology Review*, *30*(8), 1019–10129. doi:10.1016/j.cpr.2010.07.003 PMID:20708315

North Coast Women's Care Medical Group, Inc. v. San Diego County Superior Court, 189 P.3d959 (Cal. 2008).

Olshansky, E. (2003). A theoretical explanation for previously infertile mothers' vulnerability to depression. *Journal of Nursing Scholarship*, *35*(3), 263–268. doi:10.1111/j.1547-5069.2003.00263.x PMID:14562495

Rausch, M. A., & Wikoff, H. D. (2017). Addressing concerns with lesbian couples experiencing fertility treatment: Using Relational Cultural Theory. *Journal of LGBT Issues in Counseling*, *11*(3), 142–155. doi:10.1080/15538605.2017.1346494

Rogalin, C. L., & Brooks, J. E. (2018). Lesbians achieving pregnancy: The intersections of social location and the heteronormative medicalization of infertility. *Sociology Compass*, *12*(11), 1–11. doi:10.1111oc4.12637

Rostosky, S. S., Riggle, E. D. B., Horne, S. G., & Miller, A. D. (2009). Marriage amendments and psychological distress in lesbian, gay, and bisexual (LGB) adults. *Journal of Counseling Psychology*, *56*(1), 56–66. doi:10.1037/a0013609

Singh, A. A., & Moss, L. (2016). Using relational-cultural theory in LGBTQQ counseling: Addressing heterosexism and enhancing relational competencies. *Journal of Counseling and Development*, *94*(4), 398–404. doi:10.1002/jcad.12098

Sumontha, J., Farr, R. H., & Patterson, C. J. (2016). Social support and coparenting among lesbian, gay, and heterosexual adoptive parents. *Journal of Family Psychology*, *30*(8), 987–996. doi:10.1037/fam0000253 PMID:27709970

Szymanski, D. M., Kashubeck-West, S., & Meyer, J. (2008). Internalized heterosexism: Measurement, psychosocial correlates, and research directions. *The Counseling Psychologist*, *36*(4), 525–574. doi:10.1177/0011000007309489

Uchino, B. N. (2004). *Social support and physical health: Understanding the health consequences of relationships*. New Haven, CT: Yale University Press. doi:10.12987/yale/9780300102185.001.0001

United States Census. (2014). *Household characteristics of opposite-sex and same sex households ACS 2014*. Retrieved from: http://www.census.gov/acs/www

Van Der Merwe, E., & Greeff, A. P. (2015). Infertility-related stress within the marital relationship. *International Journal of Sexual Health*, *27*(4), 522–531. doi: 10.1080/19317611.2015.1067275

Vonofakou, C., Hewstone, M., & Voci, A. (2007). Contact with outgroup friends as a predictor of meta-attitudinal strength and accessibility of attitudes toward gay men. *Journal of Personality and Social Psychology*, *92*(5), 804–820. doi:10.1037/0022-3514.92.5.804 PMID:17484606

Walker, M. (2008). Power and effectiveness: Envisioning an alternate paradigm. *Women & Therapy*, *31*(2-4), 129–144. doi:10.1080/02703140802146266

Williams, S. L., Laduke, S. L., Klik, K. A., & Hutsell, D. W. (2016). A paradox of support seeking and support response among gays and lesbians. *Personal Relationships*, *23*(2), 296–310. doi:10.1111/pere.12127

Zeiler, K., & Malmquist, A. (2014). Lesbian shared biological motherhood: The ethics of IVF with reception of oocytes from partner. *Medicine, Health Care, and Philosophy*, *17*(3), 347–355. doi:10.100711019-013-9538-5 PMID:24395218

Chapter 5
Rose's Thorn:
Navigating Career and College Readiness Self-Efficacy While Aging-Out of the Foster Care System

Regina Gavin Williams
North Carolina Central University, USA

EXECUTIVE SUMMARY

This case study examines the life of Rose, a 17-year-old junior attending a public high school in a southeastern city. In the state where Rose resides, the year of "aging-out" of the foster care system is 18-years-old. With the age of 18 being such a pivotal year, Rose must not only think about her potential post-secondary options, but her ability to achieve adult self-sufficiency at such a young age as well. With no supports, this proves to be a daunting task for Rose. It becomes Rose's thorn. This chapter will explore the career and college readiness self-efficacy of Rose as she navigates her post-secondary options, builds her support networks, and discovers resources for adolescents aging out of the foster care system via her work with Dr. Williams, creator and counselor of the Students That Are Reaching Success (S.T.A.R.S.) program. Results from Rose's participation in the program will be shared and implications for counselors working with adolescents aging out of the foster care system will be reviewed.

DOI: 10.4018/978-1-7998-0022-4.ch005

INTRODUCTION

Navigating post-secondary options and preparing for adult self-sufficiency prior to high school completion is a significant barrier for adolescents aging out of the foster care system. Kirk, Lewis, Nilsen, and Colvin (2013) reported that approximately 10% of adolescents who were formerly in foster care enrolled in college. Day, Dworsky, and Weng (2013) stated that although they finish high school, youth in foster care may not be fully prepared for the academic rigors of post-secondary education. Out of the 10% of former foster care youth enrolled in college, only 4% obtained a bachelor's degree (Kirk, Lewis, Nilsen, & Colvin, 2013). High school completion for adolescents in foster care is also accompanied by a higher susceptibility for them to be suspended or expelled, repeat a grade, or even drop out of high school (Unrau, Font, & Rawls, 2012). They are also reported to be less likely to enroll in college preparatory courses compared to their peers (Day, Dworsky, & Weng, 2013).

Despite these educational barriers, Courtney, Terao, and Bost (2004) reported that more than 70% of foster care youth aspire to pursue a post-secondary education. They instead find themselves susceptible to hindrances such as mental health concerns, homelessness, and unemployment (Kirk et al., 2013). Youth in the foster care system have been removed from their families by the court system. They may be placed with relatives, in foster homes, or in group homes (Kirk et al., 2013). Longer-term placement options include being adopted or allowing them to age out of the foster care system and instead live independently. The common age for aging out of the foster care system in most states is 18-years-old. According to the U.S. Department of Health and Human Services (2016), of the near 438,000 youth in foster care, over 20,000 of these youth age out of welfare services between the ages of 18-20 annually. They are then expected to transition from foster care and directly into adulthood without any supports such as being legally reunified with their biological family members, being placed under permanent guardianship, or without being adopted (Blakeslee & Best, 2018).

According to the National Foster Youth Institute (2017) approximately 20% of youth who were in foster care will become homeless after turning 18-years-old. Adolescents aging out of the foster care system may also lose many of support networks that facilitated their transition to independent living (Hudson, 2013). This presents a detrimental impact on the career and college readiness preparation needed for their successful transition from the foster care system to post-secondary education opportunities (Gavin Williams, Baker, Williams-DeVane, 2018). Conley (2010) described "career ready" as having the content knowledge and key learning techniques and skills to begin studies in a career pathway. Achieve, Inc. (n.d.)

describe "college ready" as being prepared for post-secondary education training experiences that lead to gaining education credentials such an associate or bachelor's degree, certificate, or license.

Piel (2018) indicated that school personnel may not have identified students in their school who are in foster care and the educational implications of being in the foster care system entail. Nonetheless, Finkelstein, Wamsley, and Miranda (2002) reported that school personnel may provide the strongest connection between foster youth and their formal education. In this regard, school counselors, in collaboration with other adults in their support networks (e.g. social worker, therapist, guardian et litem), could be essential in improving the educational outcomes of foster care youth. Williams et al. (2018) indicated that by understanding the unique circumstances foster care youth encounter and by having the desire to enhance their career and college readiness, one may help to improve the potential for foster care youth gaining access to post-secondary education opportunities. Counselors are knowledgeable and professionally equipped adults who can both recognize these circumstances and help to improve the career and college readiness of foster care adolescents. Furthermore, addressing the complex identities and lived experiences of youth aging out of the foster care system from a cross-cultural counseling stance can be helpful to counselors who are assisting these youth with their transition towards adult self-sufficiency.

This chapter will examine the work with Rose, a participant in the Students That Are Reaching Success (S.T.A.R.S.) program. Rose is a student aging out of foster care who is seeking to prepare for life after high school graduation. Customized counseling interventions and cross-cultural counseling strategies that will help her to adequately prepare for the post-secondary transition, as well as allow her to explore her identities, dismantle barriers towards success, and build her support networks will be shared.

CASE NARRATIVE

When I began working with Rose, she was a 17-year-old, African American, heterosexual, cisgender female. She was a high school junior attending a public high school in a southeastern city. Rose had been in the foster care system since she was 12-years-old. Prior to being in foster care, Rose grew up in a household with a single mother and three siblings, two sisters and one brother. When her mother lost her job, she was unable to adequately care for Rose and her siblings, which resulted in high poverty for the family. This situation, coupled with an altercation that occurred between her mother and her older brother, resulted in Rose and her siblings being placed in foster care by their local social services department. Rose has since lived in various homes due to past problems with foster caregivers and the growing demands from the state's social services departments. This high mobility has led to enrollment record issues and at times, lowered Rose's educational progress as compared to her peers. In the state where Rose resides, the year of "aging-out" of the foster care system was 18. Aging out is the process in which youth transitioning from the supervision of the foster care system work towards independent living. Rose had to not only think about her potential post-secondary options but also her ability to achieve adult self-sufficiency at a young age. She had high aspirations to pursue a post-secondary education, but minimal expectations due to the multiple barriers she had experienced. Some of these barriers include high mobility, loss of support networks, separation from her mother and siblings, growing up in poverty, and lack of educational support. Rose's desire was to change her beliefs so that she could pursue a post-secondary education, but she knew very little about this process. With no familial supports or adult mentors, this proved to be a daunting task for Rose. It became Rose's "thorn." Rose's career and college readiness self-efficacy had to improve if she was to truly take the steps towards pursing post-secondary education opportunities. She needed the support of a counselor who could challenge her current thinking and provide the career and college readiness interventions that would help her to solidify her post-secondary opportunities.

INTRODUCTION TO THE COUNSELOR

I am a 33-year-old African American woman from the southeastern United States. I hold a Doctor of Philosophy degree in counseling and counselor education, a master of education degree in school counseling and a bachelor of science degree in psychology with a minor in women's studies. I am a counselor educator, a licensed professional counselor (LPC), a national certified counselor (NCC), and a National Board for Certified Counselors (NBCC) Minority Fellowship Program (MFP) Doctoral Fellow who has worked in educational and community mental health settings. Within a community mental health setting, I worked with children and adolescents predominantly from underserved backgrounds with a significant number of these clients being in the foster care system. This population of clients is important to me given my personal experiences with family members who were adopted from the foster care system. Seeing their personal struggles toward developing their social identities as well as the educational barriers they faced while in school, prompted me to learn more about how my role as a counselor can help to provide better support for youth who are in the foster care system. I specifically became interested in the level of support that must be provided as these youth transition out of the foster care system with the goal of adult self-sufficiency.

In my previous roles, I strived to provide fair and equitable access to education and mental health services to individuals and families. My counseling philosophy utilized the existing theories/approaches of Choice Theory/Reality Therapy, Cognitive Behavioral Therapy, and Person-Centered Therapy. In this regard, I focused on helping clients create a workable plan that was specific to their needs and engaged them in an evaluation process of this plan, establishing a collaborative relationship in developing and achieving set goals. I believe it was important to evaluate clients' progress in counseling, therefore if needed, I changed a plan or a goal through mutual agreement of the client. I provided structured counseling with an emphasis on having unconditional positive regard for clients where they were given the opportunity to grow and gain insight in a safe and supportive environment. I operated from a multicultural lens as to better understand the worldview of my clients, taking in to account their cultural backgrounds and environmental influences. This helped me to provide services that were individualized to better suit my client's needs. It has allowed me to adhere to the American Counseling Association's (ACA) Multicultural Counseling and Social Justice Competencies (MSJCC; Ratts, Singh, Nassar-McMillan, Butler, & Rafferty McCullough, 2015).

Currently, I serve as a Clinical Assistant Professor in a Counselor Education program at a History Black College and University (HBCU) in a southeastern city. Through my faculty role, I focus on enhancing the multicultural and social justice counseling competencies of counselors-in-training. My research focuses on the career and college readiness and adult self-sufficiency of adolescents aging out of the foster care system, training therapeutic foster caregivers, and assisting adolescents with post-secondary education and career decision-making.

CASE CONCEPTUALIZATION

The case presented within this chapter is centered around Rose, a 17-year-old high school junior. Rose was a participant in a voluntary, state-funded, county-administered program offered through a department of social services in a southeastern city. The program provided services for foster care youth, ages 13 to18, who were aging of foster care at age 18, and for youth who were voluntarily in foster care between the ages of 18 to 21. It provided a life-skills development program designed to aid participants in their transition into adulthood by gaining support in the areas of education, sustainable housing, career development, money management, health care and overall well-being.

Through a collaboration with this life-skills program, Rose was invited to participate in a program entitled, *Students That Are Reaching Success (S.T.A.R.S.)*, a six-week career and college readiness intervention program for adolescents, ages 13-19 years-old, who were aging out of the foster care system. The program consisted of one hour per week, individual counseling sessions that focus on enhancing the career and college readiness self-efficacy of the participants. I served as the creator and counselor of the S.T.A.R.S. program. With the permission of her social worker and foster caregiver, Rose agreed to serve as participant in the S.T.A.R.S program. S.T.A.R.S. was described to Rose as an individualized career and college readiness intervention program designed to help adolescents aging out of foster care become self-sufficient adults by recognizing and working toward achieving, post-secondary education goals.

Conceptual Frameworks

The Ecological Model of Human Development (Bronfenbrenner, 1979), Social Cognitive Career Theory (SCCT; Lent, Brown, & Hackett, 1994), the Cognitive Information Processing Approach (CIP; Peterson, Sampson, Lenz, & Reardon, 2002), and the American School Counselor Association Model (ASCA, 2012) were combined as the framework for the interventions for the S.T.A.R.S program. These frameworks included tenets that were relevant to influences associated with the career and college readiness of foster care youth. The blended framework provided a critical lens for examining the environmental influences and skills of persons who are historically underserved and its implications on their developmental outcomes and perceived competencies.

Understanding that hindrances exist in the lives of adolescents aging out of foster care system, Rose's personal environments and roadblocks toward success were examined via the Ecological Model of Human Development. The SCCT (Lent, Brown, & Hackett, 1994) was utilized to help Rose develop positive post-secondary aspirations. The CIP Approach (Peterson, Sampson, Lenz, & Reardon, 2002), was used to enhance Rose's career problem-solving and decision-making skills. Furthermore, the five essential components of a career intervention where utilized when creating and administering the customized counseling interventions for the S.T.A.R.S. program. These components include written exercises, individualized interpretation and feedback of career inventories, information on the world of work, modeling, and attention to building support (Brown and Ryan Krane, 2000).

Career and College Readiness Self-Efficacy Inventory (CCRSI)

(CCRSI; Baker & Parikh Foxx, 2012) was used as the measure for the S.T.A.R.S. program. The CCRSI is an instrument that consists of 14 statements to elicit respondents' beliefs about how confident one is on a set of behaviors considered to be important for college and career readiness. The CCRSI consists of a five response Likert-scale ranging from the choices "strongly agree" to "strongly disagree" and a four-factor model measuring career and college readiness self-efficacy (Baker et al., 2016) in the following areas: (a) college knowledge, (b) positive personal characteristics), (c) academic competence, and (d) potential to achieve future goals. Scores on the CCRSI can range from a score of 14 (lowest) to a score of 70 (highest). The CCRSI was used as a pre-treatment measure in order to discover which of these four factors, although all four factors were utilized in some form within the intervention program. The CCRSI was administered to Rose once per week for the six-week program duration so that she could frequently measure Rose's career and college readiness self-efficacy and note any progress made weekly.

Multicultural and Social Justice Counseling Competencies (MSJCC)

The work with Rose was also rooted in the ACA Multicultural and Social Justice Counseling Competencies (MSJCC; Ratts, et al., 2015). As the counselor, I took the time to both recognize, understand, and gain knowledge on Rose's worldview by closely examining and acknowledging her personal experiences, cultural background, attitudes, and beliefs. Rose shared how her status in foster care lowered her expectations to a pursue post-secondary education, sharing her belief that foster care youth often do not attend and cannot afford college. Rose's marginalized status was also recognized, to provide culturally responsive counseling, as well as to immerse myself in the client's environment by holding sessions in her foster home (i.e., field experiment research). Holding sessions in the foster home allowed me to further understand the client's worldview and how she was impacted daily by her home environment.

Through weekly session plans, our progress toward enhancing Rose's career and college readiness self-efficacy, and the results from Rose's participation in the program will be shared. Rose's experience as it pertained to the MSJCC model, power, privilege, marginalization, oppression, and the intersectionality of these constructs are also examined. Implications for counselors working with adolescents aging out of the foster care system will also be shared.

TREATMENT

Program Introduction

I began my work with Rose within the S.T.A.R.S. program by introducing the program's purpose and goals. The program's purpose was as follows: The S.T.A.R.S. program is designed to help adolescents aging out of foster care, think about and prepare for post-secondary education and future careers through individual counseling sessions. S.T.A.R.S. will help to prepare participants for a successful transition to higher education. A copy of the participant consent form was then given to Rose for her to review. The guardian consent form was given to her social worker and foster caregiver in order to receive permission for Rose to participate, and for sessions to be conducted at the foster caregiver's home. After the consent forms were reviewed and signed, the CCRSI (Baker & Parikh Foxx, 2012) was administered as a pre-test measure prior to the initial session. Completing this measure helped us to create an initial plan that focused on Rose's career and college readiness self-efficacy prior to conducting the interventions. Furthermore, Rose and I took that time to build rapport with one another as to develop the therapeutic relationship through this counseling process. This process, consistent with the MSJCC (Ratts, et al., 2015) allowed client and counselor to learn more about one another and discuss their backgrounds and experiences. We also discussed what we would like to accomplish during our time together to include setting goals and collaborating on an individualized plan.

First Session

Pre-CCRSI Results

Rose scored a 52 out of 70 points on the CCRSI. Her results also revealed her lowest factors were in the areas of *college knowledge self-efficacy* and *academic competence self-efficacy*. College knowledge was described as understanding: (a) the admission selections process, (b) ways to financially afford post-secondary education, (c) academic requirements for work on the college level, and (d) cultural differences in the respective post-secondary education settings (Hooker and Brand, 2010). The components for academic competence included: (a) using appropriate study skills, (b) time management strategies, (c) utilizing academic resources, (d) knowing and using your learning style, and (e) understanding how academic performance in high school relates to access to post-secondary education.

Rose did not appear to be surprised at her CCRSI results as she shared with me that she frequently becomes unmotivated to study and stay focused on her school work; she admitted that she needed help staying on track academically. Regarding college knowledge, Rose said she knew very little about her post-secondary education options, the admissions process, ways to pay for a post-secondary education, and what the college environment was like. She knew that it will help her to be successful in life but did not know the steps she needed to take to get there. She was also unaware of what career field and academic major she would be most interested in pursuing.

I reflected on my role as counselor as it related to the MSJCC model by examining and understanding the client's worldview. In this instance, it was important as the counselor to demonstrate an openness to learn about the client's cultural background, social identities, values, beliefs, and privileged and marginalized status. In doing so, it was revealed that Rose felt that possessing college knowledge was only reserved for those with the privilege and financial means and supports to gain access to post-secondary education. As a foster care youth who was marginalized, this notion lowered her expectations for feeling that she could achieve such access. Furthermore, having moved between several homes while in foster care and having worked at a fast food restaurant most evenings after school, Rose had little desire to complete homework assignments and study adequately for tests. This in turn impacted Rose's desire to stay on track academically. It was important for me to understand how this situation of power and privilege influenced Rose and her worldview. It was important to explore how these societal notions made Rose feel over the years. Rose was asked if she would like to challenge these notions by gaining more college knowledge and academic competence self-efficacy to which she agreed. The pre-CCRSI results and this feedback from Rose was used to specifically focus the treatment goals on building Rose's *college knowledge self-efficacy* and *academic competence self-efficacy*. This information helped us to develop a five-week plan for engaging Rose in lessons that were designed to enhance her career and college readiness self-efficacy. The plan also focused on building her support networks and enhancing her expectations that would then help her to be feel supported throughout her life transitions.

Individual Learning Plan (ILP)

An individual learning plan (ILP) was created for Rose (see Table 1.), a component of the CIP Approach (Peterson, Sampson, Lenz, & Reardon, 2002). The ILP allows the counselor to work alongside the client to develop specific career-oriented goals and identify various resources and activities that can be utilized to achieve these goals, followed by selecting and sequencing those activities and resources that were deemed most promising. The ILP allows the client to monitor and achieve his or her goals for career problem-solving and decision-making (Peterson et al., 2002). In this regard, it was important for Rose to learn how to be a life-long career decision-maker, which is largely emphasized by the CIP Approach.

The goals we mutually decided upon as the focus of the ILP were to: (a) explore academic majors that match career choice, (b) review the college application process (c) explore ways to pay for college, and (d) engage in short-term and long-term goal-setting. From here, we listed various activities Rose intended to engage in, the purpose/outcome of each activity, the estimated time commitment of each activity, which goal the activity corresponded with, and what priority level did the activity take.

Session Two: Shoot for the STARS - Exploring Potential Careers and Academic Major

For the second week of treatment, Rose was engaged in a session entitled, *Shoot for the STARS: Exploring Potential Careers & Academic Major*. The objective for this session was to explore careers that fit Rose's personality and interests in order to narrow down a potential academic focus in post-secondary education. During the session, I shared and reviewed the College and Career Readiness and Success Organizer (CCRS; Balestreri, Sambolt, Duhon, Smerdon, & Harris, 2014) with Rose so that she better understood the components of career and college readiness success. Rose's current knowledge regarding post-secondary education was then examined using a college knowledge questionnaire. From there, we explored academic majors and careers that aligned with the Rose's personality and interests using Holland's Code (Holland, 1959). Moreover, we explored academic major profiles using Bigfuture.collegeboard.org in order to narrow down Rose's potential academic major(s) of interest. Next, we explored careers and career information using O*Net. To end the session, Rose was given a homework assignment which was to further explore career interest(s) using O*Net and write down three facts she discovered from researching

Table 1. Individual learning plan for Rose

Activity	Purpose/Outcome	Estimated Time Commitment	Goal #	Priority
Engage in academic major exploration using the CFNC website.	Narrow down your college major choice	1-2 hours	1	1
Examine what information goes on a college application	To know what to expect when it is time to apply for college	1 hour	2	2
Explore financial aid, scholarships, and grants	Funding a college education	1-2 hours	2	3
Discuss the high school to college transition/ what life looks like 10 years from now	Develop a plan/ feel confident about the future	2 hours	3	4

Adapted from the CIP Approach (Peterson, Sampson, Lenz, & Reardon, 2002)

the career(s); write down the main things she thought she would need to put on a college application (e.g. SAT/ACT scores, personal information, etc.); and review information on the national college fair list of schools.

Work from the session revealed that Rose had a Holland code of Social, Artistic, and Enterprising (SAE). Individuals with the code for Social are considered helpers who like to work with people. Individuals with the code for Artistic are considered creators who like to work in situations where they can use their creativity and imagination. Furthermore, individuals with the code for Enterprising are considered persuaders who like to influence and lead people in order to achieve organizational goals (Holland, 1959). After exploring majors using the Holland code on O*Net, Rose showed the most career interest in the field of Early Childhood Education. Rose and I explored why this field interested her the most in which Rose replied, "I want to do something to make a difference in someone's life. I've always loved younger children and want them to have everything they need to be successful." Together, we explored how this desire to help children played out in her own life. Rose explained, "I want to make sure children are in a better place than I was growing up. I want them to have a genuine chance at being successful regardless of their life situations, and I want them to get this early in life." In using the MSJCC model, I assessed the degree to which Rose's experiences in foster care and her past barriers contributed both to her career and academic interest and her presenting issues with career and college readiness self-efficacy. Doing this aligned with the MSJCC model in that multicultural and social justice competent counselors must develop a knowledge of historical events and current issues that have shaped the past experiences of marginalized clients (Ratts, et al., 2015). Rose expressed how her marginalized identity as a child in foster care impacted her belief that she could be successful after leaving the foster care system. This information allowed me to become more informed on how to better assist Rose in making informed career decisions that will allow her to feel more supported and valued in her future. We spent time reviewing the perceived barriers that have hindered her educational process and replaced these barriers with resources and tools that allowed her to adequately explore potential academic majors and career options.

Session Three: STAR Struck - Finding the Right Post-Secondary Education Institution and Demystifying the College Application Process

For the third week of treatment, Rose was engaged in a session entitled, *STAR Struck: Finding the Right Post-Secondary Education Institution for Me and Demystifying the College Application Process*. The objective for this session was to explore post-secondary schools that had Rose's academic major of interest and where she would feel most comfortable attending. The session was also focused on examining the items a student needs to gather in order to successfully complete a college application. At the beginning of the session, we reviewed Rose's homework assignment. Next, it was important to examine the items Rose needed to feel the most comfortable in a post-secondary education environment. This list of needs was then used to narrow down Rose's college options using school finder tools.

Rose was then asked about the aspects of her identity she deemed important and how she may want these identities reflected within the college environment. Rose explained:

As an African American, it's very important for me to be around some people who look like me, where I can maybe get in some student groups centered around Black students. I also want to be in a place where I can get some support as a first-time college student, since I've never done this before. I also want to be in a smaller environment so it will be a little easier to navigate, where I can maybe make friends and get resources a little easier.

Rose and I dialogued about what aspects of her identity and characteristics of the college environment were important to her to gain a clearer picture of a college environment. She was asked to describe the ideal college environment where she would feel the most safe, supported, and valued. We then utilized a school finder tool on the Collegeboard.org website to explore colleges with various characteristics that align with Rose's needs, and delved deeper into the selected colleges by reviewing their respective websites. This aligned with the MSJCC model in that counselor and marginalized client explored the extent to which social institutions can be supportive.

Rose was then instructed to review a mock college application to see an example of what a completed college application looked like. Through this exercise, we further demystified the college application process for Rose by going over the various components of a college application. Furthermore, in preparation for a national college fair that we attended together, Rose was asked to complete a college exploration day worksheet where she researched at least three colleges/universities she was interested in learning more about. Rose was also asked to come up with three to five questions she wanted to ask an admission counselor based on the colleges she was most interested in. Through this process, Rose challenged some of her previous assumptions regarding the type of student she felt gets admitted in to college. She instead explored how various college campuses provide opportunities for students from various backgrounds to thrive both academically and socially.

Session Four: Wish Upon a STAR - Paying for College and Life in the Future

For the fourth week of treatment, Rose was engaged in a session entitled, *Wish Upon a STAR: Paying for College and Life in the Future*. The objective for this session was to explore ways to pay for post-secondary education and to examine Rose's expectations and long-term goals in adult life. The goals of the session were to increase Rose's understanding of the ways she can pay for college, particularly learning about grants and scholarships that were designed specifically for adolescents aging out of the foster care system, and components of the free application for federal student aid (FAFSA). The goal was also for Rose to examine and set realistic expectations for her future based on what she would like for her life to look like ten years from now.

Rose was guided through the exercise of examining her goal expectations and future post-secondary aspirations using SCCT (Lent, Brown, & Hackett, 2002). Rose expressed that in ten years she wanted to be fully independent, have a career as a pre-kindergarten teacher, and own a house and a car. They explored how Rose's desired future lifestyle may align with her potential career goal. It became clear that Rose desired to improve her situation by gaining adult self-sufficiency upon aging out of the foster care system. She wanted to achieve this by having the resources she deemed necessary to be independent (e.g. working towards post-secondary education, getting her driver's license, having money for college and living expenses, etc.). This made sense to me given that it is estimated that only one-third of foster care youth who have aged out of the system had basic necessities such as a driver's license or cash upon leaving the system (Pecora, Williams, Kessler, Hiripi, O'Brien, & Emerson, 2006).

I turned to the interpersonal process outlined in the MSJCC model to discuss support networks for Rose. Rose was asked, "What individuals in your life provide support for you in working towards your post-secondary education and career goals?" Here it was important for the counselor to help the client build and maintain a network that would assist the client in achieving her future goals and serve as a source of support. The Ecological Model of Human Development (Bronfenbrenner, 1979) was used to help Rose examine her environments more closely. Rose named her school counselor, social worker and foster parent as potential individuals who can serve in her support network. Rose was then asked to outline what each of these adults' roles would be in her support network and how she would specifically ask them to support her in the ways she deemed necessary to achieve adult self-sufficiency.

Session 5: Super STAR Status - Preparing for High School Graduation and Access to College

For the fifth and final week of treatment, Rose was engaged in a session entitled, *Super STAR Status: Preparing for High School Graduation and Access to College*. The objective for this session was to learn effective ways to prepare for high school graduation and entrance into post-secondary education. The goals for this session were to discuss future planning for successfully graduating from high school and entering the post-secondary education environment. A high school planning timeline was reviewed with Rose for her junior and senior years of high school and together we mapped out a plan for her high school completion. To accomplish this goal, I referred to the website mappingyourfuture.org to go over the guide to life after high school with Rose (mappingyourfuture.org, 2017). Rose asked any lingering questions she had regarding preparing for post-secondary education and her future career goals.

To close the session, we reviewed some steps Rose wanted to work on to successfully plan for high school graduation. She responded,

I would like to establish a savings account. I also want to tell my foster parents that I am really interested in studying Early Childhood Education. I would also like to obtain a summer internship or a job shadowing opportunity at a daycare or elementary school, and I want pass my classes with good grades each year.

CONCLUSION

The post-CCRSI was administered to Rose in order to see if her career and college readiness self-efficacy had improved. Results from the inventory indicated a score of 70, the highest score possible. Rose's pre- and post-CCRSI total scores indicated that there was indeed an overall improvement in her career and college readiness self-efficacy from the beginning of the S.T.A.R.S. program until the end of the program. In looking at the individual scores more closely for each of the CCRSI four factors, the intervention program helped Rose to feel more confident in her beliefs about engaging in the post-secondary education preparation and access process (i.e. college knowledge). Furthermore, as a high school junior, she had minimal exposure to the post-secondary education exploration and preparation processes. By participating in the S.T.A.RS. program, Rose explored different colleges and universities and identified a few small to mid-size institutions she would not mind learning more about. She also learned about the college admissions process (e.g., what is on a college application and what is needed to apply for college) and discovered options for paying for a post-secondary education. She also explored ways she can feel safe and supported in her identity within the college environment as well as explored academic majors and careers in order to select a potential academic major (i.e., Early Childhood Education). Moreover, Rose identified adults who can serve in her support network who can help her to be successful in her future as she ages out of the foster care system. She also agreed to re-prioritize her commitments and put academics in the forefront so that she can remain academically eligible for college.

Through my work with Rose, I was able to further understand the worldview of marginalized clients who are aging out of the foster care system. In particular, I discovered how clients in Rose's situation may come to make decisions based on past experiences and lack of access to resources and support. These insights allowed me provide more culturally responsive counseling, support and advocacy for Rose in to help her enhance her career and college readiness self-efficacy.

Recommendations for Counseling Practice

The results of the S.T.A.R.S. program and the work with Rose can have significant implications for counselors working in school and community setting who support the needs adolescents aging out of foster care. School counselors are encouraged to create educational and support programming for foster care youth in their schools. Because multiple foster care placement changes can create a barrier to high school completion and an overall disruption to the education process, school counselors are challenged to coordinate career and college readiness programming needs that will allow for foster care youth to receive an adequate amount of information regardless of when they enter in to their schools (Gavin Williams, 2016). Given the limited amount of time school counselors may have for individual counseling sessions with students, it is suggested that the S.T.A.R.S. program be adapted in to a group counseling curriculum so that school counselors are able to work with more students during a period of time. Furthermore, the CCRSI can be used as a free assessment tool for measuring career and college readiness self-efficacy and can be requested directly from the authors.

School and community counselors can attend monthly child and family team meetings that are led by the youth's social worker to address school needs, mental health concerns, and request adequate assistance for the foster care youth. Furthermore, as the MSJCC model emphasized, the counselor connecting the client to supportive individuals in social institutions can help to alter the inequities influencing marginalized clients (Ratts et al., 2015). Thus, it is important for counselors in schools and communities to introduce students in foster care to educational support programs that can appropriately and effectively assist them. Counselors must also inform community organizations and college personnel of their needs, which can, in turn, form effective collaborative relationships between the counselor and community supports. School and community counselors can also familiarize themselves with programs aimed at providing postsecondary education services to current and former foster care youth in college, helping them recognize more targeted sources of support they can receive in the post-secondary education environment.

Foster care youth experience many educational disparities, which has become more prevalent both through professional literature and in mainstream society. As such, counselors must become more familiar with their needs, thus apt to help these youth discover ways to reaching their highest potential. Through support from a counselor with enhancing her career and college readiness self-efficacy, what was once Rose's thorn, has become her symbol of overcoming. Rose now feels more empowered to not only work towards her post-secondary educational goals and academic competence, but to take the necessary steps towards achieve adult self-sufficiency with the help of her support network along the way.

REFERENCES

Achieve, Inc. (n.d.). *College and career readiness*. Washington, DC: Author. Retrieved from https://www.achieve. org/college-and-career-readiness

Baker, S. B., & Parikh Foxx, S. (2012). *Career and College Readiness Self-efficacy Inventory*. Raleigh, NC: Authors.

Balestreri, K., Sambolt, M., Duhon, C., Smerdon, B., & Harris, J. (2014). *The college and career readiness and success organizer*. Retrieved from, https://ccrscenter.org/sites/default/files/College%20and%20Career%20Readiness%20and%20Success%20Organizer%20Brief_FINAL.pdf

Blakeslee, J., & Best, J. I. (2018). Understanding support network capacity during the transition from foster care: Youth-identified barriers, facilitators, and enhancement strategies. *Children and Youth Services Review*, *96*, 220–230. doi:10.1016/j.childyouth.2018.11.049 PMID:30765899

Bronfenbrenner, U. (1979). *The ecology of human development: Experiments by nature and design*. Cambridge, MA: Harvard University Press.

Conley, D. T. (2010). *College and career ready: Helping all students succeed beyond high school*. San Francisco, CA: Jossey-Bass. doi:10.1002/9781118269411

Courtney, M., Terao, S., & Bost, N. (2004). *Midwest evaluation of the adult functioning of former foster youth: Conditions of youth preparing to leave state care*. Chicago, IL: Chapin Hall at the University of Chicago.

Day, A., Dworsky, A., & Weng, F. (2013). An analysis of foster care placement history and postsecondary graduation rates. *Research in Higher Education*, *19*, 1–17.

Finkelstein, M., Wamsley, M., & Miranda, D. (2002). *What keeps children in foster care from succeeding in school: Views of early adolescents and the adults in their lives*. New York, NY: Vera Institute of Justice.

Gavin Williams, R. (2016). The role of school counselors in the career and college Readiness of foster care youth: An ecological systems theory approach. *Journal of Counselor Leadership and Advocacy*. doi:10.1080/2326716X.2015.1133335

Holland, J. L. (1959). A theory of vocational choice. *Journal of Counseling Psychology*, *6*(1), 35–45. doi:10.1037/h0040767

Hudson, A. L. (2013). Career mentoring needs of youths in foster care: Voices for change. *Journal of Child and Adolescent Psychiatric Nursing*, *26*(2), 131–137. doi:10.1111/jcap.12032 PMID:23607825

Kirk, C. M., Lewis, R. K., Nilsen, C., & Colvin, D. Q. (2013). Foster care and college: The educational aspirations and expectations of youth in the foster care system. *Youth & Society*, *45*(3), 307–323. doi:10.1177/0044118X11417734

Kirk, R., & Day, A. (2011). Increasing college access for youth aging out of foster care: Evaluation of a summer camp program for foster youth transitioning from high school to college. *Children and Youth Services Review*, *33*(7), 1173–1180. doi:10.1016/j.childyouth.2011.02.018

Krane, N. E. (2000). Four or five sessions and a cloud of dust: Old assumptions and new observations about career counseling. In S. D. Brown & R. W. Lent (Eds.), *Handbook of counseling psychology* (3rd ed.; pp. 740–766). New York, NY: Wiley.

Lent, R. W., Brown, S. D., & Hackett, G. (2002). Social Cognitive Career Theory. In D. Brown (Ed.), *Career choice and development* (pp. 312–369). San Francisco, CA: Jossey-Bass.

Mappingyourfuture.org. (2017). *Guide to life after high School*. Retrieved from https://www.mappingyourfuture.org/guidetolife/

National Foster Youth Institute. (2017). *51 Useful Aging Out of Foster Care Statistics*. Retrieved from, https://www.nfyi.org/51-useful-aging-out-of-foster-care-statistics-social-race-media/

Pecora, P. J., Williams, J., Kessler, R. C., Hiripi, E., O'Brien, K., Emerson, J., & Torres, D. (2006). Assessing the educational achievements of adults who were formerly placed in family foster care. *Child & Family Social Work*, *11*(3), 220–231. doi:10.1111/j.1365-2206.2006.00429.x

Peterson, G. W., Sampson, J. P., Lenz, J. G., & Reardon, R. C. (2002). A cognitive information processing approach to career problem solving and decision making. In D. Brown & ... (Eds.), *Career choice and development* (pp. 312–369). San Francisco, CA: Jossey-Bass.

Piel, M. H. (2018). Challenges in the Transition to Higher Education for Foster Care Youth. *New Directions for Community Colleges*, *2018*(181), 21–28. doi:10.1002/cc.20288

Ratts, M. J., Singh, A. A., Nassar-McMillan, S., Butler, S. K., & McCullough, J. R. (2015). *Multicultural and social justice counseling competencies*. Retrieved from http://www. counseling.org/docs/default-source/competencies/multicultural-and-social-justice-counselingcompetencies. pdf?sfvrsn=20

Unrau, Y. A., Font, S. A., & Rawls, G. (2012). Readiness for college engagement among students who have aged out of foster care. *Children and Youth Services Review*, *34*(1), 76–83. doi:10.1016/j.childyouth.2011.09.002

U.S. Department of Health and Human Services Administration for Children and Families. Children's Bureau. (2016). *The AFCARS report: Preliminary FY Estimates as of October 20, 2017*. US Department of Health and Human Services. Retrieved from https://www.acf.hhs.gov/sites/default/files/cb/afcarsreport24.pdf

Williams, R. G., Baker, S. B., & Williams-DeVane, C. R. (2018). Effects of customized Counseling Interventions on Career and College Readiness Self-Efficacy of Three Female Foster Care Youth. *The Professional Counselor*, *8*(2), 159–174. https://doi-org.ezproxy.nccu.edu/10.15241/rgw.8.2.159

Chapter 6
Lucia's Journey of Bridging Two Worlds:
Counseling Latinx First-Generation College Students

Angelica M. Tello
University of Houston – Clear Lake, USA

EXECUTIVE SUMMARY

Lucia is a Latina first-generation college student (FGCS) attending a predominantly white institution, a state university in her hometown, located in a large metropolitan city in the Southern United States. While in her sophomore year, Lucia accessed counseling services on her campus to discuss having difficultly balancing school, work, and home responsibilities. In this chapter, the author discussed the challenges experienced by Latinx FGCS along with the strengths they bring to college settings. In addition, the author utilized the case study of Lucia to discuss her counseling approach for helping Latinx FGCS navigate the terrains of higher education.

DOI: 10.4018/978-1-7998-0022-4.ch006

INTRODUCTION

Lucia is a Latina first-generation college student (FGCS) attending a predominantly white institution, a state university in her hometown, located in a large metropolitan city in the Southern United States. In higher education settings, FGCS refers to students whose parents did not attend college or any postsecondary institution (Wang & Castañeda-Sound, 2008). When she entered college, Lucia began pursuing a degree in mechanical engineering. However, early on in her transition to college, she began experiencing some struggles. As a result, Lucia accessed counseling services on her campus at the start of her sophomore year. In her intake session, Lucia discussed having a difficult time balancing school, work, and home responsibilities. From an outside perspective, it could appear that Lucia's presenting concern relates to time management issues, a typical struggle college students experience. Often times, college students are viewed as a homogeneous group. However, undergraduate students are quite diverse; they hold an intersection of identities related to race, ethnicity, class, social economic status, gender, sexual orientation, and ability.

Lucia, like many Latinx FGCS, was struggling with navigating the culture of higher education (e.g., understanding degree expectations, connecting with faculty, and locating campus resources). This was coupled with Lucia also navigating issues of marginality on her campus: not seeing Latinx representation, institutional invalidation, and microaggressions. For low-income FGCS, the campus environment can provide validating or invalidating experiences, which in turn can have a positive or negative impact on their college persistence (Rendón, 1994; Rendón Linares & Munoz, 2011). Validation occurs for FGCS when "an enabling, confirming and supportive process [is] initiated by in- and out-of-class agents that fosters [the] academic and interpersonal development" of these students (Rendón, 1994, p. 44). The focused is placed on how faculty, staff, peers on campus are cultivating a welcoming and supportive environment for FGCS. Invalidating actions include "faculty who students believe are unapproachable, inaccessible, and often dehumanizing toward students" (Rendón & Munoz, 2011, p. 20). For Lucia, the invalidating actions she experienced on campus made her question if she was "college material." Lucia also experienced various forms of microaggressions on her campus. Microagressions are:

> *...subtle, innocuous, preconscious, or unconscious degradations, and putdowns, often kinetic but capable of being verbal and/or kinetic. In and of itself a microaggression may seem harmless, but the cumulative burden of a lifetime of microaggressions can theoretically contribute to diminished mortality, augmented morbidity, and flattened confidence. (Yosso, Smith, Ceja, & Solórzano, 2009, p. 281)*

Lucia's Journey of Bridging Two Worlds

In her first semester, Lucia had an engineering faculty member who questioned her openly in class whether her inner-city high school had strong enough classes to prepare her for a career in engineering. Another incident occurred when Lucia visited her academic advisor for support after she fell behind in one of her courses. The academic advisor told Lucia she seemed more suitable for a career in education instead of engineering, because Latinas typically had a difficult time completing their engineering degrees. Lucia did not share her experiences of institutional invalidation and microaggressions with others, especially those in positions of power. She learned in high school that bringing up concerns about institutional invalidation and microaggressions could cause more unwanted negative attention. For instance, school officials not believing her and the staff members retaliating with more microaggressions.

In addition, Lucia felt she was living between two worlds: her college world and the world of her upbringing. Due to the struggles she faced on campus, Lucia did not feel she belonged there. The majority of the students attending her university were white and from upper-middle class families. It was clear in class discussions that most of her peers held different life experiences. Furthermore, Lucia felt an academic pressure to separate from family which led to an internal cultural struggle. Universities tend to foster a culture of independence that is often rooted in a white, middle-class cultural expression of this value (Stephens, Fryberg, Markus, Johnson, & Covarrubias, 2012). Even though Lucia lived at home, she felt a level of disconnection from her family, because they could not relate to her college experiences. This in-between feeling Lucia experienced fed into her narrative that she was not meant to be in college, even though she was doing well in her courses and was passionate about a career in engineering.

Although the stressors experienced by Lucia and other Latinx FGCS have been well documented, most college support programs tend to only focus on helping FGCS navigate the culture of college (Tello, 2015). College counselors are often an underutilized campus resource that can help address this need (Tello, 2015; Tello & Lonn, 2017). College counselors have the skills to assist Latinx FGCS in developing coping strategies to navigate the culture of higher education and address issues of marginality (Tello & Lonn, 2017). As a counselor, I have used Narrative Therapy and the Multicultural and Social Justice Counseling Competencies (MSJCC) (Ratts, Singh, Nassar-McMillan, & McCullough, 2015) in supporting the needs of Latinx FGCS: bridging the in-between place they often experience. Latina FGCS have described living between two cultures: the culture of their upbringing and the culture of academia (Tello, 2015). In this chapter, I will discuss the challenges experienced by Latinx FGCS along with the strengths they bring to college settings. In addition,

I will utilize the case study of Lucia to discuss my counseling approach for helping Latinx FGCS navigate the terrains of higher education. Throughout this chapter, the term Latinx, a gender-neutral term for Latina/o (Castro & Cortez, 2017; Vélez, 2016) is used.

THE EXPERIENCES OF LATINX FGCS

In order to meet the needs of Latinx FGCS, it is important for counselors to understand various aspects of their experiences in college. Latinx FGCS are a growing population on college campuses (Santiago, Calderón Galdeano, & Taylor, 2015). According to the U.S. Department of Education (2017), between the years of 2000 and 2015, Latinx college student enrollment has more than doubled, a 126 percent increase from 1.4 million to 3 million students. Moreover, Latinx students represent 27 percent of FGCS enrollment (Redford & Mulvaney Hoyer, 2017). Although there is an increase in Latinx FGCS enrollment, they continue to lag behind in retention and graduation rates (Snyder, de Brev, & Dillow, 2016). Only 11 percent of the overall FGCS population earn a bachelor's degree in six years compared to 55 percent of non-FGCS (The Pell Institute, 2008), and FGCS are 71 percent more likely to leave college in their first year than non-FGCS (Pratt, Harwood, Cavazos, & Ditzfeld, 2017). These numbers are similar to the degree completion rates of Latinx college students. Only 13 percent of Latinx students completed a bachelor's degree (Fry, 2011). In order to help Latinx FGCS attain their bachelor's degree, it is important for college support professionals to understand their needs. More importantly, college counselors can play important roles in the college transition and persistence of Latinx FGCS (Tello, 2015; Tello & Lonn, 2017).

Since many FGCS come from low-income backgrounds, they often attended public schools that were underfunded. Consequently, these schools are less likely to academically prepare college-bound FGCS for post-secondary education (Lundberg et al., 2007; Prospero & Vohra-Gupta, 2007). In addition, FGCS are more likely to work more than part-time which leads these students to be less likely to participate in campus extracurricular activities (Bergerson, 2007). As a result, FGCS can struggle with balancing school, work, and home responsibilities (Tym, McMillion, Barone, & Webster, 2004). The FGCS literature often discusses how FGCS lack the cultural capital that non-FGCS receive from their parents (Lundberg et al., 2007; Sanez, Hurtado, Barrera, Wolf, & Yeung, 2007). In higher education settings, cultural capital relates to knowledge and understanding of what it means to be in college (e.g., the steps of navigating higher education, knowledge about degrees, and how to access retention resources). Furthermore, the FGCS literature often discusses FGCS' experiences as a homogenous group. However, being a FGCS is not the only identity these students hold while navigating higher education. Recent studies have highlighted that FGCS struggle with negotiating multiple identities (i.e., race, ethnicity, and class) and issues of marginality become more salient in college (Orbe, 2004, 2008; Tello, 2015). For instance, some Latina FGCS become aware of their socioeconomic status and the financial privilege of their peers (Tello, 2015). Moreover, FGCS struggle with negotiating issues of marginality in both their school and home environments (Orbe, 2004). FGCS are "disproportionately overrepresented in the most disadvantaged racial, income, and gender groups" (Lohfink & Paulsen, 2005, p. 409). For ethnic minority FGCS, their college experience may be different than non-minority FGCS. These experiences can impact the academic and social integration of ethnic minority FGCS (Lohfink & Paulsen, 2005).

Many FGCS are left to navigate these multiple identities along with participating in college (Orbe, 2004, 2008; Tello, 2015). Beyond the general challenges faced by many FGCS, Latinx FGCS experience additional barriers to college completion, such as cultural incongruence, institutional invalidation, and microaggressions (Tello, 2015; Yosso et al., 2009).

THE CHALLENGES EXPERIENCED BY LATINX FGCS

Latinx FGCS report struggling with their sense of belonging on their university campuses (Tello, 2015). Latinx FGCS report feeling in between two worlds; the world of their upbringing and the world of higher education (Tello, 2015). For Latinx FGCS, attending college can mean moving away physically and emotionally from their family and community (i.e., their cultural upbringing). Even when FGCS are traditional-age college students and live at home with their family, this internal conflict is present (Ward et al., 2012). Latinx FGCS may also feel a level of disconnection with their family. Many Latinx FGCS feel they are unable to share their college experiences with members of their family. In order to feel connected with their family members, some FGCS downplayed their college identity (Orbe, 2004). Consequently, some FGCS avoid behaviors that showcased their college studies, such as completing homework and reading their college textbooks in front of family members. These family tensions and struggles mean many FGCS renegotiate relationships with family members (Ward et al., 2012). Not only is this challenging, but Latinx FGCS are also left to navigate these experiences on their own. For FGCS, continuing their education into college creates a new aspect to their identity and some family members cannot relate to their experiences. Orbe (2004) identified this struggle as the "old" and "new" selves. If Latinx FGCS do not receive support in negotiating these old and new identities, they can feel isolated from family members, their community, and even themselves.

In addition, many Latinx students experience cultural incongruence on college campuses (i.e., a lack of cultural fit between students and their university), and the difficulties that arise can lead to issues in college persistence (Gloria & Rodriguez, 2000). This in between place and cultural incongruence is often exacerbated by experiences on their campuses of institutional invalidation, negative stereotypes, prejudices, marginalization, and microaggressions (Gonzales, Blanton, & Williams, 2002; Rodriguez, Guido-DiBrito, Torres, & Talbot, 2000; Tello, 2015; Yosso et al., 2009). These are direct and indirect messages that tell Latinx FGCS they do not belong on their college campuses. Latinx college students have reported experiencing microaggressions that could fall into three categories: (a) interpersonal microaggressions (i.e., verbal and nonverbal racial insults or slights that were directed to the students by faculty, staff, and other students), (b) racial jokes, and (c) institutional microaggressions (i.e., a hostile campus climate created by racially marginalized actions through a university's structure and practices towards students of color) (Yosso et al., 2009). Students who are able to navigate through these challenges and find support on their campuses are able to persist in college (Tello, 2015). In addition, Latinx college students who experience a cultural fit with their postsecondary institution perceive fewer barriers to their education (Gloria, Castellanos, Scull, & Villegas, 2009). In the literature on Latinx FGCS, the support college counselors can provide are often not discussed. However, college counselors have the skills to support Latinx FGCS in developing positive coping skills to navigate this in between place. College colleges can also lean on the strengths of Latinx FGCS when developing and fostering positive coping skills.

The Strengths of Latinx FGCS

Although the FGCS literature tends to focus on the challenges Latinx FGCS face, recent studies (Cavazos et al., 2010a, 2010b; Tello, 2015) have highlighted their strengths. Additionally, Latinx FGCS enrolled in higher educational settings have experienced success; they are the first in their families to attend college. Latinx college students have also reported the following coping strategies: positive reframing, positive self-talk, long-term goal setting, gaining motivation from low expectations, self-reflection, taking action, and seeking support (Cavazos et al., 2010b). Moreover, Latinx FGCS exhibit resiliency factors, such as intrinsic motivation, internal focus of control, fostering interpersonal relationships, and self-efficacy (Cavazos et al., 2010a). In order to provide culturally competent support to Latinx FGCS, it is important that college counselors ground their work in the strengths and resiliencies these students exhibit. In addition, college counselors can use the Multicultural and Social Justice Counseling Competences (MSJCC) to help.

My Experiences as a Latina FGCS

In order for college counselors to effectively support Latinx FGCS, they must reflect on their cultural identities. The Multicultural and Social Justice Counseling Competencies (MSJCC) is an important tool in helping counselors to understand the needs of their clients. The MSJCC also calls for counselors to be aware of how their cultural identities and the impact they have on the therapeutic relationship (Ratts et al., 2015).

My interest in supporting Latinx FGCS stems from my personal experiences. I am a Latina FGCS, specifically I identify my ethnicity as Mexican American. My father immigrated to the United States from Mexico as a young adult. My mother is a 4th generation Mexican American, both her parents were born in the United States but her grandparents were born in Mexico. I also come from a low-income background and was the oldest of four siblings. Additionally, I was the first person in my family to graduate from high school, college, and graduate school. I faced many of the challenges noted by researchers when I transitioned from high school to college. I was navigating college on my own, without the cultural capital my peers received from their parents or guardians. My first semester was an especially difficult time in my transition from high school to college, even though I was a commuter student completing my studies at a postsecondary institution located in my hometown.

Mid-way through my first semester in college, I contemplated dropping out. To outside observers, it might have looked like I was struggling academically, but this was not the case. I struggled with my sense of belonging on campus. I attended a predominately white research institution, and I did not see many students from my ethnic and socio-economic background on campus. As a result, feelings of marginalization were constantly on my mind. The stress that is naturally experienced in any college freshmen's transition to college was coupled with feelings of marginalization because of the saliency of my ethnic and class identities. My undergraduate university offered various programs to help FGCS transition successfully in college, and I was invited to participate in several of them. Although the programs offered academic and financial assistance, which are well documented needs of FGCS, they failed to address the socio-emotional aspects I experienced related to being the first in my family to attend college.

Early in my undergraduate experience, I began to feel that I was living in between two cultures: the culture of academia and the culture of my upbringing. I experienced a pressure of having to leave my upbringing behind. I did not feel there was a place on my university campus where I could share my experiences of being a Latina who grew up in low socio-economic background. After leaving campus every evening, I went back to a community that felt very different from the world created in college.

In order to help me process my experiences, I searched for my voice on campus, and I found it through my Latina studies courses. In these courses, I began to recognize and value my voice. Even though I came from a different background than most of my peers and faculty members on my campus, I could relate to the voices in my Latina studies courses. These were voices from the Latina scholars we read, the faculty members teaching the courses, and my peers in the classroom. I left those courses feeling empowered, and I was able to create a space that embraced me living in both cultures.

Through the support I received by faculty members who became mentors, I was able to successfully complete my first semester in college. During my remaining undergraduate years, I began finding my place on the university campus. I completed an interdisciplinary minor and certificate program. In addition, I worked on research teams, completed a research capstone project, presented at a national conference, and studied abroad twice. I ended up graduating from college in four years and immediately entered graduate school.

In graduate school, I began pursuing a career in counseling. I completed a Master's degree in Community Counseling and a doctoral degree in Counselor Education and Supervision. My driving force in graduate student was to help give back to my community, to address the mental health needs of Latinx clients. I am currently an Assistant Professor in a counseling program. My research work has focused on the counseling needs of Latinx FGCS. The counseling profession lacks literature on how high school and college counselors can support these students. Since I have a passion for supporting Latinx FGCS, I decided to begin my clinical work providing counseling services in a postsecondary setting.

My Counseling Approach

Although I shared some of the cultural identities with the clients I served in the university setting (i.e., Latina FCGS from a low-income background), I was focused on creating a therapeutic relationship that fostered a safe space for clients to share their experiences. Through this therapeutic relationship, I was able to help my clients, many who were Latinx FGCS, gain self-awareness and autonomy. This foundation is necessary for helping to foster client empowerment. Reflecting client's strengths can help increase their confidence in navigating higher education; they have the skills to bridge both worlds (i.e., the world of their upbringing and the world of higher education).

As a clinician, I lean on Narrative Therapy to help foster this therapeutic relationship with clients. Narrative Therapy also speaks to many of the cultural values of Latinx clients. In Latinx culture sharing your "testimonio" or testimony is an important component of self-reflection and learning important lessons on navigating life through oppressive systems (Delgado Bernal, Burciaga, & Flores Carmona, 2012). Narrative therapy fosters a therapeutic relationship where telling your story and re-authoring your story that is grounded in your truth are important components. Narrative Therapists believe that clients hold on to stories that can cause distress in their lives. Clients' stories are events that have taken place in their lives (Morgan, 2000). For instance, clients can hold stories about themselves, their abilities, their struggles, their competencies, their actions and achievements, and their failures (Morgan. 2000). Counselors can help clients discover other details or events that are often been overlooked by clients. This process is called re-authoring or re-storying.

Lots of narratives have been imposed on Latinx FGCS that is grounded in negative stereotypes and microaggressions. For example, Latina FGCS have shared being told directly by peers that they are were only admitted to their universities as a "token acceptance," that their admissions were based solely on their ethnicity and not their academic abilities (Tello, 2015). However, these students had strong academic performances that led to their college acceptance (Tello, 2015). Narrative Therapy can help Latinx FGCS explore their personal narrative that is grounded in their strengths (i.e., their truth) and not those that have been imposed on them.

In my clinical work, I also knew it was important to broach topics around diversity to understand the clients' intersections of identities. Since many clients are new the counseling profession, they might defer to the counselor on what is appropriate to discuss in session. Topics around race, ethnicity, class, and sexuality are often viewed in our society as being taboo. In addition, it has been well documented that Latinx college students also encounter institutional invalidation and microaggressions (Tello, 2015; Yosso et al., 2009). Therefore, I found it imperative to incorporate the Multicultural and Social Justice Competencies (MSJCC) (Ratts, Singh, Nassar-McMillan, Butler, & McCullough, 2016) into my work with Latinx college students. Utilizing the MSJCC allowed me to be multiculturally competent in my work with Latinx FGCS. Furthermore, the competencies allow for counselors to infuse multiculturalism and social justice advocacy into their sessions.

LUCIA'S JOURNEY

Through Lucia's case study, I will demonstrate how I have used Narrative Therapy and MSJCC in counseling Latinx FGCS. During the fall semester of her sophomore year, Lucia accessed counseling services on campus. When she scheduled her appointment, she stated that she needed assistance with managing her time. She was having a difficult time focusing on her studies, because she was trying to balance work and home responsibilities.

In my initial session with Lucia, I could sense she was waiting on my lead to direct the session. However, I knew it was critical to build a therapeutic relationship where Lucia felt she had autonomy. This would also help her to open up about the difficulties she was experiencing in college. In the session, Lucia shared that she was the first person in her family to graduate high school and attend college. She also identified as Latina, specifically Mexican American, and was the oldest of three siblings. Even though Lucia lived 50 minutes from the university, it was important for her to live at home to help financially support her family. She grew up in single-parent, low-income household, and she worked part-time at a bakery to help her mother pay utility bills. Lucia also described how she was majoring in mechanical engineering. As a high school student, Lucia had strong math and science grades. She also participated in an engineering group on her high school campus, and it supported her interest in becoming an engineer. Even though Lucia made a 2.9 GPA in her first year in college, Lucia reported that she struggled in her classes. She shared how it was difficult to complete homework and study for exams, because she was working and helping her mom care for her younger siblings.

Utilizing MSJCC and Narrative Therapy

Viewing Lucia's through the lens of a non-FGCS, one could assume Lucia's presenting concern related to time management. It could be easy for a college counselor to provide counseling support and resources around eliminating the work and home stressors, so Lucia could focus her attention to her studies. However, I found it important to understand the intersections of identities Lucia held and how it impacted her journey in college. Not all college students have the same needs. Utilizing the MSJCC, I created space to understand the complexities of my client's experiences. MSJCC calls for the examination of the following:

(a) understanding the complexities of diversity and multiculturalism on the counseling relationship, (b) recognizing the negative influence of oppression on mental health and well-being, (c) understanding the individuals in the context of social environment, and (d) integrating social justice advocacy into various modalities of counseling. (Ratts et al., 2016, p. 30)

Therefore, I began my therapeutic relationship with Lucia by understating our intersection of identities and their interactions with power, privilege, and oppression. The MSJCC has a four quadrant model to help clinicians understand the interactions of privilege and marginalized identities in in the therapeutic relationship (e.g., privilege counselor-marginalized client, marginalized-counselor-marginalized client, marginalized counselor-privilege client, and privilege counselor-privilege-client). Based on the MSJCC model, it appeared that my relationship with Lucia was of a *marginalized counselor-marginalized client*. Lucia and I held similar cultural identities. We are both Latinas who were FGCS and grew up in low-income households. However, it was important to note that through my educational status I have gained positional power. My graduate degrees and change is socio-economic status allowed me to hold certain privileges. Through my own self-reflection and awareness, I was conscious of not imposing my view and experiences on Lucia, especially since we held similar identities.

I then created space to understand my client's worldview. Since I know college students from marginalized backgrounds can experience institutional invalidation and microaggressions, I broached these topics in our counseling sessions. When I asked Lucia if she had experienced any hostile experiences or microaggressions on campus, Lucia shared how she felt out of place on campus and she did not belong. She questioned if getting a college degree and becoming a mechanical engineer was something she could accomplish. She did not see other students like her in the courses she was taking or represented in the faculty at the university. She described how the students in her class were from affluent backgrounds and did not have the same stressors she held regarding supporting her family and working. Her engineering classes also had only a handful of women. In passing, she heard classmates saying they cannot believe a Latina like Lucia could be successful in the class, and they did not invite her to work on group projects.

During these sessions with Lucia, I began to understand that the university environment was playing a role in her inability to focus on her academic studies. Lucia held a strong narrative that being in college was not a place for her due to the invalidating experiences she has had on campus. Based on Lucia's grades, she was doing well in her courses and still had a passion about pursuing a degree in mechanical engineering. Moreover, being an active member in her family and helping her mother pay bills was an important cultural value she held. Directing Lucia to quit her job could cause additional stressors. In addition, I knew as a counselor I could help Lucia develop coping skills with navigating the in between place that many Latinx FGCS experience.

I utilized Narrative Therapy because it allows for "opening space for the authoring of alternative stories, the possibility of which have previously been marginalized by the dominate oppressive narrative which maintains the problem" (Carr, 1998, p.486). For Lucia, the oppressive narrative was being foster by the university environment. Through the cultural invalidation she experienced, Lucia felt college was not a place for Latina FGCS. At the foundation of Narrative Therapy is the collaborative co-authoring approach of the therapeutic relationship. As a counselor, I was focused on creating a safe environment for Lucia to share her narrative. This approach of telling your story also aligns to the Latinx cultural value of *testimonios*. Delgado Bernal et al. (2012) described *testimonios* as "a process, *testimoniar* (to give testimony) is the act of recovering *papelitos guardados* – previous experiences otherwise silenced or untold – and unfolding them into a narrative that conveys personal, political, and social realties" (p. 364). Through discussing one's narrative and *testimonio*, a client can begin to understand their strengths and truth. Moreover, as a counselor using Narrative Therapy, I was able to reflect and bring to surface "new liberating stories" that were grounded in Lucia's strength.

Treatment and Progress

For Lucia, her *testimonio* and re-authored story held themes of resiliency. Even though Lucia did not have the cultural capital from her mother regarding how to navigate higher education, she was resilient. In facing the unknown of accessing higher education, Lucia had the coping skill of reaching out for support. I worked with Lucia in strengthen this re-authored narrative. For instance, I reflected how Lucia came to counseling to figure how to address the stressors in her life. Lucia also recognized she brought diverse perspectives into the classroom and it was important to share her experiences as a Latinx FGCS. Lucia felt she could help advocate for the needs of college students who belong to marginalized identities. In re-authoring her narrative, Lucia wanted to feel she belonged on campus. In order to help Lucia bridge her two worlds (i.e., the world of her upbringing and the world of higher education), she explored in counseling how that could take place. Lucia's narrative began to change from "I am not worthy of being on campus" to "I am a strong student who can bring change to my campus."

This sense of empowerment led Lucia to look for places on campus where Latinx students shared their experience and gave back to their communities. I shared with Lucia information about the university's multicultural center and her homework was to connect with the center. Through her discussions with the center on campus, Lucia was able to join a Latina Greek organization. This organization allowed Lucia to connect with peers from similar backgrounds, and she was involved in community service activities that helped her give back to her community. Being involved in Greek life provided witnesses to her new self-narrative, which is an important component of Narrative Therapy. This helped to solidify Lucia's new narrative that was grounded in her truth; Lucia has the skills and abilities to be in college. Through her work in college, she could still feel culturally connected to her community while navigating the unknown terrains of higher education.

For college counselors supporting Latinx FGCS, broaching topics around cultural identities is crucial. Due to past experiences of cultural invalidation and mircoaggressions, Latinx FGCS might not feel comfortable bringing up these discussions, especially for counselors who hold privilege identities. Even for me, as a counselor who holds multiple marginalized identities (e.g., being Mexican American woman from a low-income background), holding advanced degrees and working within a university affords me privileges. Clients who hold marginalized identities, such as Latinx FGCS, will be aware of these privileges and can feel disconnected from the therapeutic relationship from the start. As a result, counselors must work diligently to build a therapeutic relationship that is safe for Latinx FGCS clients to share various aspects of their identities and experiences. Especially since discussing microaggressions can be painful for some clients and can place them in vulnerable positions.

In helping Latinx FGCS re-author their story, finding supportive places on campuses can aid in this process. For example, Lucia was able to counter the oppressive, microagressions she received on campus with the supportive messages from the students in the Latinx Greek organization. To be involved in campus Greek Life, students must have strong academic performance and demonstrate strong leadership skills. For Lucia, this was evidence that her re-authored story was her truth. She was an academically strong student who was bringing change to her campus.

College counselors can also hold group counseling sessions, so Latinx FGCS can connect with each other and support the re-authoring of their stories. Capello (1994) conducted a study examining a specific group counseling intervention with Latina college students. The researcher created a Latina support group after hearing concerns from Latinas attending a predominantly white institution. The Latina students expressed an absence in their courses on content related to the experiences of Latinas and not having access to Latina role models (Capello, 1994).

The Latina students discussed issues around: (a) feelings of marginality (e.g., being the only students of color in their courses), (b) cultural issues on their campus (e.g., racial oppression from instructors and students), and (c) responsibilities related to carrying for siblings or children (e.g., family and cultural expectations to provide childcare) (Capello, 1994). Another reoccurring theme was that the group participants were searching for Latina role models. As a result, the researcher incorporated reading assignments from Latina writers. Capello (1994) reported that the support group helped the Latina participants strengthen their self-worth, receive cultural validation of their experiences, and make connections with other Latina college students on their campus.

CONCLUSION

College counselors have the skills to help Latinx FGCS navigate higher education. Most Latinx FGCS struggle with the institutional invalidation and microaggressions that are present on their campuses. It is crucial that counselors' practice MSJCC in their work with clients in order to be multiculturally competent. Moreover, it is important for counselors to understand the socio-political context of our client's lives. Taking only a surface impression could lead to counselors imposing what they believe the client should work on in the therapeutic relationship. Lucia's journey also illustrated the complexities of our client's identities. In order for counselors to move beyond the surface, they must understand their client's worldview and create a safe, nonjudgmental space for broaching topics regarding their cultural identities.

REFERENCES

Bergerson, A. A. (2007). Exploring the impact of social class on adjustment to college: Anna's story. *International Journal of Qualitative Studies in Education: QSE*, *20*(1), 99–119. doi:10.1080/09518390600923610

Capello, D. C. (1994). Beyond financial aid: Counseling Latina students. *Journal of Multicultural Counseling and Development*, *22*(1), 28–36. doi:10.1002/j.2161-1912.1994.tb00240.x

Carr, A. (1998). Michael White's Narrative Therapy. *Contemporary Family Therapy*, *20*(4), 485–503. doi:10.1023/A:1021680116584

Castro, E. L., & Cortez, E. (2017). Exploring the lived experiences and intersectionalities of Mexican community college transfer students: Qualitative insights toward expanding a transfer receptive culture. *Community College Journal of Research and Practice*, *41*(2), 77–92. doi:10.1080/10668926.2016.1158672

Cavazos, J. Jr, Johnson, M. B., Fielding, C., Cavazos, A. G., Castro, V., & Vela, L. (2010a). A qualitative study of resilient Latina/o college students. *Journal of Latinos and Education*, *9*(3), 172–188. doi:10.1080/15348431003761166

Cavazos, J. Jr, Johnson, M. B., & Sparrow, G. S. (2010b). Overcoming personal and academic challenges: Perspectives from Latina/o college students. *Journal of Hispanic Higher Education*, *9*(4), 304–316. doi:10.1177/1538192710380744

Delgado Bernal, D., Burciaga, R., & Flores Carmona, J. (2012). Chicana/Latina testimonios: Mapping the methodological, pedagogical, and political. *Equity & Excellence in Education*, *45*(3), 363–372. doi:10.1080/10665684.2012.698149

Fry, R. (2011). *Hispanic college enrollment spike, narrowing gaps with other groups*. Washington, DC: Pew Hispanic Center.

Gloria, A. M., Castellanos, J., Lopez, A. G., & Rosales, R. (2005). An examination of academic nonpersistence decisions of Latino undergraduates. *Hispanic Journal of Behavioral Sciences*, *27*(2), 202–223. doi:10.1177/0739986305275098

Gloria, A. M., Castellanos, J., Scull, N., & Villegas, F. J. (2009). Psychological coping and well-being of male Latino undergraduates: Sobreviviendo la universidad. *Hispanic Journal of Behavioral Sciences*, *31*(3), 317–339. doi:10.1177/0739986309336845

Gloria, A. M., & Rodriguez, E. R. (2000). Counseling Latino university students: Psychosocial issues for consideration. *Journal of Counseling and Development*, *78*(2), 145–154. doi:10.1002/j.1556-6676.2000.tb02572.x

Gonzales, P. M., Blanton, H., & Williams, K. J. (2002). The effects of stereotype threat and double-minority status on the test performance of Latino women. *Personality and Social Psychology Bulletin*, *28*(5), 659–670. doi:10.1177/0146167202288010

Hurtado, S., & Carter, D. F. (1997). Effects of college transition and perceptions of the campus racial climate on Latino college students' sense of belonging. *Sociology of Education*, *70*(4), 324–345. Retrieved from http://www.jstor.org/stable/2673270. doi:10.2307/2673270

Lundberg, C. A., Schreiner, L. A., Hovaguimian, K., & Miller, S. S. (2007). First generation status and student race/ethnicity as distinct predictors of student involvement and -learning. *NASPA*, *44*(1), 57–83.

Morgan, A. (2000). *What is narrative therapy?: An easy-to-read introduction*. Adelaide, Australia: Dulwich Centre Publications.

Orbe, M. P. (2004). Negotiating multiple identities within multiple frames: Ana analysis of first-generation college students. *Communication Education*, *53*(2), 131–149. doi:10.1080/03634520410001682401

Orbe, M. P. (2008). Theorizing multidimensional identity negotiation: Reflections on the lived experiences of first-generation college students. *New Directions for Child and Adolescent Development*, *120*(120), 81–95. doi:10.1002/cd.217 PMID:18521866

Pratt, I. S., Harwood, H. B., Cavazos, J. T., & Ditzfeld, C. P. (2017). Should I stay or should I go? Retention of first-generation college students. *Journal of College Student Retention*, 1–14. doi:10.1177/1521025117690868

Prospero, M., & Vohra-Gupta, S. (2007). First generation college students: Motivation, integration, and academic achievement. *Community College Journal of Research and Practice*, *31*(12), 963–975. doi:10.1080/10668920600902051

Ratts, M. J., Singh, A. A., Nassar-McMillan, S., & McCullough, J. R. (2015). *Multicultural and Social Justice Counseling Competencies.* Retrieved from http://www.counseling.org/knowledge-center/competencies

Rendón, L. (1994). Validating culturally diverse students: Toward a new model of learning and student development. *Innovative Higher Education, 19*(1), 33–51. doi:10.1007/BF01191156

Rendón Linares, L., & Muñoz, S. (2011). Revisiting validation theory: Theoretical foundations, applications, and extensions. *Enrollment Management Journal: Student Access, Finance, and Success in Higher Education, 5*(2), 12–28.

Rodriguez, A. L., Guido-DiBrito, F., Torres, V., & Talbot, D. (2000). Latina college students: Issues and challenges for the 21st century. *NASPA Journal, 37*(3), 511–227. doi:10.2202/0027-6014.1111

Saenz, V. B., Hurtado, S., Barrera, D., Wolf, D. S., & Yeung, F. P. (2007). *First in the family a profile of first-generation college students at four year institutions since 1971.* The Foundation for Independent Education. Retrieved from http://www.gseis.ucla.edu/heri/ PDFs/resSummary051807-Firstgen.pdf

Santiago, D. A., Calderón Galdeano, E., & Taylor, M. (2015). *Factbook 2015: The condition of Latinos in education.* Retrieved from http://www.nccpsafety.org/assets/files/library/ The_Condition_of_Latinos_in_Education.pdf

Snyder, T. D., de Brey, C., & Dillow, S. A. (2016). *Digest of Education Statistics 2015 (NCES 2016-014).* Washington, DC: National Center for Education Statistics, Institute of Education Sciences, U.S. Department of Education.

Stephens, N. M., Fryberg, S. A., Markus, H. R., Johnson, C. S., & Covarrubias, R. (2012). Unseen disadvantage: How American universities' focus on independence undermines the academic performance of first-generation college students. *Journal of Personality and Social Psychology, 102*(6), 1178–1197. doi:10.1037/a0027143 PMID:22390227

Tello, A. M. (2015). *The psychosocial experiences of Latina first-generation college graduates who received financial and cultural capital support: A constructivist grounded theory* (Doctoral dissertation). Retrieved from ProQuest. (3702397)

Tello, A. M., & Lonn, M. R. (2017). The role of high school and college counselors supporting the psychosocial and emotional needs of Latinx first-generation college students. *The Professional Counselor, 7*(4), 349–359. doi:10.15241/amt.7.4.349

The Pell Institute. (2008). *Moving beyond access: College success for low-income first-generation students.* Retrieved from http://www.pellinstitute.org/downloads/publications-Moving_Beyond_Access_2008.pdf

Tym, C., McMillion, R., Barone, S., & Webster, J. (2004). *First generation college students: A literature review.* Austin, TX: Research and Analytical Services.

U.S. Department of Education. (2018). *The Condition of Education.* Retrieved from https://nces.ed.gov/pubs2017/2017144.pdf

Vélez, V. N. (2016). Organizing for change: Latinx im/migrant parents, school decision-making, and the racial politics of parent leadership in social reform. *Association of Mexican American Educators Journal, 10*(3), 108–125.

Wang, C. D., & Castañeda-Sound, C. (2008). The role of generational status, self-esteem, academic self-efficacy, and perceived social support in college students' psychological well-being. *Journal of College Counseling, 11*(2), 101–118. doi:10.1002/j.2161-1882.2008.tb00028.x

Ward, L., Siegel, M. J., & Davenport, Z. (2012). *First-generation college students: Understanding the experience from recruitment to commencement.* San Francisco, CA: Jossey-Bass.

Yosso, T. J., Smith, W. A., Ceja, M., & Solórzano, D. G. (2009). Critical race theory, racial microaggressions, and campus racial climate for Latina/o undergraduates. *Harvard Educational Review, 79*(4), 659–690. doi:10.17763/haer.79.4.m6867014157m707l

Chapter 7
Utilization of Acceptance and Commitment Therapy (ACT) With Charlotte Underrepresented on Campus:
ACT Case Study on Campus

Chantel K. Gant
University of New Orleans, USA

EXECUTIVE SUMMARY

This chapter will focus on an underrepresented student in STEM Charlotte and the utility of Acceptance and Commitment Therapy (ACT) and how African-American college students' access to STEM careers remains low with representation of eight percent in varied STEM fields by Georgetown University Center on Education and Workforce Analysis. This chapter highlights psychological flexibility in ACT in connection with counseling an African-American female, and first-generation college student in STEM who has academic, financial, emotional, and familial stressors. A multicultural and social justice perspective (MSJCC) addresses some of the unique challenges this student faces while focusing on her holistic growth in the counseling process. Recommendations for higher education, counseling, and STEM are discussed.

DOI: 10.4018/978-1-7998-0022-4.ch007

INTRODUCTION TO THE CASE

The case study focuses on an African American, female, nineteen-year-old undergraduate premedical student majoring in chemistry. The goal is to share the counseling journey of an underrepresented student in science, engineering, and mathematics (STEM) (McGee, 2017; Palmer, Arroyo & Flowers, 2017). This case study will explore the counselor's multicultural lens to address some of the systemic factors that impact underrepresented African American college students including economic challenges, stigma, and access to resources (Palmer et al., 2017). This case will serve as a template for master's counseling graduate students in school counseling and clinical mental health counseling for working with diverse college students, to provide therapeutically sound cross-cultural counseling interventions.

OVERVIEW

Charlotte is a 19-year old sophomore African American premedical chemistry major who is on academic probation after failing her organic chemistry and physics courses. Charlotte reports studying for her courses but presents with test anxiety. Charlotte is very concerned about losing her academic scholarship as her grade point average is below the requirements. She is not sure if she can return the following semester to her university due to her financial situation and grades. Charlotte is concerned about disappointing her family due to being a first-generation college student. She has three younger sisters and wants to serve as a role model for her sisters, as her mom is a single parent, and continuously brings up financial issues in the family. Charlotte increased her work schedule to 30 hours a week at a local retail store because of her strong desire to provide financial support for her family. She does not want to burden her mom with her struggle of deciding whether or not to maintain her job while attending school. Charlotte also has hopes of breaking the family cycle of financial instability.

CASE DESCRIPTION

Charlotte is brought to the university counseling center (UCC) by a peer who saw her crying on campus. She meets with the counselor and is hesitant to talk at first as this is her first counseling session. Charlotte opens up to the counselor about growing up with both her parents in a financially stable home until age 13 when her father passed away from heart problems. She details that her family downsized to an apartment when her dad passed away. Charlotte reports coping with her father's passing. She discussed her mom becoming the sole financial provider working two jobs to support Charlotte and her three younger sisters financially.

Charlotte discusses the stress of being a premedical student in college. She tells the counselor that she wants to become a physician while struggling with her capability of succeeding in premedical studies. Charlotte expresses interest in becoming a physician to support her family financially. She continually compares herself to her roommate, who excels in premed classes at her university. Charlotte often states, "I am not good enough," and "I do not want to be a disappointment to my family." She experiences anxiety about visiting the tutoring center on campus, hoping her peers will not find out that she does not understand the course material. She reports having racing thoughts, trouble sleeping nightly for the past month, and stomach aches two to three times per week. She mentions thoughts about not being alive and not caring if she is on earth anymore. I clarified with Charlotte about whether her thoughts are more related to thoughts about death or thoughts about committing suicide. Charlotte discussed with me that she would never kill herself and has no plans to commit suicide, but occasionally thinks about death when she experiences significant academic and financial stress. She expressed that she does not want to commit suicide due to her strong faith and spirituality.

Charlotte is hesitant to attend a follow-up session due to discomfort discussing her concerns and family details with a counselor. She feels a sense of embarrassment that she is attending counseling and fears her family and friends' judgment of her. She believes that attending counseling sessions once-a-week is time-consuming with her busy schedule. Charlotte wonders if the counseling sessions will help her feel better. She decides to attend another counseling session due to experiencing overwhelming feelings of stress daily and her desire to not drain her family or friends with her issues.

LITERATURE REVIEW

Introduction

African American women made gains in college enrollment with sixty-two percent of African American women enrolled in college in 2014; however, their access to science, technology, engineering, and math (STEM) careers remained low and filled with challenges (Carnevale, Fasules, Porter, & Landis-Santos, 2016; Musu-Gillette et al. 2017; Palmer, Arroyo, & Flowers, 2017). African American first-generation college women experienced obstacles with regard to education, economic resources, and support networks (Winkle-Wagner, 2010). Historically, African American women served as pioneers in STEM similar to Katherine Johnson who was a "physicist, space scientist, and mathematician" whose work at the National Aeronautics Space Administration (NASA) was instrumental in space exploration and featured in the film *Hidden Figures* (Gigliotti, Chernin, Topping, Williams, & Melfi, 2016; Palmer, et al., 2017; Shetterly, 2016). Still, the voices of African American women in STEM are missing from prior and current research (Jackson, 2013; Young, Ero-Tolliver, Yong, & Ford, 2017). There was a shortage of African American STEM majors impacting STEM workforce development considering that "African American college students represented 11% to 13% of full-time undergraduates earning 9% of degrees in science and engineering from 2000 to 2013." (National Science Board, 2016, pp. 5 and 39). African American students can excel in STEM to increase the visibility of African Americans in STEM (Palmer et al., 2017). College counselors are instrumental in helping African American college students persist in STEM through counseling focused on their self-confidence, academic abilities, emotions, and adjustment to STEM (Henfield & Byrd, 2014). Furthermore, Fife, Bond, & Byars-Winston (2011) found that African American college students who actively practice their spirituality holistically connect achievements in STEM fields like biology and engineering to increased prestige and inherent worth. African Americans succeeding in STEM can reduce the financial gaps that exist in the African American community (Palmer et al., 2017).

African American Women's Collective Stress Experiences

Collectively, African American women have faced increased oppression across women of other ethnicities and suppression due to their gender and ethnicity (Lockett, Gasman, & Nguyen, 2018; Shahid, Nelson, & Cardemil, 2018). African American college women experienced heightened stress connected to racist experiences at Predominantly White Institutions (PWIs) (Shahid et al., 2018). African American college women who ascribed to the notion of being *The Strong Black Woman* (SBW) identified more situations of racism on campus, increased stress, and depression (Shahid et al., 2018). African American female college students' stress stemmed from multitasking, distance from support systems, financial stressors, and educational choices (Lindsey et al. 2011). Watson-Singleton (2017) found that African American women who strongly ascribed to SBW are not likely to identify the benefits of support systems, recognize or reach out for help. Thus, African American women were likely to have a lack of self-care and wellness that leads to physical health problems and mental health disorders (Chaney, Lawrence, & Skogrand, 2012). African American college women had significant sleep difficulties (Henry, Cormier, Hebert, Naquin, & Wood, 2018). Also, African American women experienced financial difficulties concerning not having financial resources due to assisting the family, shortage of job opportunities or jobs that do not suffice their experience, talents, and background compared to Caucasian peers (Chaney et al., 2012). African American women took on tremendous financial burdens to pursue higher education (Chaney et al., 2012).

AFRICAN AMERICAN COLLEGE STUDENTS' EXPERIENCES IN STEM

African American College Women in STEM

African American women pursued STEM fields at higher numbers than other women all the while not being welcomed in STEM spaces and typically not earning degrees in STEM (Ma & Liu, 2017; Morton & Parsons, 2018). O'Brien, Blodorn, Adams, Garcia & Hammer (2015) attributed lower numbers of African American women earning degrees in STEM due to prevailing notions of race as a limiting factor in them being able to earn a STEM degree. White female students in fourth grade even when not enrolled in gifted classes still have more academic gains in math than African American girls in gifted classes (Young, Young, & Ford, 2017). Warren et al., 2013 found that African American women rated photos of women in STEM careers more favorably than women in non-STEM careers possibly attributed to their limited identification with STEM. In line with self-efficacy concerns, African American women's interests in STEM careers related to how they perceive past communications and connections with educators and male classmates (Pinder & Blackwell, 2014). African American women are interested in pursuing STEM, but there is a lack of help provided to them to pursue such careers (Lockett, Gasman, & Nguyen, 2018). Leath & Chavous (2018) attributed African American women missing from STEM careers due to colleges not focusing on conducive learning spaces to meet the needs of African American women to succeed in STEM. Black women enrolled at Predominantly White Institutions (PWIs) not majoring in STEM had more fulfillment in their major, academic confidence, and belief that they could continue in their academic program (Leath & Chavous, 2018).

African American College Student Visibility in STEM

There is progress with African American college students increasingly majoring in STEM upon the start of college but persistent underrepresentation in the field (McGee, 2017 Moakler & Minsuin-Kim, 2014; Palmer, Arroyo, & Flowers, 2017). The possible explanations for small numbers of African American college students in STEM included more receptivity to pursuing social service professions where the only perceived benefit of pursuing STEM is financial (McGee, 2017). Keshishian,

Brocavich, Boone, & Paul (2010) addressed that African American students do not frequently select pharmacy as a major in comparison to Caucasian peers. White, Decuir-Cunby, & Kim (2019) indicated for African American students there is a relationship between race, belief in their ability to perform in sciences, view of self within the science field, and accomplishments in the sciences. African American college students in STEM experienced economic challenges with increasing tuition, utilizing student loans, delineating increased time to employment over course work, and mulling over grade point averages requirements for academic scholarships (Palmer et al., 2017). Carnevale, Fasules, Porter, & Landis-Santos (2016) emphasized that African American college students have significant gaps in terms of having higher income and economic stability by not pursuing STEM fields impacting their support systems, future offspring, and career development due to lack of visible mentors in STEM.

African American Women STEM Progression

African American women who explored STEM in elementary and middle school through coursework and class visits to STEM sites had a STEM foundation to thrive in college (McPherson, 2014). McPherson (2014) also found that African American women whose family explored STEM through visiting STEM centers, discussions on STEM, and interactive learning provided grounding for these women as college students. Young, Young, & Ford (2017) found that African American female students enrolled in gifted math classes in fourth grade surpassed fellow African American female peers in math not enrolled in gifted classes. O'Brien, Blodorn, Adams, Garcia & Hammer (2015) found that African American women at Historically Black Colleges and Universities (HBCUs) majored in STEM at substantial rates compared to African American women enrolled at other universities. STEM careers can provide African American women with greater access to career opportunities and more financial wellness (Farinde & Lewis, 2012). Morton & Parsons (2018) addressed that there is a strong symbolism of Black women reaching attainments like STEM fields and careers to overcome systemic challenges.

AFRICAN AMERICAN FIRST-GENERATION COLLEGE STUDENTS

A majority of first-generation students were ethnically diverse where their ethnicity and position as first-generation are imperative to explore in their educational pursuits (Ward, Siegel, & Davenport, 2012). Holman's (2014) qualitative study found that most first-generation African American college students did not find their high school counselor resourceful when guiding them in the college process highlighting their counselor's incompetence and prioritizing students who excelled in academics, sports or who were well-known. First-generation African American college students had difficulty adjusting to college with no prior blueprint for successfully matriculating through college and may feel disconnected from family members who have not experienced a similar journey (Evans & Norriega, 2011). Specifically, first-generation African American college students struggled with grades parallel to Latino first-generation college students grades that were lower than White first-generation college students (DeFrietas & Rinn, 2013). African American first-generation college students had less belief in their math abilities compared to fellow Asian and Latino first-generation college students (DeFrietas & Rinn, 2013). African American first-generation college students do not seek the services of their college career center due to their busy work schedules while attending college (Parks-Yancy, 2012). It is imperative that ethnically diverse first-generation college students feel a sense of connection to support systems to succeed in colleges where limited counseling is available (Vega & Moore, 2012). The opportunity for some first-generation African American women to attend college is a protective factor from community violence (Winkle-Wagner, 2010). Blackwell & Pinder (2014) found that African American women college graduates who were first-generation college students identified self-determination to attend college.

AFRICAN AMERICAN COLLEGE STUDENTS UTILIZATION OF COUNSELING

A majority of studies reported that African American college students underutilized counseling center services; however, there was research indicating that African American college students utilized college counseling center services at average rates (Jones, 2014; Cheng, Kwan, & Sevig, 2013; Hayes et al. 2011). Mesidor & Sly (2014) found that African American and international college students' knowledge that mental health services were available for emotional pain was more of a reason for them to utilize services. This interest in seeking counseling services connected to research studies that African American college women had favorable perceptions of counseling (Colvin, Bullock, & George, 2016). African American female college students were more likely to seek mental health resources if they were encouraged by family (Barksdale Molock, 2009; Colvin et al., 2016). African American college students had a propensity to cope by talking with Church support network or family instead of attending counseling (Harris & Wong, 2018). African American college students who assumed peer stigma about receiving mental health services were likely to have unfavorable perceptions about utilizing mental health services (Cheng et al., 2013). Masuda, Anderson, & Edmonds (2012) noted that African American college students had negative perceptions of receiving behavioral health services based on stigma and concerns about addressing personal challenges.

AFRICAN AMERICAN COLLEGE STUDENTS' SPIRITUALITY

African American women's coping mechanisms included prayer, relationship with God, and spiritual connection (Chaney, Lawrence, & Skogrand, 2012). Notably, African American women's involvement with religion helped to decrease their anxiety and depression (Cokley et al., 2013). Johnson & Reynolds (2018) identified that African American female college students who are active in their religion were more likely to apply their study skills which linked to academic achievement. Morrison & Hopkins (2019) found that African American female college students who did not utilize spirituality for a coping mechanism experienced heightened stress, increased suicidal thoughts as well as suicide attempts. Spirituality for a coping mechanism helped these young women cope with life difficulties to understand that their current struggles were only temporary (Morrison & Hopkins, 2019).

African American college students sought the solace of the Black Church due to the sense of hope and optimism before they explored clinical counseling (Harris & Wong, 2018). African American college students utilized spirituality as a resource for life situations through prayer, values, and going to Church (Brooks & Allen, 2016). African American college students who connected to their race and ethnic identity tend to be more engaged with their religion leading to a greater sense of purpose (Ajibade, Hook, Utsey, Davis, & Tongeren, 2016). Donahoo & Caffey (2010) found that African American college students finding support in the Church helps them matriculate in college.

INTRODUCTION TO COUNSELOR

I am an African American woman from New Orleans, Louisiana whose cultural identity is rooted in my family's genealogy. One of my earliest ancestors was a slave born in 1740 who lived in New Orleans. My familial line post-transatlantic slave trade is from Vacherie and Edgard Louisiana. More recently, I have found ancestors born in Virginia in the 1800s. My cultural background is African American due to my pride in my ancestor's West African roots that stem from pre-slavery to the infusion of Louisiana culture. I was taught to love my heritage and given Black history games, books, and fact cards about Black historical figures. I am rooted in my family's genealogy through understanding vastly deeper amounts of information about who they are to give me greater context about who I am. My passion for historical research includes visiting historical sites honoring civil rights leaders and feeling gratitude for their tremendous sacrifice for humanity. Thus, these civil rights leaders worked for the freedom of all. As a counselor, I work with adults of varied backgrounds to gain a sense of freedom and acceptance of self through a multicultural lens.

COUNSELING APPROACH

My counseling approach is acceptance and commitment therapy (ACT) which helps clients acknowledge and normalize difficult thoughts and emotions to gain a more open perspective on self to reach their goals while following their value system (Hayes, Strosahl, & Wilson, 1999). Humans experience pain as an inevitable aspect of life (Hayes et al., 1999). ACT encourages *psychological flexibility*, explores what was not effective in helping clients process problems, and focus on meaning from client use of language (Hayes et al., 1999). I view clients from the perspective of acceptance and focus on areas of strength and growth. I view counseling as a facilitative process in which the client and counselor work together to understand client stressors, focus on strengths, and develop goals for the client to work towards while gaining insight in the process. The counseling process will allow the client to grow and learn more about self and recognize the progress they have made in counseling. Counseling is an approach with *committed action* to help clients accept and process some of the social, economic, cultural, and institutional challenges they face throughout life (Hayes & Lillis, 2012; Pistorello, 2013).

I recognize that I have to remain mindful of my level of influence, background, growth, and evolution within the counseling profession (Ratts, Singh, Nassar-McMillan, Butler, & McCullogh, 2016). I utilize a Multicultural Social Justice Counseling Competencies (MSJCC) perspective to inform clients that we are working together for the client to find and use coping skills that work individually for their counseling needs and concerns (Ratts et al., 2016). I work with clients from the perspective that multicultural factors must be taken into consideration in that no unified coping skill works for every client (Ratts et al., 2016). I approach counseling with the mindset of ongoing learning about counseling and culture through continuing education, online resources, and research literature and textbooks (Ratts et al., 2016). Within the counseling session, I explore the client's background to gain more insight on the client, their perspective, and what works for them in counseling.

CASE CONCEPTUALIZATION

Theory

I will utilize acceptance and commitment therapy (AC) a theory developed by Steven C. C. Hayes, Dr. Kirk D. Strosahl, & Dr. Kelly G. Wilson" (1999). It is imperative that the counselor utilizing ACT and MSJCC focus on all cultural contexts relative to Charlotte from the case study including her ethnicity as African American, identity as a woman, systemic factors including first-generation college student, financial distress, employment status working 30 hours a week, and her underrepresentation in the STEM field (Masuda, 2014; Palmer, Arroyo, & Flowers, 2017). Charlotte is a daughter and sister of a collective of African American women (Masuda, 2014). The counselor utilizing ACT must focus on psychological flexibility with Charlotte to move beyond a fixed perception of herself (Hayes & Lillis, 2012; Hayes et al., 1999; Pistorello, 2013). The goal is for Charlotte to accept painful emotions and thoughts, to express her concerns, and identify her values (Hayes & Lillis, 2012; Hayes et al., 1999; Pistorello, 2013). It is essential for the counselor to evolve in an understanding of their personal identity, emotions, thoughts, strengths, and challenges for therapeutic impacts when counseling Charlotte (Hayes et al., 1999; Ratts, Singh, Nassar-McMillan, Butler, & McCullogh, 2016). The therapeutic process involves the counselor displaying adaptability with counseling interventions in ACT that align with Charlotte's perspective, culture, and background (Hayes & Lillis, 2012; Hayes et al., 1999; Ratts et al., 2016).

The counselor can follow the *ACT Case Conceptualization Form* to explore Charlotte's presenting concerns (Louma, Hayes, & Walser, 2017; Ratts, Singh, Nassar-McMillan, Butler, McCullough, 2016). Charlotte identifies academic concerns including academic probation for failing chemistry and physics, test anxiety, the possibility of losing her academic scholarship due to her grades, stress as a premed student, and worry about visiting the campus tutoring center. She identifies financial concerns as the possibility of her being unable to return to the university due to lack of finances and not wanting to burden her mom with financial stress. Her psychological presenting concerns are racing thoughts, anxiety, sleep issues, and not caring if she is alive. Charlotte's perceptions of her problems are shame and fear regarding how she believes her family and friends will view her. Her initial perspective is questioning the benefits of counseling, and her goal is to work on stress and not placing her issues on her family and friends.

As the ousnelor implementing the ACT framework I will focus on an alternative perspective of Charlotte's identified problems (Louma, Hayes, & Walser, 2017). Together, we will focus on the internal battle she is having with being a premed major and the self-critical tendencies of her intrinsic worth, academic performance, and expectations of her role within her family. I hypothesize that Charlotte does not visit the tutoring center to avoid experiencing discomfort about the difficulty of understanding her course work rather than seeking help. I wonder if Charlotte's thoughts of not being alive are to escape the emotional pain she experiences with racing thoughts, trouble sleeping as well as academic and financial stressors. I also consider that Charlotte's shame and fear about attending counseling is due to her fear of expressing her emotions and thoughts. Charlotte rationalizes not attending counseling by focusing on the time involved in the process. She uses fear, self-doubt, her extended work hours, and stalling to seek help to prevent her from moving forward. Overall, Charlotte is avoiding seeking the help of her family, friends, and counselor by masking her feelings and thoughts to protect herself from embarrassment.

The counselor's conceptualization of Charlotte includes patterns of avoidance, control and psychological inflexibility (Louma, Hayes, & Walser, 2017). There is a perpetual pattern of Charlotte not reaching out to her family, friends, or counseling center for help due to shame and self-perception concerns. There is no mention in the case study of her reaching out to her church community despite her active spirituality. In my role as counselor, I will support Charlotte seeking help as Watson-Singleton (2017) encourages counselors to gage African American women's thoughts on seeking help to promote these women help-seeking, while remaining connected to their inherent worth as African American women. Her negative self-perception defines Charlotte's inflexibility in the case in the constant messages of inadequacy she repeats to herself while describing herself academically incapable due to academic probation. Charlotte creates financial obligations in the present at her current job and her future vision of becoming a physician to provide financially for her family. She tries to match the ideal of *The Strong Black Woman* by being the model daughter and sister, academically high performing student and increasing her work hours (Shahid, Nelson, & Cardemil, 2018).

The counselor's conceptualization of Charlotte' case study is rooted in themes of multiculturalism to aid in her treatment planning (Louma, Hayes, & Walser, 2017; Ratts, Singh, Nassar-McMillan, Butler, & McCullough, 2016). The counselor identifies that Charlotte feels internal pressure to succeed in college as a first-generation college student. She has anxiety about her familial role as the oldest sibling, and intends to positively model matriculation through college in STEM. Brooks' (2015) qualitative study highlighted that African American college students want to be a positive example for their family members and enjoy pursuing their college education. Specifically, African American college students' bonds with family propels them to excel in college (Brooks, 2015). From an MSJCC perspective, Charlotte's desire to support her family connects to her belief system and values (Ratts, Singh, et al., 2016). It is pertinent that the counselor explores additional obstacles first-generation college students experience with regards to financial standing, ethnicity, and familial background (Ward, Siegel, & Davenport, 2012). First-generation college students from a lower socioeconomic background enrolled at selective universities experience internal battles adjusting to peers who have a different socioeconomic status and to family and friends who do not have a similar experiences (Rondini, 2012). Charlotte's ethnicity amid other cultural factors may lead to more difficulties for her advancement in college where ethnically diverse college students who are first-generation, and non-first generation, have similarities trying to progress through college (Davenport, 2012).

Since, the counselor is working with Charlotte, an African American woman in STEM, her connection with STEM professors, classmates, and engagement in learning are part of the case conceptualization (Leath & Chavous, 2018; Pinder & Blackwell, 2014). Charlotte's emotions should be openly addressed utilizing ACT to accept her feelings regarding engagement or disconnection on her campus with STEM faculty and support (Leath & Chavous, 2018; Pinder & Blackwell, 2014; Pistorello, 2013). Furthermore, as the counselor, I can address Charlotte's self-perception connected to her chemistry premed major because for many African American women in STEM they believe beyond their circumstances whether financial, academic, or social that a STEM career that reflects a sense of influence (Parsons, 2018; Pistorello, 2013).

In terms of case conceptualization, Charlotte recognizes that her current coping is not helping where she is overwhelmed with stress and identifies that she needed to attend a follow-up counseling session (Hayes, Strosahl, & Wilson, 1999). She is finally allowing herself to release her emotions when her peer finds her crying. Charlotte wants to succeed in college, not lose her academic scholarship, which are incentives for her to work through her thoughts, emotions, and challenges. Additionally, she is motivated to succeed by being a positive example for her siblings. Charlotte wants to be able to help her family financially, and earning a college degree would lead her closer to that goal. I will remain aware of Charlotte's academic motivation, concern about scholarship maintenance, and finances to understand what succeeding in college means for her. Gilford & Reynolds (2011) qualitative study outlined that African American college women who progress through college while experiencing obstacles went through this process to reach financial opportunities not available before and to persist in their educational aspirations regardless of familial distress.

It is essential for me to explore Charlotte's strengths to implement ACT counseling interventions (Louma, Hayes, & Walser, 2017). Charlotte is entirely driven and motivated to succeed evident being a first-generation college student while overcoming obstacles. She is passionate about earning her college degree. Charlotte loves her family and wants the best for them. She has a strong work ethic working 30 hours and attending college simultaneously. Charlotte copes through her faith and finds some value in her life. She did return for a follow-up session despite initial hesitance. Charlotte has the potential to succeed. There is strength in her culture and background for the client to explore (Sue & Sue, 2008). In line with ACT, she values her education, family, and faith (Hayes, Strosahl, & Wilson, 1999; Ratts, Singh, Nassar-McMillan, Butler, & McCullough, 2016).

MULTICULTURAL COUNSELING SOCIAL JUSTICE COMPETENCIES

The multicultural counseling social justice competencies (MSJCC) are essential to incorporate with ACT (Ratts, Singh, Nassar-McMillan, Butler, & McCullough, 2016; Hayes, Strosahl, & Wilson, 1999) Research is just starting to explore the utility of ACT with diverse populations (Masuda, 2014; Hayes & Lillis, 2012). Research studies with 20% non-Caucasian participants" have shown some efficacy of ACT with different communities; however, the results are not conclusive (Woidneck, Pratt, Gundy, Nelson, & Twohig, 2012). MSJCC includes "counselor self-awareness, client worldview, counseling relationship, counseling, and advocacy interventions" (Ratts et al., 2016, p. 3). It is essential when working with Charlotte to utilize MSJCC to understand how my background in regards to gender, race, socioeconomic status, sexual orientation, education, culture, challenges, opportunities, and influence, mingle with aspects of her background, impact working with her as a client (Ratts et al., 2016).

When utilizing MSJCC, I need to conceptualize the client concerning system factors that led to her current position (Ratts, Singh, Nassar-McMillan, Butler, & McCullough, 2016). Also, there needs to be an understanding if I as a counselor identify very closely with Charlotte that I do not project my beliefs onto Charlotte, as that would be oppressive for the client (Ratts et al., 2016). Also, I need to identify aspects of my background that are different from Charlotte and not make assumptions or generalizations based on African American women (Ratts et al., 2016). As a counselor I need to be mindful if they have a spirituality or faith background or if there is no connection to spirituality or faith of how it presents in the counseling session with Charlotte (Mengesha & Ward, 2012; Ratts et al., 2016). The MSJCC in the application with the case study includes creating a space for Charlotte to tell her story, address her background, and symptoms of racing thoughts and difficulty sleeping where the counselor listens to show that care about what is going on (Ratts et al., 2016).

As a counselor following MSJCC I would not lead Charlotte to a decision about family, as she appears to value her family, and it is not the counselor's role to make decisions for the client (Ratts et al., 2016). Mainly, the family is an essential communal collective for African Americans (Sue & Sue, 2008). Sue and Sue (2008) acknowledge that Charlotte being in a single parent family is an essential resource and beneficial without assuming a model family. Also, financially from the MSJCC perspective, Charlotte has a lack of access to resources and removing herself from her job may create a real financial hardship (Ratts et al., 2016). Even Charlotte's STEM major provides hope for financial access (Ratts et al., 2016). We can explore ways to empower Charlotte (Ratts et al., 2016). (Ratts et al., 2016). Additionally, I must make sure that I am not pressuring Charlotte academically or financially, as to avoid a power dynamic where she assumes that a certain course of action may disappoint the counselor (Ratts et al., 2016).

I can utilize MSJCC guidelines to remain educated and informed on best practices in working with client Charlotte and for my personal counselor development (Ratts, Singh, Nassar-McMillan, Butler, & McCullough, 2016). For instance, I can read empirical research articles and counseling/multicultural texts, and attend continuing education opportunities that focus on African American clients, college students, and multicultural populations (Ratts et al., 2016). Also, when working with Charlotte, I can ask for clarity if there is something that I did not know or need understanding about her perspective on life or background (Ratts et al., 2016). I can also seek community agencies or reach out to multicultural organizations on Charlotte's campus to find additional resources (Ratts et al., 2016). An MSJCC counselor can attend a cultural activities or church services connected to the client's religion to gain more understanding about client culture and beliefs, mainly since church is a significant source of inspiration in the African American community (Ratts et al., 2016; Sue & Sue, 2008).

MULTICULTURAL COUNSELING AND THERAPY

MSJCC ties into Multicultural Counseling and Therapy (MCT) which holds the same tenets of MSJCC in understanding client and my values applicable to Charlotte's case study (Halbur & Halbur, 2019). From the MCT perspective, I can ask Charlotte about experiences with racism on and off campus and the effects on her which prevent some Black women from reaching their pinnacles of achievement (Sue & Sue, 2008; Lockett, Gasman, & Nguyen, 2018). I can process that the client's hesitance to attend counseling may correlate with past experiences with helping professionals (Sue & Sue, 2008). As a counselor, I work early on to foster the counseling relationship (Sue & Sue, 2008). Sue, Ivey, and Pedersen (1996) address MCT as the counselor working beyond their position to help a client in areas where they need support due to social injustice. They also discuss that the counselor must consider multicultural factors when addressing client treatment plan goals (Sue et al., 1996). Sue et al., (1996) encourages counseling interventions that address client way of life and background. Counselors are encouraged to understand the client from multiple aspects including self, connection to culture and community, and from a global perspective (Sue et al., 19996).

TREATMENT

Initial Sessions

I will focus on client consent to receiving treatment, presenting concerns, and creative hopelessness addressing client coping effectiveness before counseling (Hayes, Strosahl, & Wilson, 1999). Then together we would explore Charlotte's statements about not wanting to be alive in the intake session utilizing ACT to express that counseling is a safe place where she can discuss distressing thoughts (Hayes et al., 1999). If Charlotte expressed suicidal thoughts, I would follow the crisis protocol to assess the client for suicide risk, address safety planning and contact a crisis response team for evaluation and hospitalization if the client is at risk for harming oneself or others ACA Code of Ethics (ACA, 2014, Standard B.2.a). Multicultural factors would be explored such as Charlotte's connection to her ethnicity, family, her familial financial situation, spirituality, job, and being a first-generation to focus on what client most needs in counseling (Davenport, 2012; Ratts, Singh, Nassar-McMillan, Butler, & McCullough, 2016;Ward, Siegel, & Davnport, 2012). An MSJCC and MCT counselor would also explore the cultural dynamics between counselor and client (Ratts et al., 2016; Sue & Sue, 2008).

Goals

Charlotte's goals are to earn a 3.0-grade point average for the semester, decrease anxiety, and to increase her self-confidence. As the counselor, my goals will be to integrate ACT with MSJCC and MCT to be multiculturally sensitive (Hayes, Strosahl, & Wilson, 1999; Ratts et al., 2016; Sue & Sue, 2016). The objectives for the 3.0-grade point average will be for Charlotte to meet with her sciences professors once a week, attend tutoring twice a week, and study two hours per night. Together we will explore what earning a certain grade point average means for the client, her family, and her community (Sue & Sue, 2016; Sue, Ivey, & Pedersen, 1996). The objective for decreasing her anxiety is for Charlotte to attend counseling once per week, practice stress relaxation activities at least three times a week, keep a journal of emotions and thoughts daily (Hayes et al., 1999). The objective for the increasing self-confidence is to attend counseling once per week, keep track of thoughts and work on accepting strengths and challenges, and journal about self-growth daily (Hayes et al., 1999).

Interventions

I will implement ACT counseling interventions focused on "psychological flexibility" namely *"acceptance, defusion, self as context, committed action, values,* and *attention to the present moment"* to work on Charlotte's counseling goals (Pistorello, 2013, p. 57). Charlotte will complete a "Values Assessment" to explore her values across academics, job, social life, community engagement, physical wellness, and spiritual life (Hayes, Strosahl, & Wilson, 1999). Thus, she can identify what values are significant to her considering her beliefs, outlook, culture, and background (Ratts, Singh, Nassar-McMillan, Butler, & McCullough, 2016). She can write down her values or use creative mechanisms to display her values while checking on her weekly progress (Pistorello, 2013). In connection to her goal of earning a 3.0-grade point average, decreasing her anxiety, and increasing her self-confidence counselor will utilize the *FEAR* model that focuses on *fusion, evaluation, avoidance*, and reasons (Hayes et al., 1999). We will then explore how her attachment to earning A's or B's, judging academic probation status, and avoiding tutoring due to concerns about peer perception has impacted her self-esteem and led to anxiety. Next, Charlotte's familial expectations about education due to African Americans focusing intensely on academic learning when their child is young will be explored (Sue & Sue, 2008). Charlotte will commit to seek help with her courses from her professor, attend tutoring weekly, and attend weekly counseling sessions until her symptoms improve (Pistorello, 2013)

In regards to Charlotte's goal of working on anxiety, exercises will be used to help her safely experience fears surrounding test anxiety and being a chemistry premed major. Techniques will be employed to help her take in discomforting, comforting, and neutral thoughts and feelings in the present (Ahles & Jenkins, n. d.; Hayes, Strosahl, & Wilson, 1999; Pistorello, 2013). Experiential exercises will also be used with Charlotte throughout treatment to help her confront symptoms of the anxiety with a greater awareness of her emotions, identification of when her thoughts race, and attention to physical symptoms like stomach aches that inform her of impending stress (Eifert & Forsyth, 2013; Sue & Sue, 2016). I will also will encourage stress relaxation activities and suggest Charlotte complete timed practice test in the test room to work on anxiety (Pistorello, 2013). Since, spirituality is a coping mechanism to decrease stress and suicidal thoughts for African American college students who adhere to spiritual practices, an MJSCC counselor can explore more about Charlotte's faith, how she practices her spirituality, and what her spirituality has taught her about acceptance and control (Hayes et al., 1999; Morris & Hopkins, 2019; Ratts, Singh, Nassar-McMillan, Butler, & McCullough, 2016; Hayes et al., 1999). Charlotte will identify actions she will take to achieve her goals, whether devoting more time to self-care through exercising, journaling, praying or meditating (Pistorello, 2013).

As a culturally competent counselor, I will focus on Charlotte's goal of increasing her self-confidence by addressing her use of negative language regarding herself to understand the impact of her self-talk on her academic mindset (Hayes, Strosahl, & Wilson, 1999; Masuda, 2014; Ratts, Singh, Nassar-McMillan, Butler, & McCullough, 2016). I will have client identify her thoughts about self, academics, work, and family to normalize that a variety of cognitions that will change (Hayes et al., 1999; Pistorello, 2013). I will utilize the "Feedback Screech Metaphor," to focus on ways Charlotte places herself in the background in her own life (Hayes et al., 1999). As an MSJCC counselor, I will work with Charlotte to help her assert herself when communicating personal needs in her family (Ratts et al., 2016). I will address Charlotte's sense of control and rules concerning her perspective taking sense of self through the activity of having her list everything she is trying to control with her self-image (Hayes et al., 1999; Hayes, & Lillis, 2012; Pistorello, 2013). Together we will explore Charlotte's self-imposed rules exploring the myth of perfection in her roles of daughter, role model, and student and her self-perception in the African American community (Hayes et al., 1999; Ratts et al., 2016). Specifically, I will focus on the purpose of self-comparison in Charlotte's life (Pistorello, 2013). A MCT theoretical lens will be employed to explore Charlotte's strengths as an African American first-generation female college student in STEM (Parsons, 2018; Sue & Sue, 2008).

From an MSJCC perspective, Charlotte can be connected to campus scholarship coordinator, financial aid counselor, work-study staff, external/internal scholarship resources as well as campus, church, and community resources (Ratts, Singh, Nassar-McMillan, Butler, & McCullough, 2016). We can also work together to explore budgeting and fiscal responsibility programs (Chaney, Lawrence, and Skogrand, 2012). Referrals can be provided to mentoring programs and academic resources on campus that provide support for African American or multicultural populations with STEM or explore national organizations due to lack of assistance given to African American women (Lockett, Gasman, & Nyugen, 2018; Russell & Rusell, 2015). Charlotte can also seek out scholarships, campus organizations, or support groups that focus on wellness, first-generation college students, or groups that align with her values system.

PROGRESS

Charlotte's progress would include her accepting her emotions and thoughts non-judgmentally even when she experiences distressing feelings or thoughts including anxiety when studying for a test or receiving a grade (Eifert & Forsyth, 2012; Hayes, Strosahl, & Wilson, 1999). Charlotte will have various experiential exercises to practice when anxious, to focus on the present and not get caught in her thoughts (Eifert & Forsyth, 2013; Hayes et al., 1999; Pistorello, 2013). Charlotte will recognize that she does not have to cope solely on her own and can seek help from family, friends, and peers (Pistorello, 2013). She will attend counseling, work on self-care to decrease the anxiety, and identify areas of confidence. Charlotte will become more aware of her patterns of behavior when she is hard on herself and the connection to stress that may present in lack of motivation in her classes (Hayes et al., 1999; Pistorello, 2013). Her plan will include attending tutoring, taking practice tests, and working on study skills for test anxiety. Her view of herself will expand with her acknowledging the multiple roles she plays and her willingness to learn more about herself (Hayes et al., 1999). Charlotte's progress will consist of knowing and moving towards the values that matter the most to her including confidence in her academics, showing love and compassion for family, and engaging in self-care (Hayes et al., 1999). Charlotte will notice progress in the reduction of her anxiety, increased self-confidence, and improved academic performance. Charlotte will recognize that she is already a success by taking on the pursuit of STEM as an African American woman and first-generation college student in a field where African American women are not as visible but can excel (Palmer, Arroyo, & Flowers, 2017; Morton & Parsons, 2018).

IMPLICATIONS FOR COLLEGE COUNSELORS

This topic is essential to the field of counseling and higher education to focus on strategies to encourage African American students in STEM to seek counseling. College counselors can provide group therapy for African American female college students who have shared experiences from single-parent families to address their concerns, share resources, and uplift one another (Gilford & Reynolds, 2011). Additional recommendations include focusing on African American college students' need for family psychoeducation on mental health and therapy (Barksdale & Mock, 2009). Specifically, it is essential for counselors to discuss religion and spirituality when counseling African American clients (Cokley et al., 2013). Directors of college counseling centers can outreach to African American college women, encouraging them to meet with a counselor and express their pain in a supportive environment

(Donovan & West, 2015). College counselors should reach out to Black college campus members across academic disciplines, offices, student organization, and individual students to understand the culture of seeking help amongst African American college students (Grier-Reed, 2013).

IMPLICATIONS FOR UNIVERSITY STEM OUTREACH AND FIRST-GENERATION COLLEGE STUDENTS

Teachers and parents need to provide STEM support starting in elementary and secondary levels for African American girls (Young, Ero-Tolliver, Young & Ford, 2017). Specific recommendations include STEM-specific academic support, online tutoring, and mentoring as well as STEM role models (Russell & Russell, 2015). It is integral to link African American women in college to group study and summer research opportunities in STEM, particularly in areas like physics (Rosa & Mensah, 2016). Researchers suggest having more African American and diverse faculty, providing multiculturalism training for faculty, and cross-enrollment for students at (PWIs) to encourage African American students to pursue careers like pharmacy (Keshishian, Brocavich, Boone, & Paal, 2010; Mock, 2009). University leaders can do more to educate African American college women outside of the classroom through science outreach and engagement, campus programming, STEM discussions, and visiting STEM facilities (McPherson, 2014). University student support and academic departments should collaborate on providing support for ethnically diverse first-generation students (Ward, Siegel, & Davenport, 2012). Brown-Nagin (2014) urge colleges with strict admission standards to emphasize the financial and support needs of first-generation college students to optimize their present condition while equalizing educational opportunities for these students.

CONCLUSION

This chapter highlighted an African America first-generation female college student in STEM who can persevere in STEM (Palmer, Arroyo, & Flowers, 2017). There was a further exploration of the financial, academic, and systemic obstacles common for African American college students in STEM (Palmer et al., 2017; Ward, Siegel, & Davenport, 2012). There are advances with more African Americans STEM majors but to retain African American women in STEM essential support needs to be accessible for supportive learning and increased faculty engagement (Leath & Chavous, McGee, 2017 Moalker & Minsuin-Kim, 2014; Palmer et al., 2017). Universities must provide needed counseling services and outreach for African

American college students to seek counseling, starting their first year of college (Palmer et al., 2017). Counselor's utilization of ACT and MSJCC can work for first-generation ethnically diverse college students in STEM to address multicultural factors in a culturally sound holistic manner that considers client culture, values, ethnicity, educational, familial and socio-economic background, emotions (Hayes, Strosahl, & Wilson, 1999; Ratts, Singh, Nassar-McMillan, Butler, & McCullough, 2016).

REFERENCES

Ahles, A., & Jenkins, J. (n. d.). *When the going gets tough the tough gets mindful: A toolkit based on the principle of acceptance and commitment therapy*. Retrieved from https://contextualscience.org/6_session_act_toolkit

Ajibade, A., Hook, J. N., Utsey, S. O., Davis, D. E., & Van Tongeren, D. R. (2016). Racial/ethnic identity, religious commitment, and well-being in African Americans. *The Journal of Black Psychology*, *42*(3), 244–258. doi:10.1177/0095798414568115

American Counseling Association. (2014). *ACA code of ethics*. Alexandria, VA: Author.

Barksdale, C. L., & Molock, S. D. (2009). Perceived norms and mental health help seeking among African American college students. *The Journal of Behavioral Health Services & Research*, *36*(3), 285–299. doi:10.100711414-008-9138-y PMID:18668368

Blackwell, E., & Pinder, P. J. (2014). What are the motivational factors of first-generation minority college students who overcome their family histories to pursue higher education? *College Student Journal*, *48*(1), 45–56.

Brooks, J. E. (2015). The impact of family structure, relationships, and support of African American students' collegiate experience. *Journal of Black Studies*, *46*(8), 817–836. doi:10.1177/0021934715609914

Brooks, J. E., & Allen, K. R. (2016). Academic persistence of African American college students attending an HBCU. *Journal of Family Issues*, *37*(6), 814–832. doi:10.1177/0192513X14540160

Brown-Nagin, T. (2014). Rethinking proxies for disadvantages in higher education: A first generation students' project. *University of Chicago Legal Forum*, (1): 433–500.

Carnevale, A. P., Fasules, M. L., Porter, A., & Landis-Santos, J. (2016). *African Americans college majors and earnings*. Retrieved from Georgetown University, Center on Education and Workforce, McCourt School of Public Policy website: https://cew.georgetown.edu/cew-reports/african-american-majors/

Chaney, C., Lawrence, F. C., & Skogrand, L. (2012). An exploration of financial coping strategies for college-educated African American working women: A research note. *Black Women, Gender, &. Families*, *6*(2), 75–94.

Cheng, H.-L., Kwan, K.-L. K., & Sevig, T. (2013). Racial and ethnic minority college students' stigma associated with seeking psychological help: Examining psychocultural correlates. *Journal of Counseling Psychology*, *60*(1), 98–111. doi:10.1037/a0031169 PMID:23356468

Cokley, K. O., Beasley, S., Holman, A., Chapman-Hilliard, C., Cody, B., Jones, B., ... Taylor, D. (2013). The moderating role of gender in the relationship between religiosity and mental health in a sample of Black American college students. *Mental Health, Religion & Culture*, *16*(5), 445–462. doi:10.1080/13674676.2012.684346

Colvin, A. D., Bullock, A. N., & George, T. (2016). Factors associated with college students' propensity towards mental health services utilization on historically Black colleges and university campuses. *Journal of Sociology and Social Work*, *4*(1), 10–19. doi:10.15640/jssw.v4n1a2

Davenport, M. (2012). Examining involvement as a critical factor: Perceptions from first-generation and non-first-generation students. In T. Hicks & A. Pitre (Eds.), *Research studies in higher education: Educating multicultural college students* (pp. 189–222). Lanham, MD: University Press of America, Inc.

DeFrietas, S. C., & Rinn, A. (2013). Academic achievement in first generation college students: The role of academic self-concept. *The Journal of Scholarship of Teaching and Learning*, *13*(1), 57–67.

Donahoo, S., & Caffe, R. A. (2010). A sense of home. The impact of church participation on African American college students. *Journal of Research on Christian Education*, *19*(1), 79–104. doi:10.1080/10656211003630471

Donovan, R. A., & West, L. M. (2015). Stress and mental health: Moderating role of the strong Black woman stereotype. *The Journal of Black Psychology*, *41*(4), 384–396. doi:10.1177/0095798414543014

Eifert, G. H., & Forsyth, J. P. (2013). *Acceptance & commitment therapy for anxiety disorders: A practitioner's treatment guide to using mindfulness, acceptance, and values-based behavior change strategies*. Oakland, CA: New Harbinger Publications Inc.

Evans, S., & Noriega, P. (2011). Institutions of higher education marketing strategies in recruiting first generation African American students. *The Consortium Journal of Hospitality and Tourism*, *15*(2), 5–24.

Farinde, A. A., & Lewis, C. W. (2012). The underrepresentation of African American female students in STEM fields: Implications for classroom teachers. *US-China Education Review*, *2*(4), 421–430.

Fife, J. E., Bond, S., & Byars-Winston, A. (2011). Correlates and predictors of academic self efficacy among African American students. *Education*, *132*(1), 141–148.

Gigliotti, D. (Producer), Chernin, P. (Producer), Topping, K. (Producer), Williams, P. (Producer), Mefli, T. & Melfi, T. (Director). (2016). *Hidden figures* [Motion Picture]. United States 20th Century Fox

Gilford, T. T., & Reynolds, A. (2011). "My Mother's Keeper." The effects of parentification on Black female college students. *The Journal of Black Psychology*, *37*(1), 55–77. doi:10.1177/0095798410372624

Grier-Reed, T. (2013). The African American student network: Creating sanctuaries and counterspaces for coping with racial microaggressions in higher education settings. *The Journal of Black Psychology*, *39*(2), 169–184. doi:10.1177/0095798413478696

Halbur, D. A., & Halbur, K. V. (2019). *Developing your theoretical orientation in counseling and psychotherapy* (4th ed.). Hoboken, NJ: Pearson Education.

Harris, J. R., & Wong, C. D. (2018). African American college students, the Black church, and counseling. *Journal of College Counseling*, *21*(1), 15–28. doi:10.1002/jocc.12084

Hayes, J. A., Youn, S. J., Castonguay, L. G., Locke, B. D., McAleavey, A. A., & Nordberg, S. (2011). Rates and predictors of counseling center use among college students of color. *Journal of College Counseling*, *14*(2), 105–116. doi:10.1002/j.2161-1882.2011.tb00266.x

Hayes, S. C., & Lillis, J. (2012). *Acceptance and commitment therapy*. Washington, DC: American Psychological Association.

Hayes, S. C., Strosahl, K. D., & Wilson, K. G. (1999). *Acceptance and commitment therapy: An experiential approach to behavior change*. New York, NY: The Guilford Press.

Henfield, M. S., & Byrd, J. A. (2014). Recruiting and retaining gifted Black students in STEM majors: Implications for college counselors. In Gifted education: Current perspectives and issues. Emerald Group Publishing Limited.

Henry, B., Cormier, C., Hebert, E., Naquin, M., & Woods, R. (2018). Health and health care issues among upper-level college students and relationships to age, race, gender, and living arrangements. *College Student Journal*, *52*(1), 7–20.

Holman, Z. A. (2014). *So you call yourself a counselor? School counselor's impact on first-generation African American college students' post-secondary aspirations* (Doctoral dissertation). Retrieved from https://search-proquestcom. ezproxy.xula. edu/docview/ 1728305099/abstract/A3297E78099F41F6PQ/1?accountid=40599

Jackson, D. L. (2013). A balancing act: Impacting and initiating the success of African American female community college transfer students in STEM into the HBCU environment. *The Journal of Negro Education*, *82*(3), 255–271. doi:10.7709/jnegroeducation.82.3.0255

Johnson, M. J., & Reynolds, A. L. (2018). Factors influencing academic success among African American college women: The impact of African American acculturation and religiosity. *The Journal of Black Psychology*, *44*(5), 403–421. doi:10.1177/0095798418777400

Jones, B. J. (2014). *Examining help-seeking attitudes in African American collegians: The role of minority student stress, out-group stress, out-group comfort, cultural congruity, and counselor racial preferences* (Doctoral dissertation). University of Texas-Austin. Retrieved from https://repositories.lib.utexas.edu/bitstream/handle/2152/26139/JONES-DISSERTATION-2014.pdf?sequence=1

Keshishian, F., Brocavich, J. M., Boone, T., & Pal, S. (2010). Motivating factors influencing college students' choice of academic major. *American Journal of Pharmaceutical Education*, *74*(3), 1–7. doi:10.5688/aj740346 PMID:20498739

Leath, S. & Chavous, T. (2018). Black women's experiences of campus racial climate and stigma at predominantly white institutions: Insights from a comparative and within-group approach for STEM and non-STEM majors. *Journal of Negro Education*, *87*(2), 125-139. doi:10. 7709/jnegroeducation.87.2.0125

Lindsey, R., Reed, S., Lyons, R., Hendricks, D., Mead, A., & Butler, K. L. (2011). Sources of stress among gender and classification for African American college students. *College Student Journal*, *45*(4), 749–757.

Lockett, A., W., Gasman, M., & Nguyen, T-H. (2018). Senior level administrators and HBCUs: The role of support for Black women's success in STEM. *Education Sciences, 8*(2), 1-12. doi:103390/edusci8020048

Louma, J., Hayes, S. C., & Walser, R. (2017). *Learning ACT* (2nd ed.). Oakland, CA: New Harbinger Publications, Inc.

Ma, Y., & Liu, Y. (2017). Entry and degree attainment in STEM: The intersection of gender and race/ethnicity. *Social Sciences*, *6*(3), 1–17. doi:10.3390osci6030089

Masuda, A. (2014). *Mindfulness & Acceptance in multicultural competency: A contextual approach to sociocultural diversity in theory & practice*. Oakland, CA: New Harbinger Publications, Inc.

Masuda, A., Anderson, P. L., & Edmonds, J. (2012). Help-seeking attitudes, mental health stigma, and self-concealment among African American college students. *Journal of Black Studies*, *43*(7), 773–786. doi:10.1177/0021934712445806

McGee, E. (2018). Black genius, Asian fail: The detriment of stereotype lift and stereotype threat in high-achieving Asian and Black STEM students. *AERA Open*, *4*(4), 1–16. doi:10.1177/2332858418816658

McGee, E., Bentley, L. (2017). The equity ethic: Black and Latinx college students reengineering their STEM careers towards justice. *American Journal of Education, 124*(1), 1-36. doi:10.1086/693954

McPherson, E. (2014). Informal in science, math, and engineering majors for African American female undergraduates. *Global Education Review*, *1*(4), 96–113.

Mengesha, M., & Ward, E. C. (2012). Psychotherapy with African American women with depression: Is it okay to talk about their religious/spiritual beliefs? *Religions*, *3*(4), 19–26. doi:10.3390/rel3010019

Mesidor, J. K., & Sly, K. F. (2014). Mental help-seeking intentions among international and African American college students: An application of the theory of planner behavior. *Journal of International Students*, *4*(2), 137–149.

Moakler, M. W. Jr, & Kim, M. M. (2014). College major choice in STEM: Revisiting confidence and demographic factors. *The Career Development Quarterly*, *62*(2), 128–142. doi:10.1002/j.2161-0045.2014.00075.x

Morrison, K. S., & Hopkins, R. (2019). Cultural identity, Africultural coping strategies, and depression as predictors of suicidal ideations and attempts amongst African American female college students. *The Journal of Black Psychology*, *45*(1), 3–25. doi:10.1177/0095798418813511

Morton, T., & Parsons, E. D. (2018). #BlackGirlMagic: The identity conceptualization of Black women in undergraduate STEM education. *Science Education*, *102*(16), 1363–1393. doi:10.1002ce.21477

Musu-Gullette, L., de Brey, C., McFarland, J., Hussar, W., Sonneberg, W., & Wilkinson-Flicker, S. (2017). *Status and trends in the education of racial and ethnic groups 2017 (NCES 2017-051)*. Washington, DC: U. S. Department of Education, National Center for Education Statistics. Retrieved from https://nces.ed.gov/pubs2017/2017051.pdf

National Science Board. (2016). *Science and engineering indicators* (NSB-2016-1). Arlington, VA: National Science Foundation. Retrieved from https://ww.nsf.gov/statistics/2016/nsb 20161/uploads/1/nsb20161.pdf

O'Brien, L. T., Blodorn, A., Adams, G., Garcia, D. M., & Hammer, E. (2015). Ethnic variation in gender-STEM stereotypes and STEM participation: An intersectional approach. *Cultural Diversity & Ethnic Minority Psychology*, *21*(2), 169–180. doi:10.1037/a0037944 PMID:25244590

Palmer, R. T., Arroyo, A., & Flowers, A. M. (2017). *The African American students' guide to STEM career*. Westport, CT: Greenwood.

Parks-Yancy, R. (2012). Interaction into opportunities: Career management for low-income, first-generation African American college students. *Journal of College Student Development*, *53*(4), 510–523. doi:10.1353/csd.2012.0052

Pinder, P. J., & Blackwell, E. L. (2014). The "Black Girl Turn" in research on gender, race, and science education: Toward exploring and understanding the early experiences of Black females in science, a literature review. *Journal of African American Studies*, *18*(1), 63–71. doi:10.100712111-013-9255-4

Pistorello, J. (Ed.). (2013). *Mindfulness and acceptance for counseling sollege Students: Theory and practical applications for intervention, prevention, and outreach*. Oakland, CA: Context Press.

Ratts, M. J., Singh, A. A., Nassar-McMillan, S., Butler, S. K., & McCullough, J. R. (2016). Multicultural and Social Justice Counseling Competencies: Guidelines for the counseling profession. *Journal of Multicultural Counseling and Development*, *44*(1), 28–48. doi:10.1002/jmcd.12035

Rondini, A. (2012). "I thought I was so dumb…": Low-income first generation college students, inequities in academic preparation and reference group theory. In T. Hicks & A. Pitre (Eds.), *Research Studies in Higher Education: Educating Multicultural College Students* (pp. 161–187). Lanham, MD: University Press of America, Inc.

Rosa, K., & Mensah, F. M. (2016). Educational pathways of Black women physicists: Stories of experiencing and overcoming obstacles in life. *Physical Review Physics Education Research, 12*(2), 1–15. doi:10.1103/PhysRevPhysEducRes.12.020113

Russell, M. L., & Russell, J. A. (2015). Black American undergraduate women at a PWI: Switching majors in STEM. *Negro Educational Review, 66*(1-4), 101–125.

Shahid, N. N., Nelson, T., & Cardemil, E. V. (2018). Lift every voice: Exploring the stressors and coping mechanisms of Black college women attending predominantly white institutions. *The Journal of Black Psychology, 44*(1), 3–24. doi:10.1177/0095798417732415

Shetterly, M. L. (2016). *Hidden figures: The American dream and the untold story of the Black women mathematicians who helped with the space race* (1st ed.). New York, NY: William Morrow.

Sue, D. W., Ivey, A. E., & Pedersen, P. B. (1996). *A theory of multicultural counseling and therapy*. Pacific Grove, CA: Brooks Cole.

Sue, D. W., & Sue, D. (2008). *Counseling the culturally diverse: Theory and practice* (5th ed.). Hoboken, NJ: John Wiley & Sons, Inc.

Sue, D. W., & Sue, D. (2016). *Counseling the culturally diverse: Theory and practice* (7th ed.). Hoboken, NJ: John Wiley & Sons, Inc.

Vega, D., & Moore, J. L. III. (2012). African American and Latino first-generation students: Implications for teachers, school counselors, university officials, parents, and students. In T. Hicks & A. Pitre (Eds.), *Research studies in higher education: Educating multicultural college students* (pp. 3–25). Lanham, MD: University Press of America, Inc.

Ward, L., Siegel, M. J., & Davenport, Z. (2012). *First-generation college students: Understanding and improving the experience from recruitment to commencement.* San Francisco, CA: Joey-Bass.

Warren, S. T., Lim, S. J., Nicholson, J., Ryalls, E. D., Cooley, S. C., Goodman, M., ... Kyles, L. (2012). The effect of participants' race and gender on perceptions of STEM and non-STEM images of women. *The International Journal of Science in Society, 4*(3), 63–73. doi:10.18848/1836-6236/CGP/v04i03/59284

Watson-Singleton, N. M. (2017). Strong Black woman schema and psychological distress: The mediating role of perceived emotional support. *Journal of Black Psychology, 43*(8), 778-788. doi: 10.11770095798417732414

White, A. M., DeCuir-Guncy, J. T., & Kim, S. (2019). A mixed methods exploration of the relationship between the racial identity, science identity, science self-efficacy, and science achievement of African American students at HBCUs. *Contemporary Educational Psychology*, *57*, 54–71. doi:10.1016/j.cedpsych.2018.11.006

Winkle-Wagner, R. (2010). College as life or death: The college choice and transition process of African American women. In T. L. Strayhorn & M. C. Terrell (Eds.), *The evolving challenges of Black college students: New insights for policy, practice, and research* (pp. 26–48). Sterling, VA: Stylus, Publishing.

Woidneck, M. R., Pratt, K. M., & Gundy, J. M., Nelson, C. R., & Twohig, M. P. (2012). Exploring cultural competence in acceptance and commitment therapy outcomes. *Professional Psychology: Research and Practice, 43*, 227-233. doi:10/1037a0026235

Young, J. L., Ero-Tolliver, I., Young, J. R., & Ford, D. Y. (2017). Maximizing opportunities to enroll in advanced high school science courses: Examining the scientific dispositions of Black girls. *Journal of Urban, Teaching, and Research*, *13*, 174–183.

Young, J. L., Young, J. R., & Ford, D. Y. (2017). Standing in the gaps: Examining the effects of early gifted education on Black girl achievement in STEM. *Journal of Advanced Academics*, *28*(4), 290–312. doi:10.1177/1932202X17730549

Chapter 8
Aaron:
Exploring the Intersection of Religion and Identity With an LDS Client

Brianne E. Scott
Idaho State University, USA

Katie K. Sacco
Idaho State University, USA

EXECUTIVE SUMMARY

The purpose of this chapter is to examine the integration of the existentialist counseling approach and MSJCC as it relates to the case study of Aaron. Authors review the case of Aaron, a college student, who identifies within the LDS faith, struggling with symptoms of depression and anxiety. The authors include a review of the foundation and history of the LDS church, as well as the modern structure and implications for counseling. The authors also describe their own cultural backgrounds and counseling approaches when working with Aaron. Following this review is a case conceptualization through an existential theoretical lens with the inclusion of short-term and long-term goals alongside a treatment plan.

DOI: 10.4018/978-1-7998-0022-4.ch008

AARON: EXPLORING THE INTERSECTION OF RELIGION AND IDENTITY WITH AN LDS CLIENT

The Church of Jesus Christ of Latter-Day Saints (LDS) reports having over 16 million members worldwide with over 6.5 million members in the United States (LDS Church, n.d. -d). Individuals within the LDS faith who identify as either an active, inactive, or an ex-member (no longer affiliated with the LDS church) may benefit from addressing their relationship with religion in counseling. Counselors and counselor educators may be hesitant to address spirituality and religion with clients or counselors-in-training due to personal biases or lack of training.

Counselors and counselor educators have an ethical duty to evaluate potential personal biases when working with a client or counselor-in-training that identifies as LDS. Active/Inactive or ex-members of the LDS faith are an underrepresented and underserved population facing stereotypes and personal biases that may negatively impact the counseling relationship. Culturally sensitive counselors engage in self-reflection on personal biases and explore the application of the Multicultural and Social Justice Counseling Competencies (MSJCC) in their work with clients.

The intent of this chapter is to explore the case of Aaron and the struggles he faces with his developing identity within the Church of Jesus Christ of Latter-Day Saints. The authors provide a brief case study to introduce the reader to Aaron, followed by the history and formation of the LDS church, and the current structure of the LDS church. The authors provide implications for counseling, as well as, an in-depth description of the main author's cultural background as it relates to this case. The authors detail an existential conceptualization and approach used when working with Aaron, including a conceptualization of Aaron and the counseling relationship using the MSJCC. The authors conclude by detailing Aaron's treatment, goals, and his current progress.

Aaron is a fictional client created for the purposes of exploring the use of MSJCC and existentialism within a counseling session. Aaron was created to represent common struggles to some members of the LDS faith, as identified by the research literature. Any similarities to any of the author's current or previous clients are purely coincidental.

CASE DESCRIPTION

Aaron is a 20 year old, heterosexual, Caucasian male enrolled in his second semester of a local college after returning from a mission served for the Church of Jesus Christ of Latter-Day Saints. He sought out individual counseling to address feelings of depression, anxiety, and isolation. He reported struggling to focus in class, feelings of irritability, and inability to fall and stay asleep during the night. Aaron identified a desire to focus on his feelings of loneliness and anxiety, due to the perceived lack of social support at the State University he attends. Aaron reported feeling judged by other students after he discloses his religion and feeling overwhelmed with balancing his schoolwork and his responsibilities in his church community.

Aaron discussed trouble connecting with the peers he interacts with at his newly assigned local ward. Until recently, Aaron played on the church basketball team and was heavily involved in teaching the young men's and mutual group activities. Aaron disclosed that he no longer wishes to be involved with these activities after being confronted by several other members regarding his absence from a few Sunday services since the beginning of the semester.

Aaron disclosed that he initially sought counseling from his bishop. Aaron and his bishop agreed that Aaron would seek guidance from LDS doctrine and meet weekly. Aaron received a priesthood blessing from the bishop during his first visit and reported, "it helped." Aaron discussed his practices of reading scripture and engaging in daily prayer and also regularly visits the local LDS temple to practice his faith. During the first several sessions, Aaron presented as hesitant and defensive when discussing his feelings and thoughts surrounding his religion. Aaron self-identified his strengths to be "being a good son, brother, and friend." From the first session, Aaron was encouraged to share openly and honestly about his experiences.

As sessions progressed, Aaron disclosed that he had not told his family and church community about seeking counseling services outside of the LDS church. Aaron feared the backlash he may receive from family for seeking counseling with a non-LDS counselor. When questioned about his decision to seek out a non-LDS counselor, Aaron stated, "I've tried doing all of the things that my bishop encouraged me to do and it's still not working. I'm still feeling lost and I'm starting to wonder if there's something wrong with me." Throughout the sessions, Aaron presented with polarizing feelings towards his faith and the LDS community. Aaron reported finding great strength within his faith and also expressed feelings of confusion and anger towards some of the teachings within the LDS doctrine. However, whenever Aaron expressed his anger, he reported feeling guilty about "questioning [his] faith" and "not putting [his] faith in the Father."

THE CHURCH OF JESUS CHRIST LATTER-DAY SAINTS

History and Formation

First established in 1830 New York by Joseph Smith, the Church of Jesus Christ of Latter-Day Saints has grown to a membership of over 15 million people on six continents (LDS Church, n.d.-a). The Church of Jesus Christ Latter-Day Saints, commonly referenced as LDS, practices their faith through the King James translation of the Bible in conjunction with the Book of Mormon. LDS faith states that salvation is earned through obedience and adherence to Gospel Principles. In accordance with the faith, a popular passage in LDS Scripture: Book of Mormon (1 Nephi 3:7) reads:

I will go and do the things which the Lord hath commanded, for I know that the Lord giveth no commandments unto the children of men, save he shall prepare a way for them that they may accomplish the thing which he commandeth them (Corporation of the President of The Church of Jesus Christ of Latter-day Saints, 1830/1981, p. 6).

Obedience is practiced by following the religious scriptures and texts.

The LDS faith commonly practices from several religious texts, which guide their faith and their interactions with the world. These texts include: The King James translation of the Holy Bible, the Book of Mormon, the Doctrine and Covenants, and the Gospel Principles (LDS Church, n.d.-c). Each of these religious texts plays a key role in the understanding and growth for a person of the LDS faith.

The Book of Mormon consists of fifteen main divisions, or books (A Brief Explanation about the Book of Mormon, 2019). According to this text, in A.D. 421, the angel Moroni sealed the records and returned them to the Lord until the Lord and Moroni presented the golden plates with the sacred text to Joseph Smith in 1823 (A Brief Explanation about the Book of Mormon, 2019). In addition to the Book of Mormon, members of the LDS faith are guided by the Doctrine and Covenants, which contain the revelations of Joseph Smith and other modern-day prophets of the LDS faith (The Doctrine and Covenants, 2013). The Doctrine and Covenants dictates 138 revelations by Joseph Smith and other modern-day prophets. The introduction to the Doctrine and Covenants states:

The Doctrine and Covenants is unique because it is not a translation of an ancient document, but is of modern origin and was given of God through His chosen prophets for the restoration of His holy work and the establishment of the kingdom of God on the earth in these days.

As previously noted in the Book of Mormon, salvation is earned through obedience to the LDS scripture and those who adhere to and live by the scripture will receive eternal life. Active members abide by The Gospel Principles to adhere to word of this religious text and the LDS faith.

The Gospel Principles are intended as a teaching tool for The Doctrine and Covenants and focuses on "answers to life's questions, [and] gain[ing] an assurance of your purpose and self-worth" (LDS Church, n.d.-b, para. 1), this text includes several aspects regarding creation, the fall of Adam and Eve, sacrament, and obedience. The message of the Gospel Principles is to "grow in your understanding and testimony of God the Father, Jesus Christ and His Atonement, and the Restoration of the gospel." (LDS Church, n.d. -b, para. 1).

Modern Day Structure

The LDS church is based on a hierarchical system, with the president of the LDS church identified as a modern day prophet. According to the LDS faith, the president of the LDS church is God's spokesman (McConkie, 1966) for active church members. LDS church doctrine maintains that the Presidency relays the word of God. The Church of Jesus Christ of Latter Day Saints official website states:

*We can always trust the living prophets. Their teachings reflect the will of the Lord, who declared: "What I the Lord have spoken, I have spoken, and I excuse not myself; and though the heavens and the earth pass away, my word shall not pass away, but shall all be fulfilled, whether by mine own voice or by the voice of my servants, it is the same" (*D&C 1:38*). (LDS church, n.d. -e, para. 3)*

The LDS presidency consists of three members: the President and two supporting counselors. The presidency is further supported by a quorum of twelve apostles, a quorum of seventy members, stake leaders, bishops, and many others that comprise the remainder of leadership within the LDS organization.

The bishop of a congregation, or ward, is called upon and appointed by the Presidency of the Church of Jesus Christ of Latter-Day Saints (LDS Church, n.d.-f). A bishop can hold any profession and is not paid by the LDS Church for their services. A bishop is responsible for teaching and disciplining the men and women in his ward and managing the ward's finances (LDS Church, n.d.-f). The bishop oversees the well being of congregation members, which includes psychological and spiritual needs (Anderson, 2008).

When a man is called to the position of ward bishop, no requirement exists for any formalized mental health training and he "immediately becomes [an] ecclesiastical counselor"(Anderson, 2008, p. 329). The bishop does attend trainings provided by the church leadership, however, "their training does not include professionally accredited curricula of counseling" (Anderson, 2008, p. 329). Active members may choose to seek guidance from the bishop in the form of spiritual counseling (Anderson, 2008). In the event that a member is in need of more services, they may seek counseling from a counselor in the community.

IMPLICATIONS FOR COUNSELING

Research for counseling strategies when working with the LDS community remains sparse, representing a dearth of practical and theoretical knowledge for practicing counselors. Several factors are to be considered when working with a member of the LDS community. A major consideration is the potential stigma associated with seeking counseling outside of the LDS community. Individuals within the LDS community who seek counseling outside of their community may fear that their counselor will devalue their personal faith and beliefs (Barlow & Bergin, 1998). Therefore, it is important for counselors to be aware of their own personalizations, biases, and spiritual identity when working with a member of the LDS community.

The biases surrounding mental health and the LDS faith have shown to be reciprocal in nature. Allen and Hill (2014) interviewed religious leaders of the LDS community and non-LDS mental health counselors with experience working with LDS clients. Both groups expressed negative biases towards the other group. The LDS religious leaders reported a "disappointing attitude about the "lack of results" when their members go through therapy" (p. 80), while the mental health counselors expressed a "specific discouragement toward LDS religious leaders" (p. 80). Because the LDS religious leaders (i.e. bishops) are integral within the LDS community and are viewed "as a local source of spiritual guidance," (Anderson, 2008, p. 329), members may view the bishop as the "divine authority" (p. 332) for all issues, spiritual or otherwise. If possible, collaboration with the bishop is encouraged to promote the wellbeing of the client.

Brown (1978) shares that collaboration between a mental health counselor and bishop can occur, with the bishop ultimately taking charge. The counselor is encouraged to "never place himself or herself above the bishop, [and] consistently recognize and respect the bishop's ecclesiastical authority" (Anderson, 2008, p. 332). To further clarify roles between bishop and counselor, Anderson (2008) suggests for mental health counselors to "shift rhetorical footing" (p. 333), by prefacing their thoughts and conceptualizations with the beginning phrase, "Professionally…," as a way to distinguish between the discipline of counseling and the ecclesiastical domain of counseling.

Accordingly, it is necessary for the counselor to examine their own biases, personalizations, and religious identity before working with members of the LDS faith. Within counseling, clients of the LDS faith may present with strong dichotomous thinking and doctrinal beliefs on what they "should" or "should not" do. To avoid harm to client, it is important for counselors to examine their own belief systems.

Counselors adhering to the ACA Code of Ethics 2014 are required to uphold C.5 Nondiscrimination on account of religion or spirituality and E.8 Multicultural Issues/ Diversity in Assessment regarding impacts of assessment and religion/spirituality.

Johns (2016) identifies ACA Code A.1.d and the importance of spirituality support networks and the introduction to Section C for the importance of counselors to attend to their own personal self-care in regards to spirituality. Johns (2016) also notes that religion and spirituality are not identified in the glossary of the ACA Code of Ethics 2014 in terms of the importance of ethical practices in regards to religion and spirituality. The assigned counselor maintains an ethical duty to recognize his or her own cultural values and beliefs.

While counselors are not expected to be value-free upon entering a counseling session they must avoid imposing their own values onto their client. Kocet & Herlihy (2013) introduced a potential strategy, ethical bracketing, to utilize when combating biases. Ethical bracketing is defined as:

the intentional separating of a counselor's personal values from his or her professional values or the intentional setting aside of the counselor's personal values in order to provide ethical and appropriate counseling to all clients, especially those whose worldviews, values, belief systems, and decisions differ significantly from those of the counselor (p. 182).

In utilizing ethical bracketing, the counselor engages in self-reflection when value conflicts arise. Ethical bracketing encourages counselors to "deliberately set aside or bracket their personal values" (p. 182) as a way to avoid imposing their values onto the client and consequently, empowering the client to focus on their therapeutic goals. In order for the counselor to set aside their personal values and beliefs, it is first necessary for the counselor to identify their own cultural identity and subsequent values and accordingly, practice cultural competence throughout counseling sessions. One significant aspect of culture within Aaron's life is defined by his religious upbringing. As his counselor, I integrated aspects of religious identity development as it relates to Aaron.

Religious Identity Development

Religious identity development remains an ambiguous concept. Despite it's documented influence in identity development (Erikson, 1968), researchers still struggle to form a consensus. Religion is known to be a significant factor in an individual's self-concept and identity development, particularly during adolescence. Petts and Desmond (2016) reported "studying religion during these developmental stages is important, as individuals undergo a number of transitions including increased independence as well as physical and emotional changes" (p. 241). In order to provide a better understanding of religious identity development, de Bruin-Wassinkmaat, de Kock, Visser-Vogel, Elsbeth, Bakker, and Barnard (2019) conducted an extensive literature review to determine a common conceptualization as it relates to religious identity development. Within the data analysis from the literature review, religious upbringing and identity are comprised of an individual's "beliefs, values, and doctrines as well as behaviors, rituals, and religious practices" (de Bruin-Wassinkmaat et al., 2019). Accordingly, contextual influence, exploration and commitment, and autonomy and choice all emerged as relevant themes within past research.

Contextual influence refers to personal interactions with significant identity agents, described as those who interact with the individual in the formation of their religious identity as well as "personal experiences like leaving home, difficult periods in life, religious organizations, traditions, customs, God and scripture, and the religious community" (p. 73). Exploration and commitment refer to the degree an individual's perceived ability to explore and question their religious identity. Defined as a "period of crisis in which alternative identities are explored prior to the making of commitments" (Layton et al., 2012, p. 158), exploration influences the choice of commitment within an individual's religious identity. Within commitment, there is a distinction between internalized and externalized commitment, with externalized commitment categorized through obligation and forced behaviors, while internalized commitment related to as an intrinsic motivation (Armet, 2009). Finally, autonomy and choice account for an individual's desire to make an independent decision in participating and practicing within the religion. While identified as significant, religion remains as only one sector of Aaron's identity; in order to provide culturally competent conceptualization and treatment, other aspects of Aaron cultural identity and his counselor's cultural identity will be considered through the Multicultural and Social Justice Counseling Competencies.

MULTICULTURAL AND SOCIAL JUSTICE COUNSELING COMPETENCIES (MSJCC)

Multicultural and Social Justice Counseling Competencies (MSJCC) outline the four developmental domains: counselor self-awareness, client worldview, counseling relationship, and counseling and advocacy interventions. The MSJCC considers potential privilege and marginalization for both counselor and client. A counselor working to incorporate the MSJCC must first engage in self-reflection to determine personal identities of privilege, marginalization, or any biases or stereotypes that may be present when working with a client. Accordingly, the counselor must then recognize the client's privilege or marginalization within the counseling relationship. Furthermore, the recognition of privilege/marginalization within each person's identity creates an opportunity for further growth and knowledge about differing cultural backgrounds. Counselors adhering to the MSJCC must also consider the institution, community, public policy, and global affairs that are impacting the client. Any counselor utilizing the MSJCC model should engage in deep exploration of self-awareness and the attitudes and beliefs, knowledge, skills, and action that impact the counseling relationship (Ratts, 2015). The counselor must be able to recognize areas of privilege and marginalization of both themselves as the counselor and their client.

Within this particular counseling relationship with Aaron, I must acknowledge my privilege with regard to education level, race, socioeconomic status (SES), and other identities. To this date, I am a college graduate and was raised in a suburban middle-class home. I identify as Caucasian and able-bodied, which allots my interactions to come from a place of privilege. Accordingly, identifying as bisexual woman creates some potential for marginalization. Aaron's privilege is acknowledged in his gender (male) and sexual orientation (heterosexual). I must consider privilege and marginalization in regards to Aaron's religion. In comparison with other national religions, LDS is considered a minority, comprising only 2.04% of the national population (Facts and Statistics, 2019). The MSJCC stipulates considerations for institution, community, public policy, and global affairs for this reason. From the first session, Aaron has identified incidences of community discrimination where he has felt isolated and judged after disclosing his religion.

A counselor must also actively engage in and demonstrate curiosity about the client's worldview (Ratts, et al, 2015). I worked to understand Aaron's interpretation of his LDS beliefs and attitudes towards the church and current practices. In the beginning sessions, Aaron disclosed that he is starting to "wonder if something is wrong with me" related to his struggle. I seek to understand where this belief originated based on his worldview and beliefs about the implications within his LDS faith. I must also consider further action and advocacy to support Aaron. To avoid unintentional harm to Aaron, I must seek supervision for any biases that arise as I work with Aaron as he discusses his religious beliefs. I may also need to complete further research to better understand the implications for counseling.

While seeking to understand Aaron's worldview, I explored Aaron's intrapersonal experience of privilege and marginalization, and accordingly discrimination, as well as, his experience of how this may impact his connections with others. Aaron discussed feeling isolated from his peers, being confronted by members of his ward, and feeling fearful of telling his family and friends that he is seeing a non-LDS counselor. I explored the ways in which Aaron is feeling marginalized in these interactions with his peers. I assisted Aaron to understand existing supports, or lack thereof, and any ways the client may be empowered when interacting with these individuals.

MSJCC suggests examining the interactions a client has with institutions and community (Ratts, et al, 2015). For Aaron, this includes examining his relationship with his church and his university community. I seek to understand Aaron's experiences of privilege and marginalization within both of these institutions and how his identities (single, male, Caucasian, LDS faith) may interplay within these interactions. I must also consider what actions can be taken to advocate for Aaron.

As a way to provide best practice to clients, counselors must acknowledge areas of privilege and marginalization for both themselves and clients and reflect on the potential implications for counseling. This includes consideration of personal biases and areas for advocacy. Based on my cultural background and personal values, it is necessary to recognize potential biases that are present when interacting with the LDS faith. It is the responsibility of the counselor to recognize any biases, engage in self-reflection, and utilize supervision/consultation when conceptualizing and working with Aaron.

COUNSELOR CULTURAL BACKGROUND AND COUNSELING APPROACH

Brianne Scott

Cultural Background. My name is Brianne Scott and I am a doctoral student enrolled in a counselor education program in the Rocky Mountain region. I am a Midwestern native, from where I completed my bachelors in psychological sciences and my masters in clinical mental health counseling. I am the eldest of my siblings and I grew up in a middle-class suburban home. I identify as a queer Caucasian woman and I as move throughout my life, I continue to recognize how my intersecting identities influence (both indirectly and directly) my worldview. From the ages of 1-6 years old, I lived on an Air Force base within the southern United States. Although I was young, I can recall our everyday lives being highly shaped and enforced by the culture of military life, particularly within the family dynamic as my father was enlisted in the Air Force. At age six, I moved with my family to the Midwest, where I have lived a majority of my life.

Religion has maintained a steady presence through my lifespan, most prominently in the Eastern Orthodox faith. I attended an Eastern Orthodox church from ages 10 to 16 years old, was baptized through this faith, and was an active member in the congregation. Particularly in my church, there was a heavy emphasis on the Holy Trinity with altars dedicated to religious figures and sacraments given each Sunday to the Father, Son, and Holy Spirit. In comparison with the Western Christian religions, the typical Orthodox church service could appear unique, as the service involves many prayers, singing/chanting specific hymns, all the scent of incense permeates the air.

Eastern Orthodox faith differs from Western Christian religions both externally (in the church's design/style of worship) as well as it's internal interpretation towards Paradise/Hell salvation. Within this faith, perfection is addressed, which explains that we are "eternally advancing to higher stages of perfection" and "the one who is damned is incapable of progress, he is unable to accept progress towards perfection" (Fr. A. Jarmus., 2018).

Whilst attending the church, I recognized the importance of religion and how powerful its presence could be in other people's lives. Now as a young adult, I have begun to research other world faiths including: Christianity, Judaism, Buddhism, as a way to promote my own understanding of religion and spirituality. While growing up in Indiana, the LDS population was not prominent, however, they were still visible. At the time, I did not have any knowledge of the faith, however, I can recall the individuals who identified within the LDS community were met with negative perceptions by others. Upon arriving in the Rocky Mountain region for my doctoral program, I became aware of the prominence of the LDS faith and have worked to further my understanding when working with clients and supervisees who identify within the LDS faith.

Counseling Approach. I view counseling as a collaborative approach, between the client and counselor. I work within the "I-Thou" approach, which can be thought of as "I am here with you." Part of my role as counselor is to walk alongside the client when they are in session and delving into sensitive topics. Accordingly, I promote a focus on the present moment, which can allow for further awareness for what the client is experiencing within each session. I do not believe it is my role to provide solutions, but rather to move alongside the client as they explore their own emotions, thoughts, behaviors, beliefs, and values.

Through my existential lens, I encourage meaning making as the client explores these different emotions and beliefs. Each client will create a different meaning based on his or her worldview and through the exploration of these deeper meanings, the client will gain further understanding about his or her own worldview. To better understand a client's worldview, I conceptualize a client through a biological, physiological, and relational lens. These different lenses allow me a more holistic view of the client and accordingly allows me to address any systemic barriers that may be present within my client's world. As a counselor, I have identified advocacy as a personal responsibility, both in and out of counseling sessions. Using the information from my research and privilege within my cultural identity, I hope to speak about injustices towards marginalized populations and promote further research and discussion regarding these topics.

I recognize that I enter counseling sessions with my own values and beliefs and without continuous self-reflection and awareness, could inadvertently affect my counseling sessions. As I navigate each session, I encourage myself to be wholly aware of any potential biases/personalization that may arise and consult when necessary. I seek to address potential areas of bias or personalization through supervision and the use of decision-making models. Kocet and Herlihy developed the Counselor Values-Based Conflict Model (2013) to specifically guide counselors working through personal bias with clients. Counselors work to create plans to engage in self-reflection and gaining further cultural competence in this process, while working closely with a supervisor and consulting with other peers as needed (Kocet & Herlihy, 2013). I value this decision making model as it outlines steps to take to increase cultural competence and greatly encourages self-reflection for the counselor to evaluate where personal biases come from and how to avoid these biases becoming a barrier when working with clients.

COUNSELING THEORY AND CONCEPTUALIZATION

Existentialism

First developed as a philosophy of humanity in the 1800s (Yalom, 1980), existential theory has been further conceptualized through an atheistic and theistic perspective (e.g., Nietzsche & Kierkegaard). Still viewed through a humanistic perspective, existential theory is predominantly known to center around the four basic assumptions: freedom, isolation, meaninglessness, and death. Within an existential lens, freedom is viewed as a person's inability to avoid making choices. However, with each choice comes a subsequent consequence and individuals have to cope with the responsibility of their choices. Isolation refers to the marked separateness that individuals will experience. This ultimate aloneness of human existence creates anxiety within a person with the recognition that one will enter and leave this world alone. Death is typically marked by a person's fear of non-being, which leads to anxiety regarding the finality of life. Finally, meaninglessness is the realization that there is no innate meaning in the world, and that meaning must be made within each person (Yalom, 1980).

From an atheistic perspective, the four assumptions are conceptualized as "an inescapable part of human existence" (Fernando, 2007, p. 227), while the theistic approach posits that the four assumptions "exist in varying degrees" (Bartz, 2009, p. 71). Accordingly, theistic existentialism introduces an additional ultimate concern: guilt and shame. While atheistic perspective disregards guilt and shame as a by-product of culture, theism posits humans as moral creatures, emphasizing guilt and shame as a fundamental category (Lewis, 1952). When feelings of shame and guilt arise, perfectionism has been identified as common defense mechanism (Kaufman, 1980).

Van Deurzen (2002), a major contributor in the research of existentialism, references the concept of perfection within the spiritual dimension of human experience, classified through the term, uberwelt. Van Deurzen (2002) posits that the counselor can conceptualize perfection as a virtue in relation to the client's creation of meaning. Theistic existential counselors can conceptualize clients on a continuum of belief in God to a search for meaning and truth (Van Deurzen, 2002). Existential counselors benefit from understanding the client in relation to four realms, or welts, of human existence.

Existential counselors utilize the concepts of the welts: umwelt, mitwelt, eigenwelt, and uberwelt to conceptualize the client in relation to existence. The umwelt is a term used to delineate the client in space; physiological needs (i.e. food/water/shelter) are the focus of the umwelt (Vontress, 1979). The client's mitwelt consists of interpersonal relationships, social identities and communication with others (i.e. sense of belonging) (Vontress, 1979). The client's eigenwelt is the world that cannot be seen by others, otherwise known as the private world (Vontress, 1979). The uberwelt unites spirituality/religion and values directly associated with that particular religion (Rowan, 2018, van Deurzen, 2002). The uberwelt is highly utilized when practicing from a theistic existential perspective. The welts are used to further conceptualize a client by examining the client through their physiological needs (umwelt), social needs (mitwelt), private needs (eigenwelt), and spiritual needs (uberwelt).

As the counselor working with Aaron, I have practiced through an atheistic existential approach to counseling, however, to account for Aaron's prominent religious identity, I have chosen to conceptualize Aaron through a theistic existentialist perspective to include the basic tenets of atheistic existentialism.

Counselors working within an existential theoretical orientation believe that humans have the ability to change and this change process is continuous throughout the lifetime (Corey, 2013, Halbur & Halbur, 2014). Existential counselors believe that individuals are continuously striving for self-actualization and authenticity. "The aim of therapy is to help the individual learn how to live" (Yalom, 1980, p. 29). Aaron described feeling judged by students after disclosing his religious beliefs and fear in regards to telling family members that he is seeing a non-LDS counselor. As an existential counselor, I conceptualized this as part of Aaron's struggle for authentic living and continued to address this within Aaron's goals for counseling. As his counselor, I worked collaboratively with Aaron to tailor his goals within counseling and to focus on our relationship dynamic to specifically meet his needs.

Additionally, counselors practicing through existentialism will tailor their interventions and conceptualizations to each client and each client's needs (Corey, 2013). Counselors recognize the importance of relationship-building with the client and strive to demonstrate compassion and understanding. Counselors are able to accomplish this by demonstrating curiosity of the client's worldview and authenticity in the counseling relationship. Throughout the counseling experience, I explored areas of privilege and marginalization, as described by the Multicultural and Social Justice Counseling Competencies (Ratts, Singh, Nassar-McMillan, Butler, & McCullough, 2015), to better understand Aaron's worldview and build the counseling relationship. Utilizing curiosity and openness, I encouraged Aaron to share his experiences and integrate relationship-building interventions such as paraphrasing and feeling reflections to show compassion and gain understanding. Existential counselors rely on relationship building interventions and basic intervention skills to guide the beginning counseling sessions.

Counselors practicing from an existential lens are given few direct therapeutic interventions to utilize with clients in session. Yalom (1980) introduced the therapist's set in which counselors strongly focus on the therapeutic relationship, their ability to interpret the client's meaning, and confronting and refocusing the client in session. I used the therapeutic set to gain further understanding of Aaron's worldview, how he may be engaging in inauthentic living, and to explore Aaron's culture. Theism posits that humans are multifaceted beings (Richards & Bergin, 2005), therefore the counselor must address all aspects of Aaron's being, including his biological, relational, and spiritual realm. Considerations for conceptualization and treatment include techniques to facilitate confrontation, awareness, and healthier ways to cope (Bartz, 2009). Further discussion of techniques utilized will be introduced in the treatment section of this chapter.

Conceptualization of Aaron

Aaron has disclosed struggles connecting with students on campus as well as the members of his new ward. Aaron also disclosed fear over his relationships with family if he chooses to disclose that he is seeing a non-LDS counselor. I conceptualized this presentation as concerns with interactions in Aaron's mitwelt and alongside the existential assumption: isolation. Further utilization of Yalom's (1980) therapist's set was used to explore these concerns and develop goals collaboratively to address Aaron's struggles with interpersonal relationships. Accordingly, the loss of connection coincides with isolation.

Additionally, Aaron presented with concerns seated in his uberwelt. Aaron discussed polarizing feelings towards his LDS faith as he draws strength from his personal practice and contrarily, expresses anger with some of the teachings. Aaron reported feelings of guilt for questioning his faith and seeking help outside of the LDS church. Within sessions, I utilized the theistic existential conceptualization of the uberwelt and discovered further cultural implications for Aaron. Aaron believed obedience to the LDS principles is essential for his salvation, however he was questioning the LDS doctrine, which has led to inauthentic living within his uberwelt (spiritual self). I collaborated with Aaron to determine his closest internal values through a value card sort and identify how his personal values may be similar or different from the external values of the LDS faith. Aaron then determined what is essential to include within his uberwelt (spiritual self) to engage in authentic living. Because Aaron had identified religion as a significant factor within his life, it is pertinent to examine his religious identity development throughout counseling.

Past research described above identified contextual influence, exploration and commitment, and autonomy and choice as significant factors within religious identity development. As it relates to Aaron, it is pertinent to examine how Aaron's contextual environment: family members, LDS community members, school peers, academic environment might influence his values, beliefs, thoughts, emotions, and decisions within session. Through self- report, Aaron reported a perceived disconnect from family members, members of the LDS community, and school peers. Understanding the role of Aaron's identity agents (family, bishops, peers) within his life helped to understand how Aaron interacts with and understands his role within his religion.

Within the concept of exploration and commitment, Aaron reported discomfort to discuss his concerns with his religion with other members of his faith. Because he has experienced difficulty within exploration of his religion, he experienced more external commitment towards his faith as opposed to internal commitment. As well, Aaron experienced an internal crisis as he develops his other emerging identities alongside his religious identity. Autonomy and choice may also play a factor through Aaron's perceived ability to question and discuss his concerns with his faith with family members and other members of the LDS community. Aaron felt his religious identity has been ascribed to him, rather than self-constructed, leading to a perceived lack of freedom and choice in constructing his own understanding of his religion. Through Aaron's own self-report, religion remains an impactful factor within his identity.

CASE HISTORY

Treatment

As discussed before in the Theistic Existentialism section, I utilized a theistic existentialism approach, to accommodate for Aaron's religious background. Goals for counseling sessions include:

Short Term Goals:

1. Identify 1-2 new social supports within community or faith.
2. Reduce symptoms of anxiety from 5 times per week to 2 times per week.
3. Reduce symptoms of depression from 5 times per week to 2 times per week.

Long Term Goals:

1. Address conflicting feelings towards LDS faith/community.
2. Identify personal values as they do and do not relate with LDS values.

I recognized that in order to safely address Aaron's feelings of depression and anxiety, a therapeutic alliance must be established. I focused the first one to two sessions on establishing this alliance with Aaron, which included addressing any concerns he may have with seeking counseling outside of his faith, working with a non-LDS counselor, and broaching the topic of religion. Patterson and Staton (2009) emphasized the importance of authenticity within the counseling session to demonstrate an authentic relationship; Yalom's (1980) Therapeutic Set is utilized throughout to foster the development of the relationship between Aaron and his counselor. Clients who are able to find meaning and authenticity within the counseling relationship are able to translate this into other relationships (Patterson & Staton, 2009; Yalom, 1980).

In an attempt to promote an authentic working relationship with Aaron, I chose to disclose my religious upbringing and background. I was aware of any transferential or countertransferential feelings that may present in session and utilized the skill of immediacy to address these feelings. To further promote a positive working relationship, I utilized additional basic counseling skills to further establish the counseling relationship, including, paraphrasing, reflection of feelings, pattern recognition, confrontation, and probing questions to better understand Aaron's worldview. As the therapeutic alliance was established, I was able to address Aaron's determined goals.

Aaron's feelings of depression and anxiety potentially stemmed from perceived isolation from the LDS community and university community. As a member of the LDS community, Aaron identifies with a dominant religion within his context and accordingly, faced discrimination from university peers and outside community. Accordingly, Aaron expressed conflicting feelings towards his faith. Questioning his faith could invoke anxiety in Aaron as it leads to questioning the stability of his religion. Kolkto (1991) states that: "a fear about the stability of [one's] testimony is a fear about the stability of something as central as the way [one] deal with reality" (p. 41).

Conceptualized through the existential given of isolation and meaninglessness, I addressed this assumption through facilitating confrontation and awareness of existential fear. Bartz (2009) reported confrontation as addressing existential fear as a way to promote growth and awareness through evocative exploration.

Evocative exploration includes identifying Aaron's emotions within session and encouraging him to sit with these emotions. These emotions can be subtle or overt via Aaron's verbal and nonverbal language. Primarily, Aaron has expressed feelings of guilt, sadness, and anger when discussing personal struggles. These identified emotions are expressed through Aaron's dialogue (i.e. when he reports feeling "lost" or "alone" when discussing lack of social support in community and the questioning of his faith) and through nonverbal indicators (i.e. crossed arms, shifting in seat, tone, and pitch of voice). The goal of this technique is to encourage exploration of conflicting feelings and gain awareness. To promote further inward orientation when exploring these difficult topics, I assigned homework through daily journal reflections (Kolkto, 1991). Aaron reported that the journal reflections have been a helpful tool that he can use outside of session when he is "feeling upset about something." The daily journaling can also be a technique to foster further awareness for Aaron. Level of awareness can vary among clients (Bartz, 2009), however the ultimate goal was to have Aaron recognize how the existential fear of isolation and meaninglessness may influence his attitudes and behaviors. Within session, I facilitated this awareness through asking open-ended questions and exploring emotions associated with isolation and meaninglessness.

Progress

Aaron has completed eight sessions of counseling to date and self-reported that his symptoms are improving. As discussed above, Aaron presented with feelings of hesitancy when he first arrived to counseling. From his intake, Aaron reported a desire to discuss his religion but did not want to be judged by his counselor. To further promote a positive, authentic working relationship, I self-disclosed my religious upbringing as a potential path to discussing religion. Aaron attributed his hesitancy due to several negative experiences with peers after disclosing his religion, which had prevented him from sharing it with others in the future. I encouraged Aaron to openly communicate when he felt misunderstood or misrepresented by me during sessions. The first several sessions focused solely on Aaron's feelings of guilt and loneliness as he navigated balancing his duties within his church, his academic obligations, and creating and maintaining relationships. As he explored his emotions related to all his self-identified duties (school, church, friendships), Aaron recognized that he was experiencing an immense amount of self-imposed pressure to succeed and struggled with reaching out to his family and friends for support. Aaron shared that his family is "incredibly important" to him and expressed a desire to reach out to them but worried about their reactions to him seeking counseling outside of the LDS faith. After 4-5 sessions exploring his concerns, Aaron felt comfortable reaching out to his parents and older brother to discuss his struggles with loneliness and anxiety. Aaron reported that while his parents and brother are supportive, he still does not feel comfortable disclosing this to others outside of his family.

Because of the added family support, he reported that he is able to focus in class and his grades are improving as a result. After some personal consideration, Aaron decided to decrease his class load from 15 hours to 12 hours. After this change, Aaron reported some feelings of guilt towards "not doing as much as I should." These feelings of guilt were further explored and Aaron discovered his feelings of guilt originated from personal expectations. He has recognized that his feelings of irritability have significantly decreased and he feels "less stressed all the time". I continue to highlight the importance of self-compassion when balancing life demands. Aaron expressed a desire to engage in more university related activities and began participating with the intramural basketball team on campus. He reported some discomfort around interacting with teammates and wants to continue to build on his relationships with his peers on the team before he disclosed his religion. Within sessions, I worked alongside Aaron to self-identify his strengths including a continued openness and courage to share his concerns and to work outside of his comfort zone. He and I continued to collaboratively explore how he will practice self-compassion within his daily life.

Aaron is currently attending LDS church services on the campus rather than at his previously assigned ward. He reports that he is re-establishing his "relationship with the Father". Aaron is continuing to experience conflicting feelings with specific doctrines within the LDS faith and feelings of uncertainty regarding his direction forward. Aaron continues to report his faith as a major strength and identifies himself as "a great son, brother, and friend." Aaron aspires to continue to establish friendships with university peers and explore how to resolve conflicting feelings with his faith.

CONCLUSION

Clients from the LDS population continue to be an underserved and underrepresented population. Those who are a part of this population continue to face biases and discrimination from the general population, including the counseling profession. With a dearth of knowledge regarding effective treatment for LDS clients, counselors could unintentionally cause undue harm and consequently create an unsafe environment for their client. In order to abide by the ACA Code of Ethics (2014), counselors are responsible to uphold multicultural competencies as it relates to clients of diverse backgrounds. In the case of Aaron, it is important to note while counselors may have experienced biases, it is essential that these biases did not affect the counseling relationship and subsequent treatment. Utilizing a theistic existential lens, the counselor conceptualized Aaron's struggles through the existential givens and welts, while accordingly addressing the MSJCC guidelines to promote awareness, advocacy, and a therapeutic working relationship. Considerations for conceptualization and treatment include further examination of marginalization of LDS population and promoting best practice when working with a member of this faith.

REFERENCES

Allen, G. E., & Hill, C. (2014). Exploring perceived attitudes of counseling between LDS religious leaders and mental health therapists. *Journal of the Association of Mormon Counselors and Psychotherapists: Issues in Religion and Psychotherapy*, *36*, 71–82.

American Counseling Association. (2014). *ACA Code of Ethics*. Alexandria, VA: Author.

Anderson, S. V. (2008). Rhetorical footing in Latter-Day Saints Counseling. *Social Thought*, *27*(4), 323–339. https://doi-org.libpublic3.library.isu.edu/10.1080/15426430802345309

Armet, S. (2009). Religious socialization and identity formation of adolescents in high tension religions. *Review of Religious Research*, *50*(3), 277–297. Retrieved from https://www.jstor.org/stable/25593742

The Association of Religion Data Archives. (2010). *County membership report: Bonneville county, Idaho*. Retrieved from http://www.thearda.com/rcms2010/r/c/16/rcms2010_16019_county_adh_2010.asp

Barlow, S., & Bergin, A. (1998). Religion and mental health from the Mormon perspective. In H. Koenig (Ed.), *Handbook of religion and health* (pp. 225–243). San Diego, CA: Academic Press. doi:10.1016/B978-012417645-4/50082-1

Bartz, J. D. (2009). Theistic Existential Psychotherapy. *Psychology of Religion and Spirituality*, *1*(2), 69–80. doi:10.1037/a0014895

Book of doctrine and covenants of the Church of Jesus Christ of Latter-day Saints. (1864). Cincinnati, OH: Publishing Committee of the Reorganized Church of Jesus Christ of Latter-day Saints.

The Book of Mormon. (1981). Salt Lake City, UT: The Church of Jesus Christ of Latter-Day Saints. (Original work published 1830)

Brown, V. L. (1978). Q&A: Questions and answers. *New Era*, *8*(9), 16–19.

The Church of Jesus Christ of Latter-Day Saints. (n.d.a). *About us*. Retrieved from https://www.mormon.org/about-us

The Church of Jesus Christ of Latter-Day Saints. (n.d.b). *Gospel principles*. Retrieved from https://www.lds.org/manual/gospel-principles/introduction?lang=eng

The Church of Jesus Christ of Latter-Day Saints. (n.d.c). *Scriptures*. Retrieved from https://www.lds.org/scriptures?lang=eng

The Church of Jesus Christ of Latter-Day Saints. (n.d.d). *Facts and statistics: United States*. Retrieved from: https://www.mormonnewsroom.org/facts-and-statistics/country/united-states

The Church of Jesus Christ of Latter-Day Saints. (n.d.e). *Prophets*. Retrieved from: https://www.lds.org/manual/true-to-the-faith/prophets?lang=eng

The Church of Jesus Christ of Latter-Day Saints. (n.d.f). *How the Church is organized*. Retrieved from: https://www.lds.org/topics/church-organization/how-the-church-is-organized?lang=eng&old=true

Corey, G. (2012). *Theory and practice of counseling and psychotherapy* (9th ed.). Belmont, CA: Brooks/Cole, Cengage Learning.

de Bruin-Wassinkmaat, A. M., de Kock, J., Visser-Vogel, E., Bakker, C., & Barnard, M. (2019). Being Young and Strictly Religious: A Review of the Literature on the Religious Identity Development of Strictly Religious Adolescents. *Identity*, *19*(1), 62–79. doi:10.1080/15283488.2019.1566067

Erikson, E. H. (1968). *Identity: Youth and crises*. New York, NY: Norton.

Fernando, D. M. (2007). Existential theory and solution-focused strategies: Integration and application. *Journal of Mental Health Counseling*, *29*(3), 226–241. doi:10.17744/mehc.29.3.r01582660404v734

Fr. A. Jarmus. (2018, December 6). The real difference between orthodoxy and the west [web log comment]. Retrieved from https://www.stnicholasonline.org/fr-andrews-blog/the-real-difference-between-orthodoxy-and-the-west

Halbur, D., & Halbur, K. (2014). *Developing your theoretical orientation*. Boston, MA: Pearson.

Johns, R. D. (2016). Stories matter: Narrative themes of counselor educators' religious and spiritual competency. *Counseling and Values*, *62*(1), 72–89. doi:10.1002/cvj.12050

Kaufman, G. (1980). *Shame: The power of caring*. Cambridge, MA: Schenkman.

Kocet, M. M., & Herlihy, B. J. (2013). Addressing value-based conflicts within the counseling relationship: A decision-making model. *Journal of Counseling and Development*, *92*(2), 180–186. doi:10.1002/j.1556-6676.2014.00146.x

Koltko, M. E. (1991). The psychological foundations of the Mormon client in counseling and psychotherapy. *Journal of the Association of Mormon Counselors and Psychotherapists*, *17*(1), 1–26. Retrieved from https://scholarsarchive.byu.edu/irp/vol17/iss1/2/

Layton, E., Hardy, S. A., & Dollahite, D. (2012). Religious exploration among highly religious American adolescents. *Identity*, *12*(2), 157–184. doi:10.1080/15283488.2012.668728

McConkie, B. (1966). *Mormon doctrine* (2nd ed.). Salt Lake City, UT: Bookcraft.

Patterson, F. L., & Staton, A. R. (2009). Adult-acquired traumatic brain injury: Existential implications and clinical considerations. *Journal of Mental Health Counseling*, *31*(2), 149–163. doi:10.17744/mehc.31.2.1p42572p01435173

Petts, R. J., & Desmond, S. A. (2016). Adolescence and emerging adulthood. In D. Yamane (Ed.), *Handbook of religion and society* (pp. 241–262). New York, NY: Springer. doi:10.1007/978-3-319-31395-5_13

Ratts, M. J., Singh, A. A., Nassar-McMillan, S., Butler, S.K., & McCullough, J.R. (2015). *Multicultural and social justice counseling competencies.* Retrieved from https://www.counseling.org/docs/default-source/competencies/multicultural-and-social-justice-counseling-competencies.pdf?sfvrsn=20

Richards, P. S., & Bergin, A. E. (2005). *A spiritual strategy for counseling and psychotherapy* (2nd ed.). Washington, DC: American Psychological Association. doi:10.1037/11214-000

Vontress, C. E. (1979). Cross-cultural counseling: An existential approach. *The Personnel and Guidance Journal*, *58*(2), 117–122. doi:10.1002/j.2164-4918.1979.tb00363.x

Yalom, I. D. (1980). *Existential psychotherapy*. New York: Basic Books.

Chapter 9
The Case of Harper, Courageous Cultural Conversations in the Counseling Room:
Overcoming Complacency With Competence and Confidence

Noreal Armstrong
Montreat College, USA

Megan Clunan
Montreat College, USA

EXECUTIVE SUMMARY

The authors will utilize the case of Harper to delineate how to counsel clients to remain true to one's personal identity, while still developing a culturally competent identity in empathetic relationship with others. Harper is coming to counseling because she is facing a move from her homogeneous cultural community in Western North Carolina to the diversity of Washington, DC. Harper states she is fearful and anxious about (1) having to set her values aside, (2) being offensive because she lacks awareness of other cultures, and (3) the unknown of what living around different religions, ethnicities, and cultures may entail. The authors will explore practical ways in which the MSJCC can be implemented in the clinical setting for the sake of counseling clients toward cultural competency. Counselors will examine the importance of counselor self-awareness, regarding marginalization and privilege, within the therapeutic relationship. The authors will provide examples of experiential, solutions focused, and group therapy interventions to help clients move toward cultural competency.

DOI: 10.4018/978-1-7998-0022-4.ch009

INTRODUCTION

According to Ratts, Singh, Nassar-McMillan, Butler and McCullough (2016) the Multicultural and Social Justice Counseling Competencies (MSJCC) are a theoretical framework to implement competency within counseling theories and practice. Through the lens of the MSJCC, the case study exemplified within this chapter is one which provides an example of therapeutic interventions for a client struggling with fear and anxiety due to a lifetime of implicit cultural complacency. The client, Harper, is coming to counseling because she is currently facing a move from her homogeneous cultural community in Western North Carolina to the diversity of Washington, DC. Harper states she wants to feel more confident about the move because it is for the purpose of her husband's recent promotion and she wants to be supportive of him, however she is fearful and anxious about (1) having to set her values aside within a much greater diverse population; (2) being offensive because she lacks awareness of other cultures; and (3) the unknown of what living around different races, religions, ethnicities and cultures may entail.

Case Description

The case of Harper addresses one client's insecurities as a result of implicit cultural complacency. The presenting issues Harper is facing are nothing new for many individuals who have grown up and remained within the community wherein they were born. *Implicit* is denoted, as it is not until Harper is faced with leaving her homogenous cultural climate is she made aware of her limited perspective of other cultures. *Implicit bias* being subconscious or unarticulated perceptions, positive or negative, directed toward an individual or group based on stereotypes (Berg-Weger, 2016).

Through Harper's presenting issues of being anxious and fearful of leaving her homogenous cultural climate, for a more culturally diverse climate, we will walk through Harper's struggle of integrating her personal identity with a culturally competent identity, fears of being offensive or offended by individuals who are different from her, and anxieties over the unknown of what living among people of different cultures may signify. Through the use of solution-focused interventions, experiential therapy, and psychoeducation group therapy techniques we will see Harper benefit from the courageous cultural conversations created within our counseling room.

Before addressing client issues, meeting clients at their personal point of understanding is essential, so let's meet Harper. Harper is a bright, caring, and open-minded client. However, in the initial intake session she discloses,

I am concerned about having to set my values aside and about losing myself. This concern is weighing on me and I am finding I can't sleep well, as I worry so much about what it will mean for me to live around people so different from me! I have never lived anywhere else. I was born and raised here in Western North Carolina, but I want to be supportive of my husband's promotion and be happy for what this means for us. The thought of living in Washington, DC just scares me.

In listening to Harper's presenting issue, it is clear that Harper is not a client who struggles with an unwillingness to learn about other cultures; however, simply struggles with the fact that her life (up to this point) has not required her to learn of other cultures. Harper, like many living within a homogenous culture wherein the people one lives around are of the same race, religion, heritage, and overall culture has an established implicit complacency when it comes to cultural competence. In fact, through Harper sharing her presenting issue, a realization occurred. Many clients within our (mine and my colleague's writing this chapter) caseload, were similar to Harper. Similarities existed in that they had the privilege to always be around and interact with people who looked and presumably thought like them. In each case, the clients struggled with being able to create experiences affording them opportunities to grow culturally, expand their knowledge, and interact with people who have endured different lived experiences; including privilege and marginalization, as noted within the MSJCC.

Notably, a part of our role as counselors is to create growth opportunities for our clients. We are charged with providing holistic care for those we counsel (American Counseling Association, 2014), part of which is that of cultural competency. Therefore, in light of Harper's presenting issues and the commonalities seen from within Harper's case across quite a few other client cases, this case study is worth examining. The counseling principles and techniques utilized within Harper's case can easily be transposed for other clients facing similar presenting issues.

Brief Literature Review of Specific Issues

The concept of counseling toward multicultural competence and action effectively has been on the forefront of the counseling profession for many years. A ProQuest literature search provided a wealth of articles going back as far as 1997. The literature search included topics on implicit bias, cultural competence in the classroom, relational-cultural theory, experiential activities in multicultural training, and social justice. The researchers in many of the articles aimed to discover (Constantine, Hage, Kindaichi, & Bryant, 2007), develop (Priester et al., 2008), and measure (Pieterse, 2008) how best to counsel clients with multiculturalism. Constantine et al., (2007) stated "the skill component of multicultural competence involves the ability to draw from an existing fund of cultural knowledge to design mental health interventions that are relevant to marginalized populations," (p. 24). For some clients, their fund of knowledge may lack influential experiences with diverse/marginalized populations and it becomes the counselor's' responsibility to provide many meaningful and engaging opportunities.

Lack of cultural self- or other-knowledge can be due to a refusal to learn or be open to various experiences, however more than not, it is due to implicit complacency. *Implicit complacency* is defined by the authors as not taking active steps to become multiculturally aware due to the perceived lack of need to do so. Individuals living within a homogeneous culture (i.e. similar race, religious affiliation, gender identity, and socioeconomic status) may never recognize the need to grow within a diversity perspective. Arguably, implicit complacency created from living in a homogeneous culture is no longer an acceptable standard of living, as society is diversifying more rapidly than ever (Berg-Weger, 2016; Boysen, 2010; Corey, 2017; Ratts et al., 2016).

Implicit complacency creates various troubling issues for individuals and society as a whole, one of which is that of implicit bias. Implicit bias presents in the form of "actions or judgments that are under the control of automatically activated evaluation, without the performer's awareness of that causation" (Greenwald, McGhee, & Schwartz, 1998, p. 1464). Such behaviors can also be labeled as *microaggressions* or *microinvalidations* (Constantine, Smith, Redington, & Owens, 2008; Sue, et al., 2007). Microaggressions are the subtle "slights and insults that targets of bias face, most of which occur without the perpetrator's awareness, whereas microinvalidations are behaviors that reject or invalidate the experiences of targets of bias" (Boysen, 2010, p.211). Examples of a microaggressions can be seen in the following statements, which at surface level may seem benign, but are quite negative in sentiment: "oh, you are smart for a girl!" or "don't cry, be a man!" Examples of microinvalidations can be seen in the following: assuming all individuals from a Hispanic background came to America illegally, or denying the fact that racism still exists in our society today.

To counsel clients toward action and away from cultural complacency we, as counselors, need to do the necessary work to become culturally aware. As counselors ourselves (the authors), we believe we must be willing to do what we ask of our clients. Holistic client care begins with us, but more specifically begins with self-awareness. The MSJCC defines the process of establishing counselor self-awareness as, "privileged and marginalized counselors develop self-awareness, so that they may explore their attitudes, beliefs, develop knowledge, skills, and action relative to their self-awareness and worldview" (Ratts et al., 2016, p. 5). Beginning with attitudes and beliefs, the MSJCC informs counselors of the need to become aware of their own social identities, power, privilege, strengths, limitations, assumptions, attitudes, and values. By understanding oneself on such levels the counselor can acknowledge differences between personal experience and the experiences of clients, and therein, create a protective barrier against allowing differences to detrimentally influence the therapeutic relationship. The counselor is also better positioned to develop greater empathy in the therapeutic work being requested of the client to address similar understandings within themselves (Corey, 2017).

In an effort to move toward cultural competence and action, engagement is required (Ratts et al., 2016). One theory that encourages active engagement with others is Relational-Cultural Theory (RCT). Grounded in feminism and psychodynamic theories (Kress, Haiyasoso, Zoldan, Headley, & Trepal, 2018), RCT is a developmental theory that centers on the importance and necessity of relationships with others as opposed to psychological individuation and separation. Counselors using RCT may encourage clients to step into situations that can develop diverse growth-fostering relationship characterized by "five good things"; (1) zest, (2) personal and relational clarity, (3) a sense of self-worth, (4) creative and productive capacities, and (5) the desire for more connection (Jordan & Harling, 2010, p.1; Kress et al, 2018). Another key element of RCT is the recognition that disconnections as well as opportunities for growth occur not only on the individual level, but at the sociocultural level (Jordan & Hartling, 2010).

Individuals within a homogeneous culture may isolate from diverse encounters and limit opportunities to develop growth-fostering relationships outside of their culture unit (Kress et al, 2018; Richardson, Hammer & Chan, 2018). RCT theorist warn that the *-isms* can impede all individuals' ability to engage and participate in growth-fostering relationships (Jordan & Hartling, 2010). In this context, implicit bias could be included. Building and fostering relationships is key for gaining cultural competence in counseling (Ratts et al., 2016). Counselors must be aware of the different-isms and forms of unearned advantage that can hinder relational growth and use the tenets of RCT in session to foster mutual empowerment and empathy and cultural competence.

INTRODUCTION TO THE COUNSELORS

Norèal Armstrong: Cultural Background and Counseling Approach

I have decided to share my cultural background in a poem. The poem is an application tool that can be used by counselors in session with clients and with supervisees. *Where I am from* is poem created by George Ella Lyon (1999). The poem has been used for a variety of purposes. In recent years it has been adapted for use in multicultural training courses to help students think and see themselves in culturally novel ways.

Where I am From

I am from books

From Pink oil moisturizer and Old Spice

From the small city with big city dreams (sweet, boring, it felt like fresh line dried sheets covering the bed)

I am from the Rose bush on the side of the house, the sweet scent floating across the kitchen,

I'm from excelling in school and community care,

From Emma-etta, and Richard Learon,

I'm from the knowledge seekers, and the funny ones,

From "Eat, sleep, and study," and "Knowledge is power"

I'm from Hallelujah, salvation, and glory, singing, clapping and shouting my troubles over

I'm from Texarkana and ancestry unknown,

Hot toddy and sweet potato pie.

From the always busy soda pop shop my granddaddy owned,

The robust smile and hardy laugh my Georgia daddy had,

My mom dusting and sweeping to Minnie, Stevie, and Al.

Hanging on the walls, sitting on shelves, our lived experiences framed and out for all to see

Knick-Knacks and scrapbooks keep the family's history

I am from these moments; these moments are me.

I grew up in an average size city in a diverse neighborhood and attended a predominantly black elementary school. By middle school my family's focus on education propelled me to the advanced classes and from then until today I have experienced the world as *the only or one of a few blacks* in a world of whites. I know the world well and I have worked hard to be an agent of change when I see a need. My cultural background taught me valuable lessons that I take with me into my sessions with clients. Working as a Licensed Professional Counselor for 10 years and a supervisor for three, I appreciate the collaboration and lessons learned from working with diverse clients. Growing up Black in America, I encountered some situations that although painful, helped me grow stronger in my self-awareness and personal development. In writing this chapter, I realized that within the counseling room, I didn't feel I had to prove who I was because of my cultural background. While counseling or supervising, I aim to be authentic and purposeful in my actions, to address cultural differences with care, and to create a safe space for clients and supervisees to grow through genuine interactions with someone who is different from them.

Over the years, I have shaped my counseling approach under a Behavioral umbrella with a Rational Emotive Behavior Therapy lens and utilize Narrative Therapy to help clients reach their goals. In addition to the ABCD model, REBT emphasizes unconditional self-acceptance (Turner, 2016). A part of living authentically (Richardson, Hammer, & Chan, 2018) is to acknowledge and accept ourselves without rating and berating based on behaviors and attributes (Sy, 2018; Turner 2016). Unconditional self-acceptance aims to help us remove the conditions upon which we judge ourselves and allows us to "change and grow while still acknowledging we are fallible and worthwhile individuals" (Sy, 2018.). I see counseling as an opportunity to help clients search themselves and find solutions to the issues they face using creative and engaging techniques. In order for counselors to help clients find who they are, we must first know who we are. We cultivate that knowledge through our actions and interactions with others.

Megan Clunan: Cultural Background and Counseling Approach

As a Licensed Professional Counselor and Licensed Mental Health Counselor who supervises post-master's interns, as well as teaches undergraduate and graduate counseling students, one of the big and consistent messages I regularly share is the following: "Do not leave you at the door. However, know you cannot bring you into the counseling room if you do not know yourself!" Knowing oneself is essential to quality therapeutic processes, as without knowing such, not only are the detrimental effects of biases likely, but therapists also "often fail to appreciate the values inherent in simply being themselves" (Corey, 2017, p. 28). I am a firm believer that all of your life experiences up to this point have led you to become the person you are today. Adlerian therapy would support such a notion wherein the view of humanity is one which sees individuals as *indivisible* from the context of life experiences. All that a person is, within any given moment, is created from interconnected elements and experiences. However, the unawareness of such often leaves therapists in a space of not utilizing what tools have naturally been provided. One tool naturally provided is that of culture.

Regarding my culture, two key components to such, are my race and gender. I am a Caucasian female. I am aware that being white automatically puts me in the majority, even if being female pushes me into the marginalized sector of the majority. I understand, even if not in full, the reality of my race signifies I am privileged. This is not to say there have not been times in my life that I have not faced racism or prejudice, because I have.

The majority of my professional career was spent in New Orleans, Louisiana and Miami, Florida. Both cities were cities wherein, although within the United States population this is not the case, I was a minority. I have been told I do not understand, I cannot help, and that my presence is not wanted because of my race or gender. While living in Miami, I saw my daughter (six years old at the time) racially prejudged by children her age because she was "too light" and her brown eyes were not "dark enough." The aforementioned are not all of my experiences, rather they are shared to simply denote that rarely (if ever) will someone go through life without such occurrences. Yet, I still understand my experiences are extremely limited compared to my fellow humans who have lived the broader minority status their whole lives and within generations of such.

Where I live now, in North Carolina, I am a majority. The city I currently live in was the last city to surrender to the North in the Civil War. On my way to work I drive past a few homes that proudly wave the Confederate Flag. This is something new for me and each time I see such a symbol, a part of my heart aches. My heart does not ache for the traditions of the South, as they are rich in history should be honored. My heart aches because the symbol of the Confederate Flag represents a symptom of greater pain for many. A representation which seemingly declares, "We do not care about the humanity that this flag represented, on various levels, the destruction of, nor do we care that the repercussions of the trauma caused by the Civil War are perpetuated by such a symbol." As counselors we are taught to "be mindful of diversity and social justice issues if we are to practice ethically and effectively" (Corey, 2017, p. 44; Lee, 2015), therefore the image of such a symbol does not just cut to my personal understanding of humanity, but into my professional perspective as well.

In fact, after first moving to the city I now live in I remember having a conversation with my colleague that has written this chapter with me about the fact that I was not quite sure what to do in the space that I had been placed. The space being one so very contrary to what my journey had led me through thus far. To which we were able to conclude that it is perhaps because of my race, my majority status, and my past experiences that I have been given such a platform to help initiate healthy change where otherwise change may not be initiated.

Social Psychology states that through the phenomena of *identification* a greater level of receptivity and understanding can be attained, as when people identify with the one sharing a message they are more likely to accept what is shared (Aronson, 2012). In other words, because I am white and now within a predominantly white cultural context I have a unique opportunity to speak out and be heard in ways minority individuals may not. The minority race may struggle to be heard even if sharing similar concepts, not because the message is different, but because they will likely be received differently (if at all) by a majority audience. For example, within counseling, if the client perceives a counselor to be similar to themselves there is a greater sense of comfort due to perceived common ground. Specifically, if one finds another to be appealing in some way, the inclination to believe and accept influence from that individual is greater (Aronson, 2012).

My experiences as a minority in the cities mentioned above and the reality that I have a unique perspective and platform where I currently am, have shaped the passions I have for counseling and educating others to never underestimate the value that is YOU. Therapists need to knowingly bring themselves into the counseling room. One's privileged or marginalized status *will* impact the therapeutic relationship; the impact being detrimental when unknown, but powerful when understood (Ratts et al., 2016). Additionally, I greatly stand on the premise that all people are intrinsically valuable: a part of what constitutes one's value being the culture from which one has come. Therefore, the concept of continuing to cultivate courageous cultural conversations is consistently a part of my counseling pedagogy. To counsel toward cultural awareness with clients I utilize concepts from Systems Theory, Experiential, and Solution Focused Theories, each of which will be explored further in the following pages.

CASE CONCEPTUALIZATION

Why the MSJCC

The MSJCC was endorsed in 2015 by the American Counseling Association (ACA), as a revision of the Multicultural Counseling Competencies (MCCs) by Sue, Arredondo, and McDavis (1992). Changes from the MSJCC include increased attention on counselor and client attitudes regarding marginalization and privilege, as well as action, for practical implementation of each domain. The four domains within MSJCC are (1) *Counselor Self-Awareness*; (2) *Client Worldview*; (3) *Counseling Relationship*; and (4) *Counseling and Advocacy Interventions*. Within each domain four subheadings exist to further elaborate on the primary domain identified. The four subheadings within each are (1) *Attitudes and Beliefs*; (2) *Knowledge*; (3) *Skills*; and (4) *Action*.

Noticeably, a key component differentiating the MSJCC from the former MCCs is that of *action*. The MSJCC provides steps throughout the competencies, for taking action, while developing cultural competence (Ratts et al., 2016). In addition to those steps, counselors are responsible for modeling and empowering clients to act and increase their knowledge by gaining new experiences. Cultural competence is no longer sufficient by itself. Simply knowing individual biases, or the various microaggressions of one culture toward another, is irrelevant without *action*. The only thing racism, discrimination, and hatred of fellow humans on the basis anything that makes one different from another, need in order to thrive is inaction (i.e. complacency). Arguably, knowledge without action is a silence which promotes such evils' thriving. Competent counselors "understand that when culturally responsive counseling is integrated with action, they become better equipped to address clients' concerns" (Ratts et al., 2016, p. 42).

Therefore, through the lens of the MSJCC, our client, Harper is invited into greater awareness and empowered toward action of developing cultural competence. In a focused clinical effort to help increase Harper's level of awareness, knowledge, skill, and action (Ratts et al., 2016), solution focused techniques, experiential interventions, and a psychoeducational group therapy process are implemented.

Solution Focused Techniques

Unlike other clients, Harper had a firm deadline. Her move was fast approaching and we needed to know we had provided her with greater clarity of self-awareness prior to her move. Therefore, we integrated a solution focused technique, *A Personal Letter on Biases*, into her individual sessions to promote further self-awareness. The rationale for choosing such an intervention was based on the premise of solution focused therapy, which is the theory that individuals get stuck in unresolved past perceptions or problems and therein become blocked in being able to move forward into future solutions.

To counsel Harper toward further self-awareness, for the sake of addressing past perceptions, Harper was given the homework assignment of *A Personal Letter on Biases*. Harper needed to be able to articulate her biases, so she could know what may have been underlying various misperceptions fueling the various fears she had regarding diversity. After all, one cannot change what one does not know!

The *Personal Letter on Biases* assignment was provided to Harper as a way to further accomplish her identified goal one (see Treatment outline on following pages). The assignment was as follows:

Write yourself a personal letter regarding your understanding of how biases, which exist presently or previously within your life developed. Choose, at minimum, one race, one gender, and one faith which differs from your own to address. To help ensure your letter is as thorough as possible try to include the following: (1) personal identification of privileged or marginalized status; (2) discussion of any preconceived notions you hold presently, or have held in the past, regarding each identified individual or group, which differs from you; (3) notation of how your identified biases were learned (i.e., family or cultural influences; who/what taught you to believe certain things about those that are different from you; earliest age you can remember when you began to think certain ways; any spoken biases; any unspoken biases); (4) examination of how personal biases regarding each of your noted categories (race, gender, faith) have impacted your life, relationships, and decisions; and (5) exploration regarding whether or not you have broken away from previously held biases (if so, how so? If not, how do they continue to impact you?).

Once the letter was written we took the time to process the information Harper shared. For some clients this process can be completed within one session, however for Harper it was over the course of two sessions. We addressed numbers one through three within one session and numbers four and five within another. We encourage you, counselor, not to hurry through this process, as the self-awareness factor is necessary in order for clients to consciously understand the various blocks or anxieties they may feel when facing the unknown.

Experiential Interventions

To address Harper's second goal (see Treatment Plan on following pages) we incorporated experiential interventions into her treatment. In an effort to provide Harper with more growth opportunities, she was challenged to find and attend a cultural event, agency, or festival in her city. She was provided a list of places that included, various faith-based institutions, behavioral residential schools, drug rehabilitation centers, cultural festivals, mental health clinics, and residential treatments. The aim was for Harper to immerse herself in a situation that was different from her daily lived experiences. Experiential activities are recognized by counselor educators as important to the education and training of counselor trainees (Kim & Lyons, 2003). Furthermore, "experiential activities are powerful means to stimulate multicultural awareness and can be used the help individuals confront and overcome racial-ethnic bias" (Kim & Lyons, 2003, p. 402).

Knowing that the use of experiential activities could help Harper meet her needs, the counselors decided to use her attending and engaging in conversation with someone at the event as an experiential activity. This was Harper's *Immersion Experience*. Harper was to attend an event or festival for a minimum of two hours, actively participant in the event and find members of the cultural group to speak with. Once that was completed, Harper was to summarize her experience and address the following; (a) what she felt and thought leading up the event, (b) the experience of attending and talking with new people, (c) how it connects to her ability to grow in her cultural awareness, and (d) how participating in an event like this could help her in the future. By completing this task, Harper took action toward becoming more culturally competent and less fearful of new people and experiences. For counselors in training "immersing oneself in the communities in which privilege and marginalized clients reside to work through the discomfort that comes with learning about privileged and marginalized clients," (Ratts et al., 2016, p. 8).

For her *Immersion Experience,* Harper decided to attend a drug rehabilitation treatment center. She admitted to choosing this place because she was aware she had a bias against people who abuse substances. Harper visited the center on two different occasions. During her initial visit, she was able to observe groups and then had an unexpected, yet meaningful conversation with one of the patients. Harper expressed her surprise by how much personal information the client shared with her during this first meeting, but was appreciative of the exposure and experience. After Harper's visits she was able to share and process her feelings, thoughts, fears and beliefs from the experience in the safety of the counseling room.

Psychoeducational Group

Systems theory understands individuals as parts of a larger whole – even if subsystems within themselves. When one change in a subsystem is made the reverberating effects create varying, and hopefully healthy, change elsewhere (Minuchin, 1993). A great arena in which to practice systems interaction and change is that of the psychoeducational group setting Corey, 2017). Therefore, for the sake of addressing Harper's second goal with a different approach, the psychoeducational group was determined beneficial as a therapeutic intervention for Harper. The aim of the psychoeducational group was to bring Harper together with other clients from diverse backgrounds: age, ethnicity, gender, sexual orientation, socioeconomic status, nation of origin, and employment to share their lived experiences dealing with current issues in society. The purpose was to have Harper engage with a heterogeneous group of clients so she could see both the similarities and differences they shared and how those differences developed and affected the daily lives of others. The overall intent was for Harper's knowledge of others and interacting with others to expand and elicit a desire to continue living a more action focused, diverse life. The group also provided a safe place for clients who had experienced injustice, inequity, and marginalization to share their stories, listen to others, and engage in solution building.

In preparing for the psychoeducational group, this author, Dr. Armstrong, invited clients whose stories could be helpful for Harper, a client of international origin, a client who is a member of the LGBTQ+ community, and a few clients of different ethnic race and gender. All clients in attendance signed consent forms and agreed to keep confidentiality. The group had three parts and met over three group sessions. Part one was icebreakers and shared stories. During part one, everyone was asked to randomly select a greeting card, pair up and answer three questions, (a) what is your name, (b) what do you do, and (c) why did you pick this card? They had five minutes to move about the room and meet as many new people as they could. Once the five minutes were up, whomever they were standing with at the moment became their "partner." They had to sit by their new partner and share what they had learned about that person. The group processed what was new learning and how the process led to understanding others who present differently.

Part two was Q&A about hot topics. The hot topics included questions about power, privilege, oppression, and current events. Videos, social media posts, and news stories were used to elicit conversations. Participants were asked directly, if they had experienced any situations of privilege or marginalization and were able to share their stories, answer questions, and respond to others. Harper was quiet during much of this group, but this author later learned; through a personal reflection that Harper was listening to understand and was still a little fearful of sharing about her anxiety and fears.

Part three was the privilege walk. This author, Dr. Armstrong, like many therapists having gone through a counselor education program, has used the privilege walk in a multicultural class. As a clinician, this author felt it would work just as well in a psychoeducational group. All clients were asked to line up across the floor and to hold hands. As various questions pertaining to privilege and marginalization were read, the goal was to take a step backward or forward while trying to still hold hands. Eventually, some hands had to be release in order to move. By the last question many were surprised by where they ended and what that meant for not only them, but how it can help them relate to others. As the clinician, this author did not have to elicit conversation; the clients had developed trust, shared freely, engaged with one another, and offered their thoughts on what it all meant.

By the end of the group, everyone felt positive about the experience and what they learned about themselves and others. Harper was able to see the value in engaging with others different from you and why it is important to develop cultural competence.

Other Theories or Principles

As noted above, the authors have integrated the MSJCC into Harper's clinical care through the use of solutions focused techniques, experiential interventions and a psychoeducational group. However, additional theories and principles exist for counselors to utilize when guiding clients toward cultural competence and awareness.

Consoli, Kim, and Meyer (2008) address the process of aiding clients in creating a value profile for the sake of further understanding oneself and others. *Values* are concepts which are intrinsic in nature and typically guiding principles of one's life. Values are expressed in the personal, professional, and interpersonal lives of individuals and often established within one's cultural context. Counselor and client behaviors flow from one's held value system. However, where personal values go unexamined, the *why* behind certain behaviors or sentiments often remain unknown.

Additionally, Erikson and Abernethy (2014) discuss a grace based approach to multicultural awareness in diversity counseling. Erikson and Abernethy (2014) shares, it is through a grace based approach of helping clients examine various *isms* healthy change can begin to occur. *Ism* is a suffix, that when added to a word (i.e., race, sex, age, etc.) denotes discrimination or prejudice (Berg-Weger, 2016). Addressing *isms* not only brings awareness, but motivation for active change to prevent and advocate against such. The rationale for addressing client *isms* within the therapeutic process comes from an understanding that when differences remain unacknowledged micro-aggressions and minimization of another's experience can occur, therein creating (at worst) or maintaining (at best) prejudice. A risk of addressing *isms* is noted, as individuals engage in this journey and awareness of their own *isms* increases, this becomes difficult to tolerate and challenges their self-image, therefore often identity work apart from long-held beliefs must also be incorporated into the counseling process (Erikson & Abernethy, 2014, p. 180).

An additional principle relevant to Harper's case is Relational-Cultural Theory (RCT). The five good things, previously mentioned are outcomes of growth fostering relationships developed when growth occurs through mutual empowerment and mutual empathy (Kress et al, 2018), people can grow toward greater mutuality and empathic possibility (Jordan & Hartling, 2010). A central tenet of RCT is that people develop through and toward relationship, which happens and is influenced by a cultural context (Jordan & Hartling, 2010). Counselors can empower clients to move toward cultural competence and action by creating opportunities for clients to build diverse and mutual relationships. Through our counseling sessions, Harper was able to build diverse and mutual relationships with her counselors and larger heterogeneous community.

TREATMENT

Goals

After assessing Harper's concerns, perceived lack of cultural awareness, and her desire to feel better about the move, the counselors' developed the following treatment plan (Table 1). Harper's treatment plan was developed utilizing solution focus strategies, experiential activities, and psychoeducational groups. The strategies and activities below can also be helpful for counselors and counselors in training to multicultural and social justice competence through knowledge, awareness, skills, and action (Ratts et al., 2016).

Table 1. Harper's treatment plan

Treatment Plan	Harper Session: 5 Date:
Problem 1:	Fear of leaving comfort of a homogeneous cultural community.
Provisional Diagnosis	V62.89 Other problem related to psychosocial circumstances; V15.89 Other personal risk factors.
Goal 1:	Client will increase knowledge of biases and perceptions of others from different backgrounds.
Objective 1:	Client will complete a My Cultural Awareness Profile (MyCAP) survey.
Objective 2:	Client will write *A Personal Letter on Biases* In session, the client will process the values, beliefs, and thoughts that developed.
Objective 3:	Client will complete homework assignments to further explore personal biases and identify origin of development.
Goal 2:	Client will increase interactions and work to understand people who are different than her.
Objective 1:	Client will attend a cultural event (i.e., festival, church service, play, etc.), engage in conversations, and journal about her experience and what she learned. *Immersion Experience*
Objective 2:	After completion of the objectives above, the client will participate in cultural competence psychoeducational group with women and men from different backgrounds.

Harper's goals were aimed at helping her address the implicit bias (Boysen, 2010) that developed due to her lack of interaction with people different from her. Living in a homogeneous (white, middle class, Christian) community provided Harper unearned privilege (Jordan & Hartline, 2010) and safety from the challenges of coexisting and accepting others. In order to be comfortable and confident in her upcoming move to Washington, D.C., Harper had to step out her comfort zone. The treatment began with Harper identifying and addressing what biases she had. In Harper's case, her worldview had not been explored or questioned.

Harper was given the My Cultural Awareness Profile (MyCAP) (Marx, 2011). MyCAP is a self-reflection tool most notably used to support teacher educators' in training culturally and globally aware teachers. It is comprised of 40 survey and short essay questions and assesses knowledge, beliefs, and understandings across four domains of cultural awareness: (1) Exploring the global world, (2) Learning about different cultures, (3) Knowing ourselves as cultural, and (4) Communicating across cultural differences (Marx, 2011). The MyCAP survey was a sufficient tool to help Harper assess her cultural awareness level. Next, Harper completed *A Personal Letter on Biases* assignment, participated in the *Immersion Experience* and actively engaged in the cultural psychoeducational group.

Progress

As Harper neared the end of counseling, we reviewed her goals, her progress, and her plan for the future. In the initial stages of treatment, Harper fought to stay surface level. She wrote down biases that were akin to stereotypes instead of her true feelings. In session, I, Dr. Armstrong, used myself in relation with Harper to help her uncover her thoughts about blacks and black women. During the process, we would check in on her comfort level to not push too far, too fast. We also modeled understanding and care by not treating her differently after she shared her true feelings. By being open and honest we provided an example of how honest connection with others can lead to growth and mutual empowerment (Jordan & Hartling, 2010) within ourselves. Through the creation and processing through of the *Personal Letter on Biases* Harper was able to develop insight into the fact that her anxieties stemmed from a lack of understanding, as well as previous modeling. She shared comments like, "I never thought of myself as prejudiced or discriminatory, but when I thought about individuals of different races and realized I felt uneasy, I realized that is what it is." One explored experience was well articulated by Harper, as she stated,

After all our talking about implicit bias and after looking at the questions that asked me to consider how I may have learned to think a certain way about different people I have one experience that seems to stand out. I can remember my parents talking

to me about how 'birds of feather flock together,' which I never took as bias, but now see that that thought caused me to think that if someone doesn't look like me then maybe I shouldn't be around them or share life with them. My parents would often say that if they saw a biracial couple out in public.

Through the solution focused tool of the personal letter, the goal being to get Harper to actively see where her thoughts and feelings were originating, Harper was able to become aware where previously she was uncomfortable and stuck.

Additionally, the *Immersion Experience* allowed Harper to engage with a group of people she held prior bias towards and encounter the diversity within the drug rehabilitation setting. In session, Harper reflected, "I was shocked at how comfortable he was telling me about his past and all he had been through. I was honored that he felt safe with me and it was cool to learn he was a believer." Through her individual time with this patient and observing groups, Harper was able to focus more on shared commonalities and experiences and less on how they were different. One of her final comments in her summary stated, "I am happy I came and realized my faith isn't a barrier but a bridge to building new relationships and I hope the patient I spoke with felt the same." Harper was able to understand how our differences can be used positively and for personal and professional growth.

Finally, the psychoeducational groups gave Harper an opportunity to engage directly with men and women of diverse backgrounds. In the first group session after sharing responses from the icebreaker activity, Harper commented, "There is so much you don't know just by seeing a person." During the next groups, while discussing hot topics, Harper was more reserved and didn't share much. It was during these groups where members were challenged to address their experiences with unearned privilege and marginalization. Harper later share that she felt a little overwhelmed in those groups because she had not experience marginalization to the same extreme and the other group members. By the last groups, Harper had a bond with one group member because they shared a few similar lived experiences. They both enjoyed the privilege walk and were surprised and where everyone stood by the end. The purpose of the activity was to show Harper and her group mates, that we all have ebbs and flows of privilege and marginalization, we experience privilege and marginalization in different ways, and we all shape our beliefs differently based on those experiences.

Overall, Harper was motivation to see a change in her life. She attended session regularly, completed the homework, pushed passed her desire to stay within the comfort of her homogeneous culture and successfully completed her goals.

CONCLUSION

The authors found integrating current issues and addressing the intersectionality of humanity in the therapeutic setting, as a valuable tool to elicit cultural growth and competence. Through examining Harper's case study, the authors hope to have provided readers with interactive and conceptual applications for eliciting cultural growth and competence wherein complacency due to unknown privilege and implicit complacency may have formerly existed.

Through hard work, patience, and the use of integrative therapeutic techniques, Harper was able to decrease her fears of moving and engaging with people of diverse backgrounds. Harper became more self-aware, self-assured, and open to learning about herself through experiencing life within a heterogeneous community. Using group therapy, experiential activities, and solution focused interventions, the authors were able to teach, model, and provide Harper with strategies she can continue to use while in Washington, D.C. It is the authors' hope that Harper shared the lessons she learned in counseling with those in her community so that they might forge past the comfort of complacency.

REFERENCES

Aronson, E. (2012). *The social animal* (11th ed.). New York, NY: Worth Publishers.

Berg-Weger, M. (2016). *Social work and social welfare: An invitation* (4th ed.). New York, NY: Routledge.

Boysen, G. (2010). Integrating implicit bias into counselor education. *Counselor Education and Supervision*, *49*(4), 210–277. doi:10.1002/j.1556-6978.2010.tb00099.x

Consoli, A., Kim, B., & Meyer, D. (2008). Counselor values profile: Implication for counseling ethnic minority clients. *Counseling and Values*, *52*(3), 181–197. doi:10.1002/j.2161-007X.2008.tb00103.x

Constantine, M., Smith, L., Redington, R., & Owens, D. (2008). Racial microaggressions against Black counseling and counseling psychology faculty: A central challenge in the multicultural counseling movement. *Journal of Counseling and Development*, *86*(3), 348–355. doi:10.1002/j.1556-6678.2008.tb00519.x

Constantine, M. G., Hage, S. M., Kindaichi, M. M., & Bryant, R. M. (2007). Social justice and multicultural issues: Implications for the practice and training of counselors and counseling psychologist. *Journal of Counseling and Development*, *85*(1), 24–29. doi:10.1002/j.1556-6678.2007.tb00440.x

Corey, G. (2017). *Theory and practice of counseling and psychotherapy* (10th ed.). Boston, MA: Cengage.

Erikson, C., & Abernethy, A. (2014). Integration in multicultural competence and diversity training: Engaging difference and grace. *Journal of Psychology and Theology*, *42*(2), 174–187. doi:10.1177/009164711404200205

Greenwald, A., McGhee, D., & Schwartz, J. (1998). Measuring individual difference in implicit cognition: The Implicit Association Test. *Journal of Personality and Social Psychology*, *74*(6), 1464–1480. doi:10.1037/0022-3514.74.6.1464 PMID:9654756

Jordan, J. V., & Hartling, L. M. (2010). *The development of relational-cultural theory*. Jean Baker-Miller Training Institute. Retrieved from https://www.researchgate.net/publication/247836552_The_Development_of_Relational-Cultural_Theory

Kim, B. S., & Lyons, H. Z. (2003). Experiential activities and multicultural counseling competence training. *Journal of Counseling and Development*, *81*(4), 400–408. doi:10.1002/j.1556-6678.2003.tb00266.x

Kress, V. E., Haiyasoso, M., Zoldan, C. A., Headley, J. A., & Trepal, H. (2018). The use of relational-cultural theory in counseling clients who have traumatic stress disorders. *Journal of Counseling and Development, 96*, 106-114. doi:10.1002/jcad.12182

Lee, C. (2015). Social justice and counseling across cultures. In B. Helihy & G. Corey (Eds.), *ACA ethical standards casebook* (7th ed.; pp. 155–168). Alexandria, VA: American Counseling Association.

Lyon, G. E. (1999). *Where I am from: Where poems come from.* Retrieved from https://www.sausd.us/cms/lib/CA01000471/Centricity/Domain/3043/I%20Am%20From%20Poem.pdf

Marx, H. A., & Moss, D. M. (2011). *My cultural awareness profile (MyCAP): A cultural awareness reflection tool for pre-service teachers*. Retrieved from http://www.nafsa.org/_/File/_/mycap_tool.pdf

Minuchin, S. (1993). *Family healing: Strategies for hope and understanding*. New York, NY: The Free Press.

Priester, P. E., Jones, J. E., Jackson-Bailey, C. M., Jana-Masri, A., Jordan, E. X., & Metz, A. J. (2008). An analysis of content and instructional strategies in multicultural counseling courses. *Journal of Multicultural Counseling and Development*, *36*(1), 29–39. doi:10.1002/j.2161-1912.2008.tb00067.x

Ratts, M., Singh, A., Nassar-McMillan, S., Butler, K., & McCullough, J. (2016). *Multicultural and social justice counseling competencies*. Alexandria, VA: American Counseling Association.

Richardson, L. L. H., Hammer, T. R., & Chan, C. D. (2018, September). Relational-cultural theory: A social justice perspective of career development in the workplace. *Career Convergence*. Retrieved from https://www.ncda.org/aws/NCDA/pt/sd/news_article/185956/_PARENT/CC_layout_details/false

Sue, D., Arredondo, P., & McDavis, R. (1992). Multicultural counseling competencies and standards: A call to the profession. *Journal of Multicultural Counseling and Development*, *70*(4), 477–486. doi:10.1002/j.1556-6676.1992.tb01642.x

Sue, D., Capodilupo, C., Torino, G., Bucceri, J., Holder, A., Nadal, K., & Esquilin, M. (2007). Racial microaggressions in everyday life: Implications for clinical practice. *The American Psychologist*, *62*(4), 271–286. doi:10.1037/0003-066X.62.4.271 PMID:17516773

Sy, M. (2018). A myth about unconditional self-acceptance [Web log post]. Retrieved from http://albertellis.org/a-myth-about-unconditional-self-acceptance/

Turner, M. J. (2016). Rational emotive behavior therapy, irrational and rational beliefs and the mental health of athletes. *Frontiers in Psychology*, *7*(1423), 1–16. doi:10.3389/fpsyg.2016.01423 PMID:27703441

Chapter 10
Deepa's Discovery:
An Examination of Intersectionality When Multiple Identities Collide – Managing Family Roles, Doctoral Work, and Clashing Eurocentric Worldviews

John J. S. Harrichand
https://orcid.org/0000-0002-3336-2062
The College at Brockport (SUNY), USA

Krista Kirk
Liberty University, USA

Joy Maweu Mwendwa
Liberty University, USA

EXECUTIVE SUMMARY

This chapter seeks to bring awareness to the multiple identities that international (graduate/doctoral counseling) students bring to college and university campuses. The multiple identities are examined through the intersectionality paradigm and the RESPECTFUL model, and apply the Multicultural and Social Justice Counseling Competencies (MSJCC). It is intended to help counselors-in-training, counselor educators, supervisors, and administrators examine current intrapersonal, interpersonal, institutional, community, public, international/global views, and potential roles related to working with clients/students/peers who comprise our growing international student population.

DOI: 10.4018/978-1-7998-0022-4.ch010

INTRODUCTION

The reasons why students pursue international study are vast and well-known. These reasons include an opportunity to explore a different culture, explore new thinking and behavior, and to improve cross-cultural knowledge and skills (Andrade, 2006; Elsharnouby, 2016; Hendrickson, Rosen, & Aune, 2011; McClure, 2007). According to the Student Exchange Visitor Program's (SEVP; U.S. Immigration and Customs Enforcement, 2018) April 2018 report, there were 1.2 million international students in the United States (U.S.) on F and M visas (F visas allow students to attend an academic institution while an M visa is reserved for students who are seeking training at a technical or trade school). The SEVP provides foreign nationals including students, and in some cases their spouse and children under the age of 21 years old, temporary admission into the U.S. to pursue a full course of academic study from an approved SEVP school or vocational or other recognized nonacademic institution (U.S. Immigration and Customs Enforcement, 2018). In 2018, eighty-five percent of international students were enrolled in associate's, bachelor's, master's, or doctoral programs; this is over a 36% increase from the number of international students studying in the U.S. a decade ago (Institute of International Education, 2018). Additionally, international students represent a significant portion of the student body in the U.S.' graduate programs (Nayar-Bhalerao, 2014; Woo, Jang, & Henfield, 2015), with an enrollment in approximately 50% of the Council for Accreditation of Counseling and Related Educational Programs (CACREP) programs (Ng, 2006). International counseling students can provide unique benefits for counseling programs because they require counselor educators to gear pedagogies to a more holistic classroom learning environment, heightening multicultural awareness for all counseling students (Behl, Laux, Roseman, & Tiamiyu, 2017). Furthermore, well trained international counseling students can return to their countries of origin to promote mental health wellness among fellow natives (Ng, 2006). Although there are many advantages to studying in a new country, international graduate students also report experiencing several difficulties when adjusting to a new country and its cultural expectations.

LITERATURE REVIEW

It can be argued that international students are part of the fabric of American society, yet their challenges go unheard and unmet (Burlew & Alleyne, 2010; Coates & Dickinson, 2012; Hyun, Quinn, Madon & Lustig, 2007; Rai, 2002). Some of the distinct experiences of international students include acculturative stress, social isolation and rejection, discrimination, homesickness, language-related issues (Arthur,

2004; Leon & Chmiel, 2013), racial and ethnic microaggressions (Houshmand, Spanierman, & Tafarodi, 2014; Ng & Smith, 2009) and the limited opportunities for clinical experience because of their speech-accent (Mittal & Wieling, 2006; Ng & Smith, 2009). Specifically, the acculturative stress experienced by international students can affect academic performance and competency in their eventual workplaces (Sherry, Thomas, & Chui, 2010).

The term acculturative stress can be defined as psychological stress associated with interpersonal issues (e.g., perceived discrimination, social isolation, inferiority, homesickness) and external factors (e.g., culture shock, communication barriers; Sandhu & Asrabadi, 1994). Although most international students experience this stress, international students from non-European countries appear to face more of these issues than those from European countries (Houshmand et al., 2014; Sherry et al., 2009). Furthermore, Lee and Rice (2007) found that international students of color felt discriminated against by traditional students, and that these traditional students believed students of European descent were considered to have the same values as U.S. Americans, thereby treating students of color differently than their European counterparts. In this particular study, these international students of color felt that the stereotyping by faculty and other students was due to a lack of knowledge about their culture, and these faculty and students failed to acknowledge the benefits that other cultures can bring to their institutions and programs. With more than half of the international students in the U.S. representing eastern and African countries (Institute of International Education, 2018), the lack of intentionality by those in the host country can only perpetuate this sense of isolation and discrimination (Houshmand et al., 2014; Leon & Chmiel, 2013). Some authors are even reporting that on top of, or perhaps as a result of these perpetuating issues, international students can also experience mental health challenges, such as psychosomatic complaints, psychological distress, depression, and anxiety (Forbes-Mewett & Sawyer, 2016; Prieto-Welch, 2016; Valencia-Garcia, Simoni, Alegria, & Takeuchi, 2012; Yoon et al., 2013).

The examination of acculturation experiences of international students suggests that adaptation may be different for some than others (Sakamoto, 2007). Among those international students of color, approximately one-third of them are female (United Press, 2011), and although no citation could be found to detail how many of these female international students in the U.S. are also mothers, one lone statistic suggested that one in 20 international female students also brought their dependent children alongside them while studying in the United Kingdom (UKCISA, 2004). It can be assumed that there is a much larger number of international student-mothers who chose not to bring their children to the host country. This large number of international student-mothers is given little to no attention in the current literature, yet the complexity within the intersectionality of their roles deserves a deeper investigation.

The phenomenon of intersectionality has many components. It is a way of understanding the conditions surrounding an individual and how the self is shaped by those multiple factors (Collins & Bilge, 2016; Crenshaw, 1991). Studies of international students' families suggest that traditional gender role expectations force adaptations on both parents (Dion & Dion, 2002), aiding in identity confusion in light of the intersection of traditional values with the host society's values (Lim, Honey, DuToit, Chen, & Mckenzie, 2016). For international student-mothers who are struggling with adapting to a new social and physical environment, in addition to the school/work transition (Myers-Walls, Frias, Kwon, Meryl Ko, & Lu, 2011), mental health challenges experienced by most international students can be exacerbated.

The role and perception of a mother has morphed over the past thirty years, trending towards more egalitarian gender roles (Donnelly et al., 2015). Yet working outside the home has illuminated many challenges that mothers are still facing when attempting to find a balance of their multiple-life roles (von Borell de Araujo, Tureta, & von Borell de Araujo, 2015). Although there is a dearth of literature on international student-mothers, many studies have investigated the experiences of traditional student-mothers and suggest that having children is a factor associated with attrition (Brown & Nichols, 2012; Dickson & Tennant, 2018; Lynch, 2008; Mason, Goulden, & Frasch, 2009; McLaughlin & Randolph, 2012). Meeting the needs of child attachment through emotional availability and responsiveness (Belsky, Houts, & Pasco Fearon, 2010; Pasco Fearon & Belsky, 2011; Hsiao, Koren-Karie, Bailey, & Moran, 2015; Sung et al., 2016), while still attending to work/school responsibilities, can foster what Blair-Loy (2003) considers competing cognitive schemas, suggesting that only a few mothers are able to combine work and motherhood without cognitive dissonance.

The complexities of navigating the intersectionality of multiple life roles can be challenging for many. With the rise of working and international-student mothers, counselors are tasked with the responsibility of utilizing innovative counseling approaches to help this population develop an overall wellness for both them and their families. The mental health challenges that appear to accompany the expectations of international student-mothers urge counselors to obtain the necessary skills needed to competently engage with this culturally sensitive population. The case study presented follows the journey and experiences of Deepa, an international student in the U.S. from India. Deepa's experiences reflect much of the challenges discussed in the literature, thus resulting in a proposed treatment plan. The conceptualization of the case utilizes the MSJCC (Ratts et al., 2015) and the RESPECTFUL model (D'Andrae and Daniels, 2001); together, they help focus the counselors' attention to the intersecting identities impacting Deepa's psychological and social development, thereby promoting her personal well-being through intentional treatment planning. Furthermore, Cognitive Behavioral Therapy (CBT) has been identified as an effective mode of treatment within cross-cultural contexts (David, Stefan, Terracciano, 2018; Hinton, Rivera, Hoffman, Barlow, & Otto, 2012; Kananian, Ayoughi, Farugie, Hinton, & Stangier, 2017; Tang, Li, Rodger, & Ballou, 2016); therefore the utilization of interventions from CBT's framework are adapted to incorporate the RESPECTFUL model's conceptualization of Deepa, as seen throughout the treatment plan.

INTRODUCTION TO THE COUNSELORS

The first author is a Christian, son, brother, friend, counselor, and educator. I am of Chinese and East Indian origins, born and raised in Guyana, South America, a Canadian by citizenship, and a foreign worker in the U.S. My cultural identity is heavily influenced by Eastern practices, which places a high value on the role of family (nuclear and extended), and respecting all individuals, most notably my elders who are the keepers of traditions and customs. Cognitive-behavioral theory (CBT) guides my theoretical approach to counseling, while my practical approach incorporates aspects of developmental, person-centered, gestalt, and family systems with CBT. I believe counseling is a process where I have the honor of accompanying other souls on the journey through life, sharing joy and pain, while moving towards wholeness and growth. This is realized and facilitated through my expression of love, i.e., acceptance, genuineness, and empathy in the counseling relationship.

The second author was born and raised in Upstate New York by a first-generation immigrant from India and a second-generation immigrant from Lebanon. As a child, there was such complexity when attempting to define my cultural identity; I was often confronted with the question, "so, what ethnicity are you?" I was raised in a household of family members who cherished their cultural roots and I value the dynamics that emerge when multiple cultural groups exist within one society. I am continually placing myself in a position to glean from those I counsel and to contribute to the multicultural awareness of those I teach. I am multifaceted in my approach to counseling and find that eclectic therapy can be helpful when navigating the complexities of the counseling journey. As a wife, a mother, and a counselor educator, I recognize the challenges involved in functioning with multiple roles. Thus, I find it to be a privilege to be in a therapeutic relationship with those who are seeking overall wellness. I believe in creating a supportive and collaborative space to open the door for meaningful change.

The third author was born in Midwest America to Kenyan parents who had come to America in pursuit of higher education. All of my formative years were lived at home in Kenya where I developed fluency in three languages: Kikamba, Kiswahili, and English. I returned to America, my other home, as a late teen, soon after I started college. My international experiences have allowed for a more intimate understanding to international student barriers. While I do have an American passport, I also navigate my professional and personal worlds via a multicultural lens. Over the years, I have returned to Kenya and to other parts of Africa to be with family, as well as for humanitarian, mission outreach, and service experiences. Currently, I serve as a counselor, counselor educator, counseling supervisor, informal and formal mentor in my local community, and as an advocate for different minority groups. For the last five years, I have formally and informally served as the International Student Liaison for the counseling department at Liberty University. I find it an honor to sit or stand across a client or a group of students. I see my role as a counselor as a sacred invitation from a client to listen, empathize, and help another human being who could be sitting at my seat. Clinically, I operate via cognitive-behavioral and person-centered theories, and infuse proverbs, storytelling, and other indigenous innovative interventions in the collaborative scripts with my clients.

CASE STUDY

This chapter's case study will center around Deepa, a female international student from India who is starting her first semester as a doctoral student in a competitive counselor education program in the south-eastern part of the United States. Her faculty supervisor refers her to see a counselor in the college counseling center after she expresses anxiety connected to the culture shock of learning in a new educational system, adjusting to living in the a new country, facing the challenges of being a new minority and having clashing ethnocentric worldviews, lacking the support of her family and community, and juggling the roles of expectant mother and busy doctoral student, all while simultaneously holding teaching assistant responsibilities.

Deepa's Case

Deepa is a first-year doctoral student in a competitive counselor education program in the south-eastern part of United States. Her home country is India where all her family reside including her husband, a business man, who has been left behind as the sole financial support for her during this time of settling down in the States. Her husband is also working to obtain an independent entrepreneur/business visa in order to join his wife while she pursues her dream of being a global counseling leader. Additionally, Deepa is pregnant and in the end of her second trimester. She has had a healthy pregnancy thus far, however, she is very anxious about her roles as a new mother and a doctoral student. Although it was a difficult decision to start school alone and pregnant, she did not wish to forgo the opportunity, especially in light of the fact that "the girl child" in her semi-rural community does not come by these chances often. Motherhood has been a personal desire for Deepa and she is meeting the expectation of bearing an heir for their family and community. She is the first born of four daughters and continually acknowledges the responsibility to set a good example for her younger sisters, two of whom are engaged to be married – an expensive season for their family.

As the eldest daughter, with the highest education level, who possesses marital status, and now lives in the first world, Deepa does not take for granted this opportunity. She is aware that advanced education is a privilege that many women in her community will never attain. While her family and community have strongly encouraged her academic advancement through her first and second degrees in education and career counselling respectively, the topic of mental health is still stigmatized. Notwithstanding, Deepa chose to pursue a counselor education doctoral degree for several reasons. First, the degree seemed to fit her academic and professional background as a career counselor at the district level where she served both within the college setting, as well as, a team member on mental health rural initiatives with the World Health Education (WHO). Second, Deepa believes that having more educators and counselors is a part of the solution in addressing mental health stigmatization in India. Finally, her personal experiences as a career counselor have led her to many formal and informal interactions that have called for advanced counseling training.

Deepa just found out that she has been awarded a teaching assistantship, which will alleviate the financial burden of tuition to allow her husband to join her. Nevertheless, it raises the concern of how she will manage this additional role, especially as she has been feeling tired after attending class and doing all of her homework. Even though she used to be a high school teacher and college career counselor in her home country, she is extremely anxious about teaching her Human Services undergraduate class. Deepa manages to talk to her husband daily but when there are prolonged shortages of electricity and Wi-Fi back home, she is unable to reach him. Deepa soon realizes that her husband is unable to accurately sympathize with her current school stressors due to the limited context he has since he is in a non-academic field, and has never traveled to America.

You work at the college counseling center where Deepa is referred by her faculty supervisor to see you. One of the notes on the referral highlights the request that Deepa would prefer working with a female counselor. In her intake, Deepa expresses two reasons for coming to see you: 1.) sadness and feelings of loneliness without having any family or support, and (2.) fear that her views will not be welcomed in her classes because she has a different education and cultural background. There is rising anxiety in teaching her classes, too, which currently has her preparing 2 – 4 hours a night to find American examples and synonyms for different words, should she be misunderstood in her lectures.

In your first session, she shares that she is concerned that her accent may get in the way of teaching and communicating accurately. She is fearful that she will be reported to the program director and subsequently lose her assistantship – hindering her husband coming to be with her. Considering she sees this as a once in a lifetime opportunity to study in America, she states that she would feel like a failure if this happens. She also tells you that she noticed that many students, her peers included, did not seem to make an effort to pronounce her name. She is contemplating whether she should just find an English alias-name to make things easier for everyone. She overheard a group of students talking about her style of dress being unprofessional when she wore a home-made tunic; though it fit the policy of the department and was comfortable for her being pregnant; she felt discriminated against.

In the third session, Deepa discusses that she feels like she cannot share in future classes because she thinks she will offend someone. In session, she struggles to talk about a situation that happened in class, stating that she feels torn talking about a professor and his response to her, because she is 'not supposed' to talk ill of professors, or those in authority. After reminding her that the counseling space is safe, she shares about her disappointment in her professor. He does not seem to believe in her, or at least validate her non-western worldview. In her view, the professor should hold a nurturing role and lead novice counselor educators; her disappointment stems from an incident in one of her introductory to counseling classes that week. The professor "questioned" (degraded) her example of international counseling, claiming that professional counseling should not recognize informal counselors. Deepa believes that teaching is a sacred profession and she continues to struggle on how to 'fully' respect her professors, as well as peers, who may be unwelcoming of her cultural beliefs.

A few minutes before Deepa leaves the session, she informs you that her husband has been granted a work visa and will be arriving a week before the baby is born – right before the end of the semester. Since he will not have a job immediately, she is struggling on how they will make ends meet being that funds are limited and they have a new baby on the way. She is unaware of any resources in her community, especially since she was informed by her insurance company (through school) that most benefits are only for American citizens. She is also concerned about who will stay with their baby when she is not home, as the role of taking care of her family falls on her and not her husband.

CASE CONCEPTUALIZATION

According to the American Counseling Association's (ACA) Code of Ethics (2014), counselors are mandated to "gain knowledge, personal, awareness, sensitivity, dispositions, and skills pertinent to being a culturally competent counselor in working with a diverse client population" (p. 8). However, within the United States' mental health system, culturally diverse populations are consistently being underserved according to Kress, Dixon, and Shannonhouse (2018). It is essential for counselors to be aware of and acknowledge their attitudes, beliefs, and biases related to enculturation. More importantly, counselors are strongly encouraged to obtain the skills necessary to engage in culturally sensitive interventions (Kress et al., 2018). In so doing, counselors become uniquely positioned to meet the needs of diverse clientele guided by the MSJCC (Ratts et al., 2015). In clinical practice and research, the MSJCC serve as an informal roadmap assisting counselors in integrating multicultural and social justice competencies, endorsed by the Association for Multicultural Counseling and Development and the American Counseling Association (Kress et al., 2018; Ratts et al., 2015). MSJCC allow counselors to conceptualize clients along four developmental domains: (1) counselor self-awareness, (2) client worldview, (3) counseling relationship, and (4) counseling and advocacy interventions. Following the MSJCC, counselors utilize culturally responsive evaluation skills when engaging with clients, intentionally seeking to understand how their worldviews, cultural backgrounds, beliefs, biases, values, and experiences of privilege and oppression are constructed by socio-historical events and current social issues (Kress et al., 2018).

Applying the MSJCC (Ratts et al., 2015) to Deepa's case, counselors are acknowledging their commitment to practice from a multicultural framework focused on action on behalf of clients, rooted in social justice. When working with Deepa, it is important for the counselor to be aware of her/his Eurocentric worldviews and her/his socio-cultural perspectives. Addressing counselor self-awareness, it is important for the counselor to initially consider her/his own attitudes, beliefs, and biases. The counselor does this by examining her/his beliefs of their own ethnic and national origins and working with international clients, systems of oppression and privilege that she/he experienced as a result of these identities, and the extent to which these beliefs influence her/his worldview. The counselor should acknowledge that individuals from her/his ethnic/national origins might have differing perspectives from her/his own related to working with international clients. Regarding action, the counselor should be aware of how her/his prior counseling experiences working with international clients might impact her/his communication with Deepa.

The counselor also needs to have an understanding of Deepa's Asian worldview and how systems of privilege and oppression are experienced by Deepa and how they shape her attitudes and beliefs. Deepa's move to the U.S. has exposed her to oppressive forces including but not limited to gender roles (motherhood: caregiver vs. provider), language (meaning of words, rate of speech), social supports (building new supports systems), financial supports, family (immediate and extended) expectations, and educational systems – U.S. vs. India (discipline, respect for authority). The counselor can gain knowledge of Deepa's worldview by reviewing research on the stigma surrounding mental health in Asian cultures, and how female concerns/motherhood are addressed "behind closed doors." The counselor can educate her/himself on the pressures (financial, social) that Deepa experiences from being an educated woman in a predominantly patriarchal society, and the need to be successful in her studies or risk bringing "shame" and with it loss of social status to herself, family (immediate and extended) and her community. The counselor can use critical thinking and analysis to understand the oppressive forces of power and privilege at Deepa's current university and department and how these forces are impacting her overall wellbeing.

Information related to the counselor's self-awareness and knowledge of the client's worldview can assist the counselor in facilitating a supportive and meaningful therapeutic relationship. This information can assist the counselor in being acutely aware of the privileged and oppressed statuses of counselor and client, and how these statuses impact the counseling relationship. The counselor needs to be aware of her/his biases and expectations when working with Deepa, including appropriate cultural cues, and how those factors inform her new life in the U.S.. The counselor can ask Deepa "what it is like to be an educated East Indian female living in the U.S." or "tell me what it is like for you to be alone and away far away from your family." Therapeutic confrontation although helpful can be harmful when working with Deepa due to the challenging nature of the technique and Deepa's East Asian culture of respecting authority. Therefore, the counselor can be aware of her/his attitudes and beliefs related to confrontation and tentatively rely on knowledge and observational cues from working with other (international) clients. The counselor can also participate in continuing education opportunities that allow her/him to be more accepting of all clients, specifically clients who are culturally diverse, which can include immersion experiences, peer supervision, and consultation.

After the counselor gains an awareness of her/his beliefs and values in working with Deepa, acknowledges Deepa's worldview, and addresses the dynamics of power, privilege and oppression in relation to the therapeutic relationship, the counselor is positioned to recommend suitable interventions for Deepa aimed at promoting social justice. The counseling and advocacy interventions the counselor will employ in working with Deepa over a six week period, is the RESPECT model, and Cognitive Behavioral Therapy (CBT) interventions, while connecting Deepa to relevant resources (e.g., international student office, support groups). The advocacy interventions for Deepa will focus on the oppression she is experiencing and how it is negatively influencing her abilities to function as a student, teaching assistant, wife, and expectant mother. The counselor can discuss how on-campus supports (e.g., International Student Office) might assist Deepa throughout her studies and positively impact her well-being. It is also important for the counselor and Deepa to discuss her goals, with the purpose of empowering her to advocate for herself within her department, the university, and local community within the U.S., so she can obtain the supports and services needed. The MSJCC are further complemented when used in conjunction with the RESPECTFUL model (D'Andrae & Daniels, 2001), to which we now turn.

Developed in 1997 by D'Andrae and Daniels (2001), the RESPECTFUL model stresses the need for an extensive, but not exhaustive, model of human diversity that has clinical utility in counseling practice. Ten factors comprise the RESPECTFUL model according to D'Andrae and Daniels (2001), which were selected because they impact the psychological development and personal well-being of clients. The factors that form the RESPECTFUL framework are outlined in the *Theories of Counseling and Psychotherapy: A Multicultural Perspective* (Ivey, D'Andrae, & Ivey, 2012, pp. 32-33), directing attention to the individual's

R – religious and/or spiritual identity
E – economic/class experiences and identity
S – sexual/gender identity
P – level of psychological maturity/development
E – ethnic/racial/cultural identity
C – chronological status and challenges
T – traumatic experiences and other threats to one's well-being
F – family history and identity
U – unique physical characteristics
L – location of residence and preferred language usage

The ten factors of the RESPECTFUL framework impact the way clients view themselves, as well as others, and also recurrently influence the way counselors create meaning from the presenting problems/challenges leading clients to seek counseling (D'Andrae & Daniels, 2001).

Based on the RESPECTFUL model (D'Andrae & Daniels, 2001) and the case study example, the counselor is tasked with, identifying Deepa's spiritual/religious identity (R) and determining the role religion/spirituality plays in her daily life was not indicated. From the case study, regarding economic class background (E), it appears that Deepa's socioeconomic status positions her in the upper-middle class bracket in India. However, in the U.S., being an international student and a teaching assistant with a small monthly stipend, an expectant mother, and having a husband who will soon join her and not be immediately employed, she qualifies as being part of the working class/working poor (Gilbert, 2002; Thompson & Hickney, 2005). The counselor needs to be mindful that Deepa's economic class in the U.S. might be a significant stressor and contributor to her presenting problems moving forward. From the case study, it appears that Deepa's sexual identity (S) is heterosexual, being married to a man and expecting a child. However, it would be part of the counselor's responsibility to assess if Deepa's sexual identity is in keeping with what is observed/known from the case study. Regarding psychological maturity (P), the case study informs us of Deepa being the oldest daughter, who received a university education qualifying her as a high school teacher and college career counselor in India. The counselor also knows Deepa was accepted into a competitive counselor education doctoral program in the U.S., and has been taking care of herself as an expectant mother, in addition to her other stressors. Deepa is from India, and therefore identifies as Indian and Asian in relation to her ethnic/racial identity (E). In correlation to Deepa's chronological/ developmental challenges (C), we are only aware of her anxiety stemming from being a new/expectant mother; she appears to have achieved her developmental milestones without incident.

From the case study, the counselor infers the presence of trauma or threats to Deepa's well-being (T), which appears to be a major stressor that has brought her into counseling. This stems from the apparent acculturative stress of her being in a new country and culture, not having the support of her family present, not feeling welcomed in her classes and supported by some faculty, feeling judged for the way she dresses, and experiencing anxiety surrounding her role as a teacher for the undergraduate course. Therefore, it is wise for the counselor to engage in ongoing assessment of Deepa along this domain. The counselor does not have much information on Deepa's family background and history (F), however from the case study, the counselor is informed that Deepa is the oldest of four girls, meaning she was called to be an example for her sisters. Deepa was able to receive an education, which is not common for females in her semi-rural community, she is married to a business man, and was able to hold a job as a high school teacher and career counselor. She values her schooling and believes that this accomplishment will impact her family and her community as well as potentially bring some change on the stigmatization of mental health in her community/country. She longs to be a mother and fulfill a family expectation to produce an heir (male child), and believes that childrearing is a responsibility fulfilled by the woman. This domain seems to be playing a significant role in Deepa's life. The counselor can also infer that Deepa is feeling judged by her fellow students for the way she dresses, and she is acutely aware that others, including her peers, professor(s), and students, do not understand her or make the effort to try and understand her. This leads Deepa to feel excluded from the U.S. culture, due to her unique physical characteristics (U) that cannot be hidden, subsequently compounding her feelings of isolation and lack of support. Finally, in relation to location of residence and language differences (L), the counselor is aware that Deepa is from India, and not the U.S., something her U.S. counterparts knowingly and unknowingly remind her of daily. Her accent is contributing to her anxiety when it comes to teaching her undergraduate course, leading her to spend upwards of four hours each night preparing for her lectures so her students may understand the analogies and examples she uses. Deepa fears her language differences will result in her losing her teaching assistantship, leading her to have to return to India without completing her doctoral degree due to the lack of financial resources. This domain is also a significant contributor of stress and anxiety in Deepa's life and will be of interest to the counselor when collaboratively working on constructing Deepa's treatment plan.

Since Deepa is a student seeking counseling services through the university counseling center where students can receive up to six sessions per semester, counseling is going to be brief. In addition to applying the MSJCC (Ratts et al., 2015) and the RESPECTFUL model (D'Andrae & Daniels, 2001), Cognitive Behavioral Therapy (CBT) interventions will be employed, due to their cultural adaptability (David et al., 2018; Hinton et al., 2012; Kananian et al., 2017; Tang et al., 2016), to address the cognitive dissonance experienced between Asian vs. Eurocentric worldviews, and to help Deepa process how her belief system plays out in this new socio-cultural context.

TREATMENT PLAN

Problem 1

Feelings of isolation and loneliness.

As evidenced by: Struggling to adjust to living in a foreign country without family; corresponding to "E-*economic/class experiences and identity*; E-*ethnic/racial/cultural identity*; and L-*location*," in the RESPECTFUL model.

As evidenced by: Inability to (frequently) communicate with husband; corresponding to "E-*economic/class experiences and identity*; and S-*sexual/gender identity*," in the RESPECTFUL model.

As evidenced by: Wrestling with the lifestyle change from collectivism to individualism; corresponding to "E-*economic/class experiences and identity*; E-*ethnic/racial/cultural identity*; F-*family history and identity*; and L-*location*," in the RESPECTFUL model.

Goal 1

Deepa will develop a support system.

Objective 1:
Identify and connect with two to three extended family members in the U.S. or local Indian community when no Wi-Fi access is available to contact husband.
Intervention 1:
Deepa will make a list of extended family members living in the US and local Indian community centers with their contact information.
Intervention 2:
Deepa will work with counselor to identify two to three contacts indicated on list with whom she feels comfortable to contact and process reasons for contacting them.
Intervention 3:
Deepa will be encouraged by counselor to contact/visit contacts once every two to three weeks in an effort to build local (U.S.) support.
Objective 2:
Identify and connect with two to three doctoral students, in and out of the school/program to whom she can share her experiences with.
Intervention 1:
Deepa will identify two to three doctoral students and their contact information, then list the pros and cons for connecting with them.
Intervention 2:
Deepa will be encouraged by counselor to set up a meeting with a different contact each week in an effort to build her social supports.
Intervention 3:
Deepa will report and process each week on her challenges and successes from contacting/meeting extended family and/or doctoral students with her counselor.

Progress

One measure of Deepa's progress is to examine her social support system. Drawing on the case study, Deepa indicated feeling isolated and lonely with no U.S. support system of her own. As Deepa identifies and connects with family members, peers, and international students on campus and across the U.S., her feelings of isolation and loneliness will hopefully subside, and her support system will hopefully grow, leading her to feel empowered, connected, and a sense of belonging.

Problem 2

Anxiety resulting from language and cultural barriers.

As evidenced by: Fear that her international views and experiences will not be welcomed in her doctoral classes; corresponding to "R-*religious and/or spiritual identity*; P-*level of psychological maturity and development*; E-*ethnic/racial/cultural identity*; F-*family history and identity*; and L-*location*," in the RESPECTFUL model.

As evidenced by: Stress and exhaustion from extensive teaching preparation for her undergraduate class; corresponding to "P-*level of psychological maturity and development*; E-*ethnic/racial/cultural identity*; T-*traumatic experiences and other threats to one's well-being*; and U-*unique physical characteristics*," in the RESPECTFUL model.

As evidenced by: Dissonance concerning gender-roles in parenting and care-giving; corresponding to "S-*sexual/gender identity*; P-*level of psychological maturity and development*; E-*ethnic/racial/cultural identity*; C-*chronological status and challenges*; T-*traumatic experiences and other threats to one's well-being*; F-*family history and identity*; and L-*location*," in the RESPECTFUL model.

Goal 1

Deepa will develop a positive self-image regarding her native language/culture and expressing them in the U.S.

Objective 1:

Participate in social skills training each week to address anxieties related to language and cultural barriers in her university setting.

Intervention 1:

Deepa will consult with her doctor to rule out any biophysical factors that are contributing/impacting to her anxiety and pregnancy.

Intervention 2:

Deepa will be educated by counselor on basic conversation skills, ways to initiate conversations, how to be assertive in conversations, and techniques to use when public speaking.

Intervention 3:

Deepa will engage in role play/imaginary scenarios with counselor, where she can practice the skills she is learning. Counselor can embody the character of student, colleague, or professor having conversations with client.

Intervention 4:

Deepa will be provided with verbal encouragements and supports as she practices the social skills she has learned, and process her experiences of using them in social interactions each week.

Objective 2:

Participate in relaxation training each week to address anxieties related to language and cultural barriers in her university setting and at home.

Intervention 1:

Deepa will learn relaxation techniques, including progressive muscle relaxation and meditation that she can use when she feels anxious.

Intervention 2:

Deepa will practice relaxation techniques during counseling session with the guidance and support her counselor.

Intervention 3:

Deepa will list social situations that make her anxious, create a plan with her counselor on when to use them, and role play and process how she will implement relaxation techniques during those moments.

Goal 2

Deepa will develop the confidence to function in multiple identities.

Objective 1:

Develop a list of strategies client can employ to feel confident in the multiple roles she possesses.

Intervention 1:

Deepa will make a list of the roles in which she feels she lacks confidence and identify the evidence for and against the lack of confidence.

Intervention 2:

Deepa will identify positive self-statements and role play with the counselor how she will implement them during moments of low confidence.

Intervention 3:

Deepa will develop a reward system to use when she utilizes positive self-statements to increase her confidence.

Objective 2:

Deepa will attend peer support groups to help her cope with her multiple roles.

Intervention 1:

Deepa will be educated by the counselor on the role and function of support groups, and will be provided with a list of support groups related to parenting for new mothers who also work.

Intervention 2:

Deepa will select and attend one support group each week to help navigate the multiple roles of student, teacher, expectant/new mother, and provider.

Intervention 3:

Deepa will process her experiences with counselor each week and develop a schedule to track her progress related to anxiety and confidence levels.

Progress

Progress on these goals will focus on Deepa's ability to manage her anxiety, which will hopefully decrease as she develops and expresses positive self-image in relation to her native language and culture in the U.S., and practices relaxation techniques. As the counselor engages in role play with Deepa, she/he should hopefully observe Deepa as less anxious as she practices basic conversational skills and verbalizes positive self-statements. Deepa's progress will also be evaluated in relation to her ability to engage in positive self-statements and the practice of relaxation techniques outside of counseling. She should hopefully feel empowered through the process of therapy, and experience lower levels of anxiety by increasing her own positive self-talk and relying less on the encouragement of the counselor, and engaging in relaxation techniques when she begins to feel anxious (especially in relation to expressing her views in class as a student, preparing to teach her undergraduate course, and preparing for motherhood and life as a woman in academia). Deepa's progress in managing her anxiety will also be evident in her being able to identify and regularly participate in peer support groups (e.g., international student, expectant mom) and becomes comfortable navigating her multiple identities.

At the end of six sessions, it is expected that Deepa will have some meaningful supports and not feel lonely and isolated, and have the capacity to regulate her anxiety by using relaxation techniques and positive self-talk. The counselor is encouraged to follow-up with Deepa, with her consent, at one, three, six, and 12 month intervals, and provide Deepa with an open invitation to return/request counseling services should the need arise.

IMPLICATIONS

The treatment plan provides a more traditional approach to the counseling process, however, counselors are encouraged to incorporate the following implications when working with international students to strengthen the therapeutic relationship while providing client-centered care in keeping with the MSJCC (Ratts et al., 2015) and the RESPECTFUL model (D'Andrae & Daniels, 2001).

Implications for Counselors Working With International Students

In general, it is important for counselors to acknowledge the courage it takes for a client to seek out counseling services. Literature (Forbes-Mewett & Sawyer, 2016; Prieto-Welch, 2016; Valencia-Garcia et al., 2012) denotes that international students underutilize counseling services. Thus, an international student client who makes the effort to come to see a counselor requires praise for this first step and ongoing effort on the counselor's part to build a strong therapeutic alliance. To this end, a counselor may consider the following measures when engaging a client who is an international student:

- The client is an expert of their culture. It is important for a counselor to be open to the client's 'teaching' on relevant cultural topics as opposed to acting along or not confirming that they are unaware. Related to this, a counselor must consider that not all experiences of an international student from the same country or the same cultural practice applies to another (e.g., Deepa's counselor is not to assume that the practice of bride-price in India is conducted in the same way as the Kenyan way of responding to the same practice).
- Utilize strength-based vs. deficient-oriented approaches in their counseling (e.g., being knowledgeable and intentionally applying the MSJCC). As such, highlighting a client's strengths is critical in growing/deepening the counseling relationship.
- Counselors can praise the client's ability to be multilingual and invite them to use their mother-tongue when needed in processing aspects of what may come up in a counseling session. "The language of the heart" may be what is best needed for the client to connect to the feelings regarding a situation, and being comfortable with this process as a counselor would ensure that what is best for the client would remain at the forefront. Translation to the counselor's language may be relevant when the client is ready to invite them to that space.
- Welcoming of topics that may be taboo and acknowledging it as such is critical and important for an international student client to remain open and build trust. Broaching the topic of the client's request for a gender-specific counselor must be accompanied with respect and sensitivity. Furthermore, inviting the client to discuss the "forbidden" within the limitations of a safe counseling space is important. It would not be advisable to dismiss what is taboo in another culture because the West does not term it as such. This safe

space may be the only space that the client gets to wrestle with the cultural differences on a topic that may be impacting them if indeed. A counselor must not assume that reflective processing is transpiring in the classroom setting.

- Growing in one's global awareness is a minor but important strategy. General geographical information about the whereabouts of your client's home country is an act that can communicate care and an interest to the client and their needs. Also, basic knowledge on current background on topics raised is an advisable idea (e.g., acknowledging that you are aware of a typhoon that devastated your client's country would demonstrate connection to them). One way of staying abreast on what is happening around the world is being intentional in the practice of reading/listening to world news from main stream entities, or to go deeper, finding the news directly from a country's news desk online.
- A counselor's commitment to participate in continuing education opportunities that focuses on international counseling topics and multicultural competence is critical. A counselor may consider participating in cultural immersion experiences both locally and internationally, visiting a cultural center, as well as taking advantage of professional international counseling conference opportunities. Locally, a counselor's awareness on what international resources are available for their client is imperative (e.g. international support groups, international education week, international and cultural fairs).

Implications for Counseling Programs and Administrators

The West trains most international counseling leaders (Hohenshill, Amundson, & Niles, 2013; Reid & Dixon, 2012). Counseling programs provide an opportunity for counselor educators and administrators to model leadership skills and empower students – both national and international. These training grounds are the spaces where leaders-in-training learn how to utilize power, privilege, and responsibility that come with the gift of higher education. Graduates return to their communities around the globe, armed with academic and professional expertise on their subject matters, and hopefully, also take with them experiential knowledge of what bridging marginalization gaps look and feel like, stemming from personal experiences. The following implications are suggestions for counselor educators and program administrators to foster strong relationships with international students in their programs.

- At the beginning of the semester, a program/department can provide an orientation for their new international students, in addition to the regular orientations. At this event, they can discuss specific program expectations, reading and understanding course syllabi, meaning of deadlines, the nature of classes including the seemingly informal set up of student-professor interaction, and allow for students to ask *any* questions.
- Avail a resource list that is comprehensive for practical international students' needs, including but not limited to: writing, editing, and tutoring services, medical and police contacts on campus, local grocery and international store details, free clothing centers (e.g., where to obtain winter coats, if relevant), food pantries and shelters, evacuation plans and routes if institution is located in such an area that utilizes these, emergency details (e.g., local hospital, fire, and police departments), religious centers (e.g., synagogues, churches, mosques, temples), and recreation centers.
- Offer formal and informal mentoring opportunities (e.g., pair new international student with senior student).
- Invite international alumni or international professionals to share their experiences of the program, as well as professional life in foreign country. This can be one of the guest speakers at the new international student orientation.
- Foster network opportunities (career fairs) with other international counseling students/interns and future employers. This is particularly important since the counseling master's degree requires a practicum and/or internship course.
- Organize round-table conversations or focus groups to discuss current cultural issues, identify needs, and address concerns that inform the supervisor and counselor-in-training relationship.
- Accept and embrace that *all* students bring their own culture – both international students and domestic students have a culture. Professors can add reflective assignments for international students to reflect on their own culture and not simply what they are learning about the 'new' [Western] culture.
- Identify a faculty member to serve as an international student liaison, who along with other faculty advisors, advocates for international students, and is able to hear and present their needs. Linked to this, faculty advisors that have a pre-determined advisee list are to be open to the idea that their advisee may be more comfortable to share with another faculty member about certain personal needs due to gender and other cultural factors. In light of this, collaboration between faculty members is strongly encouraged, remembering that the international student's needs are paramount.

CONCLUSION

The complexities in experiencing acculturative stress while navigating the intersectionality of multiple life roles can be challenging for international students, and more specifically, international student-mothers. Without the support of the institution and the mental health community, these international student-mothers are left to be consistently subjected to social isolation, discrimination, microaggressions, and lingering role confusion. The repercussions of such stress can affect the student's academic performance and future work.

In this chapter, counselors were tasked and encouraged to utilize the application of the Multicultural and Social Justice Counseling Competencies (MSJCC; Ratts et al., 2015) while conceptualizing a case study involving Deepa through a RESPECTUL model (D'Andrae & Daniels, 2001). The intersectionality paradigm illuminates the challenges that appear to accompany this culturally sensitive population and this model helps the counselor, counselor-in-training, counselor educator, and administrator to focus on the unique characteristics that formulate a client's identity. The integration of the MSJCC alongside the RESPECTFUL model provides a more culturally informed treatment approach and allows the counselor to competently meet the needs of this diverse clientele through culturally responsive evaluation.

REFERENCES

American Counseling Association. (2014). *ACA code of ethics*. Retrieved from https://www.counseling.org/resources/aca-code-of-ethics.pdf

Andrade, M. S. (2006). International students in English-speaking universities: Adjustment factors. *Journal of Research in International Education*, *5*(2), 131–154. doi:10.1177/1475240906065589

Arthur, N. (2004). *Counseling international students: Clients from around the world*. New York, NY: Kluwer Academic/Plenum. doi:10.1007/978-1-4419-8919-2

Behl, M., Laux, J. M., Roseman, C. P., Tiamiyu, M., & Spann, S. (2017). Needs and acculturative stress of international students in CACREP programs. *Counselor Education and Supervision*, *56*(4), 305–318. doi:10.1002/ceas.12087

Belsky, J., Houts, R. M., & Pasco Fearon, R. M. (2010). Infant attachment security and the timing of puberty: Testing an evolutionary hypothesis. *Psychological Science*, *21*(9), 1195–1201. doi:10.1177/0956797610379867 PMID:20713636

Blair-Loy, M. (2003). *Competing devotions: Career and family among women executives*. Cambridge, MA: Harvard University Press.

Brown, V., & Nichols, T. R. (2012). Pregnant and parenting students on campus: Policy on program implications for a growing population. *Educational Policy*, *27*(3), 499–530. doi:10.1177/0895904812453995

Burlew, L. D., & Alleyne, V. L. (2010). A pedagogical paradigm for international graduate students studying community counseling. *Journal of Counselor Preparation and Supervision*, *2*(1), 23–36. doi:10.7729/21.0113

Coates, N., & Dickinson, J. (2012). Meeting international postgraduate student needs: A programme-based model for learning and teaching support. *Innovations in Education and Teaching International*, *49*(3), 295–308. doi:10.1080/14703297.2012.703018

Collins, P. H., & Bilge, S. (2016). *Intersectionality*. Malden, MA: Polity Press.

Crenshaw, K. (1991). Mapping the margins: Intersectionality, identity politics, and violence against women of color. *Stanford Law Review*, *43*(6), 1241–1299. doi:10.2307/1229039

D'Andrea, M., & Daniels, J. (2001). RESPECTFUL counseling: An integrative model for counselors. In D. Pope-Davis & H. Coleman (Eds.), *The Interface of Class, Culture and Gender in Counseling* (pp. 417–466). Thousand Oaks, CA: Sage. doi:10.4135/9781452231846.n17

David, D., Stefan, S., & Terracciano, A. (2018). Cognitive-behavioral therapy in the cross-cultural context: An extension of the standard paradigm from individual to country/culture level- a brief introduction into a new research line. *Journal of Rational-Emotive & Cognitive-Behavior Therapy*, 1–13. doi:10.100710942-018-0303-9

Dickson, M., & Tennant, L. (2018). 'The accommodation I make is turning a blind eye': Faculty support for student mothers in higher education. *Studies in Continuing Education*, *40*(1), 76–97. doi:10.1080/0158037X.2017.1392296

Dion, K. K., & Dion, K. L. (2002). Gender and cultural adaptation in immigrant families. *The Journal of Social Issues*, *57*(3), 511–521. doi:10.1111/0022-4537.00226

Donnelly, K., Twenge, J. M., Clark, M. A., Shaikh, S. K., Beiler-May, A., & Carter, N. T. (2015). Attitudes toward women's work and family roles in the United States, 1976-2013. *Psychology of Women Quarterly*, *40*(1), 41–54. doi:10.1177/0361684315590774

Elsharnouby, T. H. (2016). Participation behavior among international students. *International Journal of Educational Management, 30*(5), 679–697. doi:10.1108/IJEM-10-2014-0139

Forbes-Mewett, H., & Sawyer, A. M. (2016). International students and mental health. *Journal of International Students, 6*(3), 661–677. Retrieved from http://jistudents.org

Gilbert, D. (2002). *The American class structure in an age of growing inequality* (6th ed.). Belmont, CA: Wadsworth.

Hendrickson, B., Rosen, D., & Aune, R. K. (2011). An analysis of friendship networks, social connectedness, homesickness, and satisfaction levels of international students. *International Journal of Intercultural Relations, 35*(3), 281–295. doi:10.1016/j.ijintrel.2010.08.001

Hinton, D. E., Rivera, E. I., Hofmann, S. G., Barlow, D. H., & Otto, M. W. (2012). Adapting CBT for traumatized refugees and ethnic minority patients: Examples from culturally adapted CBT (CA-CBT). *Transcultural Psychiatry, 49*(2), 340–365. doi:10.1177/1363461512441595 PMID:22508639

Hohenshill, T. H., Amundson, N. E., & Niles, S. G. (2013). *Counseling around the world: An international handbook*. Alexandria, VA: American Counseling Association.

Houshmand, S., Spanierman, L. B., & Tafarodi, R. W. (2014). Excluded and avoided: Racial microaggressions targeting Asian international students in Canada. *Cultural Diversity & Ethnic Minority Psychology, 20*(3), 377–388. doi:10.1037/a0035404 PMID:25045949

Hsaio, C., Koren-Karie, N., Bailey, H., & Moran, G. (2015). It takes two to talk: Longitudinal associations among infant-mother attachment, maternal attachment representations, and mother-child emotion dialogues. *Attachment & Human Development, 17*(1), 43–64. doi:10.1080/14616734.2014.981671 PMID:25482104

Hyun, J., Quinn, B., Madon, T., & Lustig, S. (2007). Mental health need, awareness, and use of counseling services among international graduate students. *Journal of American College Health, 56*(2), 109–118. doi:10.3200/JACH.56.2.109-118 PMID:17967756

Institute of International Education. (2018). *Open doors: Report on international educational exchange.* Retrieved from http://www.iie.org/opendoors

Ivey, A. E., D' Andrea, M. J., & Ivey, M. B. (2012). *Theories of counseling and psychotherapy: A multicultural perspective* (7th ed.). Thousand Oaks, CA: Sage.

Kananian, S., Ayoughi, S., Farugie, A., Hinton, D., & Stangier, U. (2017). Transdiagnostic culturally adapted CBT with Farsi-speaking refugees: A pilot study. *European Journal of Psychotraumatology*, *8*(2), 1–10. doi:10.1080/20008198.2017.1390362 PMID:29163870

Kress, V. E., Dixon, A. L., & Shannonhouse, L. R. (2018). Multicultural diagnosis and conceptualization. In D. G. Hays & B. T. Erford (Eds.), *Developing multicultural counseling competence: A systems Approach* (3rd ed.; pp. 558–590). New York, NY: Pearson.

Lee, J., & Rice, C. (2007). Welcome to America? International student perceptions of discrimination. *Higher Education*, *53*(3), 381–409. doi:10.100710734-005-4508-3

Leon, R. A., & Chmiel, J. (2013). Counseling international students: Clients from around the world. *Journal of International Students*, *3*(2), 190–192. Retrieved from http://jistudents.org/

Lim, J. W., Honey, A., DuToit, S., Chen, Y., & Mackenzie, L. (2016). Experiences of international students from Asian backgrounds studying occupational therapy in Australia. *Australian Occupational Therapy Journal*, *63*(5), 303–311. doi:10.1111/1440-1630.12307 PMID:27302157

Lynch, K. D. (2008). Gender roles and the American academe: A case study of graduate student mothers. *Gender and Education*, *20*(6), 585–605. doi:10.1080/09540250802213099

Mason, M. A., Goulden, M., & Frasch, K. (2009). Why graduate students reject the fast track. *Academe*, *95*(1), 11–16. Retrieved from https://www.aaup.org/article/why-graduate-students-reject-fast-track/#.XHdMcflKjIU

McClure, J. W. (2007). International graduates' cross-cultural adjustment: Experiences, coping strategies, and suggested programmatic responses. *Teaching in Higher Education*, *12*(2), 199–217. doi:10.1080/13562510701191976

McLaughlin, A. N., & Randolph, K. A. (2012). Development of school support scale for low-income mothers in college. *Research on Social Work Practice*, *22*(1), 68–76. doi:10.1177/1049731511415122

Mittal, M., & Wieling, E. (2006). Training experiences of international doctoral students in marriage and family therapy. *Journal of Marital and Family Therapy*, *32*(3), 369–383. doi:10.1111/j.1752-0606.2006.tb01613.x PMID:16933440

Myers-Walls, J. A., Frias, L., Kyong-Ah, K., Meryl Ko, M. M., & Lu, T. (2011). Living life in two worlds: The stress of Asian international graduate student parents and spouses. *Journal of Comparative Family Studies*, *42*(4), 455–478. Retrieved from https://www.jstor.org/stable/41604463. doi:10.3138/jcfs.42.4.455

Nayar-Bhalerao, S. (2014). *Perceptions of international students in CACREP-accredited counseling programs* (Doctoral Dissertation). Retrieved from ProQuest Dissertations and Theses database. (UMI No. 3568184)

Ng, K. M. (2006). International students in CACREP accredited counseling programs. *Journal of Professional Counseling, Practice, Theory, & Research*, *34*(1-2), 20–32. doi:10.1080/15566382.2006.12033821

Ng, K. M., & Smith, S. D. (2009). Perceptions and experiences of international trainees in counseling and related programs. *International Journal for the Advancement of Counseling*, *31*(1), 57–70. doi:10.100710447-008-9068-7

Pasco Fearon, R. M., & Belsky, J. (2011). Infant-mother attachment and the growth of externalizing problems across the primary- school years. *Journal of Child Psychology and Psychiatry, and Allied Disciplines*, *52*(7), 782–791. doi:10.1111/j.1469-7610.2010.02350.x PMID:21214546

Prieto-Welch, S. L. (2016). International student mental health. *New Directions for Student Services*, *2016*(156), 53–63. doi:10.1002s.20191

Rai, G. S. (2002). Meeting the educational needs of international students: A perspective from US schools. *International Social Work*, *45*(1), 21–33. doi:10.1177/0020872802045001312

Ratts, M. J., Sing, A. A., Nassar-McMillan, S., Butler, S. K., & McCullough, J. R. (2015). *Multicultural and social justice counseling competencies.* Retrieved from http://www.counseling.org/knowledge-center/competencies

Reid, L. M., & Dixon, A. L. (2012). The counseling supervision needs of international students in US institutions of higher education: A culturally-sensitive supervision model for counselor educators. *Journal for International Counselor Education*, *4*(1), 29–41. Retrieved from https://digitalscholarship.unlv.edu/cgi/viewcontent.cgi?article=1032&context=jice

Sakamoto, I. (2007). A critical examination of immigrant acculturation: Toward and anti-oppressive social work model with immigrant adults in pluralistic society. *British Journal of Social Work*, *37*(3), 515–535. doi:10.1093/bjsw/bcm024

Sandhu, D. S., & Asrabadi, B. R. (1994). Development of an acculturative stress scale for international students: Preliminary findings. *Psychological Reports*, *75*(1), 435–448. doi:10.2466/pr0.1994.75.1.435 PMID:7809315

Sherry, M., Thomas, P., & Chui, W. (2009). International students: A vulnerable student population. *Higher Education*, *60*(1), 33–46. doi:10.100710734-009-9284-z

Sung, S., Simpson, J. A., Griskevicius, V., Kuo, S. I., Schlomer, G. L., & Belsky, J. (2016). Secure infant-mother attachment buffers the effect of early-life stress on age of menarche. *Psychological Science*, *27*(5), 667–674. doi:10.1177/0956797616631958 PMID:26980153

Tang, J. Y., Li, C., Rodger, R. F., & Ballou, M. (2016). Ethnic differences in the effectiveness of cognitive behavioral therapy combined with medication: Comparing Asian American and white psychiatric patients. *Asian Journal of Psychiatry*, *24*, 46–50. doi:10.1016/j.ajp.2016.08.012 PMID:27931905

Thompson, W. E., & Hickey, J. V. (2005). *Society in focus: An introduction to sociology* (5th ed.). Boston, MA: Allyn & Bacon.

UKCISA. (2004). Broadening our horizons: International students in UK universities and colleges. London: UKCISA.

United Press. (2011). *Foreign student numbers in U.S. hit record*. Retrieved from http://www.upi.com/ Top_News/US/2011/11/14/Foreign-student-numbers-in-US-hit-record/UPI-58861321323005/

U.S. Immigration and Customs Enforcement. (2018a). *SEVIS by the numbers: Biannual report on international student trends*. Retrieved from https://www.ice.gov/doclib/sevis/pdf/byTheNumbersApr2018.pdf

U.S. Immigration and Customs Enforcement. (2018b). *Student and exchange visitor program*. Retrieved from https://www.ice.gov/sevis

Valencia-Garcia, D., Simoni, J. M., Alegria, M., & Takeuchi, D. T. (2012). Social capital, acculturation, mental health, and perceived access to services among Mexican American women. *Journal of Consulting and Clinical Psychology*, *80*(2), 177–185. doi:10.1037/a0027207 PMID:22329824

von Borell de Araujo, B., Tureta, C., & von Borell de Araujo, D. (2015). How do working mothers negotiate the work-home interface? *Journal of Managerial Psychology*, *30*(5), 565–581. doi:10.1108/JMP-11-2013-0375

Woo, H., Jang, Y. J., & Henfield, M. S. (2015). International doctoral students in counselor education: Coping strategies in supervision training. *Journal of Multicultural Counseling and Development*, *43*(4), 288–304. doi:10.1002/jmcd.12022

Yoon, E., Change, C., Kim, S., Clawson, A., Clearly, S. E., Hansen, M., ... Gomes, A. M. (2013). A meta-analysis of acculturation/enculturation and mental health. *Journal of Counseling Psychology*, *60*(1), 15–30. doi:10.1037/a0030652 PMID:23163612

Chapter 11
Hiking With Heidi:
A Multicultural Approach to Ecotherapy

Bonnie Carter King
Midwestern State University, USA

EXECUTIVE SUMMARY

The following chapter describes the experience of counseling a woman named Heidi (name and identifying details changed to protect confidentiality) using Ecotherapy and the Multicultural Counseling Competencies. The chapter describes Heidi and her presenting problems, an introduction of the author, and the author's unique approach to counseling, the application of theory to her work with Heidi using existential and systems theories, as well as practicing in nature. The goals and progress that was made in their journey together through the counseling relationship is described. Throughout their journey together, Heidi utilized her strengths, which empowered her to make changes in her life that were beneficial for her growth, health, and happiness by implementing changes in her life that fully honored the complexity of her humanity.

DOI: 10.4018/978-1-7998-0022-4.ch011

INTRODUCTION

The following chapter describes the experience of counseling a woman named Heidi (name and identifying details changed to protect confidentiality) using Ecotherapy and the Multicultural Counseling Competencies of Ratts, Singh, Nassar, Butler, amd McCullough (2016). Heidi is a woman in her early thirties who came to counseling for debilitating depression, a poor work/life balance, and a lack of joy and purpose. The chapter describes Heidi and her presenting problems, an introduction to myself and my unique approach to counseling, the application of theory to my work with Heidi using existential and systems theories, as well as practicing Ecotherapy, or counseling in nature. The goals and progress made in our journey together through the counseling relationship is described. Throughout our journey together, Heidi utilized her strengths, which empowered her to make changes in her life that were beneficial for her growth, health and happiness by implementing changes in her life that fully honored the complexity of her humanity.

Heidi

Heidi is a woman in her early thirties from California. Having grown up is a small town with an Irish-German and Catholic background, she was one of many siblings in her home. Heidi was a bit shy, and reluctant to see a counselor. She mentioned that it was the first time she had tried counseling and came at the encouragement of her psychiatrist. Heidi is a white woman of petite build. She dressed formally, and her attire matched the expectations of her role as an attorney. I noticed almost immediately how difficult it was for her to decipher what was causing her depression in our first session, except that her work was stressful and tedious, and that she had been unhappy at her job for some time. Heidi seemed disconnected from her emotions and had a hard time vocalizing her feelings. She had trouble sharing hobbies, things she enjoyed, or personal interests. It is as though she had never found the things she enjoyed, or that she had forgotten them. People who experience depression often lose pleasure in activities that were once enjoyable.

Heidi stated that she had been struggling with depression that she described as "medication resistant" for the better part of a year, and that at one point she had experienced suicidal ideations. She did not attempt to take her own life, but the thoughts scared her, and eventually led her to seek the help of a psychiatrist. Heidi was prescribed a variety of high dose medications, that were helping some, but Heidi still had very low life-satisfaction. Heidi struggled to sleep at night and to wake in the morning, and she met each day with dread. On the weekends she spent most of her time in bed watching reality television. At times she "forced" herself out of the house for dinner with friends or her husband, but she stated that she did not enjoy this time socializing. In fact, she had lost pleasure in almost all of the activities that she had previously enjoyed. Further, it seemed the concept of "self-care" was something she had not practiced much in her daily life outside of basic care for her physical needs and hygiene.

When asked about her goals for therapy, Heidi shared that she wanted to increase positive feelings in her life and to manage her depression. She wanted to have more satisfaction and feelings of joy. She also wanted to engage more frequently in household responsibilities to decrease the burden on her husband; who had taken on the majority of the household chores due to her lack of energy and intense workload.

Heidi's Family and Background Information

Heidi was one of many siblings with working class parents. There were financial difficulties she experienced in her upbringing, and she stood out as academically gifted from a young age. Heidi worked hard from the time she was young until now, often receiving validation from teachers that she rarely received at home. Heidi's parents are married, and she described their relationship with her and with each other as "distant." She felt like an outsider in her own home and stated that the words "I love you" were not used in her household growing up, and that hugging and physical affection were extremely rare.

She described her parents as often either critical or distant. They were physically present but not overly involved. The small town in which she was raised is flat compared to the rest of California, so she did not have access to mountains, forests or the ocean that are often associated with California and the Pacific Northwest. She did not engage in many extra-curricular activities or recreational sports as a child. She did, however, join clubs that would help her achieve her academic goals such as debate club, but never reported particularly enjoying these activities.

Due to this lack of closeness, Heidi chose to rarely spend time with family for holidays and avoided doing so when possible. She described a distant relationship with siblings, sharing that she had little in common with them. She does not adhere to the religious upbringing of her family and described herself as "agnostic leaning toward atheist." Heidi's work ethic was a strong part of her value system from a very young age. As a self-described "over-achiever," she had received scholarships for her undergraduate admission to university and immediately went to law school upon graduation. It was expected by her teachers and peers that she would succeed academically and in her career. She plowed through job after job, as an entry level attorney at a law firm working long hours to pay off her law school student loans. Later she moved to a more stable yet equally demanding position in a state government office, overseeing the laws, procedures and functions of the agency. She received a promotion relatively quickly and was soon overseeing and re-writing almost all of the procedural manuals and aligning practices of the agency with the laws. She also traveled to litigate in court throughout the state. Her efforts had resulted in a comfortable salary for her, however extreme work hours plagued her from about 6:30 a.m., until exhaustion set in, late in the evening hours.

Heidi is happily married and has been partnered with her husband for her entire adult life. The couple started as "high school sweethearts," and have managed to stay together throughout college, first careers, and now as young adults settled into their respective careers. She describes her husband as supportive and stated that he "picked up the slack" at home when it came to cooking cleaning and caring for their dogs. He worked from home and his career was flexible and less demanding than Heidi's. They had no children, and the couple did not intend on growing a family larger than the two of them.

INTRODUCTION TO THE COUNSELOR: CULTURAL BACKGROUND

At the time I met Heidi, I was a Licensed Professional Counselor with a small private practice. I had worked in a variety of clinical settings including community counseling, inpatient drug rehabilitation, and in school counseling settings. I had just completed a Ph.D. in Counselor Education and had previously earned a master's degree in Professional Counseling. I am a cisgender white woman from the Southern United States. I was raised in a suburban, middle class household with two parents, a Judeo-Christian upbringing, and I had access to well-rated public schools. I was afforded many privileges in my childhood of which I am aware, such as healthy food, participation in extra-curricular activities ranging from swim-team and music lessons, to dance and drama club. I had access to and an expectation of university attendance when I came of age, a safe neighborhood where I was free to play, ride my bike, and socialize without fear, and the economic and psychological benefits of growing up in a two-parent household. I had a community of caring adults and children around me, and as a white person in a predominantly white community, I was part of the majority and experienced white privilege and therefore a lack of "otherness" that many non-majority people of color experience in such communities. These privileges have inherently impacted my life in a variety of ways, and I'm aware that these privileges have provided me an advantage to achievement in ways that others lacking these privileges may not have had access. As a culturally competent counselor it is important to understand one's own privilege and power in order to be aware of personal values and societal dynamics that can impact the counseling relationship (Ratts et al., 2016).

Counseling Approach

I view the counseling process as collaborative. I assume that the client is the expert on their life and that they ultimately know what is best for them. I believe that while people do not always naturally have the training to achieve their goals at first, they do have the ability to find the answers they are seeking to make their lives as meaningful as possible. I believe that they can learn the tools to heal and grow. I utilize an existential theoretical orientation and a systems approach to counseling, which means I believe that people are searching for meaning in their lives and that all behaviors have a purpose. Some of those purposes can be love, personal identity, freedom, and the search for life's greater meaning. I also believe that people are impacted by the families with which they live, as well as the systems of which they are apart in society. How one copes with his or her reality can cause internal struggles as well as strengths. For me, the goals of therapy come from a collaborative effort between myself and my clients. I focus on helping my clients access strengths to accomplish their goals and find greater insight into their lives through a collaborative therapeutic process.

When appropriate and desired, I utilize Ecotherapy in the counseling relationship. Research supports the idea that humans benefit greatly from interaction with the natural world. Benefits such as increased focus (Kaplan, 1995), decreased stress (Leather, Pyrgas, Beale & Lawrence, 1998), benefits from exercise (Doucette, 2004), and deeper connection to spirituality (Roscoe, 2009; Softas-Nall & Woody, 2017) can be experienced as a result to increased exposure to nature. As my relationship developed with Heidi it became clear that she could benefit from spending some of our counseling sessions in nature. I also strive to continuously continue to grow as a culturally competent counselor. This means having an awareness of my own cultural identity as well as the client's culture, and how those aspect of identity could manifest in the counseling relationship. I actively seek to educate myself on cultural aspects of the client's identity that can be relevant in our sessions. By gaining a deeper understanding of the client's ethnicity in society, cultural traditions, sexual orientation, gender identity, religious and spiritual, or other major components of the client's intersecting identities, I can seek to serve them in a more comprehensive manner. Ecotherapy is inherently multicultural, as all cultures connect to the natural world for survival in the most basic sense, and humans of all cultures connect to the world in aesthetic and spiritual ways. Further, ecotherapy can occur in a variety of locations, and be a great equalizer. In the traditional office setting the client comes to the counselor's office space, which can at times contribute to an unequal dynamic as the client views the credentials of the counselor hanging on the wall, and sits in a space of another (King, 2015). The natural world is a neutral space, and the inherent benefits of spending time in nature can be accessed by anyone.

CASE CONCEPTUALIZATION

Ecotherapy

''Ecotherapy is an emerging form of therapy that enlarges the traditional scope of treatment to include the human-nature relationship'' (Hasbach, 2012, p. 116). Individuals who spend time in nature can improve their mental health (Berman, Kross, Krpan, Askren, Burson, Deldin, Jonides, 2012; Bowler, Buyung-Ali, Knight, & Pullin, 2010; Bratman, Hamilton & Daily, 2012; Houlden, Weich, Porto de Albuquerque, Jarvis, & Rees, 2018; Louv, 2005), self-esteem, (Schreyer, Williams, Haggard, Easley, Passineau, & Driver, 1990) and stress levels (Hartig, Mang, & Evans, 1991; Leather et al., 1998). Anxiety disorders, depression, and other physical health problems all decrease in communities in which individuals have access to more green space compared to urban areas (Maas, Verheij, De Vries, Spreeuwenberg, Schellevis, & Groenewegen, 2009). People also report a deeper connection to spirituality and meaning making while spending time outdoors (Roscoe, 2009; Softas-Nall & Woody, 2017).

Counseling activities in nature can allow clients to process feelings more deeply while exploring goals and positive personal qualities (Reese & Myers, 2012). Further, experiencing the counseling relationship outdoors can increase equity and ameliorate the power differential in the counseling relationship (King, 2015). Nature provides a neutral space that helps decrease stigma (Becker, 2010). Counseling in nature utilizes the innate therapeutic benefits of the outdoors (Buzzell & Chalquist, 2009; Hasbach, 2012). Experiences such as outdoor and group activities can support healthier views of the self, greater belief in one's capabilities, and increased creativity (Berger, 2006). The use of metaphor is also abundant in this type of counseling which can help facilitate insightful processing in the counseling relationship (Reese & Myers, 2012). The natural environment and the possible activities and relationships that may ensue in natural environments can facilitate a non-threatening, stigma-free environment in which the counselor can be viewed as simply another person, instead of a threatening authority figure (Becker, 2010).

Existential Approach to Counseling in Nature

Existential psychotherapy is focused on living authentically, exploring purpose, personal meaning, and choice and responsibility. Existential counselors approach human suffering through the lens of meaning and purpose. They believe that when humans are out of alignment with their authentic selves or when they are lacking in meaning and purpose, that they suffer (Corey, 2017). This existential disconnect can inform the client when a change needs to occur in their lives, and can be very useful for helping them shape their existence in the ways that help them live with authenticity. Counselors can help by exploring themes in the client's life related to the givens of existence such as meaning and purpose, life and death, responsibility vs. freedom, and connectedness vs. isolation (Capuzzi & Gross, 2011). Heidi was certainly struggling to find, meaning and purpose driven living when she started counseling. She was working so hard that she rarely found time to care for herself, which left little time to ponder her short existence on earth, and how she wanted to spend that time. This lack of meaning and purpose led to an existential vacuum (Corey, 2017) that manifested in depression. Therefore, this theory is appropriate for work with Heidi given the specific nature of her presenting problems.

Existential theory is also a perfect fit when examining the ever-turbulent human relationship with the natural world. Ecotherapists have recognized a dissociation that occurs between humans and the natural world that has emerged since the industrial revolution and human dependence on technology has permeated and deeply influenced societal patterns. Technology and industrialization have led humans away from connecting with the life-giving natural world (Adams, 2005). Existential therapists would describe this phenomenon and the feelings that can emerge for humans because of this disconnect as an existential vacuum (Capuzzi & Gross, 2011), otherwise known as anxiety due to the lack of meaning or non-connection that exists between one's self and the natural environment (Adams, 2005).

The human desire to control and manipulate the natural world, though it has become normal, has led to a separation of the self from the natural world, which can lead to an existential vacuum (Adams, 2005). Humans, by respecting and attempting to preserve nature in its natural state, can experience a spiritual connectedness to self and the world. The hectic and fast-paced lives of many citizens in the United States leave little time for self-reflection, spending time in nature, or striving to preserve nature. Adams (2005) asserted that the domination of nature through development leaves a spiritual emptiness in the individual. Therefore, a re-connection with nature and acceptance of oneself could be the keystone of existential counseling practice in natural environments. Due to Heidi's disconnection with her inner desires, her body, and recreational activities that she enjoyed, I felt like incorporating Ecotherapy into our practice could help her reconnect to herself and nature.

Multicultural and Social Justice Counseling Competence With Heidi

Over the past thirty years, counselors have worked to embrace diversity and to train counselors to effectively work with groups of varied individuals. The American Counseling Association (ACA) has officially endorsed The Multicultural and Social Justice Counseling Competencies (MSJCC) (Ratts et al., 2016), which builds upon the work of Sue, Arrendondo and McDavis (1992) to reflect the ever-evolving complexities of multicultural counseling. The MSJCC include both developmental domains and aspirational domains which the counselor can utilize to improve their counseling skills with diverse populations.

As counselors in the profession become more inclusive and aware, the MSJCC outline the need for counselors to recognize both the counselor and the client's power, privilege and marginalization in society, as well as the impact these forces can have on clients in society and the counseling relationship. The developmental domains include: (1) counselor self-awareness, (2) client worldview, (3) counseling relationship, and (4) counseling and advocacy interventions (Ratts et al, 2016). The following aspirational competencies include: attitudes and beliefs, knowledge, skills, and action. As counselors it is important to understand one's self in relation to the client in addition to the views of the client. We can also analyze factors that can impact the counseling relationship, which can help counselors work with specific populations by gaining appropriate attitudes, knowledge, skills and actions to help their clients.

Cultural Identities in the Counseling Relationship

The MSJCC includes developmental domains such as (a) counselor self-awareness, (b) client worldview, (c) counseling relationship, and (d) counseling and advocacy interventions (Ratts et al., 2016). Culturally competent counselors work hard to apply the developmental domains and aspirational competencies to their practice with all clients. The following section applies the developmental domains of the MSJCC competencies, to my work with Heidi. The aspirational competencies of attitudes and beliefs, knowledge, skills, and action are also applied.

Counselor Self-Awareness

As a cisgender, white, American woman from a Judeo-Christian background in my early thirties, I have many privileges in society in terms of access and opportunity. I am aware that these privileges shape my world view. My client was also a cisgender white woman in her early thirties raised in a Christian background, however her childhood economic status was working class, whereas I came from a middle-class background. We both had advanced college degrees and both experience a level of middle-class economic comfort. In these ways we experienced some cultural similarities. Because of these similarities I had to be careful to ensure I did not make attitudinal assumptions based on my cultural background. I listened to her worldviews to try to understand her upbringing and how it shaped her, as well as her morals and guiding principles that shape her actions. As women, we both experience a level of marginalization in society due to a lack of male privilege. As a counselor, I was aware of this and listened for ways in which this aspect of her cultural identity may have impacted her development, while being mindful not to imbue her journey with my own judgements, experiences or assumptions. While challenging, I achieved this by staying actively aware of my personal values and when those might be creeping to my awareness and distracting me from listening to her. I also tried to actively compare our experiences to discern what my emotional reactions were to her that were connected to my personal experiences as a woman, versus what was objective and rooted in her personal worldviews. This helped me to stay focused specifically on her concerns and personal understanding of being a woman in society. To explore the possibility of whether or not marginalization as a woman in society impacted her, I asked specific, open-ended questions about her feelings as a woman in her workplace, in society in general, and at home. Throughout our time together we learned that there were certain aspects of female socialization that had impacted her ability to set boundaries, stand up for herself at work, and utilize assertive communication. Further, due to feeling like she was not in a power position because of her gender, she felt less empowered at work to assert herself. This later became an area of focus, and we worked together to take action in this area. Heidi critically examined her position in the workplace and advocated for change in a variety of ways to improve her standing at work.

Client Awareness

Heidi is in an egalitarian marriage, one in which both partners took on housework, worked outside of the home, and chose roles in their relationship according to their unique skills and life circumstances. Heidi's husband took on the bulk of the household chores, because he had a flexible schedule and worked from home. Due to Heidi's hectic schedule, it made sense for him to manage the household responsibilities. She felt a bit insecure about his share of the work, as she felt it was unequal, while also admitting that she had very little time to complete the tasks due to her work schedule. Equality in the relationship was important to Heidi, and she felt guilt by feeling as though she was unable to divide tasks at home in an equitable manner. I acknowledged her attitudes and values pertaining to her beliefs about relationships, and worked with Heidi to create goals that would support her ability to contribute in the ways she felt were appropriate in her relationship.

Heidi's differences with her family of origin regarding religious beliefs and socio-economic status impacted her relationship with them. Her beliefs were processed in the counseling relationship in relation to her family of origin. Heidi identified as agnostic, while her family is devoutly Christian. While she felt confident in her beliefs, it was a source of disconnect in her relationship with her family. We processed feelings related to feeling different and unaccepted because of her beliefs. She also shared feelings about the upward mobility she experienced that was not experienced by the rest of the family. The counseling relationship became a safe space for her to feel accepted while discussing these sensitive issues. By accepting her beliefs and by focusing on her as a client, I was able to support her as she shared many aspects of her complex identity. It was unnecessary for us to take action as it pertained to her religious beliefs or her socioeconomic status, as she was comfortable in her religious identity and proud of her success. She was also accepting of the religious identities of her family members. We were able to process some personal feelings of guilt related to her socioeconomic trajectory, and the lack of acceptance she felt by her family. The counseling relationship provided a safe space for her to process her feelings surrounding these topics of importance to her.

The Counseling Relationship

An awareness on the part of myself and Heidi's differences, as well as cultural similarities helped shape our counseling relationship. In some ways our similarities made it easy to relate, but in many ways our beliefs and personalities were drastically different. It was important that I empathize with her without over-identifying or making assumptions about her that were rooted in my own worldview. I utilized skills of self-awareness and an attitude of genuine curiosity. Through this curiosity a genuine rapport grew in which we were able to explore feelings that were not readily accessible to Heidi. I worked to balance a relationship of authenticity and openness while making the sessions focused on Heidi and her experiences. I did not reveal much about myself in order to focus on Heidi and her concerns throughout the relationship, and the advocacy interventions suggested were focused on Heidi, as opposed to my own biases, which could have filtered into the relationship due to some of our cultural similarities.

Counseling Interventions and Advocacy

Upon exploration of feelings of marginalization in the workplace, Heidi and I took action by exploring her socialization as a woman. We explored how internalized beliefs about her gender and microaggressions she had received in the workplace changed her behavior, and prevented her from setting healthy boundaries with co-workers. Heidi expressed that while she excelled at work, she constantly felt pressure to succeed, and as a result, struggled to set boundaries that could help her have a more balanced life. Due to her strong work ethic and the pressure she felt to succeed as a female in a leadership role, it was difficult for her to engage in self-care if it meant saying no to a work task or project. Some of our work included acknowledging fears related to her marginalized status as a woman, ways in which she was socialized that led her to feel as if setting boundaries were not possible, and the feeling of needing to work harder than others in order to be respected as a superior in her role as leader. She also stressed that she felt a pressure to be liked by those below her and above her in the hierarchy. This led to feelings of resentment when she took on the work tasks of others to complete tasks more quickly to please her superiors. Through awareness of these drives and the emotional components behind them such as a need to please, and fear of losing her job or position, she was able to make decisions about how and what she would like to change. Heidi and I discussed ways that she could advocate for herself in the workplace and co-created a plan that helped her feel more comfortable at work.

TREATMENT: HIKING WITH HEIDI AND THE COUNSELING RELATIONSHIP

The following goals were addressed in counseling with Heidi: 1) Help Heidi identify and verbalize factors that were contributing to her depression; 2) explore family of origin issues that could be contributing to unhealthy patterns of behavior; 3) examine existential concerns such as meaning making; the inevitability of death, isolation vs. connectedness, and responsibility vs. freedom; 4) utilize insights gained to create healthier patterns of functioning and to increase life satisfaction. As our time together progressed, I also wanted to incorporate Ecotherapy into my approach with Heidi. She seemed like a perfect candidate, and I felt she might benefit from the many positive aspects of spending time in nature such as exercise, relaxation and stress reduction, increased focus, and trying a new activity that could help her increase satisfaction in recreational activities and life in general (Berman et al., 2012; Bowler et al., 2010; Bratman et al., 2012; Hartig et al., 1991; Leather et al., 1998; Louv, 2005; Schreyer et al.,1990). Heidi and I engaged in Ecotherapy to help facilitate exploration, goal setting and behavioral change.

Ecotherapy

A few weeks into our counseling relationship, I brought up the possibility of taking our work outside. I mentioned that with some clients walking and talking in nature can be very beneficial for their progress. I explained some of the inherent benefits to spending time in nature such as improved mood (Berman et al., 2012), decreased depression and anxiety (Maas et al., 2009), increased focus, stress decreases (Kaplan, 1995), and the ability to access the mood boosting benefits of exercise (Doucette, 2004).

Walking or hiking in nature with depressed clients can be especially healing because people who experience depression often lack energy and motivation. While exercising and engaging in enjoyable activities that can help the client feel a sense of achievement can be helpful, it can often be difficult to get out of bed, let alone exercise. When counselors set the counseling relationship outdoors, getting to the appointment can be the push the client needs to experience the benefits of nature and exercise. With a caring professional aware of the personal needs of the client, the natural environment can be a calming, neutral space in which to process material. This was especially helpful for Heidi, as she was unsure what sorts of recreational activities she enjoyed. By walking outside together, I thought that maybe this could be a healthy habit she actually enjoyed.

In our first outdoor session we met at a nature preserve with a medium length trail. I knew the trail very well, so I could plan our walk for the appropriate amount of time and maximum privacy on the trail. Heidi really enjoyed the experience. She stated that it was something that she had never done before, but that she felt healthier, more grounded and invigorated after our session, and agreed to meet again at the trail. This journey led us for another six or so sessions on and off the trail. There are some issues that can be processed in the total privacy of an office, but most of the time we were alone on the trail and we could discuss freely most of the issues and goals mentioned above. I updated my informed consent with her and shared that there are some challenges to confidentiality. We came up with a plan in case someone she knew saw us walking. She chose to give them no explanation and just a quick hello or short introduction if necessary. We chose not to disclose to anyone that I was her counselor. It turned out that we never needed the plan, but it made us both feel at ease about protecting her confidentiality in a semi-public space.

Her relationship with the natural world continued to grow outside of the counseling relationship. Soon she was taking her dogs for longer walks and including both her husband and the dogs on hikes in the nature preserve without me. She even scheduled vacations around natural beauty and specific walks she could take. This was quickly becoming a hobby, a form of self-care, and a way to de-stress and reconnect to herself. I was thrilled to be able to share with her the benefits of spending time in nature together. Heidi's time hiking in nature was the beginning of reconnecting to herself.

Goal 1: Identify and Verbalize Factors Contributing to Depression

Heidi and I worked together in the assessment phase of counseling to give voice to the problems she was experiencing in her life. Heidi had never been to counseling before, and the process of talking about feelings was daunting. She felt uncomfortable sharing intimate details about her life, but became more comfortable with the process as we continued to build a relationship of trust. For this stage of the process we stayed indoors. It seemed safer to get comfortable with one another in a completely private space. Even after trust had been established, I noticed it was difficult for her to express feelings in a less than general way, or connect feelings with patterns of behavior or circumstances in her life. As our relationship grew, and we uncovered authentic concerns with which Heidi was grappling, themes emerged related to over-work, a lack of balance in her work and recreational life, and a lack of pleasure and interest to most activities in her life. Heidi worked so hard for so much of her life that she did not even know what recreational activities she enjoyed. She had rarely tried any, and when she was engaging socially or in hobbies or activities, she felt guilty about not working, or exhausted from working so hard. A goal became to help her explore and incorporate activities that were enjoyable into her life. One of these activities became hiking once we started having sessions on the trail and Heidi found that it was a very enjoyable activity for her.

Goal 2: Explore Family of Origin Issues

Throughout our time in counseling, we explored her family of origin and how the dynamic in her family influenced her worldview and outlook on life. By verbalizing feelings about her family, she came to identify her family as distant, cold and stoic. When asked questions about a proud moment, happy times and family traditions, she had difficulty identifying many positive memories in her family of origin. She had three other siblings, but described herself as an outsider in a large Catholic family. She did not identify with the religion of the family and did not develop close relationships to her parents and siblings. While I listened, I started to wonder how these moments impacted her, because she shared the history as fact in an unemotional way. She claimed that the dynamic did not really affect her, and had difficulty connecting emotionally to the lack of love and care she had received in her family. She shared that she avoids family events if possible. As the first person in her family to attend college, she had received some negative treatment because of the differences in her academic aptitude growing up. It became apparent that many of her emotional needs were not attended to in her family as she came of age, and that validation from her parents was something that she had never received. Because the need for love, recognition, and validation were not met in her family of origin, we explored existential themes related to connectedness vs. isolation, and how lack of validation impacted some of her current ways of coping. She was able to articulate that she had stopped asking for her needs to be met, and thus had suppressed her needs and wants for so long that she struggled to even identify what many of them were. As we discussed some of these themes on the trail, I found that the dynamic of walking side by side made it easier for her to share about some of the aspects of her life that were more painful. A lack of direct eye contact, the movement and exercise, and the serenity of the landscape made it easier to express some very personal aspects of her life.

Strengths

We also explored her strengths and how she managed to positively cope with not getting her needs met. She found a positive and healthy relationship with her now husband and formed a bond that provided emotional support and friendship. She managed to nurture that relationship for many years and give positive support and friendship to her partner. Heidi had close friends, and an altruistic spirit. She also had a wry sense of humor that emerged more frequently as our relationship developed during our time together. Heidi was intelligent and could use that intelligence to educate herself on ways to manage depression, and to gain insight on self-care strategies. Finally, Heidi had confidence in her role at work, her ability to take risks to succeed, and confidence in her ability to work for what she wanted and to attain goals. This will and deep determination were major strengths that she could apply to her entire life to create a life that felt meaningful and fulfilling. In fact, her feelings of competence already contributed meaningfully to her self-esteem. The confidence that came from reconnecting with her body on the trail and even bringing her dogs and her husband out to the nature preserve outside of our sessions, helped contribute to a sense of accomplishment by engaging in self-care, mastering a trail, and as experiencing the positive effects of exercise and relaxing impact that spending time in nature had on her mental health.

Understanding Culture

Heidi understood how poverty may have impacted the dynamic in her family, and therefore empathized with the mindset of her parents. In her large family, the attention and energy went into literally putting food on the table, which may have left little time for support for extra-curricular activities, and even emotional support. She also shared that culturally her family is non-emotional and pragmatic. That approach, combined with financial stress could easily lead to the family dynamic she described. I had to be careful to discern between how these dynamics may have impacted Heidi without filtering her experience through my values or ideas of what I thought a family should provide for their child, particularly because our socio-economic childhood expereinces were different. I focused on her feelings, and how these factors shaped her into the woman she became. Through this process of listening I started to wonder if her ambition derived in large part from a combination of the economic insecurity she experienced as a child as well as an outlet for validation from receiving a good grade, or attention from a teacher. We explored these hypotheses and Heidi decided that these ways of coping made sense given the circumstances of her upbringing. We then discussed how these coping strategies of over-dependence on academic achievement and work were useful for her at one time, but that now the behavior was hurting her in many ways instead of helping her. While experiencing nature on the trail, we utilized metaphors and engaged in mindfulness exercises aimed at reconnecting with a sense of "just being." The insight she developed through talk therapy and mindfulness activities in nature helped her understand her patterns of coping, while learning new coping skills. She was then able to change the habits that were no longer serving her and incorporate new skills to help her life a life that felt meaningful and authentic.

Goal 3: Exploring Existential Concerns

Meaning Making

From the existential lens through which I conceptualized my work with Heidi, I was curious about what gave her life purpose and meaning. We all have guiding principles, dreams, relationships, or a passion that gives our life meaning and purpose. For some it is family, others religion, some their job, a running hobby, travel, their partnerships, their art, or any passion that makes life motivating and fulfilling. I wanted to know about Heidi, and what fueled her motivation for intentional living. At first Heidi had a difficult time pinpointing what gave her life meaning. She had a great deal of substance and an important life-giving existence, but it was difficult to wade through the depression to identify those important relationships and passions. Heidi's main motivation in life was hard work. She had learned that hard work would get her stability, independence, and the ability to depend on herself. She had enormous strengths in the form of self-sufficiency and the ability to create, work hard, and support herself. She did not need to depend on others for her livelihood and received validation in the form of promotions. These successes led to feelings of security in her life that were positive for her.

However, the anxiety she experienced that comes with an overdeveloped sense of independence became harmful to Heidi. These feelings of being overworked eventually led to depression. She felt stuck in an unbalanced work situation in which she was neglecting every other important part of her life. She struggled to assert healthy boundaries and self-care, which put both her physical and mental health in danger, and even put strain on her marriage. While her work was important (she helped to legally create an infrastructure in her city to support victims of crime), she did not feel connected to the help she was providing for others, as she was stuck behind a desk, disconnected to the impact her policy had on actual people. Further, the amount of work she was doing in many ways served as a way to avoid feelings of emptiness, an existential vacuum, and other negative feelings that are part of the human experience.

Authenticity and the Inevitability of Death

Heidi had identified her need to please others and find security in patterns that were no longer serving her. That young person who had to work so hard to experience financial security, and validation through hard work from others had achieved it, and Heidi was no longer fulfilled. Now it was time to ask herself what actually brought her joy and fulfillment. What was it that Heidi wanted in her life outside of security and validation through work? These were questions that she had not even dared to ask herself, because she was so busy and exhausted striving for security. Upon exploration, it was obvious that Heidi could benefit from setting boundaries around work, engaging in self-care, and trying new recreational activities to find authenticity and fulfillment in her life. Heidi has a solid identity, she knew who she loved and what she did not like. She just needed a little help to find out what did bring her joy, purpose and fulfillment. Heidi shared that she was an animal lover and enjoyed volunteering at the local shelter helping the veterinarians and vet techs. She felt good helping the animals and it was intellectually stimulating to her. As we continued to work together, Heidi was able to start putting boundaries in place in her work life to make time for things she enjoyed. Volunteering at the shelter was too difficult at first but making time to go on walks with her own dogs was a manageable activity she could incorporate once she started setting boundaries at work.

Responsibility Vs. Freedom

As mentioned previously, work-life balance became a major goal for Heidi in our work together. Heidi and I explored many factors that led to her inability to set boundaries between her work and home life. Waking early in the morning and leaving later in the evening characterized her work life. Throw on a lengthy commute and a job with an "on-call" responsibility, and Heidi was overloaded. She stated that even when she was home she was often working in front of the television into the late evening hours. She struggled with sleep, often staying up late at night only to be exhausted every morning. We worked together to create small changes such as no phone in the bedroom, creating better sleep hygiene, making a weekday rule of no laptops at home and other small changes that were reasonable to incorporate. Heidi admitted that she placed more pressure on herself than her employers did, and that she felt a need to please others and to never let her superiors down. We connected this extreme emotional need to her upbringing, the need to please her teachers, distinguish herself, and validate her self-worth through achievement. We worked to shift her barometer of self-worth to look within and seek validation on her own set of values. We explored her fears around security, celebrating attitudinal strengths that were motivational and life giving, while challenging beliefs that were harmful to Heidi's peace of mind. We were also aware of societal expectations of women and explored her upbringing related to gender roles and societal expectations of women. While she did not consciously believe in traditional gender roles, she did express anxiety around her status as a high-ranking employee. This anxiety manifested in her belief that she had to work harder and be more likeable than other employees to maintain their respect and her position. While some of this anxiety is rooted in very real sexism and lack of equity in many workplaces in America, it was beneficial to process these feelings to make deliberate decisions about how much she was willing to sacrifice. We processed how much of these feelings were a direct reflection of her environment, and how much of these behaviors were rooted in fear to help her change behaviors accordingly.

Connectedness vs. Isolation

Heidi found strength in her relationship with her husband, who had been her partner for the better part of two decades. She expressed a desire to spend more meaningful time with him, share more enjoyment and fun together, and to help him with more housekeeping and practical chores around the house. The depression she had experienced also kept her from engaging in social activities with friends, and even when she was physically present in her relationships she felt distant, and did not enjoy these encounters, feeling tired, irritable and in a "down" mood. Part of Heidi's plan involved adding more social activities to her life once she made more room for rest, and self-care. Once she started to implement changes in her work/life balance, she made more room for enjoyable friendships as well. She met her friends at the park with her dogs, and started making more couples' dates with friends. She even started planning nature-based trips with her husband that were semi "off the grid," meaning it was more difficult for work to reach her while she was on vacation. She realized that she had many vacation days accrued that she had not used, and so she started taking the time off that she had earned. This concentrated time with her husband, exploring new places, hobbies, and activities, ignited excitement in her life and re-invigorated her relationship. Heidi's life satisfaction started to gradually improve.

Goal 4: Utilizing Insights to Create Healthier Patterns of Functioning

Heidi did hard work to explore wants and needs, family of origin issues, existential themes, and beliefs and patterns of behavior that were no longer serving her. She bravely examined societal factors that influenced her well-being as a woman in a position of leadership in the workplace. Heidi changed negative habits such as overworking and managed diffuse boundaries that were impacting her well-being. These changes allowed her time to explore activities and self-care that enhanced her life. Through awareness of deeper motivations and coping strategies that no longer served her, she examined beliefs and patterns of behavior that she deemed inauthentic. Heidi engaged in hikes with me while we worked on goals in the counseling relationship. As a result, Heidi became passionate about hiking, and used it as a tool for self-care, connection with her pets, partner, and friends. She even started centering vacations around challenging natural environments. Heidi explored other recreational activities that were life-enhancing and asked herself difficult questions about what she wanted her life to look like now and in the future, to create the most meaningful life possible. She took major steps to change her life to reflect an existence that was most meaningful to her.

Progress

Throughout the counseling relationship, Heidi and I were able to address a variety of goals including: 1). helping her identify and verbalize issues that were contributing to her depression; 2) exploring family of origin issues that could be contributing to unhealthy patterns of behavior; 3) examining existential concerns such as meaning making, authenticity and the inevitability of death, isolation vs. connectedness, and responsibility vs. freedom; 4) utilizing insights gained to create healthier patterns of functioning to increase life satisfaction. We also engaged in Ecotherapy to help facilitate exploration, goal setting and behavioral change.

Heidi was able to successfully articulate feelings and life circumstances that contributed to her feelings of depression to identify specific changes that she could engage in to start to feel more fulfilled in life. Heidi was able to uncover unhealthy coping skills that began in childhood to cope with feelings of worthlessness in her family of origin. While recognizing that these coping skills were helpful at the time, she realized that over-working to feel secure and worthwhile was no longer working for her, and she was able to set boundaries related to work to help her feel more balanced in her life. We processed feelings, and she was able to build skills to combat negative beliefs by tracing feelings back to unmet needs in her family. We discussed her personal values, wants, needs and fulfillment. Heidi defined what she wanted in her life and took steps to start living instead of just working. While Heidi could not articulate what brought her joy at the beginning of our time together, eventually she shared a whole host of interests related to caring for animals and spending time in nature. She harnessed her courage to try hiking, which opened her up to trying a variety of other activities. When we ended our time together, Heidi's sleep had improved, her interest and energy for life had increased, and she had changed some major habits that had impacted her physical and mental health. She asked herself hard questions related to meaning and purpose, and redefined what she was willing to tolerate in order to live a life that felt authentic to her. I was grateful to spend time with such an intelligent, courageous client. I am often impressed and amazed by how adaptable and strong my clients are, and Heidi was a true inspiration.

CONCLUSION

I am constantly in awe of the way nature can transform people. My own relationship with nature has informed this perspective, as well as the great deal of literature emerging that supports using nature to help improve both physical and mental health outcomes. My journey with Heidi including using Ecotherapy, and a multicultural, existential approach. Ecotherapy is inherently cross cultural, as nature is so deeply connected to the life of all people on earth. We cannot sustain life without it, and various cultures have connected in spiritual, practical, and aesthetic ways throughout the entirety of history. Therefore, layering a nature-infused approach is fairly easy to incorporate for most clients. In addition to ethically incorporating nature into our counseling relationship, I utilized the MSJCC and examined my own views, biases and worldview in order to get a deeper understanding of how my identity could interfere with or enhance the counseling relationship. I also examined Heidi's world views, paying attention to her perspectives to make sure I was respecting her values. I used the developmental and aspirational competencies of the MSJCC to enhance my work with Heidi. Through my work with Heidi I grew as an existential ecotherapist and strengthened my multicultural counseling skills. I was thrilled to work with Heidi as a counselor, and was honored to help her on her journey of living a more connected, joyful and authentic life.

REFERENCES

Adams, W. W. (2005). Ecopsychology and phenomenology: Existential analysis. *Journal of the Society for Existential Analysis*, *16*(2), 269–283.

Becker, S. P. (2010). Wilderness therapy: Ethical considerations for mental health professionals. *Child and Youth Care Forum*, *39*(1), 47–61. doi:10.100710566-009-9085-7

Berger, R. (2006). Using contact with nature, creativity and rituals as a therapeutic medium with children with learning difficulties: A case study. *Emotional & Behavioural Difficulties*, *11*(2), 135–146. doi:10.1080/13632750600619430

Berman, M. G., Kross, E., Krpan, K. M., Askren, M. K., Burson, A., Deldin, P. J., & Jonides, J. (2012). Interacting with nature improves cognition and affect for individuals with depression. *Journal of Affective Disorders*, *140*(3), 300–305. doi:10.1016/j.jad.2012.03.012 PMID:22464936

Bowler, D. E., Buyung-Ali, L. M., Knight, T. M., & Pullin, A. S. (2010). A systematic review of evidence for the added benefits to health of exposure to natural environments. *BMC Public Health*, *10*(1), 456. doi:10.1186/1471-2458-10-456 PMID:20684754

Bratman, G. N., Hamilton, J. P., & Daily, G. C. (2012). The impacts of nature experience on human cognitive function and mental health. *Annals of the New York Academy of Sciences*, *1249*(1), 118–136. doi:10.1111/j.1749-6632.2011.06400.x PMID:22320203

Buzzell, L., & Chalquist, C. (2009). *Ecotherapy: Healing with nature in mind*. San Francisco, CA: Sierra Club Books.

Capuzzi, D., & Gross, D. R. (2011). *Counseling and psychotherapy: Theories and interventions*. Pearson.

Corey, G. (2017). *Theory and practice of counseling and psychotherapy* (10th ed.). Boston, MA: Cengage.

Doucette, P. A. (2004). Walk and talk: An intervention for behaviorally challenged youths. *Adolescence San Diego*, *39*(154), 373. PMID:15563045

Hartig, T., Mang, M., & Evans, G. W. (1991). Restorative effects of natural environment experiences. *Environment and Behavior*, *23*(1), 3–26. doi:10.1177/0013916591231001

Hasbach, P. H. (2012). Ecotherapy. In P. H. Kahn Jr & P. H. Hasbach (Eds.), *Ecopsychology: Science, totems, and the technological species* (pp. 115–139). Cambridge, MA: MIT Press.

Houlden, V., Weich, S., Porto de Albuquerque, J., Jarvis, S., & Rees, K. (2018). The relationship between greenspace and the mental wellbeing of adults: A systematic review. *PLoS One*, *13*(9), 1–35. doi:10.1371/journal.pone.0203000 PMID:30208073

Kaplan, S. (1995). The restorative benefits of nature: Toward an integrative framework. *Journal of Environmental Psychology*, *15*(3), 169–182. doi:10.1016/0272-4944(95)90001-2

King, B. (2015) *The shared experiences of counselors who practice in natural environments.* Retrieved from https://scholarworks.uno.edu/td/203

Leather, P., Pyrgas, M., Beale, D., & Lawrence, C. (1998). Windows in the workplace, sunlight, view, and occupational stress. *Journal of Environment and Behavior*, *30*(6), 739–762. doi:10.1177/001391659803000601

Louv, R. (2005). *Last child in the woods: Saving our children from nature-deficit disorder.* Chapel Hill, NC: Algonquin Books.

Maas, J. J., Verheij, R. A., de Vries, S. S., Spreeuwenberg, P. P., Schellevis, F. G., & Groenewegen, P. P. (2009). Morbidity is related to a green living environment. *Journal of Epidemiology and Community Health*, *63*(12), 967–973. doi:10.1136/jech.2008.079038 PMID:19833605

Ratts, M. J., Singh, A. A., Nassar, M. S., Butler, S. K., & McCullough, J. R. (2016). Multicultural and Social Justice Counseling Competencies: Guidelines for the Counseling Profession. *Journal of Multicultural Counseling and Development*, *44*(1), 28–48. doi:10.1002/jmcd.12035

Reese, R. F., & Myers, J. E. (2012). EcoWellness: The missing factor in holistic wellness models. *Journal of Counseling and Development*, *90*(4), 400–406. doi:10.1002/j.1556-6676.2012.00050.x

Roscoe, L. J. (2009). Wellness: A review of theory and measurement for counselors. *Journal of Counseling and Development*, *87*(2), 216–226. doi:10.1002/j.1556-6678.2009.tb00570.x

Schreyer, R., Williams, D. R., Haggard, L., Easley, A. T., Passineau, J. F., & Driver, B. L. (1990). Episodic versus continued wilderness participation—implications for self-concept enhancement. In A. T. Easley, J. F. Passineau, & B. L. Driver (Eds.), The use of wilderness for personal growth, therapy, and education (General Technical Report RM-193, pp. 23–26). Fort Collins, CO: Rocky Mountain Forestand Range Experiment Station.

Softas-Nall, S., & Woody, W. D. (2017). The loss of human connection to nature: Revitalizing selfhood and meaning in life through the ideas of Rollo May. *Ecopsychology*, *9*(4), 241–252. doi:10.1089/eco.2017.0020

Chapter 12
Flying With Eddie:
Complicated Grief in the Military

Emeline Carol Eckart
University of Indianapolis, USA

EXECUTIVE SUMMARY

Over 2.4 million American service men and women were deployed overseas between 2001 to 2011. Families of these service members include over one million spouses and two million children under the age of 18. There is a growing need for counselors to understand the mental health needs of military service men and woman, and the unique aspects of military culture. This chapter will demonstrate how to practically apply the Multicultural and Social Justice Counseling Competencies (MSJCC) to counseling work with the military population through a case study.

INTRODUCTION TO THE CASE

Case Description

Eddie calls my private practice office for counseling, stating that he recently lost a friend in an accident and people are urging him to talk with someone. He states he is in the military and does not want to see a counselor on base because he does not want anyone to find out he is in counseling. He is tearful on the phone and asks for the first available time slot. I previously served fourteen years in the military as an aviator before becoming a counselor. I schedule him for an intake the very next day.

DOI: 10.4018/978-1-7998-0022-4.ch012

Eddie arrives promptly at the office in jeans and a collared shirt. He is groomed, though his eyes are swollen and red. He appears nervous as I invite him into the counseling space. When asked what brings him into counseling today, Eddie tears up. Eventually, he blurts out that his best friend, who was in the same aviation squadron as him, died. A week ago his friend was completing an annual flight evaluation in marginal weather, and Air Traffic Control lost radar on the airplane. Three days later the plane was found in the ocean underneath the area where the plane had been operating. Both pilots died in the incident.

Since that time Eddie reports difficulty sleeping and eating. He reports increased use of alcohol. He no longer drives his own car but instead drives his best friend's car around. He is in shock about the mishap and is angry the squadron has started to continue normal operations. Eddie states that he knows the squadron needs to continue workups before they leave on their six-month deployment in three weeks. He is not sure whether he can go on this deployment, whether it is safe for him to fly an aircraft under these circumstances. He is concerned that if he does not go on this deployment, it will impact his career. "I just can't get myself together!"

I utilize a biopsychosocial assessment during the intake session to assess the psychological, social, and cultural factors that impact Eddie. Eddie is from a middle-class background, in which his parents urged him to seek scholarship opportunities for college. Eddie is a white male who entered the Naval Academy after high school. Upon his graduation from the Naval Academy, he entered the pilot training program in the Navy and became a helicopter pilot. He has served as an active duty officer for five years and is currently on a tour of sea duty that is three years in duration. Eddie is 27 years old, identifies as Catholic, and is a Lieutenant (O-3) (Redmond et al., 2015) in the Navy. He is scheduled to leave for deployment onboard a ship in three weeks. He has been married for five years and has no children. He and his wife live off base. He states no family history of mental illness or substance use. Eddie reports this is the first time he has experienced a significant death in his life. Eddie reports that there are some negative aspects of the military, but overall, he enjoys his occupation and lifestyle.

Literature Review

The military as a social institution has a distinct culture, and within the larger culture, subcultures are based on an individual's affiliation with a specific branch of the military, such as the Navy, Air Force, or Army, etc. (Branson, 2017). In April 2019, the Navy reported a total force of 332, 507 active duty members and 101, 018 reserve members (www.navy.mil). Men and women who are part of the Navy are involved in various careers that include aviation, navy seals, search and rescue, medical, cryptology, meteorology, navigation, explosive ordinance disposal, etc. (www.navy.mil). A unique aspect of the Navy is the sailor's experience with "shipboard life" during their sea tour, which they rotate with a shore tour (Wilcove, Schwerin, & Kline, 2009, p. 446). During a sea tour a sailor typically leaves for a six-month deployment on board a US Fleet ship or submarine, and is forward deployed to strategic locations around the globe.

Redmond et al. (2015) summarized the structure and culture of the US military for those who may not have an understanding of that culture. Service members learn military cultural norms during their indoctrination training, which teaches military personnel how to think, communicate, and interact with each other. Individual thinking transforms from individualist to collectivist thinking that focuses on completing the mission. Service members learn a new communication style, which emphasizes professionalism in greetings (e.g., using *sir* or *ma'am*), and common military terms and acronyms (e.g., *galley* means *dining room*; *O-6* stands for *Captain*) (Redmond et al., 2015). Additionally, service members learn new ways of interacting, in which salutes replace handshakes. Rules of interaction focus on following a chain of command and maintaining professional relationships with coworkers.

Within the military culture, a member's social status depends on the subculture with which they identify. Subcultures include differences common to many groups of people such as gender, sexual orientation, social class, race, ethnicity, and age, but there are additional subcultures in the military (Branson, 2017). Each service branch has a distinct culture, and rivalries exist between services, as evidenced in the annual Army vs. Navy football game. An individual's rank identifies him or her as part of another subculture, comprised of officers or enlisted personnel (Gleeson & Hammer, 2014). Additional subcultures exist based on an individual's job duty assignment, for example, pilots, sailors, shipmates, and "grunts" (Redmond et al., 2015). Aspects of military culture common to most service members include a lack of control over assignments and deployment dates, exposure to combat or life-threatening situations, lack of sleep or rest during operations, and high expectations for performance (Branson, 2017).

An example of a specific subculture in the US Navy is the aviation component. Aviation service men and women deploy on the same ship as sailors, though identify as aviators and maintain a distinct identity from their shipboard peers. Movies such as *Top* Gun depict a culture of aviators with attitude who participate in dangerous operations (Simpson, Bruckheimer, & Scott, 1986). The risks inherent in the aviation duty assignment are discussed often. Aircraft mishaps are due to either mechanical or human error, with aircrew/human error explaining the majority of mishaps (Alkov & Gaynor, 1991). During deployment aviation missions occur primarily at night, causing fatigue and stress which can lead to degraded pilot performance (Neri & Sheppell, 1994). The Navy spends a considerable amount of time emphasizing aircrew coordination training in which pilots monitor each other for signs of work overload and stress, and readily admit the psychological or physical stressors that can impact an individual's ability to complete a mission (Alkov & Gaynor, 1991).

Military culture also impacts the families of service members. Often a military spouse hierarchy develops based on the rank of the active duty spouse (Redmond et al., 2015). The family might live in a certain geographic location based on the service member's current duty assignment (Russo & Fallon, 2015). Other cultural differences include whether the family lives on or off base, whether they utilize health care at a base or civilian medical facility, and what school the child attends (DeGraff, O'Neal, & Mancini, 2016). When they become adults, some military children refer to themselves as *military brats* to summarize their frequent relocation and inability to call one place home (Wertsch, 1991).

A unique aspect of military culture is the deployment cycle and how it impacts service members and their families (Redmond et al., 2015). The five stages of the deployment cycle include predeployment, deployment, sustainment, redeployment, and postdeployment (Pincus, House, Christenson, & Adler, 2007). Hicks, Lenard, and Brendle (2016) described each of these five stages of deployment in their research with military families. During predeployment, service members work long hours in preparation for leaving and experience tension and anxiety about leaving. The deployment phase occurs during the first month of separation and is characterized by feelings of anger, frustration, grief, and loneliness. During the deployment stage, the service member and family adjust to life without the service member present. The redeployment stage is filled with anticipation and expectations about the return home, and sometimes frustration due to high expectations of a positive return. In the last stage, postdeployment, emotional needs must be reconsidered as the service member reintegrates into civilian culture.

The values of military culture are summarized as a warrior mentality and extend into every aspect of a military member's life (Redomond et al., 2015). Military culture values physical and mental strength (O'Brien, Keith, & Shoemaker, 2015). Service members learn to adapt and overcome challenging situations and to think from a collectivist perspective that emphasizes group cohesion (Branson, 2017; Canfield & Weiss, 2015). "Obedience, discipline, self-sacrifice, trust, and courage" are key military values (Redmond et al., 2015, p. 14). Values such as mental toughness and self-reliance help service members tolerate difficulties and emotional distress. Individuals with problems are perceived as weak and may be rejected or viewed as a liability to completing the mission (Bryan, 2016).

Castro, Kintzle, & Hassan (2015) compiled a list of common thoughts, emotions, and behaviors of combat veterans from discussions with veterans or counselors. Thoughts include being proud of one's service, and "people will think I am weak if I ask for help…showing emotions is a sign of weakness" (Castro et al., 2015, p.

301). Emotions include being angry, sad, happy to be alive, and lonely. Common behaviors include not being able to sleep, constantly feeling on edge, and not being able to calm down. The authors recommended increasing service members' self-awareness of their thoughts, emotions, and behaviors so they can recognize when they might need the assistance of a mental health practitioner.

Many of the cultural values listed above are protective factors, however, they can also be risk factors for a service member's mental health. Mental toughness and self-reliance can lead to avoiding problems, not asking for help when it is needed, and rejecting social support (Bryan, 2016). Service members who discuss problems instead of solutions may be seen as unmotivated or complaining, and subsequently may be rejected by peers. Additionally, a social dominance orientation exists within the military, in which members of the dominant group stigmatize members of the out-group if they do not conform to the dominant mentality (Johnson, Rosenstein, Buhrke, & Haldeman, 2013). Many service members will not voluntarily seek counseling and will only attend counseling if ordered by their command or given an ultimatum by a family member (Canfield & Weiss, 2015).

Additional barriers to seeking mental health treatment for soldiers are: shortcomings in a counselors' understanding of military culture, career concerns, mental health concerns, and evaluation of mental health issues (Eckart & Dufrene, 2015). Service members become frustrated at having to explain basic aspects of the culture to therapists who have little knowledge of military culture. Service members are concerned that seeking mental health treatment might negatively impact their careers, in terms of duty assignments, confidentiality, and promotions. Concerns about mental health include a stigma against receiving help. Finally, mental health issues are often assessed incorrectly or inaccurately, so that those who seek help do not receive the treatment they need (Zinzow et al., 2013).

To effectively help clients that are service members, counselors need to understand military culture, subcultures, social norms, and values. A therapist can better understand a client's worldview by considering military service as an extension of an individual's identity (Strom et al., 2012). Strom et al. pointed out that a counselor's direct experience serving in the military would enhance cultural competence with clients. In a study assessing 89 health care providers for military cultural competence, the authors found that participants with military exposure had increased knowledge of military culture compared to participants with no military exposure (Meyer, Hall-Clark, Hamaoka, & Peterson, 2015). However, the authors warned that a counselor may also make false assumptions about a client when a counselor's culture is similar to a client's culture.

Other considerations for counseling military members center on the member's schedule. Once a service member enters counseling, it is important to consider interventions the service member can use while on deployment or during extended periods away from the counselor. These interventions might include journaling, books, teleconferencing, email contact, and long-term homework (Eckart & Dufrene, 2015). Other counselors implement *smart books* (Bryan, 2016, p. 167), small notepads that allow a service member to write down coping statements or lessons from therapy and carry them discreetly in a uniform. A therapist should continually modify and adapt treatment approaches to meet the needs of each client.

INTRODUCTION TO THE COUNSELOR

Cultural Background

My background includes growing up as a white female in U.S. culture and serving as an officer in the U.S. military. I am the middle child in a single-parent family raised in the Midwest. I received a Reserve Officer Training Corps (ROTC) scholarship to attend college and upon graduation was required to enter the military. Because I had a college degree, I entered the military as an officer, where I completed nine years of active duty service, four years of select reserve duty, and currently serve in an inactive reserve status. My husband is an active duty service member who currently resides in a separate geographic location from me and my daughter, because of his duty assignment and our future plans upon his retirement.

Being an aviator in the Navy opened my eyes widely to the privilege and oppression that exist in the United States of America and other parts of the world. In 2001, when I entered the military, restrictions placed on females precluded them from participating in combat operations, some job duty assignments (e.g., being assigned to a submarine), and some military occupational specialties (MOS). In January of 2013, the Department of Defense rescinded the direct combat exclusion rule that had been in place since 1994 (Segal, Smith, Segal, & Canuso, 2016). There were few females in the pilot training program, and an immense amount of pressure to meet the program's high expectations was both physically and mentally demanding.

I had the privilege of being an officer, but I also experienced oppressive acts such as sexual harassment and gender bias. During my first deployment in 2004, my assigned ship had recently become integrated, meaning females were allowed. At that time, females were only present in the officer ranks, and I was one of three females on the entire ship. On my second deployment, I was the only female in my helicopter detachment of 35 personnel, though there were other females present on that ship.

Visiting other countries while in the Navy, I realized the privilege that Americans have, even as one of a few females present. In Oman, American females were told they needed to have their heads and knees covered before going out in the town. In other countries, such as India, women sat backward on scooters, holding their babies while males zoomed down the street. I was shocked to see the sacrifice some individuals would make to find more privilege in life when we rescued boatloads of migrants trying to go to America with nothing but oranges and the clothes they were wearing. Most of them were women and children. Even as I conducted rescue operations during Hurricane Katrina, I saw the privilege and oppression that is present in US society.

Counseling Approach

My approach to counseling is first to form a therapeutic alliance with the client. Using a feminist approach, I form a therapeutic relationship that is egalitarian and addresses any imbalances, i.e., between the therapist as expert and the client (Otting & Prosek, 2016). Sessions start by asking the client, "how would you like to use your time today?" Intake sessions usually begin by asking clients if they can tell me a little bit about what brought them in. My theoretical orientation is solution-focused, so I focus on what the client is experiencing, how they are experiencing it, and what they would like the future to look like when the problem is no longer present (Froerer & Connie, 2016). During intake sessions, I will ask clients to "tell me more about that" if I need clarification. I want to know and understand clients' worldviews so I can empathize with them.

My perspective that a session should be about the client's needs limits my level of self-disclosure with firm boundaries. I have received feedback that I can be very direct, yet still empathic. I believe some of these characteristics come from my military background. I learned a lot about boundaries through the division of officers and enlisted personnel. From my experience, it is easier to keep those boundaries if there is less self-disclosure. As a counselor and counselor educator, I begin a relationship with firm boundaries and limited self-disclosure, and those things can be relaxed at a later time if needed. Some clients ask about the military pictures in my office, and I answer by objectively telling them what I did in my previous career. The majority of clients who ask also have a military background or experience with someone in the military. In the case of Eddie, I feel it is important to disclose my military background as a way to let him know that I understand military culture, yet I also recognize that his worldview and experience in the military is different from mine.

CASE CONCEPTUALIZATION

The next section of this chapter focuses on case conceptualization of Eddie. Symptoms and presenting problems are used in case conceptualization to formulate a treatment plan. The symptoms the client describes and I observe are crying, trouble sleeping, trouble eating, and increased use of alcohol. The problems are grief and problems related to deployment. Thus, goals focus on decreasing symptoms and formulating solutions to the problems. At this time, Eddie appears to present with normal bereavement, though if his symptoms worsen, that may be changed to adjustment disorder (American Psychiatric Association, 2013).

Theory

When working with the military population, it is important for counselors to consider the amount of time they will have with a client to implement interventions and for clients to begin the process of change. Solution-focused therapy is a brief therapy with a concentration on client strengths, what the client would like to happen in the future, how things will be different when the problem no longer exists, and solution-oriented talk that does not focus on the problem (Seponski, 2016). Solution-focused brief therapy (SFBT) is collaborative, as the therapist believes the client has the solutions for his or her problem. Criticism of SFBT includes the theory being too simplistic and dismissive of client problems (Froerer & Connie, 2016).

In SFBT, interventions seek to increase client awareness and maintain a present and future focus. Solutions always come before the problems (De Shazer, 1988). For Eddie, the solution is to overcome his grief and join his squadron on deployment. If something is not working, the client is encouraged to try something different. Any time the client thinks about a past moment, it is to determine an exception when the problem was not present or when the client reacted differently (Cepeda & Davenport, 2006). The therapist focuses on what is working for the client. I want to ask about what is working, what has worked, and what might work. Acknowledging exceptions allows a client to recognize previous success in a given problem area and that solutions exist for a given problem. SFBT holds that small changes can lead to more significant changes. For Eddie, a small change in the impact of his grief will lead to more of his feelings changing related to the loss he recently experienced. As will be discussed later, Eddie acknowledges that not talking to his command about his grief is not helping him. Therapists emphasize that problems are caused by life transitions and do not indicate pathology. Considering the stigma against mental health treatment in the military (Eckart & Dufrene, 2015), it is important to normalize Eddie's experience of grief.

Therapists help clients achieve small changes by asking scaling questions (De Jong & Berg, 2013). When asking scaling questions Eddie can be asked how he rates his experience of grief (6 or 7), and what would need to happen for that to be a 5 instead. The *miracle question* is used to talk with clients about how things will be different when the problem no longer exists (Strong & Pyle, 2009). Conversation about the miracle question focuses on action and perceptions that help the client begin to create the solution to his or her problem, emphasizes behavioral descriptions of what that will look like (De Jong & Berg, 2013). I ask Eddie to describe how he will know he is no longer grieving his friend, what will be different, and how will he feel.

De Jong and Berg (2013) introduced a staged approach to forming solutions in SFBT. The stages are describing the problem, developing goals, finding exceptions, feedback, and evaluating client progress. These stages focus on the future and empower the client to resolve the problem. The language used in SFBT focuses on solution talk as opposed to problem talk. Thus, increased solution talk indicates progress in a client. Clients may shift their language from helplessness to taking control and becoming empowered to change things. Eddie can recognize areas in his life where he does have control in his life and can be empowered to make different choices, such as choosing to cope with alcohol or not. Compliments are given to the client on his or her progress toward a goal (De Jong & Berg, 2013). When a client is asked a scaling question, a change in number is another indication of progress. The stages of SFBT serve as a framework for the counseling session.

Multicultural and Social Justice Counseling Competencies (MSJCC)

Counselor/Client Intersectionality

Ratts et al. (2016) depicted a framework that indicates the privileged and oppressive statuses of counselor and client. When counseling Eddie, the quadrant that summarizes the therapeutic relationship is that of marginalized counselor–privileged client, given a male client receiving counseling from a female counselor. However, this interaction represents a snapshot in time, and it is possible for the counselor and client to consider themselves in more than one quadrant throughout the counseling session. For example, when discussing the military, both myself and Eddie experience privileged status due to our identities as officers, although a gender difference remains.

Developmental Domains and Competencies

The developmental domains in the MSJCC are: counselor self-awareness, client worldview, the therapeutic relationship, and counseling and advocacy interventions. Competencies within these domains are: attitudes and beliefs, knowledge, skills, and action (Ratts et al., 2016). By applying these domains and competencies, counselors are committing to a multicultural practice that includes the action of social justice when considering interventions for clients.

Counselor Self-Awareness

When working with Eddie, I must first consider my own attitudes, beliefs, and biases. I can examine my beliefs about being an individual who previously served in the military and the privilege of being an officer. I can also examine my beliefs about the oppression that occurred in the military due to my status as a female. When counseling Eddie, it is important for me to be aware of any feelings I have about the privilege white male officers experience. I can then explore how these beliefs impact my worldview. I acknowledge that other members of the military will have a different perspective than my own. In regard to action, I have spent a considerable amount of time immersed in military culture. I can be aware of how my military experience impacts my communication and how I talk with Eddie about his experience. *Counseling Military Families: What Mental Health Professionals Need to Know* (Hall, 2008) is a book I use a resource to separate my experiences in the military from the experience of my clients, and to review approaches to working with military members.

Client Worldview

To understand the client's worldview, I can understand the privilege and oppression the client experiences and how those experiences shape the client's attitudes and beliefs. Eddie is experiencing oppression for several reasons related to military culture. First, senior individuals in command make decisions that impact Eddie without his input, such as the decision to resume normal operations. Second, he is experiencing concerns about his career if he does not go on deployment. He has a loss of control over when he can leave on deployment and how that will impact his career, thus feels oppression. Additionally, he does not want anyone in the military to know that he is going to counseling, suggesting a stigma against mental health issues oppressing individuals who experience them.

To gain knowledge about Eddie's worldview, I can review research on mental health stigma in the military, and how career and confidentiality concerns may impact a client's decision to seek counseling (Eckart & Dufrene, 2015). I can use critical thinking and analysis to understand the oppressive force of power in the military and those senior to Eddie, and how that power impacts the client. The oppression this client feels contributes to his problems in several ways. First, the client is not reaching out to his military community for support but is coping by self-medicating with alcohol instead. Additionally, Eddie is not discussing his problems and loss with his command, so they are not aware of how much these events have impacted him. They are also not aware of his career concerns. If he discusses these concerns with them, there may be more solutions to choose from that will still allow him to meet his goals.

To better understand Eddie's worldview, I can stay current with the literature on counseling the military population. Prosek et al. (2018) developed competencies for counseling military populations that "offer a framework and foundational principles and practice for working with military-connected clients" (p. 88). These competencies are based on research and are considerations for counselors working with military clients.

Counseling Relationship

Counselor self-awareness and knowledge of the client's worldview can help me determine how the privileged and marginalized statuses of both Eddie and myself impact the therapeutic relationship. Thus, I ask the client things such as "tell me what being in the squadron is like for you" or "tell me what it would be like to tell a senior officer your concerns about leaving for deployment." For example, one way in which the marginalized status of myself in the military could impact the counseling relationship is in a situation where I use therapeutic confrontation. I might not use therapeutic confrontation because of my experiences with males in the military. In order to manage this I can be aware of my attitudes and beliefs about confronting a client in the military and rely on the knowledge and skills I have used when working with other clients. Ratts et al. (2016) suggest counselors know when it is appropriate to discuss topics such as power and stereotypes. In the case of Eddie, one way to manage the privilege and oppression present in the therapeutic alliance is to acknowledge that Eddie and I had similar experiences in the military yet that differences also exist.

In terms of action, I can participate in continuing education that focuses on being accepting of clients. When working with Eddie, this means accepting his wish to maintain confidentiality due to the stigma about mental health. I can also collaborate with colleagues when I feel I am not remaining objective or accepting of the client's choices (Sheperis & Sheperis, 2015).

Counseling and Advocacy Interventions

Once I gain self-awareness about working with Eddie, acknowledge Eddie's worldview, and discuss power, privilege, and oppression as they impact the therapeutic relationship, I can suggest appropriate interventions that promote social justice. In this case, Eddie has three weeks before leaving on deployment. SFBT is an appropriate counseling theory to use, as well as interventions that can be completed during deployment, such as books, email contact, journaling, and teleconferences (Eckart & Dufrene, 2015). Advocacy interventions for Eddie focus on the oppression Eddie is experiencing and how that is impacting his ability to formulate realistic solutions. I might try to help Eddie reflect on his thoughts about leaving for deployment and what is hindering him from telling his senior officers about his concerns. I can also discuss how military culture might support Eddie during this time and influence his well-being, as the military family takes care of its members. It is appropriate for myself and Eddie to discuss goals in terms of how he can advocate for himself so that the military can give him some of the support he needs.

Competencies for Counseling Military Populations

In 2016, the Military and Government Counseling Association appointed a task force to develop the Competencies for Counseling Military Populations (CCMP). "The intention of the CCMP is to provide a research-based set of guidelines that represent military considerations through the lens of a counselor professional identity" (Prosek et al., 2018, p. 88). Seven core competencies serve as the framework for the CCMP: military culture, ethics, system features, assessment of presenting concerns, identity development, treatment, and advocacy. These fall within the MSJCC competencies as seen in Table 1.

Table 1. Alignment of CCMP competencies within the MSJCC competencies (Prosek et al., 2018; Ratts et al., 2016)

Attitudes and Beliefs	Knowledge	Skills	Action
Ethics	Military Culture	Assessment of Presenting Concerns	Advocacy
	Identity Development	Treatment	
	Systems		

Military Culture

"Military culture represents general information about the functioning and worldview of military service members and their families" (Prosek et al., 2018, p. 88). Specifically, in this component counselors are "aware that differences in experiences may exist between Veterans who previously served and Service members/Veterans who currently serve, as well as Veterans who served in different areas" (p. 88). In Eddie's case, it is important for me to recognize that my military experiences occurred almost ten years before counseling Eddie and may have been very different from his experiences. Additionally, counselors should be aware of differing worldviews between civilians and military members. I am currently in civilian employment outside the military, so I will naturally have a different current worldview than my client.

Identity Development

The identity development component "represents the whole person concept of military life including one's personal identity as a Service member and connection to mission and core values of working as a military Service member across the lifespan" (Prosek et al., 2018, p. 89). In counseling Eddie, I start to understand how Eddie's sense of self relates to his occupational role and how his military rank influences his sense of self. Additionally, he may tie his career progression to his identity. Therefore, concerns about his mental health status impacting his career might ultimately affect his sense of self.

Systems

The systems component "represents general information about how Service members' families, spouses, and children experience the nature and structure of the military lifestyle" (Prosek et al., 2018, p. 90). It includes deployment, long periods of separation, and consequences of injury. When counseling Eddie, I want to acknowledge the stress of leaving for deployment and how it impacts the client. I also consider the emotional demands of the military and the impact of a high-risk occupation on the individual and family members. I consider Eddie's sources of support, such as marital and family support. Additionally, with Eddie's concerns about leaving for deployment, it is important to consider how his absence will impact his family system. From an SFBT perspective, the client discusses how the family system has handled past deployments and what solutions the family will implement while he is away.

Assessment of Presenting Concerns

The next component lists common clinical concerns of military members seeking counseling services. The list includes military stigma against seeking mental health treatment, as well as TBIs, PTSD, secondary and vicarious trauma, substance use, suicidality, and military sexual trauma (Prosek et al., 2018). Since Eddie expresses concern about stigma against mental health, making it difficult for him to talk with his command about his recent loss, I can advocate for him by discussing how important it is for him to seek mental health treatment and work toward addressing that stigma. Eddie also admits to increased alcohol use. Heavy drinking is often normalized within the military, therefore an individual might not recognize a substance use problem (Fuehrlein et al., 2016).

Treatment

The treatment component addresses unique concerns when treating military members, as well as research-based approaches to treatment and best practices. I understand how military care systems work and what services they may offer its members (Prosek et al., 2018), such as adjunctive services including talking with a chaplain, utilizing peer support, or incorporating physical therapy. I can help Eddie develop coping skills and continually assess social support and substance use. I determine Eddie's social support, including support from his command, and discuss his increased alcohol use and develop alternative coping strategies as well.

Ethics

The ethics component describes ethical considerations for counselors working with military members as well as counselors reflecting on their motivation to work with this population (Prosek et al., 2018). The task force recommends that counselors receive experiential training in working with military clients and learn the legal requirements for documentation and disclosure of records. Additionally, counselors who also identify as military members should assess for countertransference. I decide to seek additional supervision/peer consultation while working with Eddie, due to the possibility of countertransference. This section also discusses considering a community referral for military members if needed. In this case, Eddie felt more comfortable with a community counselor, so it is important that I maintain the confidentiality Eddie is requesting.

Advocacy

Finally, the advocacy component addresses "counselors' ability to understand and influence individual, system, and public policy efforts to increase access to mental health resources for military-connected clients and promote the role of counseling professionals working with military populations" (Prosek et al., 2018, p. 93). Counselors can advocate for approaches that use a wellness model and are strengths-based. Counselors support decreasing mental health stigma within the military and actively assist service members in self-advocacy strategies. Eddie feels self-advocacy is best in consideration of whether he is able to leave for deployment or not. Once Eddie has made this decision, I can help him advocate for himself to his command.

TREATMENT

Goals

In SFBT the counselor and client collaborate on treatment goals so the client can determine the best solutions for the problem. When formulating goals with Eddie, it is important to remember that he only has three weeks before leaving on deployment. Therefore, goals need to be short-term. I ask what the future will be like when the problem is no longer present, and Eddie expects that he will no longer be so reactive to the tragic death of his friend. Therefore, the first goal is to process the feelings of grief and loss that are present. The second goal is to address Eddie's feelings about the upcoming deployment and advocate for the best solution with one member in his command in the next two weeks. The third goal is for Eddie to recognize how military culture affects how he is experiencing his problems and to list more effective coping skills. I use solution-talk and a future focus when communicating with Eddie about meeting these goals (Froerer & Connie, 2016).

Goal 1: Processing Grief

I choose to use psychoeducation to help Eddie process his feelings of grief and loss. Kubler-Ross proposed a grief model with five stages: denial, anger, bargaining, depression, and acceptance (Sheperis & Sheperis, 2015). Sharing this model with Eddie can help normalize some of the feelings he is currently experiencing and give him hope about the future stage of acceptance.

Worden (2008) emphasized that the space provided in counseling for processing bereavement is more important than an intervention. In many other areas of life, the client may be trying to hold it together to avoid being too emotional, trying to act a certain way, or trying to hide feelings. Eddie states that he has tried to do his best at work, but often when he gets into his car for lunch, he is overwhelmed and begins sobbing at the loss of his friend. He recognizes that by not talking to others in his command about how he is feeling, he is trying to hide his feelings. He wants to maintain the perception that he can handle this and still go on deployment so it will not impact his career. Eddie and I talk about the stages of grief, and Eddie views himself as currently being in the denial stage and at times the anger stages. I recommend that Eddie read *On Death and Dying* (Kubler-Ross, 1970) while he is on deployment and journal about his feelings to continue processing his grief while he is not attending bi-weekly counseling sessions.

Goal 2: Individual Advocacy

The stated goal is for Eddie to decide what is best for him in terms of leaving for deployment and then advocate for himself by discussing this with a senior member of his command. Scaling questions can be very insightful while discussing this goal. When asked how ready he feels to leave for deployment on a scale of one to ten, with one being not ready and ten being ready to leave tomorrow, Eddie states he is currently at a five. When asked what would need to happen to change that number to five and a half, Eddie states he wishes he had more time and is afraid that if he does not leave on time, it might impact his career.

I then ask Eddie for exceptions: "Does everyone always make the whole deployment?" and, "Are there any penalties for those that do not?" Eddie remembers that two pilots split a previous deployment and were still able to accrue enough flight hours to qualify as an aircraft commander or otherwise avoid impacting their careers. Eddie states that he has been planning for this deployment and would like to be a part of it, but he feels that he needs more time to prepare since this tragedy happened. He states that he feels the best solution would be to meet his squadron on deployment two to four weeks later than the scheduled date.

After identifying this solution, the next step is to discuss is how Eddie can advocate for himself. I ask Eddie if he has ever felt comfortable talking with anyone in the command about something like this. Eddie identifies his department head as such a person and decides to ask his department head if he can join the squadron two to four weeks into the deployment because he is having some difficulty dealing with the mishap and needs a little more time to "get his head on straight" before he flies an aircraft overseas. Eddie and I also discuss how it is important for Eddie to discuss his career concerns and ask his department head how leaving late for deployment might impact his career. Eddie decides that he will do this before his next session.

Goal 3: Awareness of Military Culture

In this goal, I help Eddie explore how military culture might be hurting or helping with his current problem, including military cultural norms related to confidentiality and mental health stigma. He describes an environment in which service members handle their own problems and are mocked if they do not meet standards or act tough. He wishes he could be more courageous in managing his feelings about the mishap and that he could talk to others, but he does not want others to view him as too weak. The inability to do a job is a sign of weakness; asking for more time could be interpreted as not being part of the team.

I also discuss how military culture is helping Eddie with this problem and focus on his strengths. We discuss how other military members might be supportive of Eddie and help him get through this time as a team, despite his fears of being seen as weak. One of Eddie's strengths is the courage to seek help and to speak with his department head about leaving later for deployment. It also takes courage to recognize that it might not be safe to perform his job and to admit he fears retribution on his career. In many ways, Eddie is adapting to the situation and managing it. We also discuss self-reliance and how there are times in the military when one does need to talk with someone else.

Finally, I discuss Eddie's increase in alcohol use. Eddie states that he usually drinks at the end of the day when he is alone. I am aware that military culture promotes drinking, and alcohol misuse can be problematic (Ijamanta & Lasebikan, 2016). Alcohol use in military aviators is associated with an increased risk for safety (Gates, Duffy, Moore, Howell, & McDonald, 2007). For this reason, I decide to use the Alcohol Use Disorders Identification Test (AUDIT), to gather information on the quantity and frequency of alcohol consumption (Stevens & Smith, 2018). Eddie reports drinking every day since the mishap, and usually has three to four drinks, although occasionally he consumes more than that. Stevens and Smith (2018) recommend counselors utilize psychoeducation on the effects of alcohol which includes poor judgement, endangering self or others, and negative effects on cognitive functioning. Eddie and I identify some people that Eddie can reach out to for support during these times. We also talk about journaling and reminding himself about good times he shared with his friend. Eddie is able to identify that feeling alone is a trigger for his drinking, so we discuss alternative activities for his leisure time. Eddie mentions that he could also go running or watch a movie to keep his mind off being left alone without his friend. He also recognizes that it is important to spend time with his wife prior to leaving for deployment. I also talk with Eddie about the possibility of attending an Alcoholics Anonymous (AA) meeting. He does not wish to pursue an AA meeting at this time, but I do provide him a list of meeting times and locations.

Progress

Goal 1: Processing Grief

One measure of Eddie's progress is to look at his symptoms. During the intake session, Eddie reported having trouble sleeping and eating and also feelings of anger toward his squadron. As therapy continues, Eddie's physiological responses will hopefully subside so that he will be able to sleep and eat better and therefore will be able to meet some of his basic needs. Maslow (1954) proposed a hierarchy in which basic physiological needs (e.g., shelter, food) must be met before one can move up the hierarchy to safety and security, belongingness, esteem, and self-actualization. An individual is at a higher level of mental health when the basic needs are met.

Another measure of progress is forward movement through the stages of grief. However, this may be a long-term process, and it is common for clients to move forward and then revert to a previous stage (Sheperis & Sheperis, 2015). Journaling is an effective way to track the stages of grief.

Goal 2: Individual Advocacy

Progress on this goal depends on Eddie following through with his decision to talk with his department head about the possibility of leaving for deployment at a later time. Improved responses to the scaling question of how ready Eddie feels to leave on deployment also indicate progress. Eddie stated he is currently at a five. As the deployment approaches, I would expect this number to go up. If it does not, Eddie and I can discuss what is stopping him from being ready for deployment. We may need to reconsider the solution and try an alternative. In SFBT, if something is not working, it is time to try something else (Froerer & Connie, 2016).

Goal 3: Awareness of Military Culture

Progress in this goal is indicated by Eddie's awareness of how he is feeling and where those thoughts and values originate. Keeping a feelings journal should be very effective, in which Eddie writes down his feelings, reflects on the events that precipitated those feelings, and reflects on any cultural values that might influence how he is feeling. In this way, Eddie can separate his feelings from cultural factors that might be influencing them. He can learn to honor his feelings and recognize when he might be placing judgment on those feelings. Eddie can understand that military culture has some excellent values but also has some values and behaviors that are maladaptive. In this way, Eddie can begin to advocate for himself, allow for his feelings, and realize mental health issues need not be stigmatized. Progress on this goal would also be indicated by a decrease in the frequency and amount of alcohol consumed, and utilizing the alternative coping strategies that were discussed.

CONCLUSION

Ratts et al. (2016) discussed the importance for counselors to reflect on the intersecting identities of the counselor and client and how that impacts the process of therapy. This chapter specifically focuses on the intersecting identities of current and former members of the military. Military culture can serve as a protective factor for military members, but it may also be a risk factor in terms of mental health (Bryan, 2016). The Competencies for Counseling Military Populations (CCMP) serve as a framework for counseling military clients (Prosek et al., 2018), and these competencies fall within the MSJCC and can help counselors reflect on the intersecting identities of counselor and client (Ratts et al., 2016). A case study illustrates the practical application of the CCMP and MSJCC.

REFERENCES

Alkov, R. A., & Gaynor, J. A. (1991). Attitude changes in Navy/Marine flight instructors following an aircrew coordination training course. *The International Journal of Aviation Psychology*, *1*(3), 245–253. doi:10.120715327108ijap0103_5

American Psychiatric Association. (2013). *Diagnostic and statistical manual of mental disorders* (5th ed.). Arlington, VA: American Psychiatric Publishing.

Eckart, E. C., & Dufrene, R. L. (2015). Barriers to mental health counseling for soldiers. *Journal of Military and Government Counseling*, *3*(1), 40–55. Retrieved from http://acegonline.org/wp-content/uploads/2013/02/JMGC-Vol-3-Is-1.pdf

Branson, Y. (2017). Military cultural competency. In J. Beder (Ed.), *Caring for the military: A guide for helping professionals* (pp. 3–9). New York, NY: Routledge/Taylor & Francis Group.

Bryan, C. J. (2016). Suicidal behavior among military personnel and veterans. In N. D. Ainspan, C. J. Bryan, & W. E. Penk (Eds.), *Handbook of psychosocial interventions for veterans and service members: A guide for the non-military mental health clinician* (pp. 159–169). New York, NY: Oxford University Press; doi:10.1093/med:psych/9780199353996.003.0014

Canfield, J., & Weiss, E. (2015). Integrating military and veteran culture in social work education: Implications for curriculum inclusion. *Journal of Social Work Education, 51*(sup1), S128–S144. doi:10.1080/10437797.2015.1001295

Castro, C. A., Kintzle, S., & Hassan, A. M. (2015). The combat veteran paradox: Paradoxes and dilemmas encountered with reintegrating combat veterans and the agencies that support them. *Traumatology, 21*(4), 299–310. doi:10.1037/trm0000049

Cepeda, L. M., & Davenport, D. S. (2006). Person-centered therapy and solution-focused brief therapy: An integration of present and future awareness. *Psychotherapy (Chicago, Ill.), 43*(1), 1–12. doi:10.1037/0033-3204.43.1.1 PMID:22121955

De Jong, P., & Berg, I. K. (2013). *Interviewing or solutions* (4th ed.). Belmont, CA: Thomson Brooks/Cole. doi:10.1093/acrefore/9780199975839.013.209

De Shazer, S. (1988). *Clues: Investigating solutions in brief therapy*. Ontario, Canada: Penguin Books.

DeGraff, A. N., O'Neal, C. W., & Mancini, J. A. (2016). The significance of military contexts and culture for understanding family well-being: Parent life satisfaction and adolescent outcomes. *Journal of Child and Family Studies, 25*(10), 3022–3033. doi:10.100710826-016-0471-0

Froerer, A. S., & Connie, E. E. (2016). Solution-building, the foundation of solution-focused brief therapy: A qualitative Delphi study. *Journal of Family Psychotherapy, 27*(1), 20–34. doi:10.1080/08975353.2016.1136545

Fuehrlein, B. S., Mota, N., Arias, A. J., Trevisan, L. A., Kachadourian, L. K., Krystal, J. H., ... Pietrzak, R. H. (2016). The burden of alcohol use disorders in US military veterans: Results from the National Health and Resilience in Veterans Study. *Addiction (Abingdon, England), 111*(10), 1786–1794. doi:10.1111/add.13423 PMID:27061707

Gates, T., Duffy, K., Moore, J., Howell, W., & McDonald, W. (2007). Alcohol screening instruments and psychiatric evaluation outcomes in military aviation personnel. *Aviation, Space, and Environmental Medicine, 78*(1), 48–51. PMID:17225482

Gleeson, T. D., & Hemmer, P. A. (2014). Providing care to military personnel and their families: How we can all contribute. *Academic Medicine, 89*(9), 1201–1203. doi:10.1097/ACM.0000000000000368 PMID:24979291

Hall, L. (2008). *Counseling military families: What mental health professionals need to know*. New York, NY: Taylor & Francis Group, LLC.

Hicks, J. F., Lenard, N., & Brendle, J. (2016). Utilizing filial therapy with deployed military families. *International Journal of Play Therapy*, *25*(4), 210–216. doi:10.1037/pla0000032

Ijomanta, I. N., & Lasebikan, V. O. (2016). Lifetime and 12 months prevalence of alcohol use and alcohol use disorders among soldiers residing in a military community in Ibadan. *Substance Use & Misuse*, *51*(6), 722–732. doi:10.3109/10826084.2016.1153111 PMID:27070029

Johnson, W., Rosenstein, J. E., Buhrke, R. A., & Haldeman, D. C. (2013). After "don't ask don't tell:" Competent care of lesbian, gay and bisexual military personnel during the DoD policy transition. *Professional Psychology, Research and Practice*, *1*(1), 1–9. doi:10.1037/a0033051

Kubler-Ross, E. (2000). *On death and dying*. New York, NY: Macmillan.

Maslow, A. H. (1954). *Motivation and personality*. New York, NY: Harper & Row.

Meyer, E. G., Hall-Clark, B. N., Hamaoka, D., & Peterson, A. L. (2015). Assessment of military cultural competence: A pilot study. *Academic Psychiatry*, *39*(4), 382–388. doi:10.100740596-015-0328-7 PMID:26054708

Neri, D. F., & Shappell, S. A. (1994). The effect of combat on the work/rest schedules and fatigue of naval aviators during Operations Desert Shield and Desert Storm. *Military Psychology*, *6*(3), 141–162. doi:10.120715327876mp0603_1

O'Brien, C., Keith, J., & Shoemaker, L. (2015). Don't tell: Military culture and male rape. *Psychological Services*, *12*(4), 357–365. doi:10.1037er0000049 PMID:26524277

Otting, T. L., & Prosek, E. A. (2016). Integrating feminist therapy and expressive arts with adolescent clients. *Journal of Creativity in Mental Health*, *11*(1), 78–89. doi:10.1080/15401383.2015.1019167

Pincus, S. H., House, R., Christenson, J., & Adler, L. E. (2007). *The emotional cycle of deployment*. St. Louis, MO: West Point Parents Club. Retrieved from http://www.west-point.org/parent/wppc-st_louis/Deployment/TheEmotionalCycleofDeployment.pdf

Prosek, E. A., Burgin, E. E., Atkins, K. M., Wehrman, J. D., Fenell, D. L., Carter, C., & Green, L. (2018). Competencies for counseling military populations. *Journal of Military and Government Counseling*, *6*(2), 87–98.

Ratts, M. J., Singh, A. A., Nassar, M. S., Butler, S. K., & McCullough, J. R. (2016). Multicultural and social justice counseling competencies: Guidelines for the counseling profession. *Journal of Multicultural Counseling and Development, 44*(1), 28–48. doi:10.1002/jmcd.12035

Redmond, S. A., Wilcox, S. L., Campbell, S., Kim, A., Finney, K., Barr, K., & Hassan, A. M. (2015). A brief introduction to the military workplace culture. *Journal of Prevention. Assessment & Rehabilitation, 50*(1), 9–20. PMID:25547167

Russo, T. J., & Fallon, M. A. (2015). Coping with stress: Supporting the needs of military families and their children. *Early Childhood Education Journal, 43*(5), 407–416. doi:10.100710643-014-0665-2

Segal, M. W., Smith, D. G., Segal, D. R., & Canuso, A. A. (2016). The role of leadership and peer behaviors in the performance and well-being of women in combat: Historical perspectives, unit integration, and family issues. *Military Medicine, 181*(1S), 28–39. doi:10.7205/MILMED-D-15-00342 PMID:26741899

Seponski, D. M. (2016). A feminist-informed integration of emotionally focused and solution-focused therapies. *Journal of Family Psychotherapy, 27*(4), 221–242. doi:10.1080/08975353.2016.1235430

Sheperis, D., & Sheperis, C. (2015). *Clinical mental health counseling: Fundamentals of applied practice*. Upper Saddle River, NJ: Pearson.

Simpson, D., Bruckheimer, J., & Scott, T. (1986). *Top gun* [Motion picture]. United States of America: Paramount Pictures.

Stevens, P. W., & Smith, R. L. (2018). *Substance use counseling theory and practice*. New York, NY: Pearson.

Strom, T. Q., Gavian, M. E., Possis, E., Loughlin, J., Bui, T., Linardatos, E., ... Siegel, W. (2012). Cultural and ethical considerations when working with military personnel and veterans: A primer for VA training programs. *Training and Education in Professional Psychology, 6*(2), 67–75. doi:10.1037/a0028275

Strong, T., & Pyle, N. R. (2009). Constructing a conversational "miracle": Examining the "miracle question" as it is used in therapeutic dialogue. *Journal of Constructivist Psychology, 22*(4), 328–353. doi:10.1080/10720530903114001

Wertsch, M. E. (1991). *Military brats: Legacies of childhood inside the fortress*. New York, NY: Harmony Books.

Wilcove, G. L., Schwerin, M. J., & Kline, T. (2009). Quality of life in the US Navy: Impact on performance and career continuance. *Military Psychology*, *21*(4), 445–460. doi:10.1080/08995600903206362

Worden, W. (2008). *Grief counseling and grief therapy: A handbook for the mental health practitioner*. New York, NY: Springer. doi:10.1891/9780826101211

Zinzow, H. M., Britt, T. W., Pury, C. S., Raymond, M., McFadden, A. C., & Burnette, C. M. (2013). Barriers and facilitators of mental health treatment seeking among active-duty army personnel. *Military Psychology*, *25*(5), 514–535. doi:10.1037/mil0000015

Chapter 13
Navigating Toxic Masculinity in Clients as a Beginning Therapist

Jeffrey K. Christensen
Lewis and Clark College, USA

Justin D. Henderson
Lewis and Clark College, USA

Cort M. Dorn-Medeiros
https://orcid.org/0000-0002-6595-7503
Lewis and Clark College, USA

Ian Lertora
Texas Tech University, USA

EXECUTIVE SUMMARY

The purpose of this chapter is to provide counseling students with a framework that will allow them to broach gender with male clients and to navigate conversations that may elicit anxiety for beginning counselors. This will be done through the case example of Whitney, a graduate student who just started internship. Her client is Rick, a client in his 50s, who is coming to services because of receiving a DUI and needing to complete counseling for his diversion mandate. Whitney is younger than Rick and has the experience of having some discomforting exchanges with him, such as remarks on how "bright" she is and a passing comment her outfit. The strategies proposed in this case study are grounded in the Multicultural and Social Justice Counseling Competencies and in Relational Cultural Theory and will give students a framework for understanding clients who may respond like Rick.

DOI: 10.4018/978-1-7998-0022-4.ch013

INTRODUCTION

To see problematic examples of patriarchy in our culture, one doesn't have to look far. Recent headlines have highlighted our society's growing awareness of patriarchy's impact. The multiple cases of sexual assault and misconduct brought against Harvey Weinstein spurred by the Me Too movement (Frye, 2018; Serres, 2017), and the sexual assault allegation hearings of Justice Brett Kavanaugh as brought against him by Dr. Christine Blasey Ford (Brown, 2018), serve as clear examples of how divided our nation is when it looks at patriarchy, and of its continued impact on those who experience it. Some can see the oppressive force clearly, and indeed, may have suffered from it, while others would dismiss such claims, discredit those who speak out against patriarchy, or worse yet, justify oppressive acts simply as "boys being boys."

In learning about toxic masculinity, it may be helpful to be reminded of the parable of the fish who lives its entire life within its modest fishbowl. After months of neglect in which grime can be seen, when asked of the condition of the water, the fish replies, "What's water?"

Patriarchy is everywhere in our world and – much like the parable – since we live our day-to-day in this environment, the grime often goes unnoticed. It can be helpful to understand this when faced with a client who, because of their positionality of privilege, is not only unable to acknowledge how their rigid conformity to gender norms may adversely affect themselves and others, but may have even internalized these scripts to a point of valuing it as an aspect of their identity.

To understand toxic masculinity, it is necessary to know the concept of hegemonic masculinity, which is a strict adherence to gender roles by enforcing restrictions of behaviors that fall outside gender norms and support the existing systemic socio-political factors that favor men (Connell & Messerschmidt, 2005). Toxic masculinity is a subset of hegemonic masculinity and can be defined as a drive to dominate and endorse misogynistic and homophobic views and is characterized by employing socially destructive behaviors to do so (Parent, Gobble, & Rochlen, 2018).

Holding a place of compassion for those who exhibit maladaptive and rigid gender norms may be difficult for some beginning clinicians, especially those who have been on the receiving end of toxic masculinity. This may involve having the lived experience of physical and psychological harm, anger, sadness, and fear from sexual objectification, bullying and its lasting effects, and the many other ways that this form of oppression can negatively impact individuals (Baugher & Gazmararian, 2015). It is with some humility that the authors, who have varied privileges and positionalities themselves, attempt to write about this very complex issue and to do so in a way that can serve beginning clinicians in a way that is both empowering to their personhood and therapeutic for their clients. Thus, we will introduce Relational Cultural Theory (RCT) and the Multicultural and Social Justice Counseling Competencies (MSJCC) as useful frameworks for working with clients exhibiting this form of masculinity (Miller, 1976; Ratts et al., 2015)

It is our hope that this case example will be relevant for all clinicians, regardless of their positionalities. It is also important to mention, that the client and the counselor presented in this chapter are completely fictional, though an amalgam of many varied clients and supervisees that the authors have interacted with. Lastly, this work could not be done without the input from numerous colleagues that are too many to individually mention, but that the primary author will be forever grateful to. So without further ado, let's talk about navigating toxic masculinity.

Literature Review

In the early 1980s, an investigation into the social inequity of students in Australian high schools revealed that there was a hierarchical structure in place for boys and that their place in this hierarchy was rooted in how actively they projected their gender identity and masculinity (Kessler et al., 1982; Connell, 1983). From this, a proposed model of multiple masculinities was developed to explain the influence of power relations within those masculinities, and from that model came the term hegemonic masculinity (Carrigan, Connell, & Lee, 1985; Connell, 1987).

Displays of hegemonic masculinity are characterized by adherence to strict gender roles and engaging in behaviors that reinforce the existing power structures that favor men. This type of masculinity in Western societies is generally the standard for which "real men" are described (Kupers, 2005) and is built upon the domination of women, establishing a hierarchy of intermale dominance (Connell, 1987; Hearn, 2012), and the stigmatization of homosexuality (Frank, 1987; Wood, Lambert, & Jewkes, 2007). Displays of hegemonic masculinity could include a ruthless and highly competitive nature, an inability or unwillingness to express emotions other than anger, a devaluation of women and feminine attributes, and a strong reluctance to display any form of behavior that could be construed as weak or vulnerable in the eyes of others (Brittan, 1989; Kupers, 2005). The hegemonic norm is generally embodied as the "ideal man" and while most men do not adhere to the hegemonic ideal in their day-to-day lives, there is still an undercurrent of worry that others would perceive them as less masculine because of their deviations (Connell & Messerschmidt, 2005).

However, not all aspects of hegemonic masculinity are negative. A man's competitiveness to win at sports, to be a reliable provider for his family, or to do well in his career, are also aspects of hegemonic masculinity, and are traits that are culturally accepted and valued (Kupers, 2005). Thus, the term *toxic masculinity* is necessary, because it defines the aspects of hegemonic masculinity that are socially and relationally destructive, such as the use of violence to dominate others, misogynistic views and practices, and homophobia.

Most of the literature around toxic masculinity is theoretical, though some efforts have been made to study it empirically. Parent & Moradi (2009) developed the Conformity to Masculine Norms Inventory-46 (CMNI-46) and found that the subscales of Winning, Power Over Women, and Heterosexual Self-Presentation displayed greater intercorrelations than with other scales on the inventory demonstrating evidence of toxic masculinity. This finding has been replicated in other studies using the same inventory (Iwamoto, Corbin, Lejuez, & MacPherson, 2014; Parent, Moradi, Rummell, & Tokar, 2011). Further, investigations found that men who strongly adhere to the dominance-heterosexual-misogyny triad of masculine norms were more likely to report engaging in negative online behaviors (Parent, Gobble, & Rochlen, 2018). Additionally, studies have shown that men who exhibit and value more traditional masculinity norms report greater maladaptive interaction styles (Coughlin & Wade, 2012; Rochlen, McKelly, Suizzo, & Scaringi, 2008) and negatively impacting relationship quality for both heterosexual and homosexual couples (Burn & Wade, 2005; Wade & Donis, 2007).

With regards to masculinity, strict adherence and enforcement of gender norms, to the extent of toxicity, is damaging in multiple areas. The negative impact of toxic masculinity is evident to those who are the targets of its marginalization and oppression. What is often less apparent is the manner in which toxic masculinity causes harm to the very men who employ it—most often by injuring relationships, increasing isolation, and suppressing pain and suffering (Isenhart, 2005). Thus, while toxic masculinity will likely not be the initial focus of treatment, there is justification for mental health counselors to address it in their work with clients. In the case example presented below, we wanted to demonstrate how toxic masculinity could be breached, when the client's focus for treatment does not directly address this issue.

INTRODUCTION TO THE CASE

Rick is a 53-year old, Caucasian male who comes to treatment to fulfill a mandate of diversion after receiving a DUI two months ago. Rick's primary occupation is a medical transporter, in which he drives patients from hospitals and clinics to nursing facilities or their homes, and he has been doing this job for about 10 years. Before that he worked various construction jobs, but transitioned to this new line of work after sustaining an injury on the job that has resulted in chronic back pain and an inability to do the hard labor required for his job. Upon receiving his offense, he has been unemployed, though expresses hopes to resume his position once he completes his mandates for diversion.

Rick was previously married and is now divorced. He has three children, a 12-year-old daughter, a 16-year-old son from his previous marriage, and a 28-year-old son from an earlier relationship, from which he is estranged. He reports that "everything he does is to provide for his two younger children, unlike how his parents provided for him and his younger siblings." He denies a history of mental illness, though wonders whether his mom suffered from bipolar disorder, despite no formal diagnosis. Aside from his back pain, he doesn't report any other medical conditions as relevant.

Initial assessments of his drinking have Rick drinking a few beers a night, with some heavier episodes on the weekends. These episodes average to be around 8-12 drinks, and only a few times does he report blacking out from these episodes. Rick has a budding awareness of drinking too much, and is open to exploring strategies to lessen the impact. He sees his recent offense as an isolated incident and is unsure whether he needs to lessen his drinking, but knows he needs to be more responsible with his drinking, as it has affected his job and ability to provide for his family. While he is mandated to seek counseling, the decision is up to Rick to pick an approved site, and he chooses the college's community clinic due to its sliding scale fee, reporting that he needs to be conservative with his finances.

INTRODUCTION TO THE COUNSELOR

Whitney is a 24-year-old, white, heterosexual cisgender female, who has known that she wanted to be a counselor since she was twelve years old. Her older sister had a lot of difficulties growing up and when she had to be hospitalized for a really severe eating disorder, it was a stressful time for her parents and her whole family. Whitney reports having a high regard for her parents. Her mom is a college professor of women's studies and her dad is a computer engineer. They always provided for her and were supportive of her studies and decision to go to graduate school. For Whitney, having to witness her parents' confusion and reported helplessness to take care of her older sister, cemented her desire to become a counselor to specialize working with young adolescents and women around eating disorders.

Whitney grew up white in a predominantly white, middle-upper class neighborhood in the Pacific Northwest. She has an understanding how this upbringing gave her privilege, though reports still having a lot to learn before she feels confident in her multicultural competence in working with clients with different social locations than herself. Whitney reports her diversity class was helpful in pointing out concepts like power and oppression and that her mom has been a great resource in helping her understand how regularly these concepts play out on a societal level.

With regards to Whitney's work with clients from different social locations than hers, she plans to embody a space of openness and humility, so that her clients can understand her openness to talk about anything. She identifies with Relational Cultural Theory and considers it be a central basis for her work, as she believes that it is through a mutual empathic relationship that individuals heal and grow. Whitney reports feeling RCT is a good fit for her style and values and will try to be mindful of its core tenets throughout her work with clients.

Role as Supervisor for Whitney

To reiterate, Whitney and Rick are fictional, though a combination of some of the supervisees and clients that we have worked with. For myself (the first author), I have had to learn several lessons about the privileges that come from being an able-bodied, heterosexual, cis-gender male, who holds a position of authority as a supervisor and professor in a counseling program. Originally uncomfortable with having power, I have had to accept the power inherent in my roles and the greater responsibility that it comes with. Thus, when supervising my students, as well as counseling clients, broaching the topic of my various social locations is an absolute necessity, especially if any of those locations could negatively impact what my supervisees or clients feel able to share.

In this instance, my work with Whitney would include broaching my social locations, with specific regard to my gender, and how discussing her observations about Rick and his presentation of masculinity may be influenced by my own maleness. I would normalize any difficulty that my locations may bring and also make it a point to articulate my understanding and acknowledgement that this form of oppression is very present in our society, and painful to those who have experienced it (which we all have, myself included). Should any of my actions or words be conceived as patriarchal, I would make it a point to receive this feedback with humility, acceptance, and to ensure that my further actions not silence or oppress those that I hope to counsel and supervise.

My ever-evolving understanding of patriarchy, in particular, comes from a foundation of having multiple women in my life whom I look up to and respect, and who have been and are adversely affected by this form of oppression. For example, my Chinese grandmother was sold into slavery at a young age in China and was subsequently "bought back" when it was decided that she was pretty enough to marry off into a wealthy family. My mother and older sister have had to deal with minimizations of their intelligence and expertise, usually in the form of sexual objectification (and additional oppressions due to their positionalities of being women of color). I have also learned from women in my romantic relationships, who have experienced physical abuse, sexual abuse and sometimes both, perpetrated against them by men.

In my intention to be a supportive and responsible grandson, son, brother, and partner, I have striven to learn about those experiences with openness and understanding. I have done my best to provide whatever assurances I could that I would not recapitulate those past wrongs, but rather, participate in creating a healthier version of masculinity. Thus, I feel a personal responsibility to use my privilege appropriately, to help guide future clinicians, regardless of their gender identities and experiences of patriarchy, to understand how to integrate both awareness and experience into being the best clinicians possible for their clients.

The second author is a college educated, White, temporarily able-bodied, pansexual, U.S born, cis-gender man. The third author is a White, transgender and gender nonconforming, queer, currently able-bodied, counselor educator who works as a tenure-track Assistant Professor at a small, liberal arts college in the US.

Case Description (1st Encounter)

Upon first meeting Whitney for the intake assessment, Rick was cordial and polite enough, hearing Whitney discuss the limits of confidentiality and having few questions about counseling and the clinic's role to fulfill his mandate for his diversion. During the intake, Rick's answers were short and succinct, and when questions go into his own drinking patterns and past abuse he may have suffered, Rick appears confused and asks "Why is that important?"

Whitney responds that the assessment is used to help with identifying treatment goals that the client may have and for treatment planning. Rick's response is blunt with each word emphasized "Easy. My goal is to just complete the requirements for diversion so I can just get my job back." A short pause with unwavering eye contact. "The plan for treatment is everything that would help me get that." Whitney asks if he would prefer she leave it blank and Rick responds with "just put not relevant or…whatever."

After an hour, the following questions of the assessment progresses with terse responses until the intake assessment finishes, with Rick paying the clinic fee and departing. He doesn't say goodbye, leaving Whitney wondering if she did anything wrong.

Theoretical Case Conceptualization of First Encounter With Rick

In conceptualizing this case, we will first introduce the core tenets of RCT and MSJCC. Relational-Cultural Theory evolved from the work of Jean Baker Miller's *Toward a New Psychology of Women* (1976) and emerged from the recognition that traditional models of human development and psychotherapy were built from the Western values of individualism and insufficient as indicators of social and psychological maturity. Miller and other theorists criticized the lack of attention of these models to the relational experiences of women and others in marginalized groups (Comstock et al., 2008). Without attending to the many contextual and relational experiences of others, and the interplay of societal power levied against those from marginalized groups, inaccurate pathologizing could occur (Robb, 2006). It is through mutually positive connections with others that individuals develop and only through understanding the full contexts of the sociopolitical and relational aspects of individuals, can mutual connection be made (Duffey & Somody, 2011).

A core tenet of RCT is that through mutually empathic, growth-fostering relationships can healing take place. For mental health counselors to effectively practice from this framework, intentional efforts to help clients identify and deconstruct behaviors or thought processes that can prevent them from forming growth-fostering relationships with others (Comstock et al., 2008). This attention to how thoughts and behaviors move one towards connection or disconnection is known as *relational awareness* and should individuals engage in growth-fostering connections with others, the "five good things" occur, which include: (a) a greater sense of zest; (b) increased self-worth; (c) a better understanding of self, others, and interpersonal relationships; (d) a greater belief to act effectively with the world; and (e) a greater sense of connection and more motivation to continue to connect with others (Miller, 1986, p. 3). Another central tenet of RCT theorists is that while all individuals yearn for connection, they may still demonstrate behaviors antithetical to this purpose, due to feelings of vulnerability and to avoid reliving past experiences of rejection, social exclusion, or other forms of victimization (Miller & Stiver, 1997). This is known as the central relational paradox, and it is important for counselors to be aware of, as these very same behaviors or attitudes, are generally a symptom of underlying pain and shame (Comstock et al., 2008).

Using the Multicultural and Social Justice Counseling Competencies (Ratts et al., 2015) provides a useful framework for understanding clients in different social locations. In looking at the four developmental domains of (a) counselor self-awareness, (b) client worldview, (c) counseling relationship, and (d) counseling and advocacy interventions, allows counselors to conceptualize the necessary foundation for developing therapeutic rapport and establishing positive connection. For this particular case example it is imperative to be aware of and respond to the various social locations of both the client and the counselor, to situate Rick's concerns in a larger and broader social context. Specifically, the domains of counselor self-awareness (from a place of marginalization in this instance), with understanding client's worldview (from a place of privilege), becomes particularly salient here.

A clear identity difference between Rick and Whitney is gender identity. In understanding this client's worldview, it is entirely plausible that Rick's history of masculine gender socialization as a cisgender man may have taught him to guard against interpersonal contexts that evoked a significant degree of emotional and interpersonal vulnerability. Additionally, given that Rick is a middle-aged white cisgender man raised in the United States, there is a greater likelihood that he was raised with masculine gender norms that promote interpersonal independence and dominance over interdependence and cooperation (Englar-Carlson 2006; Jordan 2018). Since the very act of engaging in counseling services as a client presupposes a help-seeking need from others, it seems likely that Rick would have not sought counseling had it not been mandatory (Mahalik, Good, & Englar-Carlson 2003). Taking these contexts and factors into consideration, toxic masculinity would contribute toward a stratification of the therapeutic relationship, in which Rick may explicitly or implicitly enter the relationship under the pretense that mutuality and connection are not only impossible, but potentially detrimental toward his sense of identity and wellbeing.

Toxic masculinity, in many respects, would likely emerge in the counseling relationship as Rick experiences conflict between the need to address his concerns and the strain brought about by his gender socialization. An example of how this could be enacted in counseling would be a tendency on Rick's part to dismiss Whitney's competency as a cis woman and a desire to establish a sense of control and dominance in the counseling relationship. This can be seen in his discomfort of the intake questions that sparked on areas of vulnerability, and his responses were geared in taking control of the session. Indeed, it is likely that Rick was offended at Whitney's questions, for if he were to answer honestly, it would have meant admitting to a form of vulnerability and weakness. Whitney's positionality of a white, cisgender woman who was much younger than him likely made his response more severe, as societally, Rick has more power based off his social locations, and holding onto that power (whether consciously or subconsciously) is how he was socialized to behave.

In supervision, Whitney expressed a concern that maybe she wasn't competent enough and questioned her expertise and knowledge to productively work around Rick's substance use and to help him with his mandate. Her identified preference for being a counselor who presents as open and caring to provide her clients a space to be at ease and see her as trustworthy, was shaken, due to Rick's defensive and brusque demeanor.

From staff discussions about Rick with her supervisor and fellow counseling student colleagues, questions were raised about Whitney's countertransference with Rick. Did his being an older male have any influence on her comfort and ability to be his counselor? Upon reflection, Whitney agreed that she felt more pressure to be seen as competent, and held a fear that Rick would "see through her façade" and view her not as a professional, but a twenty something graduate student, with limited knowledge and training.

Upon further reflection and prompts from her supervisor and colleagues, Whitney begins to see the disempowering effects of toxic masculinity as it was enacted in the counseling session with Rick. This in turn allowed Whitney to reflect on the larger societal influences of being a younger women in a hegemonic masculine culture. Older men have generally held places of authority in her life, and in some ways, she recognizes that Rick has a similar place in her mind, despite the reality that she has more power in that relationship. Because Rick shares some of the characteristics from those with authority over her in the past, that was sufficient for her to feel a sense of intimidation at Rick's evaluation of her ability as a counselor. Whitney considers this new awareness and continues her studies, curious to see what her work with Rick will continue to reveal about herself and her ability to counsel older male clients.

Case Description (2nd-5th Sessions)

With the intake assessment completed, Whitney begins to collaborate with Rick on his treatment goals and specifies the criteria he needs to comply with to successfully manage his diversion. Once the diversion criteria is recorded in a formalized treatment plan, Rick appears more at ease, reporting being more hopeful of getting his job back and able to provide for his family again. While there is some dissatisfaction at having to provide random UAs with an outside agency and to continue counseling, Rick is pleased at the progress he is making to move on with his life.

Future sessions begin to explore Rick's triggers for drinking, which include feelings of loneliness and dissatisfaction with one of his supervisors at work (a woman). Rick also mentions wishing he could spend more time with his children, to which he sees his lack of job and his ex-wife's challenging behaviors as an impediment. Whitney validates Rick's frustrations and questions how these feelings may relate to his drinking. Rick responds surprised at Whitney's observation, and responds, "Hey, not bad. You're actually pretty bright." Whitney observes that Rick changes the subject to other counselors he didn't connect well with for the remainder of the session.

In the fourth and fifth sessions, Whitney continues to check in around Rick's progress with his life, hearing about his hopes for resuming his job and exploring his behaviors and cognitions that influences his drinking. She notices that he compliments her at the end of most of her interventions, with statements such as, "you know what you're doing," and "you're going to be good at this when you're done." At the end of the fifth session, Rick comments on Whitney's business casual clothing as he's about to leave: "You know, red is a really good color on you, you should wear it more often."

Case Conceptualization of These Encounters With Rick

With Whitney's successful collaboration with Rick on treatment goals that he had personal investment with, therapeutic rapport was starting to develop. Statements that he made regarding hope of furthering his goals for getting his job back and resuming a positive role with his family are evidence of this.

Because the therapeutic relationship is developing, Rick may be experiencing an increased threat of interpersonal emotional intimacy as he becomes more appropriately vulnerable in session with Whitney. As discussions revolve more around his drinking, the triggers that influence it, and his vulnerability at not having enough power to see his children as often as he would like, he engages in a process of reasserting power by establishing himself as someone who is qualified to comment on her abilities as a therapist. This is seen with his comments on how well she is doing, and, while this could be an honest appraisal of her skills, that there is a tone of surprise is telling. By speaking as if Whitney is an exception to the norm, Rick is doing what he can to retake control of the session when questioned about an area of possible vulnerability. As the rapport continues to develop, evidence starts to surface of Rick objectifying and sexualizing Whitney, via comments of her dress and suggestions on how she should present herself to him and others. This is a method to regain power and to avoid experiences of dependence on another, specifically Whitney. The struggle *against* mutuality and pursuit *toward* domination would be a clear demonstration of enacted toxic masculinity.

Whitney's social locations, as we can see, matter a great deal in this context. For her, the client may act out a recapitulation of larger societal forces, institutions of power, cultural messages, and cultural values as they relate to patriarchy and power. Rick may automatically ignore or minimize her competence, skills, education, and experience because she is a cis woman and is far younger than he. Whitney has likely experienced this in other contexts, though in a clinical setting, where she does have more power than Rick, his responses may not elicit the attention it deserves. As a cis woman and a counselor with training and skills, she has a greater awareness of both the process and content that are contributing towards Rick's substance abuse. This may be more difficult for her to realize this given his behaviors to position himself above her via his evaluative comments on her competency, and Whitney's own socialization of deferring to older white males.

In consulting with her supervisor and colleagues, Whitney brings up Rick's comment about her clothing and they begin to process how the statement impacted her, and where it may be coming from for Rick. Whitney initially wonders whether she allowed the comment by choosing to wear the clothing that she did, or if she gave any indication to Rick that he could make such comments, but this is quickly corrected by her fellow students and supervisor. Whitney was discomfited by Rick's comment and begins to question the rapport she developed with him. Was she truly competent, or was his engagement with therapy stemming from something else?

In examining Rick's history with women, patterns start to emerge. His conflict with his woman supervisor, the frayed relationship with his ex-wife, and hints of discord from his biological mother are all evidence of Rick's problematic approach with women. A key theme in toxic masculinity is dominance over others, especially women, and Rick's comments on Whitney's competence and appearance were all attempts at this. Whitney did not encourage Rick's comments towards her; this is a process of socialization that began long before counseling, but his tendencies to dominate and control women certainly has a negative impact on his relationships with others. This is likely not limited to just women, as toxic masculinity builds itself on dominance of other males as well (Connell & Messerschmidt, 2005; Kupers, 2005).

The challenge for Whitney, as the counselor, would be to find what Relational Cultural Theory describes as "good conflict," which is to use conflict and differences toward connection. By broaching her gender and what it means for Rick to talk about areas of sensitivity with a younger woman, Whitney would not only re-establish herself as a counselor (thus regaining power), but it can help Rick understand how his actions marginalize and stratify his own sense of isolation. It may even help him see how these behaviors have negatively impacted his relationships with others. While Rick's goals are to complete the requirements of his diversion, he is doing so to provide for his children, thus, investigating how these behaviors affect his relationship with others is beneficial, because it will likely limit the quality of his admittedly valuable relationships with his children.

Case Description (6th-12th Sessions)

Whitney and Rick are at the mid-point of his diversion requirement and the session begins with reviewing Rick's progress on his treatment plan. Rick is making good progress in that he has identified clear triggers to his drinking, has established coping skills for some of the triggers, and has learned several strategies he could use to lessen the harm of his drinking. In further collaborating with Rick on any changes he would like to make to his treatment plan, he reports that he is fine with the progress and being able to check in with Whitney about the previous week's events. Whitney and Rick then decide to continue looking at Rick's coping skills and how his triggers to drink continue to impact his life.

Once the course of treatment is agreed upon, Whitney brings up Rick's comments on her dress and asks Rick his motivations for making that comment. Rick is confused, stating that he was just trying to compliment her on her fashion sense. Whitney, aware of Rick's discomfort, begins to broach how it is for him to talk about his drinking and other areas of vulnerability, such as his wish to be with his children and sadness that he's not, his coping with alcohol for loneliness, with her, a much younger woman. Rick is unsure how to respond and Whitney allows for him to be in silence. "I guess it's...fine?"

Whitney asks, "Is this a little uncomfortable now?" to which Rick responds "Kinda..." Whitney then normalizes the discomfort and responds that her positionality as a younger woman paired with her being his counselor might seem odd for Rick and that if it does, it's okay. Whitney then reviews his progress in treatment and points out his goal is not to just complete diversion, but to regain his job so he can provide for his family. Rick agrees. Whitney then goes on to talk about how his comments of her dress and his evaluative comments on her clinical practice may have had an undesired effect, and she wonders if he has had problems working with women before.

Rick is obviously confused and after a few moments of silence and looking for a proper response, he admits to having had problems with women before. Whitney listens to the several examples that Rick gives, taking note that a lot of his story centered on women closest to him, such as his mom and ex-wife. Once he finishes Whitney summarizes what she heard from his stories and comments, "It's not that we have to talk about your relationships with women, Rick; that is ultimately up to you. But if this is a pattern in your life, I think it's realistic that these patterns could extend to other people, especially those you really care about. For example it could affect both of your children, as this pattern doesn't just stop with women."

Rick is listening attentively and after some moments he asks for clarification of this "pattern," which Whitney then discloses how the comments he gave her could have the impact of silencing others, or making others want to distance themselves from him, due to them being somewhat punitive and patronizing. Rick asks if she felt that way in response to his comments, to which she replies, "That actually doesn't really matter. What does is that you interact with those you care about in a way that is more true to how you want to come across and more true to who you are." Rick agrees with this, and the rest of the session is spent on how he would like to be regarded by his children as someone they could rely on and trust. He briefly reports missing his oldest son, from whom he has been estranged for nearly ten years. Rick explains that this was due to his being too hard on his son. "But that's how my dad was with me, so..."

As Rick begins to retell his own experiences of his upbringing, the session is nearing its end, and Whitney once again broaches how it was for Rick to discuss these areas with her a young women. Rick is more sincere when he shares that he had thought about how Whitney was closer to his children's ages than his, and that he might have had some doubts about her ability to help him, but that he is now okay with working with her. At the end of the session, Rick thanks Whitney for her time and just before leaving, turns to her and says, "Hey, I'm sorry if those patterns upset you in anyway. I didn't mean it if it did." Whitney just smiles and says that all is fine and that she would see him the following week.

The remainder of the sessions continue to go into Rick's drinking patterns and his thoughts around drinking, with some time devoted to ensuring a healthy relationship with his children and exploring some of his learned habits from his upbringing. By the time of their final session, Rick reported having had some successful interactions with his ex-wife, and was more satisfied with the last few visits he had with his children. He even reported considering reaching out to his oldest son, to see if there was any chance of making reparations, though he was unsure when he would do this. Nonetheless, after Whitney reviewed all the progress Rick made in his treatment, and demonstrated the letter that was necessary for Rick's success in his diversion program, they wished each other well and successfully terminated treatment.

Case Conceptualization of Sessions 6-12

The intervention that Whitney employed with Rick in many ways represents the ideal outcome for broaching gender with a client that exhibits traits of toxic masculinity. That Whitney broached Rick's comments about her dress sooner rather than later, rather than wait for another opportunity based off Rick's continued comments was important, as it established Whitney as the professional and allowed her to regain her power and agency. Also, her broaching was therapeutic, as it highlighted symptoms of behaviors that would further Rick's isolation, which he identified as a trigger for his drinking. Nonetheless, Rick's confusion over how to respond was warranted, as he was likely grappling with several internal conflicts: an instinct to reassert dominance over the session, the unfamiliar sense of trust and rapport he established with Whitney, and also his need to successfully complete treatment, for which he was dependent on her. At the height of this ambivalence, Rick risked being open and honest with her, which Whitney was able to normalize and redirect towards his goal of being closer to his children.

In this instance, Whitney was able to employ strategies from RCT in a fundamental way. Specifically, she was able to highlight Rick's relational paradox patterns, showing him that his attempts to be closer with others actually had the effect of distancing himself from them (Comstock et al., 2008). In addition, she was able to employ mutual empathy and authentic presence in a way that allowed Rick to do the same. Should Rick have tried to re-establish control of the session when he was confused, or make such comments to minimize Whitney's interventions, then the strategies Whitney employed would remain relatively unchanged (her open curiosity about the intention of his comments, coupled with an interest in how such behaviors might influence his sense of isolation with those he cares about, and subsequent drinking).

Should these efforts still prove to bear little or no fruit, then a possible recourse would be to continue exploring Rick's triggers and behaviors around drinking, and if necessary, set boundaries on any future comments about her appearance. While this may have a deleterious effect on the therapeutic alliance, it does provide Rick with a clear message that such behavior will not be tolerated within the counseling setting, and demonstrating that such comments may not be tolerated in others either.

TREATMENT

Treatment with Rick, and those like him, would most likely unfold in several phases. Since Rick is seeking help initially out of a mandatory requirement, the first phase of treatment would focus on orienting Rick to the counseling process—including an exploration into the reasons why Rick may find it beneficial to participate in counseling outside of his mandate. The goal here is to encourage Rick to have a higher degree of investment into counseling outside the mandates of his diversion. Whitney would be listening for opportunities to build positive help-seeking attitudes with Rick and noting potential barriers to help-seeking that may relate directly to his masculine gender role socialization process (Addis & Mahalik, 2003). Given the possibility of clients exhibiting defensiveness, this may take some time, though looking for opportunities to link client's goals with mandated criteria is a helpful strategy when building rapport. It should be noted that toxic masculinity, in this phase, could be demonstrated by a dismissal of the counseling process, a dismissal of the counselor, or both.

The next phase of treatment would involve a greater degree of exploration into Rick's life including his drinking behaviors, cultural values and socialization, his worldviews and personal values, motivations, relationships, and strengths. It could be beneficial in this phase to explore the client's relationship with their emotions, what they were socialized to do with distressing emotions, and to explore potential connections between drinking behaviors and attempts at emotional regulation.

The therapeutic relationship would, at this point, have developed a greater degree of closeness and trust. Toxic masculinity could emerge in this phase as a threat response to the growing mutuality and vulnerability Rick may feel as he opens up to Whitney. Rick's relational history and cultural socialization may leave him to believe that he is violating masculine norms opening up his emotional vulnerabilities to Whitney. He may respond to this potential threat activation in several different ways--all of which are attempts to create disconnection and to compensate for a felt loss of relational power and control. Rick may attempt to challenge the therapeutic boundary by inquiring into Whitney's life, coming onto her, or attempting to produce some form of reciprocal aid outside of payment for services. He may also attempt to increase the distance in the relationship by becoming more defensive in session, not engaging in the counseling process with openness and authenticity, or terminating counseling altogether.

The last phase of treatment would involve a more transparent and direct exploration into unhelpful internalized and rigid socialized ideologies of masculine gender role socialization that contribute toward Rick's sense of disconnection, lack awareness about his emotional life, and potentially his drinking concerns. With Whitney's help, Rick could learn to relate to women in a different way, using the counseling relationship as a launching pad to engage in different, more meaningful relationships with people. In this phase, toxic masculinity is identified in the moment-to-moment interactions with others and self, while being modulated by more flexible identity scripts and behaviors. This would allow for a working stage in the counseling process where Rick is able to experiment with new prosocial behaviors, reduce or eliminate drinking behaviors, express distressing emotions, and engage in non-sexualized interpersonal intimacy for the benefit of his own growth and wellbeing.

Table 1. Rick's Treatment Plan

Concern: Problematic drinking behaviors
Goal: Reduce problematic drinking behaviors
Objective 1: Identify triggers to drinking
Objective 2: Identify historical and cultural factors that contribute to drinking
Objective 3: Explore alternatives to drinking
Concern: Difficulty creating and maintaining close intimate relationships
Goal: Rick will create and maintain close intimate relationships
Objective 1: Identify barriers to relationship building
Objective 2: Identify social and cultural contexts that influence problematic interpersonal behavior
Objective 3: Identify and express vulnerable emotions in current relationships

CONCLUSION

Working with male clients around their toxic masculinity can be a tricky endeavor, as its very nature is an impediment to the counseling process, and unlikely the reason clients are entering therapy. In addition, given that patriarchy is everywhere in our society, there is the likelihood that clinicians have had adverse experiences with this form of oppression, making the risks for countertransference much greater. However, given how toxic masculinity further isolates men and negatively impacts them and their relationships, mental health counselors need to give it the attention it deserves, despite the feelings of vulnerability that may arise.

A commitment to developing the multicultural and social justice competencies required of counselors is a life-long endeavor, as the many systemic factors that influence marginalization and privilege are increasingly complex. Courage is a necessity in developing multicultural competence and beginning clinicians can find comfort that in doing so, they expand their ability to establish real therapeutic rapport and provide a space where both they and their client can learn and benefit from each other's experiences. To become a competent counselor requires growth, which in turn requires courage, but in doing the work necessary to effectively work with all clients, we enhance the quality of our work a hundredfold, and it is this that distinguishes the great clinicians from passable ones.

REFERENCES

Addis, M. E., & Mahalik, J. R. (2003). Men, masculinity, and the context of help seeking. *The American Psychologist*, *58*(1), 5–14. doi:10.1037/0003-066X.58.1.5 PMID:12674814

Baugher, A., & Gazmararian, J. (2015). Masculine gender role stress and violence: A literature review of future directions. *Aggression and Violent Behavior*, *24*, 107–112. doi:10.1016/j.avb.2015.04.002

Brittan, A. (1989). *Masculinity and Power*. New York: Basil Blackwell.

Brown, E. (2018). California professor, writer of confidential Brett Kavanaugh letter, speaks out about her allegation of sexual assault. *The Washington Post*. Retrieved from https://www.washingtonpost.com/investigations/california-professor-writer-of-confidential-brett-kavanaugh-letter-speaks-out-about-her-allegation-of-sexual-assault/2018/09/16/46982194-b846-11e8-94eb-3bd52dfe917b_story.html?noredirect=on&utm_term=.97cd05a2f8d2

Carrigan, T., Connell, R. W., & Lee, J. (1985). Toward a new sociology of masculinity. *Theory and Society*, *14*(5), 551–604. doi:10.1007/BF00160017

Comstock, D. L., Hammer, T. R., Strentzsch, J., Cannon, K., Parsons, J., & Salazar, I. I. G. (2008). Relational-cultural theory: A framework for bridging relational, multicultural, and social justice competencies. *Journal of Counseling and Development*, *86*(3), 279–287. doi:10.1002/j.1556-6678.2008.tb00510.x

Connell, R. W. (1983). *Which way is up? Essays on sex, class, and culture*. Sydney, Australia: Allen and Unwin.

Connell, R. W. (1987). *Gender and power*. Sydney, Australia: Allen and Unwin.

Connell, R. W., & Messerschmidt, J. W. (2005). Hegemonic masculinity: Rethinking the concept. *Gender & Society*, *19*(6), 829–859. doi:10.1177/0891243205278639

Coughlin, P., & Wade, J. C. (2012). Masculinity ideology, income disparity, and romantic relationship quality among men with higher earning female partners. *Sex Roles*, *67*(5-6), 311–322. doi:10.100711199-012-0187-6

Duffey, T., & Somody, C. (2011). The role of relational-cultural theory in mental health counseling. *Journal of Mental Health Counseling*, *33*(3), 223–242. doi:10.17744/mehc.33.3.c10410226u275647

Englar-Carlson, M. (2006). Masculine norms and the therapy process. In M. Englar-Carlson & M. A. Stevens (Eds.), *In the room with men: A casebook of therapeutic change*. Washington, DC: American Psychological Association. doi:10.1037/11411-002

Frank, B. (1987). Hegemonic heterosexual masculinity. *Studies in Political Economy*, *24*(1), 159–170. doi:10.1080/19187033.1987.11675562

Frye, J. (2018). From Politics to Policy: Turning the Corner on Sexual Harassment. *Center for American Progress*. Retrieved from https://www.americanprogress.org/issues/women/news/2018/01/31/445669/politics-policy-turning-corner-sexual-harassment/

Hearn, J. (2012). A multi-faceted power analysis of men's violence to known women: From hegemonic masculinity to the hegemony of men. *The Sociological Review*, *60*(4), 589–610. doi:10.1111/j.1467-954X.2012.02125.x

Isenhart, C. E. (2005). Treating substance abuse in men. In G. E. Good & G. R. Brooks (Eds.), *The new handbook of psychotherapy and counseling with men*. San Francisco, CA: Jossey-Bass.

Iwamoto, D. K., Corbin, W., Lejuez, C., & MacPherson, L. (2014). College men and alcohol use: Positive alcohol expectancies as a mediator between distinct masculine norms and alcohol use. *Psychology of Men & Masculinity*, *15*(1), 29–39. doi:10.1037/a0031594 PMID:25705133

Jordan, J. V. (2018). *Relational-cultural therapy* (2nd ed.). Washington, DC: American Psychological Association. doi:10.1037/0000063-000

Kessler, S. J., Ashenden, D. J., Connell, R. W., & Dowsett, G. W. (1982). *Ockers and disco-maniacs*. Sydney, Australia: Inner City Education Center.

Kupers, T. A. (2005). Toxic masculinity as a barrier to mental health treatment in prison. *Journal of Clinical Psychology*, *61*(6), 713–724. doi:10.1002/jclp.20105 PMID:15732090

Mahalik, J. R., Good, G. E., & Englar-Carlson, M. (2003). Masculinity scripts, presenting concerns, and help seeking: Implications for practice and training. *Professional Psychology, Research and Practice*, *34*(2), 123–131. doi:10.1037/0735-7028.34.2.123

Miller, J. B. (1976). *Toward a new psychology of women*. Boston, MA: Beacon Press.

Miller, J. B. (1986). *What do we mean by relationships?* (Work in Progress No. 22). Wellesley, MA: Stone Center Working Paper Series.

Miller, J. B., & Stiver, I. P. (1997). *The healing connection: How women form connections in therapy and in life*. Boston, MA: Beacon Press.

Parent, M. C., Gobble, T. D., & Rochlen, A. (2018). Social media behavior, toxic masculinity and depression. *Psychology of Men & Masculinity*. doi:10.1037/men0000156

Parent, M. C., & Moradi, B. (2009). Confirmatory factor analysis of the Conformity to Masculine Norms Inventory-46. *Psychology of Men & Masculinity*, *12*, 339–353. doi:10.1037/a0021904

Parent, M. C., Moradi, B., Rummell, C. M., & Tokar, D. M. (2011). Evidence of construct distinctiveness for conformity to masculine norms. *Psychology of Men & Masculinity*, *12*(4), 354–367. http://dx.doi.0rg/10.1037/a0023837. doi:10.1037/a0023837

Robb, C. (2006). *This changes everything: The relational revolution in psychology*. New York: Farrar, Straus & Giroux.

Rochlen, A. B., McKelley, R. A., Suizzo, M. A., & Scaringi, V. (2008). Predictors of relationship satisfaction, psychological well-being, and life satisfaction among stat-at-home fathers. *Psychology of Men & Masculinity*, *9*(1), 17–28. doi:10.1037/1524-9220.9.1.17

Serres, N. S. (2017). Sexual harassment in the workplace in a #MeToo world. *Forbes*. Retrieved from https://www.forbes.com/sites/forbeshumanresourcescouncil/2017/12/20/sexual-harassment-in-the-workplace-in-a-metoo-world/#6ea3ae615a42

Wade, J. C., & Donis, E. (2007). Masculinity ideology, male identity and romantic relationship quality among heterosexual and gay men. *Sex Roles*, *57*(9-10), 775–786. doi:10.100711199-007-9303-4

Wood, K., Lambert, H., & Jewkes, R. (2007). Showing roughness in a beautiful way: Talk about love, coercion, and rape in South African youth sexual culture. *Medical Anthropology Quarterly*, *21*(3), 277–300. doi:10.1525/maq.2007.21.3.277 PMID:17937250

Chapter 14
Mondays With Mac:
An Interpersonal Journey of Cultural Humility

Cort M. Dorn-Medeiros
https://orcid.org/0000-0002-6595-7503
Lewis and Clark College, USA

Jeffrey K. Christensen
Lewis and Clark College, USA

Ian Lertora
Texas Tech University, USA

EXECUTIVE SUMMARY

The purpose of this chapter is to "paint a picture of the counseling process" through rich description of how the Multicultural and Social Justice Counseling Competencies (MSJCC) can be applied through a model and stance of cultural humility, rather than a blanket state of achieving "cultural competence" in cross-cultural counseling. The mission of this chapter to convey the critical nature of accounting for the first author's ("counselor") positions of privilege, including positions of racial, age, socioeconomic status, and legal status privileges, over the client ("Mac"), and recognizing how cultural humility needs to be evoked within the counselor in order to apply tenants of the MSJCC as well as the counselor's interpersonal and relational-cultural approach to counseling and facilitating client growth and healing.

DOI: 10.4018/978-1-7998-0022-4.ch014

INTRODUCTION TO THE CASE

A counselor's ability to provide effective, compassionate care to an intersectionally diverse clientele is of critical importance. Both counselors-in-training (CIT) and professional counselors can often struggle with how to broach topics of difference with their clients. Broaching racial differences between counselor and client is often experienced as particularly difficult. Bringing up and addressing racial differences in the counseling room, particularly for White counselors, may trigger a range of emotions from anxiety to a concept known as *White fragility* (DiAngelo, 2018). White counselors and CIT may also struggle with addressing broader race-related topics including systemic racism, White supremacy, and the impact of racially-based microaggressions and microassaults on the mental health and overall wellbeing of their clients of color.

While any counselor, regardless of racial identity, may find race a sensitive topic, White counselors in particular can be challenged with effectively assessing, diagnosing, and treating their clients of color in a culturally competent manner. White counselors may also run the risk of perpetuating interpersonal and systemic racism and White supremacy unless they practice with not only cultural competency but race-based competency. The foundation of practicing with race-based competency is the ability to build and sustain rapport with clients of color (Hipolito-Delgado & Reinders-Saeman, 2017). The very beginning of this process for White counselors is coming from a stance of *cultural humility*.

Cultural humility refers to the ability to take on, and understand, the stance and perspective of the other within interpersonal relationships (Hook, Davis, Owen, Worthington Jr., & Utsey, 2013). Through focusing on self-humility, on what we *don't* know about the other person(s), and likely *won't* experience due to our own social locations and privilege, we can broach race-related and other topics of cultural difference in a respectful manner that acknowledges one's own privilege and power in the therapeutic relationship. In contrast to cultural competence, cultural humility requires a lifelong learning practice (Tervalon & Murray-Garcia, 1998). There is no end goal or expectation that one, particularly one coming from positions of power and racial privilege, can possibly know or experience the same things as their clients.

This chapter will focus on the case of Mac, a senior African American man who presented for mandated alcohol and drug treatment after being arrested for drug possession. I (the first author) was a newer counselor when Mac was put on my caseload at an outpatient treatment center for co-occurring issues. As a White, queer, transgender and gender nonconforming counselor living in a predominantly White city, newly graduated from my masters in counseling program at a predominantly White institution, I experienced some anxiety upon first meeting Mac. This anxiety was born out of my own internalized racism as the result of living in a country shrouded in White supremacy. Through learning a stance of cultural humility, and working on my own cultural identity development and race-based competency, Mac and I were able to develop a close therapeutic relationship over the course of nearly a year of weekly Monday afternoon meetings.

This chapter includes, (a) a brief case narrative, (b) client data including Mac's personal background and presenting problems, (c) a literature review relevant to the current case, (d) an introduction to myself, the first author, as counselor and my approach to helping, (e) a case conceptualization, (f) treatment strategy including goals and overall progress, and (g) a conclusion. It should be noted that while "Mac" is loosely based on an actual client of mine, all of his identifying information has been changed for confidentiality purposes. It is also noted and acknowledged that as I, the first author, am White, this chapter is filtered through the White experience and perspective of working cross-culturally with an African American man. The intent of this chapter and presented case is not to generalize this experience to *all* work with African Americans or clients of color. While all counselors and CIT may find this chapter useful, this chapter is written specifically for White counselors and CIT working with clients of color. This chapter also provides some experiences and insights into how counselors may go about practicing cultural humility as the foundation to using interpersonal and relational interventions to provide culturally competent services to their clients.

CASE NARRATIVE

On a warm Spring morning, Mac, a black male in his mid-60s, walked into the barely marked, neutral colored building of an outpatient treatment center. Nearly a dozen people sat in a moderately sized lobby with only posters of anti-drug ads decorating the walls. Some people flipped through old magazines with the delivery addresses cut out while others stared off in silence hoping no one would try to strike up a conversation. Upon walking up to the counter, Mac was greeted by Alice, a White woman in her mid-40s. Alice had commanded the front desk area for nearly a decade. When asked how he could be helped, Mac began a minutes long monologue about not needing to be in treatment, stating "...you (White) people put me here." Alice asked Mac to lower his voice. Mac spoke louder. He continued, stating "... everyone here is racist! You won't even let me speak my mind!" Although his intake appointment was scheduled for the usual one and a half hours, Mac insisted he would be there no longer than a half hour or else "...there would be hell to pay." Once again, Alice told Mac to "calm down" or else his counselor would tell the court he was resistant, uncooperative, and threatened clinic staff. Muttering under his breath, Mac walked away from the window, took a seat, and rolled his eyes at the *People* magazines littering the side tables.

Mac had lived in the Pacific Northwest (PNW) most of his adult life after relocating from the east coast of the United States (US) in his mid-20s. Mac had been legally mandated to outpatient treatment following a police incident a few weeks prior. Mac liked to remind all those around him that he was *really* from New Jersey and did not care for life in his current town. Mac came from a lower socioeconomic (SES) background and was predominantly raised by his grandmother. Mac had one younger brother who still lived on the east coast. Mac's brother was born with severe cognitive and developmental disabilities and had lived in supportive housing for several years. As often as he was able, Mac would send his brother cards and letters and slip in a few of his own dollars to help out.

On one Spring evening, Mac was approached by a police officer while taking a nap in his car. Mac reported he was used to being approached by police. He was routinely pulled over when driving his 1970s era Cadillac and had grown accustomed to keeping his composure even though he rarely received a straight answer when he asked why he was being pulled over. On this particular evening when the officer tapped on his car window, Mac was angry. He reported verbally "exploding" at the police officer who then reported cause to search Mac's car. Mac was subsequently arrested for being in possession of a controlled substance (PCS). As Mac had no prior convictions on his record, he was given the option to engage in court mandated counseling services, including regular drug screens, for a minimum of one year in exchange for getting his PCS charge dismissed.

Mac expressed a lot of anger upon initially entering counseling services and particularly objected to providing random, weekly urine analyses (UAs) that had to be observed by a UA technician. Mac was often reprimanded by predominantly White administrative personnel at the counseling center for behaving "inappropriately" and threatened with termination (likely leading to incarceration) if he could not "behave." As a black male, Mac had been through decades of historical, intergenerational, and personal trauma rooted in the pervasiveness of White supremacy and racial oppression in the US. As a black male living in a predominantly White city in the PNW, Mac had experienced years of personal and legal harassment. This was Mac's first engagement in any type of counseling or therapy.

Client Data

Background

Mac, age 66, heterosexual, cisgender, African American male, who has never been married and currently lives in subsidized housing in a moderately sized city in the PNW. Mac lives alone, is not currently in a romantic relationship and reports his last serious relationship was over ten years ago. Mac has been on social security disability insurance (SSDI) for almost ten years following a major car accident where he incurred severe trauma to his left leg and spine. Mac walks with a slight limp and uses a cane. Prior to his car accident, Mac worked predominantly manual labor jobs and warehousing. He holds a high school diploma and identifies as Christian though reports he mainly attends church services for the social aspect. Mac grew up in New Jersey with one younger brother, Robert, who was born with severe cognitive and developmental disabilities. Mac and Robert were predominantly raised by their paternal grandmother in a racially and ethnically diverse neighborhood. Mac grew up in a lower socioeconomic bracket and states his grandmother was strict but dedicated to providing for him and his brother. Mac's grandmother passed when he was 25, prompting his move across the country to join his girlfriend who had relocated for work.

Mac reports little contact with his mother and father growing up and states the only memory he has of his parents include their use of alcohol and beatings with a belt, "...to keep us in line". Mac believes both of his parents are deceased but is not sure as he has had no contact with them in several decades. Robert lives in supportive housing back in New Jersey and he and Mac remain in close contact through phone calls and letter writing. Mac reports having a couple of friends in his church but rarely sees them outside of weekly services. He states he experiences episodes of intense loneliness which can culminate in substance use, mainly alcohol and crack cocaine. Mac states during these episodes he also frequently solicits sex workers. Mac reports drinking alcohol on a regular basis, consuming three to four lite beers per day, but his crack cocaine use comes in binges. Mac states he can go a few months without using crack cocaine and will then use several times per day for two or three weeks straight, increase his alcohol use to include hard liquor, and simultaneously engage in risky behaviors including unprotected sex and occasionally driving while under the influence. Upon entering treatment, Mac does not identify as having any substance use or mental health concerns and states his only problem is the court system.

Presenting Problem

Mac was arrested on a PCS charge after a police officer found crack cocaine in his car. Mac was parked in a downtown area known for substance use and prostitution and was approached by the police officer for sleeping in his car. He has been mandated to a minimum of one year of outpatient treatment to address his substance use and mental health. Mac reports experiencing a lot of anger in his everyday life and is quick to lose his temper with others. Mac states he often feels lonely because he lives alone and has not had a romantic relationship in a long time. He does not believe he was addicted to any substance but did report symptoms related to his alcohol and cocaine use including using and/or drinking for longer periods of time than intended (impaired control), withdrawing from his relationship with his brother and not attending church when he was using (social impairment), and engaging in risky behaviors, such as engaging in unprotected sex and driving while under the influence, when he was in one of his "binges". Mac reported his main motivation to change his substance use was to meet the requirements to drop his pending legal charges.

Mac also reported he felt down more days than not, though he denied feeling depressed. Mac, rather, described periods of "extreme loneliness" where he would experience low appetite, difficulty sleeping, and lack energy to take care of daily activities such as checking his mail, attending doctor appointments, and going to church. Mac would experience cravings for crack cocaine every few months and would "indulge" for weeks at a time. Mac also reported having frequent thoughts that no one genuinely cared about him and that the few friends he did have only liked him because he would give them rides or do favors for them on the weekends.

Upon intake, Mac was given full mental health and American Society of Addiction Medicine (ASAM) assessments. Mac was given preliminary diagnoses of Moderate Cocaine and Alcohol Use Disorders and Dysthymic Disorder.

LITERATURE REVIEW

Significant mental health disparaities exist between people of color and White people in the United States (US). Black/African Americans are approxiamtely 10% more likely than White Americans to report severe psychological distress and to experience feelings of worthlessness, hopelessness, and sadness (Centers for Disease Control [CDC], 2016). In 2014, however, only 9.4% of African Americans actually received mental health treatment or counseling compared to 18.8% of White Americans (SAMHSA, 2015). Despite facing greater psychological stressors, people of color remain less likely than their White counterparts to receive mental health counseling (CDC, 2016; Banks, 2018). White counselors also maintain notably lower rates of retention for clients of color than they do for White clients (Banks, 2018; Meyer & Zane, 2013; Wintersteen, Mensinger, & Diamond, 2005). One reason why these discrepencies may occur is clients of color tend to view issues of race and ethnicity as important to address in counseling sessions while White clients, and White counselors, do not find as much salience in discussing race-related issues (Meyer & Zane, 2013; Wintersteen et al., 2005). In a ground-breaking study on access to mental health care, Kugelmass (2016) also found that Black/African American middle-class clients seeking mental health care were significantly less likely to receive an initial call back from mental health counselors than White middle-class clients.

One of the most salient aspects of the case presented in this chapter is the involvement of the legal system in Mac's treatment. While the fifth edition of the Diagnostic and Statistical Manual of Mental Disorders (DSM-5; American Psychiatric Association, 2013) removed legal involvement from substance use disorder diagnostic criteria, most substances of use and abuse (e.g. heroin, methamphetamine, non-prescribed opiates, cocaine, etc.) remain illegal. The US's war on drugs has decimated black communities and lead to a wildly disproportionate number of African Americans incarcerated on drug charges (Rosenberg, Groves, & Blankenship, 2018). African Americans are nearly five to seven times more likely than White Americans to be incarcerated for drug-related charges (Carson & Sabol, 2012). An in-depth analysis of working with legally mandated clients, and managing clinical expectations of court systems, is outside the scope of the current chapter. However, it is strongly recommended that counselors and CIT who are working with legally mandated clients consider how police involvement and legal processing can have a traumatic impact on their clients of color (Evans & Clay, 2018).

White fragility, a term coined by Robin DiAngelo (2018), is defined by discomfort and defensiveness among White persons when confronted with racial disparities. These disparities can include aspects of unrecognized White privilege, interpersonal and systemic racial inequalities, and social and political injustice. White counselors can inadvertently and unknowingly uphold White supremacist notions, and support aspects of systemic racism, if they do not increase their own cultural awareness through cultural identity work (Malott, Schaefle, Paone, Cates, & Haizlip, 2019). Many White individuals in the US grow up with the narratives that skin color does not matter, everyone is equal, and opportunities are available to all if only they would pull on their boot straps hard enough (DiAngelo, 2018).

Professional counselors and counselors-in-training (CIT) are required to adhere to professional and ethical standards of culturally competent practice, including the ability to effectively work with racially and ethnically diverse populations (American Counseling Association, 2014; Ratts, Singh, Nassar-McMillan, Butler, & McCullough, 2015). Yet race is often avoided in the counseling room, particularly among White counselors working with clients of color (Bartoli, Bentley-Edwards,

Garcia, Michael, & Ervin, 2018). White CIT may often carry unrecognized White privilege (Larke & Larke, 2009) and even professional counselors are often hesitant to address racial differences out of anxiety, hopelessness, and fear of misspeaking or being misunderstood (Sue, Rivera, Capodilupo, Lin, & Torino, 2010).

Historically, research has demonstrated the critical importance for counselors to acknowledge racism, its impact on communities of color, and the dangers of "color blind" attitudes towards race on their clients of color (Gushue & Carter, 2000; Gushue & Constantine, 2007; Neville, Worthington, & Spanierman, 2001). The Multicultural and Social Justice Counseling Competencies (MSJCC; Ratts et al., 2015) provide a multidimentional model that encompasses four counseling dyads: (a) privileged counselors working with marginalized clients, (b) marginalized counselors working with privileged clients, (c) privileged counselors working with privileged clients, and (d) marginalized counselors working with marginalized clients. The dimensions of "privileged" and "marginalized" in this context are intersectional and take into account the multiple identities of both counselor and client. In other words, no one counselor or client in any given situation is only privileged or only marginalized. Take, for example, a White female counselor working with a Black male client. The counelor would hold racial privilege but in any given moment in the counseling session may be in a marginalized position regarding issues of sex and gender. While this is a very basic example, it demonstrates the fluidity of identities that occur between counselor and client throughout the course of a counseling session. To practice cultural competence, CIT and professional counselors are required to remain insightful and mindful of how and when theses identities shift within session and to address accordingly with their clients.

The MSJCC (Ratts et al., 2015) require that CIT and professional counselors strive to increase self-awareness regarding attitudes and beliefs, gain knowledge, and hone the skills necessary to effectively address issues of power and privilege in the counseling room. For example, CIT and professional counselors must demonstrate a level of self-awareness where they are able to acknowledge their own racial privilege and its advantages in greater society. White counselors who do not effectively address their own White fragility are at risk of remaining defensive when clients of color bring up their own experiences of racism and racial disparities either inside or outside of the therapy room. Such defensiveness stemming from White fragility is antithical to culturally competent practice.

More recent literature has continued to advocate for race-based competencies to be included in counselor training (Hipolito-Delgado & Reinders-Saeman, 2017; Spanierman & Smith, 2017). Addressing and exploring racial identity and racism in counseling sessions can increase positive therapeutic outcomes for clients of color (Day-Vines, Bryan, & Griffin, 2013; Hipolito-Delgado & Reinders-Saeman, 2017). White counselors who practice with race-based competency are able to more effectively build rapport with clients of color, broach topics of racial differences and inequalities between the counselor and client, and validate the impact of racism on their clients of color which may include trauma responses (Day-Vines et al., 2013; Helms, Nicolas, & Green, 2010; Hipolito-Delgado & Reinders-Saeman, 2017; Malott et al., 2019).

Race-based competency (Hipolito-Delgado & Reinders-Saeman, 2017; Spanierman & Smith, 2017) and cultural competency (Ratts et al., 2015) are similar in offering guidelines of best practices for effective, culturally attuned mental health treatment for a racially and ethnically diverse clientele. Cultural competence is typically used as a broad, foundational framework that takes into account all cultural differences between counselor and client and how they inform different positions of privilege and marginalization in the therapy room and out in greater society. Cultural competence includes attending to racial and ethnic differences but also includes other aspects of the cultural experience such as gender identity, sexuality, socioeconimic status, religion and/or spirituality, education level, etc. Race-base competency, in contrast, specifically highlights the importance of racial identity development, racial differences/similarities between counselor and client, and exploring the impact of systemic racism on a client's mental health and wellbeing. Practicing with cultural competence can be seen as a foundation to build upward into race-based competence.

To approach a client with cultural humility means to acknowledge difference, not to run away from it. White counselors struggle to retain clients of color. Why? Newer counselors, in particular, can often fear bringing up differences, particularly racial differences, for fear of alienating clients of color. Or from ingrained White social norms that say talking about race is being racist (DiAngelo, 2018). From what we know in the literature, however, *not* acknowledging differences between counselor and client can lead to the client either feeling invisible (or "unseen" by the counselor), experiencing microaggressions from the counselor, or possibly assuming the counselor does not see race as an important factor in the client's life or important to the counselor-client relationship (Day-Vines et al., 2013; Sue, 2010).

INTRO TO THE COUNSELOR

Cultural Background

I, the first author, am a White, transgender and gender nonconforming, queer, currently able-bodied, counselor educator in my early 40s employed as a tenure-track Assistant Professor at a small, liberal arts college in the US. My ethnic background is predominantly Portuguese and French. I come from a family where education was highly emphasized as was fitting into social and cultural norms. My father attended a four year college and I received a lot of guidance and assistance in managing higher education processes such as taking standardized tests and applying for college. I grew up in an upper-middle socioeconomic (SES) bracket in the northeastern part of the US. I was raised Catholic and attended Catholic school from kindergarten through 12th grade. I do not currently practice Catholicism, and my Jewish partner and I are raising a family in the Jewish traditions. I am an out queer person and due to my physical appearance (masculine of center, visible tattoos, very short hair) most people I interact with assume my queer identity.

I was raised having very little knowledge or awareness of what it meant to be White. Only in my adult years did I even understand that, as a White person, I had a culture. I grew up thinking White meant *normal* or *regular* and only other (non-White) persons had a cultural background. Unconsciously, my assumption was that White equaled American. It wasn't until my undergraduate years in college when, during a sociology class, I was tasked with writing about how my sociocultural background influenced my presence at a large, private, and very expensive university in Boston, MA. I struggled. I procrastinated. I knew my father's family was Portuguese and my mother's family was predominantly French. I asked family members about cultural traditions and they also struggled to come up with specific examples of how or what our culture was, what it meant, and how we practiced it. I stretched my writing to barely meet the ten page requirement. When I received my paper back some weeks later, my professor had written in large print on the last page, "What does it mean to be White?"

In the years since, I have only begun the process of uncovering and unlearning my own unconscious biases, my own internalized racism, and truly understanding what it really does mean to be White. This process has not been linear nor will it ever be complete. Coming from a stance of cultural humility, it is crucial that I continue the work, continue the self-reflection, critical inquiry, difficult discussions, and interpersonal challenges of combating racism and oppression. I am now in a place where I do not experience much defensiveness or anxiety when discussing race, racism, or racial inequities. However, this has only come after years of struggling with my own White fragility and feelings of hopelessness, ineptitude, and ineffectiveness. It is my hope in that sharing this personal experience, White counselors and CIT can understand the process of unlearning racism is never ending. It is important to acknowledge that while this work is difficult, it does not compare to the ongoing struggles of communities of color impacted by the weight of systemic oppression.

While the case example in this chapter will be written from my (first author) experiences, I also have two co-authors. The second author is is a multiracial person of color, a cisgender, heterosexual male, who is currently able-bodied. He was raised in a predominantly ethnic middle-class family that held more collectivist views with a value of education. He is currently on faculty at a small, liberal arts college in the US. The third author is a Latino son of immigrants, straight, currently able-bodied, counselor educator who grew up in a predominantly white lower middle class neighborhood. The third author is currently on faculty at a large research university in the US. The second author and I have worked together as professional counselors at a community-based agency for co-occurring disorders prior to academic collaborations including the present chapter. The third author also has extensive clinical experience with diverse client populations. All authors are dedicated to advancing equity and social justice in professional counseling and advocating for culturally attuned practices in mental health treatment.

In identifying our social locations as authors, we encourage the reader to reflect on how the subjectivity of our thoughts, expressed beliefs, conceptualizations, and interpretations of, and within, the counseling relationship are filtered through our various positions of power and privilege. By engaging in this exercise of revealing social locations we embrace transparency in regards to potential biases that may impact our judgment and ability to connect. In opening discussions in this manner we open the door to difficult conversations about power and privilege, or a lack of, which can lead to deeper understanding, empathy, and connectedness with clients from backgrounds that may be different from our own.

Counseling Approach

Prior to getting my PhD in Counselor Education, I worked as a Licensed Professional Counselor primarily with a diverse clientele of corrections populations and mandated clients in various co-occurring treatment centers. I take a client-centered, interpersonal (Rogers, 1959; Newhill, Safran, & Muran, 2000) and relational-cultural (Miller, 1976) approach to counseling. I adamantly believe actively cultivating a strong therapeutic alliance (Bordin, 1979) provides the critical groundwork for change. As a White counselor, it is crucial that I actively practice cultural humility in every counseling session, client interaction, and even conceptualizing cases particularly when engaging in interpersonal and relational work with clients of color (Hook et al., 2013; Tervalon & Murray-Garcia, 1998).

While there is no one formula or trajectory for counseling with all clients, I typically spend the first one or two sessions getting to know a client, their interpersonal style, and immediately focus on building rapport. While having one or two sessions to ease into the counseling relationship is wonderful, building a therapeutic alliance with clients needs to begin immediately. How do we establish rapport with clients? How do we know if we have a solid working alliance with our clients? One model I have used is using Bordin's (1979) conceptualization of the working alliance as counselor and client being in alignment on the goals and tasks of treatment and attending to the bond between counselor and client. This model fits well with the practice of cultural humility as it requires a highly collaborative effort between counselor and client to develop treatment goals and specific tasks. It also fits well with interpersonal and relational-cultural approaches that require the counselor to remain attentive to therapeutic ruptures, subsequent rupture repair, and increase relational awareness (Comstock et al., 2008; Newhill et al., 2000).

While I own and acknowledge the privilege I have in the counseling room, both racial privilege and holding power in the counselor role, I rarely position myself as an expert. Mac had already experienced severe trauma over the years rooted in systemic, intergenerational, and historical oppression and racism. Practicing humility meant doing whatever I could to flatten the power differentials in the room. I admitted I had no personal experience with police involvement. I had no idea what it must be like to get pulled over frequently and asked where I was going and with whom. I had never experienced being bullied, harassed, or assaulted because of my race. I also acknowledged some areas to which I could relate as a queer person (e.g. safety concerns, finding "your people" at a large event) while verbally acknowledging our experiences would still never be equal due to my racial privilege.

In working with a diverse clientele, I think creatively about how to best engage the specific person sitting across from me. For some clients, this could look like something as simple as having myself or the client write or draw out thought bubbles for treatment plan goals and tasks. This is part of the collaborative process. Sometimes visualizing the process of goal planning can feel more collaborative than having me type into a computer during session. Stories or even news from the media or popular culture can be brought into the room as they relate to the client. In the case of Mac, as described below, he liked to bring in the newspaper that was published by a local black organization and talk about the various headlines. After Mac had brought it in a couple of times, I began to pick it up myself during the week and glance at the headlines ahead of time. It made for a more rich conversation when I had some knowledge ahead of time and could speak more competently about its contents. It was also a way to attend to the therapeutic relationship while also increasing my cultural awareness of Mac's community.

Case Conceptualization

This case is conceptualized using a framework of cultural humility, interpersonal and relational-cultural theory (RCT) treatment approaches, and the MSJCC (Hook, 2013; Miller, 1976; Newhill et al., 2000; Ratts et al., 2015; Tervalon & Murray-Garcia, 1998). While cultural humility has been defined above, it is important to note what this looks like in practice.

Through practicing cultural humility, I spent the first session practicing two essential elements: validation and exploration. The first session with Mac was spent validating his frustrating and dehumanizing experience of being arrested, incarcerated, and mandated to treatment. It was not my place to question his experience. Due to my racial privilege, I would likely never have the experiences he had gone through both during his childhood and in the here-and-now. I could likely walk into any treatment center in my city and see people who looked like me in positions of power. Most of my treatment would probably be centered in Whiteness, complete with group handouts and expectations that family members take time away from work to attend my weekly Family Group.

It was also important during the first session to broach the topic of racial difference between myself and Mac. When broaching racial difference between counselor and client it is crucial to use direct language. White counselors have often been socialized to notions of "color-blindness" and/or taught that talking about or recognizing race is rude (Gushue & Constantine, 2007; Neville et al. 2001). Hence, White CIT and professional counselors may talk around race or expect the client to bring up racial differences. Newer counselors, in particular, may fear that bringing up race will cause a therapeutic rupture. However, by broaching the topic of race, challenging our own White fragility, and coming from a stance of cultural humility, we are communicating to our clients that we see them, we acknowledge that we are different, and that we do not have the same experiences in the world because of these differences. In broaching race with Mac, I asked during the first session how he felt having a White counselor. Mac initially looked surprised, smiled and stated, "You know you're White?" While this statement was made in jest, Mac elaborated that he had never heard a White person acknowledge their own race. He did not know yet how he felt having a White counselor.

For members of marginalized communities experiences of isolation, shame, and humiliation can have an adverse effect on forming mutually positive relationships and reinforce strategies to disconnect despite wanting to connect with others. Relational Cultural Theory refers to this as the central relational paradox (Birrell & Freyd, 2006; Duffey & Somody, 2011; Hammer, et al., 2016; Miller & Stiver, 1997). This concept may become particularly salient when clients of color may, understandably, perceive more risk in engaging with a White counselor (Morgan Consoli & Marin, 2016). By forming new and healing human bonds, the hurt of disconnection can be addressed and the strategies for disconnection unlearned. This understanding in RCT is known as relational awareness (Comstock et al., 2008). The first place to start with Mac was taking in his cultural context and ask open-ended questions to gather more information about his relational worldview.

Using the MSJCC framework is a useful lens in conceptualizing Mac (Ratts et al., 2015). In looking at the four developmental domains of (a) counselor self-awareness, (b) client worldview, (c) counseling relationship and, (d) counseling and advocacy interventions, in relation to counselor and client positionality, one could begin to formulate the necessary foundations for laying a productive therapeutic rapport (Ratts et al., 2015). Mac being an African American male in a predominantly White city, means a high likelihood of his experiencing racism, either blatant overt forms, or subtle microaggressions. This is substantiated with his claims of everyone “being racist” and how “White people put me here!” Thus, Mac’s worldview is one of experienced racism, that must be acknowledged before any meaningful rapport and trust could be established (Sue, 2010).

According to the MSJCC (Ratts et al., 2015) CIT and professional counselors are required to practice ongoing self-reflection and strive towards increasing self-awareness in order better serve culturally diverse clients. Such reflexive practice can take many forms and include examples such as attending professional training, engaging in personal counseling, and discussing race-related topics in clinical clinical supervision. Competencies around counselor self-awareness become particularly salient, as the counselor needs to be aware of the inherent power imbalances within society, and how the oppressive force of racism can undermine healthy relationships and trust with others (Comstock et al., 2008). It must be noted that this level of awareness needs to be brought up, especially if the counselor presents from a positionality that Mac’s past oppressors share.

The competency of skills, with special consideration to broaching and taking steps to understand how historical events of Mac’s lifetime, may have impacted him, becomes equally crucial. However, validating Mac’s experiences as unjust, and making it clear that careful action will be taken to ensure that the counseling relationship will not recapitulate past wrongs, can go a long way to establishing a trusting relationship.

Upon further conversations, the counselor finds out that Mac was an advocate during the Civil Rights movement and is still active in advocating for racial equality. Mac even brings in local African-American newspapers to share with the counselor as a springboard to talk about some of the advocacy roles he participated in during his youth, which he recounts with pride. These conversations sometimes go into Mac’s experiences with racism, and its influence on his using substances, which could never have transpired, had the counselor not broached race and let Mac know that it would be safe to discuss this topic, if he chose to.

TREATMENT

As Mac was in a mandated treatment, many parts of the program structure were predetermined with little room for customization. There were three phases of treatment and passage through these phases was determined by a formula based on time, consistent attendance at required groups, weekly individual counseling sessions, and providing random, negative UAs. If a UA came back positive for any substance that was not legally prescribed, clients could be legally penalized including moving back a treatment phase, attending additional outside support meetings, or even be given a weekend jail sanction. Mac was required to attend a series of groups including Early Recovery, Relapse Prevention, Family, Men's Group, and a Recovery Maintenance group. Mac also opted to take Dialectical Behavioral Therapy (DBT) as an optional group during his third phase of treatment.

Of course having one treatment program for all clients is in many ways the antithesis of providing culturally competent services. In such situations, it is important to take a critical stance and ask, and reflect upon, the following questions: Who developed the treatment sequence? Who makes the overall clinical decisions? Is this a racially, ethnically, and intersectionally diverse group of people? If not, how do White cultural expectations of treatment providers and supervisors translate to clients of color? Are these services trauma-informed? Where are the opportunities for advocacy if, and when, needed? While these questions can be crucial to reflect upon and discuss in clinical supervision, this is also where the interpersonal relationship between counselor and client is critical. Especially within a structured program where options may be limited, the therapeutic relationship and interpersonal work in counseling sessions provides the base for trust, transparency, validation, and creativity.

The following provides a brief synopsis for Mac's treatment goals, examples of objectives and tasks related to those goals, and overall progress. Mac's treatment plan was developed collaboratively as discussed above. As Mac's overarching goal was to meet the requirements of his legal mandate, he wanted to prioritize the goal of remaining sober from drugs and alcohol for at least the year of his required treatment.

Goals

The primary goals for Mac's treatment were, (a) abstain from crack cocaine and alcohol use, (b) reduce symptoms of dysthymia, (c) increase social connections and positive supports in Mac's community.

Objectives

The primary objectives related to Mac's treatment goals were, (a) Mac will be able to demonstrate consistent attendance at required treatment functions and provide negative UAs when requested, (b) Mac will be able to identify, practice, and regularly implement a minimum of five coping strategies when he is feeling down and low energy, (c) Mac will be able to identify a minimum of two positive, mutually beneficial relationships with people his community.

Tasks

The tasks related to Mac's objectives and goals were, (a) Mac will attend all treatment groups and appointments as scheduled. He agrees to call his primary counselor if he will miss a treatment activity due to illness or emergency, (b) Mac will call the UA phone line every day to see if his number has been called for a random UA, (c) Mac will learn, and demonstrate, a minimum of five effective relapse prevention skills to maintain sobriety, (d) Mac will attend a biweekly walking group at his local senior center where he picks up his daily newspaper, and (e) Mac will attend weekly 12-step meetings at his local club that primarily serves the African American community.

Progress

Mac's progress began slowly. This is not unusual for individuals entering counseling or drug and alcohol treatment for the first time. Particularly for mandated clients having gone through the difficulties of the court system, engaging in treatment services for the first time can be extremely anxiety provoking. Mac missed several scheduled groups in the beginning phase of treatment. He also had a few positive UAs for cocaine and several diluted UAs which may have indicated alcohol use. However, Mac was making progress engaging in the groups he did attend with several group counselors commenting on how supportive he was to other group members. As Mac's primary counselor, I was attentive to giving him this feedback on a regular basis. Rather than further traumatize Mac by finger wagging for missed groups, I focused on the positive relational progress he was making with the treatment community.

After the first month, Mac's attendance greatly improved. He began to make social connections in his groups and enjoyed the attention he received from his fellow group members for his dry sense of humor. He began consistently abstaining from drugs and alcohol and providing negative UAs. Mac also actively participated in his individual counseling sessions and we began to explicitly talk about our racial, gender, and age differences. Mac would like to "quiz" me on "black events" in the media, ask me about older black actresses and singers he was sure I would not know, and would express empathy towards me if he saw something in the news that impacted the lesbian, gay, bisexual, transgender, and queer community. If one of my reflections did not seem to land in session, I was careful to call attention to it and inquire about what was going on for Mac in that moment. Our working alliance become stronger after a few months of treatment and ongoing reflective practice.

Attending social groups and outside support meetings was difficult for Mac. It was a task that involved heavy negotiation between us. Mac had expressed a desire for more friends whom with whom he felt a genuine, authentic connection that did not involve substance use. He also stated being social and out in the community had historically helped reduce his dysthymia symptoms. When our therapeutic relationship felt strong enough, I challenged him about what his barriers were to trying out the senior walking group or attending the 12-step meeting at his local club. Mac demonstrated emotional vulnerability and admitted he was fearful of being rejected from his peers at the senior center and anxious that the 12-step meeting would trigger him to think about using cocaine and alcohol. We spent a lot of time processing how Mac was able to build authentic relationships with his peers in treatment. We also reflected on our relationship and what parts of our relationship made Mac feel safe, understood, and supported. We discussed how he would identify these things in outside relationships. I was patient and let Mac have his own timeline for when he felt ready to try. I was not the expert of his experience. After nearly five months, Mac went for a walk with his senior group and began attending 12-step meetings.

Mac's progress was not as linear as presented here. He relapsed in the second phase of his treatment and was only permitted to remain where he was due to his honesty around drinking. Mac would still express anger in court if he felt he, or one of his treatment friends, was being treated unfairly. He went through periods of not attending his social groups, retreating to his apartment, and becoming down and withdrawn. But due to the strong relationships he had built in treatment not only with me as his primary counselor but also his group leaders and fellow clients, he always returned to try again. Mac graduated from treatment in a little over a year.

CONCLUSION

That counselors are able to provide effective services to all clients, regardless of their demographic, is not only expected of mental health professionals, it's also an area of complying with ethical practice (ACA, 2014). It is necessary for clinicians, regardless of experience, to continue to be active in exploring their attitudes and beliefs towards marginalized populations and to be active in seeking knowledge of how specific systems of oppression have historically oppressed others, in order to implement the necessary skills to articulate this knowledge in a meaningful way to clients. Doing so not only validates marginalized clients' experiences of social injustices, but provides them a safe space to continue to discuss how these oppressive systems continue to affect them, as they certainly do.

The work required to get to a place of competence requires courage and a willingness to experience vulnerability, especially if clinicians are doing so from a position of privilege. Unfortunately this work is never fully done, as the complexity of how these oppressive systems operate, requires a lifelong commitment to learning about and understanding. However, by taking the necessary steps to develop these multicultural and social justice counseling competencies, then the chances for a healthy therapeutic rapport expands a hundredfold, and from it, a positive learning experience for both the client and the clinician. For if our marginalized clients can't discuss how systems of oppression have adversely impacted them in counseling, then where can they do so, outside of their community? It is not only our clients' rights to be afforded such a space, it is our responsibility to provide it.

REFERENCES

American Counseling Association. (2014). *American Counseling association code of ethics*. Retrieved from https://www.counseling.org/docs/default-source/default-document- library/2014-code-of-ethicsfinaladdressc97d33f16116603abcacff0000bee5e7.pdf?sfvrsn=5d6b532c_0

American Psychiatric Association. (2013). *Diagnostic and statistical manual of mental disorders (DSM-5®)*. Washington, DC: American Psychiatric Pub.

Banks, B. M. (2018). University mental health outreach targeting students of color. *Journal of College Student Psychotherapy*, 1–9. doi:10.1080/87568225.2018.1539632

Bartoli, E., Bentley-Edwards, K. L., García, A. M., Michael, A., & Ervin, A. (2018). What do White counselors and psychotherapists need to know about race? White racial socialization in counseling and psychotherapy training programs. In *Whiteness and White Privilege in Psychotherapy* (pp. 80–96). New York, NY: Routledge.

Birrell, P. J., & Freyd, J. J. (2006). Betrayal and trauma: Relational models of harm and healing. *Journal of Trauma Practice*, *5*(1), 49–63. doi:10.1300/J189v05n01_04

Bordin, E. S. (1979). The generalizability of the psychoanalytic concept of the working alliance. *Psychotherapy (Chicago, Ill.)*, *16*(3), 252–260. doi:10.1037/h0085885

Carson, E. A., & Sabol, W. J. (2013). Prisoners in 2012. *NCJ, 239808*, 11. Retrieved from https://www.bjs.gov/content/pub/pdf/p12tar9112.pdf

Centers for Disease Control. (2016). *Health, United States, 2015, with special feature on racial and ethnic health disparities*. Retrieved from https://www.cdc.gov/nchs/data/hus/hus15.pdf

Comstock, D. L., Hammer, T. R., Strentzsch, J., Cannon, K., Parsons, J., & Salazar, I. I. G. (2008). Relational-cultural theory: A framework for bridging relational, multicultural, and social justice competencies. *Journal of Counseling and Development*, *86*(3), 279–287. doi:10.1002/j.1556-6678.2008.tb00510.x

Day-Vines, N. L., Bryan, J., & Griffin, D. (2013). The Broaching Attitudes and Behavior Survey (BABS): An exploratory assessment of its dimensionality. *Journal of Multicultural Counseling and Development*, *41*(4), 210–223. doi:10.1002/j.2161-1912.2013.00037.x

DiAngelo, R. (2018). *White fragility: Why it's so hard for white people to talk about racism*. Boston, MA: Beacon Press.

Evans, L., & Clay, C. (2018). Solidarity, double consciousness, and collective emotion work: Understanding negative black health outcomes resulting from systemic police terror. In *Inequality, crime, and health among african american males* (pp. 185–206). Bingley, UK: Emerald Publishing Limited. doi:10.1108/S0195-744920180000020009

Gushue, G. V., & Carter, R. T. (2000). Remembering race: White racial identity attitudes and two aspects of social memory. *Journal of Counseling Psychology*, *47*(2), 199–210. doi:10.1037/0022-0167.47.2.199

Gushue, G. V., & Constantine, M. G. (2007). Color-blind racial attitudes and white racial identity attitudes in psychology trainees. *Professional Psychology, Research and Practice*, *38*(3), 321–328. doi:10.1037/0735-7028.38.3.321

Hammer, T. R., Crethar, H. C., & Cannon, K. (2016). Convergence of identities through the lens of relational-cultural theory. *Journal of Creativity in Mental Health*, *11*(2), 126–141. doi:10.1080/15401383.2016.1181596

Helms, J. E., Nicolas, G., & Green, C. E. (2010). Racism and ethnoviolence as trauma: Enhancing professional training. *Traumatology*, *16*(4), 53–62. doi:10.1177/1534765610389595

Hipolito-Delgado, C. P., & Reinders-Saeman, R. (2017). What do allies do?: Providing culturally responsive counseling to communities of color. *Interamerican Journal of Psychology*, *51*(2), 214–225.

Hook, J. N., Davis, D. E., Owen, J., Worthington, E. L., & Utsey, S. O. (2013). Cultural humility: Measuring openness to culturally diverse clients. *Journal of Counseling Psychology*, *60*(3), 353–366. doi:10.1037/a0032595 PMID:23647387

Kugelmass, H. (2016). "Sorry I'm not accepting new patients" an audit study of access to mental health care. *Journal of Health and Social Behavior*, *57*(2), 168–183. doi:10.1177/0022146516647098 PMID:27251890

Larke, P., & Larke, A. (2009). Teaching diversity/multicultural education courses in the academy: Sharing the voices of six professors. *Research in Higher Education*, *3*, 1–8.

Malott, K. M., Schaefle, S., Paone, T. R., Cates, J., & Haizlip, B. (2019). Challenges and coping mechanisms of Whites committed to antiracism. *Journal of Counseling and Development*, *97*(1), 86–97. doi:10.1002/jcad.12238

Meyer, O. L., & Zane, N. (2013). The influence of race and ethnicity in clients' experiences of mental health treatment. *Journal of Community Psychology*, *41*(7), 884–901. doi:10.1002/jcop.21580 PMID:25400301

Miller, J. B. (1976). *Toward a new psychology of women*. Boston, MA: Beacon Press.

Miller, J. B., & Stiver, I. P. (1997). *The healing connection: How women form connections in therapy and in life*. Boston, MA: Beacon Press.

Neville, H. A., Worthington, R. L., & Spanierman, L. B. (2001). Race, power, and multicultural counseling psychology: Understanding White privilege and color-blind racial attitudes. In J. G. Ponterotto, J. M. Casas, L. A. Suzuki, & C. M. Alexander (Eds.), *Handbook of multicultural counseling* (pp. 257–288). Thousand Oaks, CA, US: Sage Publications, Inc.

Newhill, C. E., Safran, J. D., & Muran, J. C. (2000). *Negotiating the therapeutic alliance: A relational treatment guide*. New York, NY: Guilford Press.

Ratts, M. J., Singh, A. A., Nassar-McMillan, S., Butler, S. K., & McCullough, J. R. (2015). *Multicultural and Social Justice Counseling Competencies*. Retrieved from https://www.counseling.org/docs/default-source/competencies/multicultural-and-social- justice-counseling-competencies.pdf?sfvrsn=20

Rogers, C. R. (1959). *A theory of therapy, personality, and interpersonal relationships: As developed in the client-centered framework* (Vol. 3). New York, NY: McGraw-Hill.

Rosenberg, A., Groves, A. K., & Blankenship, K. M. (2017). Comparing Black and White drug offenders: Implications for racial disparities in criminal justice and reentry policy and programming. *Journal of Drug Issues*, *47*(1), 132–142. doi:10.1177/0022042616678614 PMID:28966392

Spanierman, L. B., & Smith, L. (2017). Roles and responsibilities of White allies: Implications for research, teaching, and practice. *The Counseling Psychologist*, *45*(5), 606–617. doi:10.1177/0011000017717712

Substance Abuse and Mental Health Services Administration. (2018). *National-level comparison of mental health estimates from The National Survey on Drug Use and Health (NSDUH) and other data sources*. Retrieved from https://www.samhsa.gov/data/sites/default/files/cbhsq- reports/NSDUHC2MentalHealthEst2018.pdf

Sue, D. W. (2010). *Microaggressions in everyday life: Race, gender, and sexual orientation*. Hoboken, NJ: John Wiley & Sons.

Sue, D. W., Rivera, D. P., Capodilupo, C. M., Lin, A. I., & Torino, G. C. (2010). Racial dialogues and White trainee fears: Implications for education and training. *Cultural Diversity & Ethnic Minority Psychology*, *16*(2), 206–214. doi:10.1037/a0016112 PMID:20438159

Tervalon, M., & Murray-Garcia, J. (1998). Cultural humility versus cultural competence: A critical distinction in in defining physician training outcomes in multicultural education. *Journal of Health Care for the Poor and Underserved*, *9*(2), 117–125. doi:10.1353/hpu.2010.0233 PMID:10073197

Wintersteen, M. B., Mensinger, J. L., & Diamond, G. S. (2005). Do gender and racial differences between patient and therapist affect therapeutic alliance and treatment retention in adolescents? *Professional Psychology, Research and Practice*, *36*(4), 400–408. doi:10.1037/0735-7028.36.4.400

Chapter 15
Lucille:
Cross Cultural Counseling With Older Adult Populations

Elise Johns
Nicholls State University, USA

EXECUTIVE SUMMARY

The percentage of the population in the United States comprised of older adults (65+), sometimes referred to as Baby Boomers (birth year 1946 – 1964) and the Silent Generation (birth year 1925 – 1945), is steadily on the rise. This population is often overlooked and has a unique subset of issues when it comes to counseling competencies. Layered multicultural competencies affecting these individuals include race, gender, sexual orientation, religion, and ageism. Counseling concerns related to age include but are not limited to loss of autonomy, loss of physical ability, loss of loved ones, and changing definition of self. From an existential therapeutic background blended with Cognitive Behavioral Therapy (CBT) interventions, the author reviews the case study of Lucille with a focus on therapeutic intervention and Multicultural and Social Justice Counseling Competencies (MSJCCs).

DOI: 10.4018/978-1-7998-0022-4.ch015

INTRODUCTION

This chapter will explore the use of Multicultural and Social Justice Counseling Competencies (MSJCC) and existential therapy to address the needs of 88-year-old client Lucille who has just been placed in an assisted living facility. The use of an existential framework along with interventions from other theoretical orientations such as mindfulness and Cognitive Behavioral Therapy (CBT) will be interwoven to address therapeutic goals as outlined by both client and therapist. The existential theories of Irvin Yalom and Viktor Frankl as well as the history of existential therapy will be outlined as a backdrop for understanding Lucille's existential concerns. MSJCC's provide the framework to review Lucille's multicultural identity and intersections of ethnicity, gender, and religion.

CASE DESCRIPTION

Lucille is an eighty- eight-year-old female who lives in an assisted living facility. Lucille identifies as Jewish American, having emigrated from Europe in 1948 at the age of 19. Lucille currently lives alone. Her husband and two of her three children are deceased. She has also lost many of her close friends to terminal illness in recent years. Her remaining lifelong friends who were once a support system are now scattered across the country living with their relatives or in nursing homes. They rarely get a chance to speak on the phone and Lucille struggles to text or write letters due to deteriorating eyesight. Lucille is a grandmother to five grandchildren. Her surviving daughters and grandchildren convinced Lucille to move to an assisted living facility when she was no longer able to drive and began having minor difficulties with her activities of daily living (ADL's). She speaks to her daughters frequently on the phone but rarely sees them in person. One daughter lives a five-hour drive away and the other daughter who lives in the same city cannot come visit frequently due to her own declining health. Lucille's grandchildren visit once every few months but rarely call. She does not reach out to her daughters or grandchildren but waits for them to reach out to her. She is worried she will be perceived as a burden or bothersome if she is constantly calling and asking them to visit. She sometimes avoids calls from her daughter who is ill as she states speaking to her child and not being able to care for as she did her whole life created a sense of intense guilt. Lucille mainly stays to herself and has made no friends at the assisted living facility despite numerous community activities and invitations to social events at the facility. Lucille states anxiety about her deteriorating eyesight inhibits her from participating in social events, as she feels she will be judged. She states feelings of loneliness and feeling like an outsider. Lucille states openly to the staff that she is struggling with her loss of independence and sometimes feels useless, however will deny making these statements if confronted by daughter or grandchildren. Lucille states she is frequently tired and eats little of the meals that she has delivered to her room. Lucille identifies heavily with her faith and spends much of her time in her room reading her religious texts. She believes many of the individuals in her assisted living facility identify as Christian and states due to this she feels uncomfortable discussing faith with them.

Older Adults as a Multicultural Population

Erickson described this last stage of life as "ego integrity vs. despair", characterized by a slowing down in productivity and reflection on one's life and accomplishments (Cavanaugh & Blanchard-Fields, 2010; Glover, 1998). Reflection on one's life may result in both positive and negative feelings for individuals; many of which could be productively sorted through in counseling. Statistics show that as many as one in four older adults experience a health concern such as depression (Newman, 2017). By the year 2050, the number of individuals over the age of 60 is predicted to make up 22% of the world's population (World Health Organization, 2002). Individuals 85 and older have the highest suicide rate in the United States (National Council on Aging, 2018). Access to mental health care and trust of the mental healthcare system are both hurdles to getting older adults to counseling (Newman, 2017).

Older adults (65+) face a host of specific concerns that may have an adverse effect on their mental health. Individuals that make up this population are mainly from two generational cohorts: Baby Boomers (born 1946 – 1964) and the Silent Generation (born 1925 – 1945) (U.S. Department of Health and Human Services, 2015). Many concerns deal with physical health and include both chronic and terminal illness that were not present earlier in life. Along with illness and the natural progression of age, comes loss of loved ones to include spouses, children, friends, siblings, and parents (Cavanaugh & Blanchard-Fields, 2010). Watching loved ones struggle with aging adds an added layer of difficulty to aging oneself. Included with aging and possible physical health concerns are frequent doctors' visits. These may present a problem for multiple reasons; (1) transportation, as loss of vision and ability to drive may come with aging and (2) difficulty in retrieving health records due to a deficit in understanding of technology. Many medical records are now digitized. Focus groups have shown older adults to struggle with using modern technology including tablets and computers (Vaportzis, Clausen & Gow, 2017). Life challenges including loss of vision, deficits in understanding technology, loss of ability to drive, and compromised ability to perform activities of daily living all contribute to a loss of autonomy.

Loss of loved ones may affect older adults on multiple levels. In addition to a grieving process for the loss of a loved one, an older individual may be left grieving the loss of their primary support system, while struggling to form new bonds of friendship and/or romantic relationships (Meyers, 2007; Cavanaugh & Blanchard-Fields, 2010). Experiences such as these may contribute to a sense of isolation and/or loss of support system.

A lack of financial resources contributing to deficit in autonomy and financial stressors related to long-term care can both impact older adults. Due to mounting financial pressures, many Americans have not been able to adequately save and prepare for later in life. A deficit in financial resources affects long term care options, and their ability to pay for care. Many individuals find themselves in the work force years after planned retirement. Ever changing technological advances call for constant training in the workplace, which can be challenging for older adults. In addition, there is a widening chasm in age due to individuals staying in the workforce longer. This may cause older adults to feel out of place or challenged by inter-generational differences in communication, social behaviors, and habits of work (Dison, Richard, & Rollins, 2003). Experiences such as these can contribute to a loss of autonomy and anxiety about the future in addition to a changing sense of self .

Many of the aforementioned difficulties can be exacerbated by the cultural phenomenon of ageism. When seeking out counseling, as well as in daily life, older adults may run into ageism. Ageism is prejudice and or discrimination of an individual based on their age (Meyers, 2007). The most frequent type of ageism identified by the individuals experiencing it comes in the form of jokes; becoming the butt of a joke that is directed at old age. Another prevalent form of ageism that older individuals must contend with is being ignored or not taken seriously. This becomes particularly precarious when it comes to medical and psychological care (Dittmann, 2003). The media rarely helps the situation, as older adults are frequently portrayed as comic relief or unable to do things on their own and highly functionally dependent on others. Even with public campaigns direct at positive images of aging well, the negative images seem to persist in media, politics, and culture (Angus & Reeve, 2006).

Ageism has been dubbed a "threat to aging well" (Angus & Reeve, 2006).

So how does one age well? There is a growing field of research directed at ways to foster resiliency and combat negative stereotypes of aging (Angus & Reeve, 2006; Dittmann, 2003; von Humbolt, Leal, & Pimenta, 2014). Dr. Levy at Yale University completed a longitudinal study with results indicating, of the participants, individuals with positive self-perceptions of aging lived 7.5 years longer than individuals with negative perceptions of aging (Dittmann, 2003). A study conducted by von Humbolt, Leal, and Pimenta (2014) identified spirituality, perceived health, leisure, professional status, income, household, sense of coherence, and adult children as significant predictors of adjustment toward aging. Of the significant predictors, spiritualty was the strongest participant reported predictor if adjustment toward aging (von Humbolt, Leal, & Pimenta, 2014). Spirituality has been identified as a component of life that grows stronger throughout life and provides and anchor for many during times of stress. When appropriate, focusing on spirituality can be a way to foster resiliency and a sense of independence in clients who already possess a strong sense of spirituality (Langer, 2004).

A successful counselor need incorporate both information on ageism as well as resiliency. Focusing on a strengths perspective that highlights strengths and personal control can be efficacious. A strengths perspective assumes the following views: "1) People are responsible for, and capable of making their own decisions, 2) People are often able to direct their lives more than they realize; they have some freedom to choose even if their options are restricted by environmental variables or are inherent biological or personality predispositions, and 3) People are continuously motivated to address their basic psychological and abstract self-actualization needs. (Langer, 2004, pg. 615)". Another important characteristic for the successful counselor is to acknowledge differences in perception and experience. Glover (1998) states that older adults hold opinions similar to younger adults on life satisfaction and self-efficacy. An area of suggested difference in perception and experience between older and younger adults is life change. Life change exists in many forms. As a younger adult frequently change exists in an unrestricted presentation such as moving from single to married or moving from college to career. Many of these changes provide opportunities for growth. As an older adult many changes are restricted such as moving from being married to losing a spouse or moving from free range of mobility and function to restricted range of mobility and function (Glover, 1998). It is important to view these changes and response to these changes from an appropriate and inclusive therapeutic viewpoint, as responses to these changes may vary greatly. Glover (1998) cites Warnick (1995) making the argument that many of these transitions or changes experienced later in life may be experienced as traumas and to be effective clinically they should be viewed as such.

Other factors contribute to a positive therapeutic alliance. Advocacy is an important component for facilitating positive therapeutic growth in older adults. Becoming familiar with and advocating for important laws impacting older adults such as health care reform is important for both client and counselor. Being knowledgeable and able to link clients to appropriate referrals and resources is knowledge that should be acquired when working with older adults. There are healthcare and government assistance programs available in addition to support groups and activist groups that exist (Dixon, Richard, & Rollins, 2003). Linking older adult clients with resources can be an important step in decreasing isolation and fostering a sense of community. When appropriate, including activities such as benefits planning and possible career counseling or vocational counseling for a current career or second career should also be looked at as therapeutic considerations. (Dixon, Richards, & Rollins, 2003). Activities such as *The Wheel of Wellness* that require to look at lived experiences from a holistic viewpoint are also useful in analyzing mental physical, social, and emotional resources a client may possess and how to structure these resources so that client may maximize their potential (Myers, Sweeney, & Witmer, 2000). Above all, each client must be viewed as an individual with a unique set of lived experiences that remains the expert on their life; past, present, and future.

INTRODUCTION TO THE COUNSELOR

I currently teach and practice in the Southern Region of the United States which is the same region in which I grew up and have lived my entire life. I identify as an able-bodied, middle class, middle age, white cisgender female. My professional identity involves being active in the American Counseling Association, Association for Adult Development and Aging Division and engaging in both research and advocacy efforts for the older adult population. The approach to counseling is taken in this chapter is an eclectic individual approach. An existential theoretical focus in conjunction with Cognitive Behavioral Therapy (CBT) interventions will be used for the case study. I personally identify as an existential counselor with a Feminist lens; focusing on inter and intrapersonal relationships as well as building in community involvement and advocacy for self and others into the counseling relationship. I believe the counseling relationship is a collaborative process. Growth is paramount to the counseling process; client growth as well as growth within the client/counselor collaborative process. My experience includes working with clients of all ages from five and older. I have worked with hospice, in a community mental health agency as a clinician and agency director, and as a clinician in private practice in addition to currently working as a professor in a graduate counseling program.

CASE CONCEPTUALIZATION

Existential Therapy

Drawing heavily on inspiration from existential philosophy, existential therapy has the goal of helping individuals resolve inner conflicts that arise from confrontation of existence (Sharf, 2011; Yalom, 1980; Frankl, 1946). In the 19th century, philosophers such as Kierkegaard, Jaspers, and Nietzsche wrote extensively and popularized this style of thinking. Kierkegaard focused emphasis and attention on individuals' desire to be eternal or everlasting. Confronting the human desire to be eternal is mirrored in the work of Irvin Yalom in his existential principal of "death anxiety." Yalom (2009) identified death anxiety as a universal given and described the ways death anxiety shapes a person's internal and thereby external experience. Death anxiety as defined by Yalom (2009); "anxiety about nothing is really anxiety about death (p. 22)." Death anxiety is a defining force of human nature as it is postulated that one uses this anxiety to propel forward and motivate choices; either challenging death directly by risk taking or hiding from death by being cautious (Yalom, 2009). Yalom (2009) discusses the "best arguments" to alleviate death anxiety as those outlines by Epicurus, "1) the mortality of the soul, 2) the ultimate nothingness of death, 3) the argument of symmetry (79)." In working with clients confronting death anxiety, Yalom introduces these concepts early as he states many individuals find these ideas helpful in reminding them of the universal nature of their own personal concerns (Yalom, 2009).

Existential therapy has a focus on understanding self in the present while reviewing the importance of the past and postulating the future. The goal of existential therapy is to "set clients free" (Schneider & Krug, 2010, p. 9). Freedom may take many forms but typically shows itself to be the ability to exercise choice within natural and self-imposed limits, which are set forth by society, such as language and cultural norms. Frankl (1946) discussed the last great freedom of all as the freedom of internal choice. Even if all external choices are made for an individual, the individual may still obtain internal control of thoughts. Choice, control, and responsibility play out throughout existential thought. Inherent in taking control of something (action, thought, etc.) is the idea of making a choice; either conscious or subconscious. Freedom in an existential context comes with choice and limitations. All freedoms have limitations because all choice has limitations. Making a choice for one option means one has given up a second option. Some limitations are natural and do not involve choice. Natural limits are considered things that place an individual at a deficit of control; for example, death, and aging (Schneider & Krug, 2010).

Much like the topic of existential philosophy, individuals writing on the topic of Existential therapy have varying views on the topic of individual existence, choice, responsibility, and freedom. Yalom (1980) theorized that one confronts the quality and make-up of life through confrontation of the four givens of human existence: freedom, death, meaningless, and isolation. Internal conflicts and subsequent emotions arise from confronting these givens. For example, confrontation of death arouses urgency. Life and therefore its quality, is comprised of one's relationship to these four givens and the extent to which an individual will engage in confrontation, exploration, and integration of these givens (Schneider & Krug, 2010).

In *Mans Search for Meaning*, Viktor Frankl begins his work with a brief autobiography relevant to personal meaning and then discusses his theory which he has termed Logotherapy. Frankl (1946) defines logotherapy as the following, "Logotherapy focuses on the future, that is to say, on the meanings to be fulfilled by the patient in his future. (Logotherapy, indeed, is meaning-centered psychotherapy) (p.98)." Will to meaning, a personal desire to find meaning, is stated as a primary motivation in life. This will to meaning can be set off course by existential frustrations; "1) existence itself, i.e. the specifically human mode of being; (2) the meaning of existence; and 3) the striving to find a concrete meaning in personal existence… (Frankl, 1946, p. 101)." Distress evolves out of existential frustration. Resolving this frustration and distress is a result of finding ones will to meaning. Logotherapy suggests three paths to find one's will to meaning. These paths involve relationships with self and other, perceived suffering, and being productive or creating.

While there are numerous approaches to existential therapy; the basic tenants remain the same: freedom, choice, responsibility, relationship to self and others and how one makes meaning of these to create and maintain sense of self. The task set out before an existential counselor is to view clients as holistic beings regarding their past and present states of being as well as conscious thoughts and unconscious driving forces (Schneider & Krug, 2010). Existential therapy is a theoretical orientation not often operationalized by intervention. While, few in number, there are existential interventions to aid clients in their process.

Existential therapy provides a broad and flexible framework from which to conceptualize a client. This flexibility can be especially helpful when working with older adults reviewing present emotional distress from a lifespan perspective (all lived experience, events, and emotions, that have culminated in their present world view and view of self). A focus on relationship with self and other and the ability to change and define these relationships from a perspective of responsibility, choice, and freedom may give a client the tools to see themselves differently at different stages of life and incorporate all of those versions of self into a definition of who they currently are. For example, if a client has defined self as a caregiver their entire adult life because they were caring for children and then they find themselves in a position where they are no longer caring for their children, this change in life circumstance could drastically effect how a client makes meaning of life and self. Clients are empowered through the aspects of choice and responsibility and making meaning of life and self. The flexibility of existential therapy also lends itself to incorporating use of other theoretical modalities and interventions at particular stages of client development to aid growth process.

Other Applicable Theories or Models

In addition to the few existential interventions that exist, interventions from other theoretical orientations fit nicely with the concepts outlined by existential therapy. As previously mentioned, numerous other therapeutic interventions can be used alongside existential therapy to aid in facilitating client growth toward sense of self and discovering client meaning and purpose in life. Art Therapy can be particularly useful when a client is at a loss for words and/or feels stuck at a particular point of the therapeutic process. Through art therapy, a client can project feelings, images, thoughts outward onto whatever they are choosing to create. Art projects can be given specific directives or clients free choice of expression. Art therapy can be particularly useful in processing complex emotional concerns such as grief and loss. Often clients may state they struggle with creativity, however many projects such as collage and abstract painting are functional for individuals at all artistic levels. The therapist can also facilitate a discussion with the client concerning creativity more as the outward expression of emotional self rather than the need to produce the end result of an artistic masterpiece. Using art therapy can also serve to break up the process of traditional talk therapy and through engaging the client in a new way provide an avenue to explore previously untapped emotional territory (Malchiodi, 2007).

Narrative therapy and life review can be of particular use when addressing older adult clients. Narrative therapy is a therapeutic approach in which an individual looks back and writes the story of their life. When working with individual clients from an existential theoretical perspective this can aid in defining sense of self as well as looking forward to future meaning. Frequently self-narratives of older adults contain themes of loss whether it be person, place, thing, ability or all of the above. Narrative therapy provides a way to deconstruct the current negative narrative and reconstruct a new narrative with the help of a therapist or clinician (Kropf & Tandy, 2008). Narrative therapy focuses on the client as the expert and remains non-blaming, allowing for the distinction to be made between an individual and a problem with a focus on control. Narrative Therapy techniques include putting together a narrative to analyze meaning and deconstructing a narrative ("19 Narrative therapy", 2018). A study conducted analyzing narrative therapy (8 sessions) in 47 adult individuals with depressive symptoms showed clinically significant improvement in 53% of participants when compared to benchmark research outcomes (Vronmans, Schweitzer & Lowe, 2010). In an existential framework, the use of narrative therapy gives an older adult client a tool to look back at life in its entirety and/or specific sections of lived experience and take control of the narrative while working towards making meaning. Both narrative and art therapy also have an aspect of "creating and doing", which as stated above is one of Frankl's (1946) components of making meaning. The use of techniques and interventions that focus on client creating can be empowering for client while working on the existential goal of making meaning.

Cognitive Behavioral Therapy (CBT) interventions can also be useful when working with older adults from an existential perspective. Intrusive thought patterns and habitual negative behaviors and coping patterns which are hinderances to the client growth process can be addressed using CBT interventions in conjunction with existential therapy. CBT focuses on the triad of feelings, thoughts, and actions and therefore CBT based interventions are targeted at these specific points. Using an intrusive thought record may help an individual target longstanding negatives belief and restructure them to aid in development toward a more positive holistic outlook on self and meaning. Analyzing the frequency of these thoughts and emotional effect they have on a daily basis can provide motivation toward change. Focusing on what are called cognitive distortions, faulty ways of thinking, can heighten client's awareness of their control over these patterns. Some of these patterns include judgement, overgeneralization, all or nothing thinking, blaming and a fallacy of fairness (Craske, 2017). Mindfulness based interventions such as deep breathing exercises that help clients focus on the present can be incorporated as another useful strategy. Therapists are beginning to use these interventions as mindful based CBT. (Hindman, n.d.). Interventions such as these aid the existential therapeutic outcome by giving the client a method to focus on the present concept of self and meaning without becoming overwhelmed by emotions, thoughts, and feelings from past or projected onto future. With a wealth of lived experience and possible uncertainty about the future due to concerns about changing health, finances, and/or family structure; CBT and mindfulness-based interventions provided a tool for older adult clients gain a level of control over negative thoughts and emotions while maintaining a current sense of self.

Grief Counseling techniques such as the Kubler Ross (1973) stages of grief (denial, anger, barging, depression, acceptance) may also be a useful framework to incorporate into therapeutic practice with older adults. This model, which has been updated since its initial conception, allows for individuals to view grief on a continuum with a cyclical nature which may help conceptualize layered grief over a lifetime. Individuals may struggle at different times with how grief that they previously believed to be resolved is currently affecting them, leading to emotions of guilt and frustration. Grief reactions may come in many forms such as chronic grief reactions, delayed grief reactions, exaggerated grief reactions, and masked grief reaction which may, depending on the individual, happen simultaneously or independent of each other. Prolonged grief happens typically with the client's awareness and realization that there has been no adequate resolution to their grief due to an incompletion of the tasks of grieving. Masked or somatic grief typically involved clients being unaware of unresolved grief likely because at the time of a loss their grief was repressed or absent. Exaggerated grief is difficult to define and may manifest in numerous ways depending on the individual (Worden, 2018).

The goal of grief therapy is to aid the client in mourning and resolve grief in an appropriate manner for the client based on their grief expression (Worden, 2018). With the variety of ways that grief may manifest itself throughout a lifetime, it is likely that most individuals will experience at least one event in the course of their lifetime from which they experience grief. Many individuals will experience numerous grief events by the time they reach the older adult stage of life. For an existential therapist it may be important to process grief experienced by an individual, lasting effects of that grief, and how the individual's grief process has affected their meaning making process and view of past and current self-identities. Techniques previously mentioned, such as narrative therapy and art therapy may be beneficial in this process as these techniques provide clients with new and creative ways to express emotions. CBT and mindfulness-based interventions may also be implemented in conjunction with grief therapy to aid in decreasing frequency of intrusive thoughts and memories related to past grief events.

Multicultural Social Justice Counseling Competencies (MSJCC)

In the following section the MSJCC's will be outlined as they were applied to the case of Lucille. Factors relevant to this case will be highlighted and reviewed. It is important to acknowledge that below analysis was relevant to this specific counselor and client and will change significantly based on the individuals involved.

Counselor Self -Awareness

As a counselor, I believe self-awareness is a cornerstone of the foundation of our professional make up. It is something that I incorporate frequently in my courses as well as with supervisees. When working with Lucille, I had to first acknowledge and attitudes and beliefs that I held based on privilege and marginalization. I identify as an able-bodied, middle class, middle age, white cisgender female. I acknowledge that my multicultural identity carries within it some inherent privilege; specifically, white privilege and able-bodied privilege, to name a few. I also had to acknowledge any assumptions, attitudes, values, beliefs, and biases. Acknowledging these from an open and honest standpoint can be difficult for counselors. Even though I work with older adults frequently, I acknowledge biases and values prior to working with each individual client, as I believe one should. I had a very close relationship with my grandmother when she was alive. This past relationship has to be acknowledged for me, because if not acknowledged, it can affect my bias and beliefs about a client as well as possibly set up a situation for countertransference with a client. When working with older adult female identifying clients, this is a component of self-awareness I constantly check in with myself on, in order to ensure that I am treating each client as the individual that they are.

Knowledge, skills, and action are also components of this standard. I made sure I researched and addressed any assumptions, biases, attitudes, and beliefs as well as regularly checked in with myself for any noted instances of the aforementioned. I focused attention on how my privilege comes with certain advantages and how I am affected by those advantages. In this instance, because Lucille identified as a Jewish American and moved to America from Europe during a tumultuous time in world history; I researched different facets of her multicultural identity. While acknowledging that she would always be the expert in the room on her lived experiences, I chose to review information on religion, time period, historical context, and immigration. I also looked into resources on gradual loss of eyesight and changes in physical ability. Lucille would frequently reference her religion as well as events that happened around the time she first took up residence in the United States. I explained to Lucille the research I had done and would make sure to ask questions based on research when it intersected with Lucille's life story or life meaning. Lucille stated she greatly appreciated this, and that this made her feel more comfortable and able to be genuine in sessions even though there was a large age difference between the two of us.

Client World View

Lucille identified as a cisgender Jewish American female. She stated she no longer identified as able bodied due to loss of visual abilities and deficits in functioning related to activities of daily living. She also identified as a mother and a wife (even though her husband was deceased). Lucille acknowledged that inherent in her multicultural identity was marginalization related to age, non-able bodied, and religion. She acknowledged how she was affected by these components. She also acknowledged how she wanted to change her perceptions of and reactions to these personal identifiers. For example, she would get very angry when people would speak loudly to her. She stated her hearing was perfectly fine and that it made her very angry that people would assume that either because she was an older adult and/or because she was losing her sight, that she must also be losing her hearing. Lucille was very aware of stereotypes that she had felt were placed on her at various points in her life and acknowledged that she felt she had internalized some of them while others very much angered her. She was very open to acquiring new knowledge and increasing her skill set. When working with Lucille I focused on the following skill acquisition: "acquire culturally responsive assessment skills to identify limitations and strengths when working with privilege and marginalized clients; acquire culturally responsive conceptualization skills…; acquire culturally responsive cross-cultural communication skills…(Ratts, Singh, Nasser-McMillan, Butler, & McCullough, 2016, p. 8)." All skills listed in this section of MSJCC's is equally important, however, after an assessment of this individual client and my personal awareness, these are the ones that stuck out as most relevant. I looked into finding any community resources that would be of assistance as well. There was a very supportive Jewish community in the area in which Lucille lives with numerous outreach and support programs. There was also a nonprofit agency that trained individuals to be companions for individuals losing their eyesight. This nonprofit provided a wealth of information and resources that I could pull from.

Counseling Relationship

As mentioned above, Lucille and I expressed differing multicultural identities with various levels of privilege and marginalization. During the first counseling session Lucille actually started the discussion by making a joke about our age difference when she first sat down in session. I used this humor to facilitate an open honest discussion about similarities and differences. We both addressed our multicultural identities and their differences. We focused attention on areas where we differed in regard to privilege. We agreed to acknowledge and discuss those differences if they expressed themselves in the counseling relationship. Lucille stated she took great pride in her ethnic and religious identity and stated she would like to share her knowledge with me related to those parts of her identity. She stated that the discussions that we had surrounding our individual multicultural identities were very empowering for her because she felt like she was heard. Lucille stated that she believed in the end, she was more open to counseling due to this.

Counseling and Advocacy Interventions

Interpersonal advocacy interventions were addressed by using empowerment-based theories to address internalized privilege and oppression. This will be address subsequently under the Progress section of this chapter. I n the beginning sessions, as Lucille worked through her personal narrative, we discussed to follow MSJCC's:

the degree to which historical events, current issues, and power, privilege, and oppression contribute to the presenting problems expressed by privileged and marginalized clients; assist privileged and marginalized clients with developing self-advocacy skills to promote multiculturalism and social justice …(Ratts, Singh, Nasser-McMillan, Butler, & McCullough, 2016, p. 11).

Interpersonal and Institutional advocacy interventions intersected as many of her interpersonal connections were within the residential community in which she lived. Advocacy was employed as Lucille began to re-develop her support network. Lucille engaged in advocacy through family sessions and residential community involvement. Family sessions were incorporated so that Lucille could share components of herself and world view with family, and they could work together to integrate this information into their family culture. Lucille became more active in her assisted living facility and by connecting more with others, realized that there were other Jewish individuals in residence. She started a weekly meeting in which she reviewed her religious texts. The group was successful and acquired many individuals that did not identify as Jewish as well. At times a few staff members would also join in. Lucille was also connected with the non-profit that worked with visually impaired individuals. This added a variety of resources for her in addition to a companion who came multiple times a week for visits and to help with her vision transition.

TREATMENT

Goals

Lucille's goals aligned with concerns relevant to an older adult population as addressed previously in the review of literature. Lucille's main expressed goal was to increase her sense of autonomy in her present situation. She expressed that her lack of autonomy was in direct conflict with her sense of self, as such she was struggling with, not only who she currently was, but her views of who she had been. Increasing sense of autonomy spoke to Lucille finding her "will to meaning". As addressed by Frankl (1946), the search for meaning in one's life is constantly evolving and changing. While Lucille's "will to meaning" had once been to leave something positive behind for her children and grandchildren; the deaths of two of her children and her husband changed that. She found herself expressing a sense of meaninglessness. In conjunction with increasing autonomy, creating a sense of meaning in the present was important to Lucille. Another of Lucille's goals was to process the grief of the deaths of loved ones, both family and friends. She stated she had suffered numerous losses of her lifetime and felt she was at various degrees of acceptance and healing with them all. Losing her children was the hardest and according to her the one she struggled the most with as a sense of unfairness. These were the primary goals that Lucille wanted to focus on throughout the course of her counseling sessions.

As a therapist, elements of concern for Lucille were an increasingly depressed mood (frequency, severity, duration) with client expressed hopelessness, client lack of social interaction and increasing isolation, decrease in appetite, and lack of interest in activities she previously enjoyed. The therapeutic goal was to increase autonomy as well as use CBT and mindfulness to combat negative intrusive thoughts and stay in the present moment so that client could focus on a new definition of self and meaning. Processing grief was interwoven throughout the therapeutic goals as grief was an integral part of the clients lived experience and as such presented itself at numerous stages in the counseling process. Therapist and client reviewed goals and agreed on goals as well as check-ins at regular intervals to determine progress toward goals.

Progress/Outcome

Dezelic and Ghanoum (2015) outlined a brief therapy protocol for individual and group existential therapy to aid in fostering self-awareness, self-reflection, self-connection, self-acceptance, self-transcendence, transforming existential crisis and despair, and discovering meaning and purpose in life among other client specific goals. Existential therapy in this workbook is seen as a growth process and focuses on the inner and outer worlds – being self in relation to self and being self in relation to other (anything/anyone outside of self). The outline for the 8 session protocol is as follows: 1) introduction to concepts; 2) exploring meaning; 3) exploring human essence through mind, body, and spirit; 4) inner resources and strengths; 5) existential aspects; 6) suffering and meaning; 7) personal growth and transformation; 8) living meaningfully (Dezelic & Ghanoum, 2015). This outline, although not strictly adhering to an 8-week format, was used as the framework for Lucille's sessions. Within this framework, existential methodologies used were analysis, Socratic questioning, and paradoxical intention. Throughout the process interventions from other theoretical orientations were blended in on a need-based basis. As this was curriculum used with Lucille; progress towards goals and therapeutic relationship will be discussed under the 8-part outline provided.

In the first session introductions and concepts were reviewed. We both reviewed our multicultural identities and discussed goals for counseling. I briefly discussed existential counseling and Lucille introduced me to who she was as she saw things. We also used the *Wheel of Wellness* (Myers, Sweeney, & Witmer, 2000) technique to complete an assessment of Lucille's current resources and the way she used her time. As mentioned previously, this therapeutic approach analyzes individuals across the following life dimensions: social, emotional, intellectual, physical, occupational and spiritual. This is depicted as a circle divided in to 6 pieces. Each dimension is represented by a piece of the circle. The client fills out the aspects of their life that align with each dimension thus creating a visual representation of how balanced or unbalanced these dimensions are. Lucille listed nothing in her social dimension, a significant amount of health concerns in her physical dimension, loss of identified occupation (mother) in her occupational dimension, and her religious identity in her religious dimension. We revisited this activity toward the conclusion of Lucille's sessions. At this point it had changed drastically. In her social section she listed family visits and phone calls, events at her residential facility, a religious group she started and the occasional shared meal. In her physical section she added to her list of physical concerns a list of things related to health and physical ability she was grateful for. For example, hearing. Lucille was grateful for hearing as she now would listen to her books on tape as well as podcasts. Her previous list only listed loss of sight which had inhibited her greatly cherished ability to read. She also added the ability to listen to books and podcasts to her intellectual dimensions list. Lucille recorded for herself a reading of her final wheel exercise so that she could listen to it and be reminded of the balance she had created in her life.

Exploring meaning as a second phase of counseling lasted 5 sessions for us. During this time Lucille and I engaged in narrative therapy and began to look at how she was defining herself at the time (not capable, not a mother, a burden, sick) versus how she previously defined herself (proud, confident, mother, wife, strong). We discussed redefining her current world view. This caused significant distress for Lucille and we would stop to take break and engage in mindful breathing exercises to refocus the sessions. At this juncture we also employed the use of a CBT thought record to engage in thought discrimination. Lucille dictated her personal narrative into a tape recorder as opposed to writing it, which was her idea. She later kept the tape with the idea of giving it to one of her grandchildren.

Exploring human essence according to Dezelic and Ghanoum (2015) involves discussing the intersections of body mind and spirit. Lucille, who identified strongly with her faith, began to see her faith as a way to combat her negative feelings about her deteriorating eyesight. It is at this juncture that she decided she would explore making connections with individuals at her residence and used faith as a way to start conversations when she had previously been reticent to bring up her faith. She stated this felt very empowering and she began to feel increasingly less isolated.

Focusing on inner resources/strengths was also very strongly tied to religion for Lucille. At this juncture we checked in on progress. We also pulled out Lucille's life narrative for a second time and assessed it from a strengths-based perspective. She was able to identify numerous characteristics such as her intelligence and sense of humor that she identifies as strengths that she believed she possessed. In discussions of her will to meaning, the themes of her grandchildren and her religion came up frequently.

Existential aspects explore the "tragic triad" of guilt, death, and unavoidable suffering ; as well as the "neurotic triad" of depression, aggression, and addiction (Dezelic & Ghanoum, 2015). Lucille stated resonated deeply with the tragic triad. We spent time focusing on her emotions and her anger at the unfairness of life at times; mainly the losses of her husband and child. We built on the work we had already done with her life narrative and defined concept of self from a strength's perspective.

Suffering and meaning are important components of existential therapy as well as the sixth stage of the Dezelic and Ghanoum (2015) therapy protocol. Clients are asked to review their success and meaning in life based on Frankl's statement, "suffering ceases to be suffering at the moment it finds meaning (Dezelic & Ghanoum, 2015; p. 75)." This exploration comprised 5 or 6 sessions of my time with Lucille. We went through the losses she had suffered throughout her life with a focus on the previously mentioned strengths perspective and resiliency. We reviewed loss of loved ones through a grief counseling lens. Lucille was able to discuss her losses due to changes in living situation (moving to the assisted living facility, etc.) from a strength's perspective. She was also able to make progress mourning the death of her husband and change in her identity as a wife to a widow which she stated was a huge "mountain to overcome." She continued to struggle with her perceived loss of identity as a mother which she related to the loss of a child and being unable to currently care for her living child who was ill. She stated the latter more so than the former influenced this perception.

The personal growth and transformation component of Dezelic and Ghanoum (2015) therapy protocol was blended with the living meaningfully component of the therapy protocol. These two components comprise sessions seven and eight in the brief therapy protocol. Living meaningfully as outlined by Dezelic and Ghanoum (2015), involves looking at the how, what, where, when, and who. Questions such as ; "how have I grown from my experience, where do I see new possibilities..., who is making a difference in my life and am I making a difference in someone else's life?," are relevant questions for review (Dezelic & Ghanoum, 2015, p. 95). In the sessions leading to termination, as well as our last session, we reviewed Lucille's progress. Lucille was able to take responsibility in her decision-making process and thus take control of her life. Instead of assuming she was a burden if she reached out to family, she began to regularly call family members and request they come visit. She was able to accept, with minimal negative emotion, if they were unable to talk or visit at the time and they would frequently call her back. She stated she also felt more emotionally closer with her immediate family following a family session in which she was able to share pieces of her past experiences with family members that were integral parts of her multicultural identity. More frequent members from family members meant that they were there to help her communicate with friends via letter and text. Lucille began to look forward to this more frequent communication and bean to engage more frequently in activities at the assisted living facility in order to have new information to share with family when they visited. As previously mentioned, Lucille also started a group at the assisted living facility to discuss and study Jewish religion. She also reached out to the local agency with resources for individuals with impaired vision. She received a lot of information as well as a companion that made weekly visits to her and helped her acclimate to her surroundings and declining vision by doing things like adding safety pins to all her black clothes. This allowed Lucille to feel more independent and, in her words, "less self-conscious" because she was able to dress herself again without help and know that her clothing matched. Lucille stated that she felt as though she was recreating her sense of autonomy.

CONCLUSION/ IMPLICATIONS FOR COUNSELORS

Older adults face marginalization and ageism in society. In addition, older adults face new life challenges such as declining health, loss of loved ones, loss of autonomy, loss of physical function and cognitive abilities, loss of primary support systems, financial concerns and anxiety about the future. Counselors need to be aware of these factors as well as their own multicultural identities and competencies when working with older adults. A focus on older adults' multicultural identity and areas of privilege and marginalization is an important lens through which to view the counseling relationship. Counseling from an existential theoretical perspective with a focus on resiliency may be a useful modality when working with older adults. In addition, blending in other modalities such as narrative may help navigate an individual's wealth of lived experience and provide a new perspective from which to view things.

REFERENCES

Angus, J, & Reeve, P. (2006). Ageism: A threat to "aging well" in the 21st century. *Journal of Applied Gerontology, 25*(2), 137–152. doi: 1doi:0.1177/0733464805285745

Cavanaugh, J., & Blanchard-Fields, F. (2010). *Adult development and aging* (6th ed.). Belmont, CA: Wadsworth Publishing.

Craske, M. (2017). *Theories of psychotherapy series: Cognitive behavioral therapy* (Revised edition). American Psychological Association. doi:10.1037/0000027-000

Dezelic, M., & Ghanoum, G. (2015). *Meaning-Centered Therapy Manual: Logotherapy & Existential Analysis Brief Therapy Protocol for Group and Individual Sessions: 8 Session Format*. New York: Palace Printing and Design.

Dittmann, M. (2003). *Fighting ageism: Geropsychologists are striving to stop negative stereotypes and meet the growing mental health needs of older adults*. PsycEXTRA Dataset. doi:10.1037/e30112203-027

Dixon, C. G., Richard, M., & Rollins, C. W. (2003). Contemporary issues facing aging americans: Implications for rehabilitation and mental health counseling. *Journal of Rehabilitation*, *69*(2), 5–12.

Frankl, V. (1946). *Man's Search for Meaning: An Introduction to Logotherapy*. New York: Simon & Schuster.

Glover, R. J. (1998). Perspectives on aging: Issues affecting the latter part of the life cycle. *Educational Gerontology*, *24*(4), 325–331. doi:10.1080/0360127980240403

Hindman, R. (n.d.). Integrating mindfulness into CBT. *The Beck Institute*. Retrieved from https://beckinstitute.org/integrating-mindfulness-cbt/

Kropf, N., & Tandy, C. (1998). Narrative therapy with older clients: The use of a "meaning-making" approach. *Clinical Gerontologist*, *18*(4), 3–16. doi:10.1300/J018v18n04_02

Langer, N. (2004). Resiliency and spirituality: Foundations of strength perspective counseling with the elderly. *Educational Gerontology*, *30*(7), 611–617. doi:10.1080/03601270490467038

Malchiodi, C. (2007). *The art therapy sourcebook*. New York: McGraw – Hill.

Myers, J. (2007). Combating ageism: Advocacy for older persons. In C. C. Lee (Ed.), *Counseling for social justice* (2nd ed.; pp. 51–73). Alexandria, VA: American Counseling Association.

Myers, J. E., Sweeney, T. J., & Witmer, J. M. (2000). The wheel of wellness counseling for wellness: A holistic model for treatment planning. *Journal of Counseling and Development*, *78*(3), 251–266. doi:10.1002/j.1556-6676.2000.tb01906.x

19 . Narrative Therapy Techniques. (2018, August 10). Retrieved from https://positivepsychologyprogram.com/narrative-therapy/

National Council on Aging. (2018). *Healthy aging facts*. Retrieved from www.ncoa.org

Newman, K. (2017). *A look into older adults state of mind*. Retrieved from www.usnews.com

Ratts, M., Singh, A. A., Nasser-McMillan, S., Butler, S. K., & McCullough, J. R. (2016). Multicultural and social justice counseling competencies: Guidelines for the counseling profession. *Journal of Multicultural Counseling and Development*, *44*(1), 28–48. doi:10.1002/jmcd.12035

Ross, E. K. (1973). *On death and dying*. London: Tavistock Pubs. doi:10.4324/9780203010495

Schneider, K. J., & Krug, O. T. (2010). *Theories of psychotherapy series: Existential humanistic therapy*. Washington, DC: American Psychological Association.

U.S. Department of Health and Human Services. (2015). *Administration on aging: Aging statistics*. Retrieved from: http://www.aoa.acl.gov/Aging_Statistics/index.aspx

von Humbolt, S. V., & Leal, I. (2017). Older adults adjustment to aging: The impact of sense of coherence, subjective well-being and socio-demographic, lifestyle and health related factors. *European Psychiatry, 41*. doi:10.1016/j.eurpsy.2017.01.1134

von Humbolt, S. V., & Leal, I. (2017). Older adults adjustment to aging: The impact of sense of coherence, subjective well-being and socio-demographic, lifestyle and health related factors. *European Psychiatry, 41*. doi:10.1016/j.eurpsy.2017.01.1134

Vromans, L., Schweitzer, R. D., & Lowe, R. (2010). Narrative therapy for adults with major depressive disorder: Improved symptom and interpersonal outcomes. *Psychotherapy Research*, *21*(1), 4–15. doi:10.1080/10503301003591792 PMID:20306354

Vromans, L., Schweitzer, R. D., & Lowe, R. (2010). Narrative therapy for adults with major depressive disorder: Improved symptom and interpersonal outcomes. *Psychotherapy Research*, *21*(1), 4–15. doi:10.1080/10503301003591792 PMID:20306354

Warnick, J. (1995). *Listening with different ears: Counseling people over 60*. Ft. Bragg, CA: QED Press.

Worden, J. (2018). *Grief counseling and grief: A handbook for the mental health practitioner*. New York, NY: Springer Publishing Company, LLC. doi:10.1891/9780826134752

World Health Organization. (2002). *Active Aging: A policy framework*. Geneva, Switzerland: Author.

Yalom, I. (1980). *Existential psychotherapy*. New York, NY: Basic Books.

Yalom, I. (2009). *Staring at the sun: Overcoming the terror of death*. San Francisco, CA: Jossey Bass.

Compilation of References

19. Narrative Therapy Techniques. (2018, August 10). Retrieved from https://positivepsychologyprogram.com/narrative-therapy/

Abbott, D. A., Springer, P. R., & Hollist, C. S. (2012). Therapy with immigrant Muslim couples: Applying culturally appropriate interventions and strategies. *Journal of Couple & Relationship Therapy*, *11*(3), 254–266. doi:10.1080/15332691.2012.692946

Abdo, G. (2005). Islam in America: Separate but unequal. *The Washington Quarterly*, *28*(4), 7–17. doi:10.1162/0163660054798717

Abdullah, T., & Brown, T. L. (2011). Mental illness stigma and ethnocultural beliefs, values, and norms: An integrative review. *Clinical Psychology Review*, *31*(6), 934–948. doi:10.1016/j.cpr.2011.05.003 PMID:21683671

Abdul-Rauf, M. (2007). *The Islamic view of women and the family*. Alexandria, VA: Al-Saadawi Publications.

Abraído-Lanza, A. F., Echeverría, S. E., & Flórez, K. R. (2016). Latino immigrants, acculturation, and health: Promising new directions in research. *Annual Review of Public Health*, *37*(1), 219–236. doi:10.1146/annurev-publhealth-032315-021545 PMID:26735431

Abu-Hilal, M., Al-Bahrani, M., & Al-Zedjali, M. (2017). Can religiosity boost meaning in life and suppress stress for Muslim college students? *Mental Health, Religion & Culture*, *20*(3), 203–216. doi:10.1080/13674676.2017.1324835

Achieve, Inc. (n.d.). *College and career readiness*. Washington, DC: Author. Retrieved from https://www.achieve. org/college-and-career-readiness

Adams, W. W. (2005). Ecopsychology and phenomenology: Existential analysis. *Journal of the Society for Existential Analysis*, *16*(2), 269–283.

Adashi, E. Y. (2015). A same-sex infertility health insurance mandate in Maryland? *Journal of the American Medical Association*, *314*(1), 15. doi:10.1001/jama.2015.6562 PMID:26151251

Addis, M. E., & Mahalik, J. R. (2003). Men, masculinity, and the context of help seeking. *The American Psychologist*, *58*(1), 5–14. doi:10.1037/0003-066X.58.1.5 PMID:12674814

Adler, A. (1964). *The individual psychology of Alfred Adler: A systematic presentation in selections from his writings* (H. L. Ansbacher & R. R. Ansbacher, Eds.). New York, NY: Harper Perennial. (Original work published 1956)

Ahles, A., & Jenkins, J. (n. d.). *When the going gets tough the tough gets mindful: A toolkit based on the principle of acceptance and commitment therapy*. Retrieved from https://contextualscience.org/6_session_act_toolkit

Ajibade, A., Hook, J. N., Utsey, S. O., Davis, D. E., & Van Tongeren, D. R. (2016). Racial/ethnic identity, religious commitment, and well-being in African Americans. *The Journal of Black Psychology*, *42*(3), 244–258. doi:10.1177/0095798414568115

Ali, O. M., Milstein, G., & Marzuk, P. M. (2005). The Imam's role in meeting the counseling needs of Muslim communities in the United States. *Psychiatric Services (Washington, D.C.)*, *56*(2), 202–205. doi:10.1176/appi.ps.56.2.202 PMID:15703349

Alkov, R. A., & Gaynor, J. A. (1991). Attitude changes in Navy/Marine flight instructors following an aircrew coordination training course. *The International Journal of Aviation Psychology*, *1*(3), 245–253. doi:10.120715327108ijap0103_5

Al-Krenawi, A., & Graham, J. (2005). Marital therapy for Arab Muslim Palestinian couples in the context of reacculturation. *The Family Journal (Alexandria, Va.)*, *13*(3), 300–310. doi:10.1177/1066480704273640

Allen, G. E., & Hill, C. (2014). Exploring perceived attitudes of counseling between LDS religious leaders and mental health therapists. *Journal of the Association of Mormon Counselors and Psychotherapists: Issues in Religion and Psychotherapy*, *36*, 71–82.

Al-Waqfi, M., & Forstenlechner, I. (2010). Stereotyping of citizens in an expatriate-dominated labour market: Implications for workforce localisation policy. *Employee Relations*, *32*(4), 364–381. doi:10.1108/01425451011051596

Amari, S., Nassar-McMillan, S., Amen-Bryan, S., & Misenhimer, M. M. (2013). Counseling Arab Americans. In C. C. Lee (Ed.), *Multicultural issues in counseling: New approaches to diversity* (4th ed.; pp. 87–104). Alexandria, VA: American Counseling Association.

American Counseling Association. (2014). *ACA code of ethics*. Alexandria, VA: Author.

American Counseling Association. (2014). *ACA Code of Ethics*. Alexandria, VA: Author.

American Counseling Association. (2014). *ACA code of ethics*. Retrieved from https://www.counseling.org/resources/aca-code-of-ethics.pdf

American Counseling Association. (2014). *American Counseling association code of ethics*. Retrieved from https://www.counseling.org/docs/default-source/default-document- library/2014-code-of-ethicsfinaladdressc97d33f16116603abcacff0000bee5e7.pdf?sfvrsn=5d6b532c_0

American Psychiatric Association. (2013). *Diagnostic and statistical manual of mental disorders* (5th ed.). Arlington, VA: American Psychiatric Publishing.

American Psychiatric Association. (2013). *Diagnostic and statistical manual of mental disorders (DSM-5®)*. Washington, DC: American Psychiatric Pub.

Amer, M. M., & Awad, G. H. (2016). *Handbook of Arab American psychology* (1st ed.). New York, NY: Routledge.

Anderson, S. V. (2008). Rhetorical footing in Latter-Day Saints Counseling. *Social Thought, 27*(4), 323–339. https://doi-org.libpublic3.library.isu.edu/10.1080/15426430802345309

Andrade, M. S. (2006). International students in English-speaking universities: Adjustment factors. *Journal of Research in International Education, 5*(2), 131–154. doi:10.1177/1475240906065589

Angus, J, & Reeve, P. (2006). Ageism: A threat to "aging well" in the 21st century. *Journal of Applied Gerontology, 25*(2), 137 – 152. doi: 1 doi:0.1177/0733464805285745

Ansbacher, H., & Ansbacher, R. (Eds.). (1956). *The individual psychology of Alfred Adler: A system presentation in selection from his writings*. San Francisco, CA: Harper & Row.

Aprahamian, M., Kaplan, D. M., Windham, A. M., Sutter, J. A., & Visser, J. (2011). The relationship between acculturation and mental health of Arab Americans. *Journal of Mental Health Counseling, 33*(1), 80–92. doi:10.17744/mehc.33.1.0356488305383630

Armet, S. (2009). Religious socialization and identity formation of adolescents in high tension religions. *Review of Religious Research, 50*(3), 277–297. Retrieved from https://www.jstor.org/stable/25593742

Aronson, E. (2012). *The social animal* (11th ed.). New York, NY: Worth Publishers.

Arthur, N. (2004). *Counseling international students: Clients from around the world*. New York, NY: Kluwer Academic/Plenum. doi:10.1007/978-1-4419-8919-2

Asazawa, K. (2015). Effects of a partnership support program for couples undergoing Fertility treatment. *Japan Journal of Nursing Science, 12*(4), 354–366. doi:10.1111/jjns.12074 PMID:25780939

Bakali, N. (2016). *Islamophobia: Understanding Anti-Muslim Racism Through the Lived Experiences of Muslim Youth*. Rotterdam: Sense Publishers. Retrieved from http://ezproxy.augusta.edu/login?url=http://search.ebscohost.com/login.aspx?direct=true&db=nlebk&AN=1429086&site=eds-live&scope=site

Baker, S. B., & Parikh Foxx, S. (2012). *Career and College Readiness Self-efficacy Inventory*. Raleigh, NC: Authors.

Balestreri, K., Sambolt, M., Duhon, C., Smerdon, B., & Harris, J. (2014). *The college and career readiness and success organizer*. Retrieved from, https://ccrscenter.org/sites/default/files/College%20and%20Career%20Readiness%20and%20Success%20Organizer%20Brief_FINAL.pdf

Banks, B. M. (2018). University mental health outreach targeting students of color. *Journal of College Student Psychotherapy*, 1–9. doi:10.1080/87568225.2018.1539632

Barksdale, C. L., & Molock, S. D. (2009). Perceived norms and mental health help seeking among African American college students. *The Journal of Behavioral Health Services & Research*, *36*(3), 285–299. doi:10.100711414-008-9138-y PMID:18668368

Barlow, S., & Bergin, A. (1998). Religion and mental health from the Mormon perspective. In H. Koenig (Ed.), *Handbook of religion and health* (pp. 225–243). San Diego, CA: Academic Press. doi:10.1016/B978-012417645-4/50082-1

Bartoli, E., Bentley-Edwards, K. L., García, A. M., Michael, A., & Ervin, A. (2018). What do White counselors and psychotherapists need to know about race? White racial socialization in counseling and psychotherapy training programs. In *Whiteness and White Privilege in Psychotherapy* (pp. 80–96). New York, NY: Routledge.

Bartz, J. D. (2009). Theistic Existential Psychotherapy. *Psychology of Religion and Spirituality*, *1*(2), 69–80. doi:10.1037/a0014895

Baugher, A., & Gazmararian, J. (2015). Masculine gender role stress and violence: A literature review of future directions. *Aggression and Violent Behavior*, *24*, 107–112. doi:10.1016/j.avb.2015.04.002

Baumann, A. A., Kuhlberg, J. A., & Zayas, L. H. (2010). Familism, mother-daughter mutuality and suicide attempts of adolescent Latinas. *Journal of Family Psychology*, *24*(5), 616–624. doi:10.1037/a0020584 PMID:20954772

Becker, S. P. (2010). Wilderness therapy: Ethical considerations for mental health professionals. *Child and Youth Care Forum*, *39*(1), 47–61. doi:10.100710566-009-9085-7

Behl, M., Laux, J. M., Roseman, C. P., Tiamiyu, M., & Spann, S. (2017). Needs and acculturative stress of international students in CACREP programs. *Counselor Education and Supervision*, *56*(4), 305–318. doi:10.1002/ceas.12087

Belsky, J., Houts, R. M., & Pasco Fearon, R. M. (2010). Infant attachment security and the timing of puberty: Testing an evolutionary hypothesis. *Psychological Science*, *21*(9), 1195–1201. doi:10.1177/0956797610379867 PMID:20713636

Ben-Ari, A., & Livni, T. (2006). Motherhood is not a given thing: Experiences and constructed meanings of biological and nonbiological lesbian mothers. *Sex Roles*, *54*(7-8), 521–531. doi:10.100711199-006-9016-0

Berger, R. (2006). Using contact with nature, creativity and rituals as a therapeutic medium with children with learning difficulties: A case study. *Emotional & Behavioural Difficulties*, *11*(2), 135–146. doi:10.1080/13632750600619430

Bergerson, A. A. (2007). Exploring the impact of social class on adjustment to college: Anna's story. *International Journal of Qualitative Studies in Education: QSE*, *20*(1), 99–119. doi:10.1080/09518390600923610

Berg-Weger, M. (2016). *Social work and social welfare: An invitation* (4th ed.). New York, NY: Routledge.

Berman, M. G., Kross, E., Krpan, K. M., Askren, M. K., Burson, A., Deldin, P. J., & Jonides, J. (2012). Interacting with nature improves cognition and affect for individuals with depression. *Journal of Affective Disorders, 140*(3), 300–305. doi:10.1016/j.jad.2012.03.012 PMID:22464936

Berry, J. W., Phinney, J. S., Sam, D. L., & Vedder, P. (2006). Immigrant youth: Acculturation, identity, and adaptation. *Applied Psychology, 55*(3), 303–332. doi:10.1111/j.1464-0597.2006.00256.x

Bettner, B. L., & Lew, A. (2005). *Raising kids who can.* Connexions.

Birrell, P. J., & Freyd, J. J. (2006). Betrayal and trauma: Relational models of harm and healing. *Journal of Trauma Practice, 5*(1), 49–63. doi:10.1300/J189v05n01_04

Bitter, J. R. (2014). *Theory and practice of family therapy and counseling* (2nd ed.). Belmont, CA: Brooks/Cole, Cengage Learning.

Blackwell, E., & Pinder, P. J. (2014). What are the motivational factors of first-generation minority college students who overcome their family histories to pursue higher education? *College Student Journal, 48*(1), 45–56.

Blair-Loy, M. (2003). *Competing devotions: Career and family among women executives.* Cambridge, MA: Harvard University Press.

Blakeslee, J., & Best, J. I. (2018). Understanding support network capacity during the transition from foster care: Youth-identified barriers, facilitators, and enhancement strategies. *Children and Youth Services Review, 96*, 220–230. doi:10.1016/j.childyouth.2018.11.049 PMID:30765899

Bleich, E. (2011). What is Islamophobia and how much is there? Theorizing and measuring an emerging comparative concept. *The American Behavioral Scientist, 55*(12), 1581–1600. doi:10.1177/0002764211409387

Boivin, J., Griffiths, E., & Venetis, C. A. (2011). Emotional distress in infertile women and failure of assisted reproductive technologies: Meta-analysis of prospective Psychosocial studies. *BMJ (Clinical Research Ed.), 342*(feb23 1), d223. doi:10.1136/bmj.d223 PMID:21345903

Book of doctrine and covenants of the Church of Jesus Christ of Latter-day Saints. (1864). Cincinnati, OH: Publishing Committee of the Reorganized Church of Jesus Christ of Latter-day Saints.

Bordin, E. S. (1979). The generalizability of the psychoanalytic concept of the working alliance. *Psychotherapy (Chicago, Ill.), 16*(3), 252–260. doi:10.1037/h0085885

Borneskog, C., Lampic, C., Sydsjö, G., Bladh, M., & Skoog Svanberg, A. (2014). How do lesbian couples compare with heterosexual *in vitro* fertilization and spontaneously pregnant couples when it comes to parenting stress? *Acta Paediatrica (Oslo, Norway), 103*(5), 537–545. doi:10.1111/apa.12568 PMID:24456297

Bowler, D. E., Buyung-Ali, L. M., Knight, T. M., & Pullin, A. S. (2010). A systematic review of evidence for the added benefits to health of exposure to natural environments. *BMC Public Health, 10*(1), 456. doi:10.1186/1471-2458-10-456 PMID:20684754

Boysen, G. (2010). Integrating implicit bias into counselor education. *Counselor Education and Supervision, 49*(4), 210–277. doi:10.1002/j.1556-6978.2010.tb00099.x

Bozorgmehr, M., Ong, P., & Tosh, S. (2016). Panethnicity revisited: Contested group boundaries in the post-9/11 era. *Ethnic and Racial Studies, 39*(5), 727–745. doi:10.1080/01419870.2015.1081959 PMID:27182093

Branson, Y. (2017). Military cultural competency. In J. Beder (Ed.), *Caring for the military: A guide for helping professionals* (pp. 3–9). New York, NY: Routledge/Taylor & Francis Group.

Bratman, G. N., Hamilton, J. P., & Daily, G. C. (2012). The impacts of nature experience on human cognitive function and mental health. *Annals of the New York Academy of Sciences, 1249*(1), 118–136. doi:10.1111/j.1749-6632.2011.06400.x PMID:22320203

Bratton, S., Ray, D., Rhine, T., & Jones, L. (2005). The efficacy of play therapy with children: A Meta-analytic review of the outcome research. *Professional Psychology, Research and Practice, 36*(4), 376–390. doi:10.1037/0735-7028.36.4.376

Brittan, A. (1989). *Masculinity and Power.* New York: Basil Blackwell.

Bronfenbrenner, U. (1979). *The ecology of human development: Experiments by nature and design.* Cambridge, MA: Harvard University Press.

Brooks, J. E. (2015). The impact of family structure, relationships, and support of African American students' collegiate experience. *Journal of Black Studies, 46*(8), 817–836. doi:10.1177/0021934715609914

Brooks, J. E., & Allen, K. R. (2016). Academic persistence of African American college students attending an HBCU. *Journal of Family Issues, 37*(6), 814–832. doi:10.1177/0192513X14540160

Brown, E. (2018). California professor, writer of confidential Brett Kavanaugh letter, speaks out about her allegation of sexual assault. *The Washington Post.* Retrieved from https://www.washingtonpost.com/investigations/california-professor-writer-of-confidential-brett-kavanaugh-letter-speaks-out-about-her-allegation-of-sexual-assault/2018/09/16/46982194-b846-11e8-94eb-3bd52dfe917b_story.html?noredirect=on&utm_term=.97cd05a2f8d2

Brown, L. (2010). *Feminist therapy.* Washington, DC: American Psychological Association.

Brown-Nagin, T. (2014). Rethinking proxies for disadvantages in higher education: A first generation students' project. *University of Chicago Legal Forum*, (1): 433–500.

Brown, V. L. (1978). Q&A: Questions and answers. *New Era, 8*(9), 16–19.

Brown, V., & Nichols, T. R. (2012). Pregnant and parenting students on campus: Policy on program implications for a growing population. *Educational Policy*, *27*(3), 499–530. doi:10.1177/0895904812453995

Bryan, C. J. (2016). Suicidal behavior among military personnel and veterans. In N. D. Ainspan, C. J. Bryan, & W. E. Penk (Eds.), *Handbook of psychosocial interventions for veterans and service members: A guide for the non-military mental health clinician* (pp. 159–169). New York, NY: Oxford University Press; doi:10.1093/med:psych/9780199353996.003.0014

Burke, N. J., Hellman, J. L., Scott, B. G., Weems, C. F., & Carrion, V. G. (2011). The impact of adverse childhood experiences on an urban pediatric population. *Child Abuse & Neglect*, *35*(6), 408–413. doi:10.1016/j.chiabu.2011.02.006 PMID:21652073

Burlew, L. D., & Alleyne, V. L. (2010). A pedagogical paradigm for international graduate students studying community counseling. *Journal of Counselor Preparation and Supervision*, *2*(1), 23–36. doi:10.7729/21.0113

Burnett, J. A. (2009). Cultural considerations in counseling couples who experience fertility. *Journal of Multicultural Counseling and Development*, *37*(3), 166–177. doi:10.1002/j.2161-1912.2009.tb00100.x

Buzzell, L., & Chalquist, C. (2009). *Ecotherapy: Healing with nature in mind.* San Francisco, CA: Sierra Club Books.

Caballero, T. M., Johnson, S. B., Muñoz Buchanan, C. R., & DeCamp, L. R. (2017). Adverse childhood experiences among Hispanic children in immigrant families versus US-native families. *Pediatrics*, *140*(5), e20170297. doi:10.1542/peds.2017-0297 PMID:28993445

Camara, S. K., Katznelson, A., Hildebrandt-Sterling, J., & Parker, T. (2012). Heterosexism in context: Qualitative interaction effects of co-cultural responses. *The Howard Journal of Communications*, *23*(4), 312–331. doi:10.1080/10646175.2012.722836

Canfield, J., & Weiss, E. (2015). Integrating military and veteran culture in social work education: Implications for curriculum inclusion. *Journal of Social Work Education*, *51*(sup1), S128–S144. doi:10.1080/10437797.2015.1001295

Capello, D. C. (1994). Beyond financial aid: Counseling Latina students. *Journal of Multicultural Counseling and Development*, *22*(1), 28–36. doi:10.1002/j.2161-1912.1994.tb00240.x

Capuzzi, D., & Gross, D. R. (2011). *Counseling and psychotherapy: Theories and interventions.* Pearson.

Carlson, J., & Slavik, S. (Eds.). (1997). *Techniques in Adlerian psychology*. Washington, DC: Accelerated Development.

Carlson, J., Watts, R. E., & Maniacci, M. (2006). *Adlerian therapy: Theory and practice*. Washington, DC: American Psychological Association. doi:10.1037/11363-000

Carnevale, A. P., Fasules, M. L., Porter, A., & Landis-Santos, J. (2016). *African Americans college majors and earnings*. Retrieved from Georgetown University, Center on Education and Workforce, McCourt School of Public Policy website: https://cew.georgetown.edu/cew-reports/african-american-majors/

Carr, A. (1998). Michael White's Narrative Therapy. *Contemporary Family Therapy*, *20*(4), 485–503. doi:10.1023/A:1021680116584

Carrigan, T., Connell, R. W., & Lee, J. (1985). Toward a new sociology of masculinity. *Theory and Society*, *14*(5), 551–604. doi:10.1007/BF00160017

Carson, E. A., & Sabol, W. J. (2013). Prisoners in 2012. *NCJ, 239808*, 11. Retrieved from https://www.bjs.gov/content/pub/pdf/p12tar9112.pdf

Carter, D. J., & Rashidi, A. (2004). East meets West: Integrating psychotherapy approaches for Muslim women. *Holistic Nursing Practice*, *18*(3), 152–159. doi:10.1097/00004650-200405000-00007 PMID:15222603

Castro, C. A., Kintzle, S., & Hassan, A. M. (2015). The combat veteran paradox: Paradoxes and dilemmas encountered with reintegrating combat veterans and the agencies that support them. *Traumatology*, *21*(4), 299–310. doi:10.1037/trm0000049

Castro, E. L., & Cortez, E. (2017). Exploring the lived experiences and intersectionalities of Mexican community college transfer students: Qualitative insights toward expanding a transfer receptive culture. *Community College Journal of Research and Practice*, *41*(2), 77–92. doi:10.1080/10668926.2016.1158672

Cavanaugh, J., & Blanchard-Fields, F. (2010). *Adult development and aging* (6th ed.). Belmont, CA: Wadsworth Publishing.

Cavazos, J. Jr, Johnson, M. B., Fielding, C., Cavazos, A. G., Castro, V., & Vela, L. (2010a). A qualitative study of resilient Latina/o college students. *Journal of Latinos and Education*, *9*(3), 172–188. doi:10.1080/15348431003761166

Cavazos, J. Jr, Johnson, M. B., & Sparrow, G. S. (2010b). Overcoming personal and academic challenges: Perspectives from Latina/o college students. *Journal of Hispanic Higher Education*, *9*(4), 304–316. doi:10.1177/1538192710380744

Centers for Disease Control and Prevention. (2016). *Adverse childhood experiences (ACEs)*. Retrieved from https://www.cdc.gov/ violenceprevention/acestudy/index.html

Centers for Disease Control. (2016). *Health, United States, 2015, with special feature on racial and ethnic health disparities*. Retrieved from https://www.cdc.gov/nchs/data/hus/hus15.pdf

Cepeda, L. M., & Davenport, D. S. (2006). Person-centered therapy and solution-focused brief therapy: An integration of present and future awareness. *Psychotherapy (Chicago, Ill.)*, *43*(1), 1–12. doi:10.1037/0033-3204.43.1.1 PMID:22121955

Chabot, J. M., & Ames, B. D. (2004). "It wasn't 'let's get pregnant and go do it':" Decision making in lesbian couples planning motherhood via donor insemination. *Family Relations*, *53*(4), 348–356. doi:10.1111/j.0197-6664.2004.00041.x

Chan, C. D., Core, D. N., & Band, M. P. (2018). Privilege and oppression in counselor education: An intersectionality framework. *Journal of Multicultural Counseling and Development*, *46*(1), 58–73. doi:10.1002/jmcd.12092

Chandra, A., Martinez, G. M., Mosher, W. D., Abma, J. C., & Jones, J. (2005). Fertility, Family planning, and reproductive health of U.S. women: Data from the 2002 National Survey of Family Growth. *Vital and Health Statistics*, *23*, 22–31. PMID:16532609

Chaney, C., Lawrence, F. C., & Skogrand, L. (2012). An exploration of financial coping strategies for college-educated African American working women: A research note. *Black Women, Gender, &. Families*, *6*(2), 75–94.

Chang, R., & Page, R. C. (1991). Characteristics of the self-actualized person: Visions from the East and West. *Counseling and Values*, *36*(1), 2–10. doi:10.1002/j.2161-007X.1991.tb00772.x

Cheng, H.-L., Kwan, K.-L. K., & Sevig, T. (2013). Racial and ethnic minority college students' stigma associated with seeking psychological help: Examining psychocultural correlates. *Journal of Counseling Psychology*, *60*(1), 98–111. doi:10.1037/a0031169 PMID:23356468

Ciftci, A., Jones, N., & Corrigan, P. W. (2013). Mental health stigma in the Muslim community. *The Journal of Muslim Mental Health*, *7*(1), 17–32. doi:10.3998/jmmh.10381607.0007.102

Coates, N., & Dickinson, J. (2012). Meeting international postgraduate student needs: A programme-based model for learning and teaching support. *Innovations in Education and Teaching International*, *49*(3), 295–308. doi:10.1080/14703297.2012.703018

Cokley, K. O., Beasley, S., Holman, A., Chapman-Hilliard, C., Cody, B., Jones, B., ... Taylor, D. (2013). The moderating role of gender in the relationship between religiosity and mental health in a sample of Black American college students. *Mental Health, Religion & Culture*, *16*(5), 445–462. doi:10.1080/13674676.2012.684346

Cole, E. R. (2009). Intersectionality and research in psychology. *The American Psychologist*, *64*(3), 170–180. doi:10.1037/a0014564 PMID:19348518

Coll, C. G., Surrey, J., & Weingarten, K. (1998). *Mothering against the odds: Diverse Voices of contemporary mothers*. New York, NY: The Guilford Press.

Collins, P. H., & Bilge, S. (2016). *Intersectionality*. Malden, MA: Polity Press.

Colvin, A. D., Bullock, A. N., & George, T. (2016). Factors associated with college students' propensity towards mental health services utilization on historically Black colleges and university campuses. *Journal of Sociology and Social Work*, *4*(1), 10–19. doi:10.15640/jssw.v4n1a2

Comstock, D. L., Hammer, T. R., Strentzsch, J., Cannon, K., Parsons, J., & Ii, G. S.II. (2008). Relational-cultural theory: A framework for bridging relational, multicultural and social justice competencies. *Journal of Counseling and Development*, *86*(3), 279–287. doi:10.1002/j.1556-6678.2008.tb00510.x

Conley, D. T. (2010). *College and career ready: Helping all students succeed beyond high school*. San Francisco, CA: Jossey-Bass. doi:10.1002/9781118269411

Connell, R. W. (1983). *Which way is up? Essays on sex, class, and culture*. Sydney, Australia: Allen and Unwin.

Connell, R. W. (1987). *Gender and power*. Sydney, Australia: Allen and Unwin.

Connell, R. W., & Messerschmidt, J. W. (2005). Hegemonic masculinity: Rethinking the concept. *Gender & Society*, *19*(6), 829–859. doi:10.1177/0891243205278639

Consoli, A., Kim, B., & Meyer, D. (2008). Counselor values profile: Implication for counseling ethnic minority clients. *Counseling and Values*, *52*(3), 181–197. doi:10.1002/j.2161-007X.2008.tb00103.x

Constantine, M. G., Hage, S. M., Kindaichi, M. M., & Bryant, R. M. (2007). Social justice and multicultural issues: Implications for the practice and training of counselors and counseling psychologist. *Journal of Counseling and Development*, *85*(1), 24–29. doi:10.1002/j.1556-6678.2007.tb00440.x

Constantine, M., Smith, L., Redington, R., & Owens, D. (2008). Racial microaggressions against Black counseling and counseling psychology faculty: A central challenge in the multicultural counseling movement. *Journal of Counseling and Development*, *86*(3), 348–355. doi:10.1002/j.1556-6678.2008.tb00519.x

Cook-Masaud, C., & Wiggins, M. I. (2011). Counseling Muslim women: Navigating cultural and religious challenges. *Counseling and Values*, *55*(2), 247–246. doi:10.1002/j.2161-007X.2011.tb00035.x

Corey, G. (2012). *Theory and practice of counseling and psychotherapy* (9th ed.). Belmont, CA: Brooks/Cole, Cengage Learning.

Coughlin, P., & Wade, J. C. (2012). Masculinity ideology, income disparity, and romantic relationship quality among men with higher earning female partners. *Sex Roles*, *67*(5-6), 311–322. doi:10.100711199-012-0187-6

Courtney, M., Terao, S., & Bost, N. (2004). *Midwest evaluation of the adult functioning of former foster youth: Conditions of youth preparing to leave state care*. Chicago, IL: Chapin Hall at the University of Chicago.

Craske, M. (2017). *Theories of psychotherapy series: Cognitive behavioral therapy* (Revised edition). American Psychological Association. doi:10.1037/0000027-000

Crenshaw, K. (1991). Mapping the margins: Intersectionality, identity politics, and violence against women of color. *Stanford Law Review*, *43*(6), 1241–1299. doi:10.2307/1229039

D'Andrea, M., & Daniels, J. (2001). RESPECTFUL counseling: An integrative model for counselors. In D. Pope-Davis & H. Coleman (Eds.), *The Interface of Class, Culture and Gender in Counseling* (pp. 417–466). Thousand Oaks, CA: Sage. doi:10.4135/9781452231846.n17

Dahl, B., & Malterud, K. (2015). Neither father nor biological mother. A qualitative study about lesbian co-mothers' maternity care experiences. *Sexual & Reproductive Healthcare: Official Journal of the Swedish Association of Midwives*, *6*(3), 169–173. doi:10.1016/j.srhc.2015.02.002 PMID:26842641

Daneshpour, M. (2017). *Family therapy with Muslims*. New York, NY: Routledge/Taylor Francis Group.

Davenport, M. (2012). Examining involvement as a critical factor: Perceptions from first-generation and non-first-generation students. In T. Hicks & A. Pitre (Eds.), *Research studies in higher education: Educating multicultural college students* (pp. 189–222). Lanham, MD: University Press of America, Inc.

David, D., Stefan, S., & Terracciano, A. (2018). Cognitive-behavioral therapy in the cross-cultural context: An extension of the standard paradigm from individual to country/culture level- a brief introduction into a new research line. *Journal of Rational-Emotive & Cognitive-Behavior Therapy*, 1–13. doi:10.100710942-018-0303-9

Day, A., Dworsky, A., & Weng, F. (2013). An analysis of foster care placement history and postsecondary graduation rates. *Research in Higher Education*, *19*, 1–17.

Day-Vines, N. L., Bryan, J., & Griffin, D. (2013). The Broaching Attitudes and Behavior Survey (BABS): An exploratory assessment of its dimensionality. *Journal of Multicultural Counseling and Development*, *41*(4), 210–223. doi:10.1002/j.2161-1912.2013.00037.x

de Bruin-Wassinkmaat, A. M., de Kock, J., Visser-Vogel, E., Bakker, C., & Barnard, M. (2019). Being Young and Strictly Religious: A Review of the Literature on the Religious Identity Development of Strictly Religious Adolescents. *Identity*, *19*(1), 62–79. doi:10.1080/15283488.2019.1566067

De Jong, P., & Berg, I. K. (2013). *Interviewing or solutions* (4th ed.). Belmont, CA: Thomson Brooks/Cole. doi:10.1093/acrefore/9780199975839.013.209

De Shazer, S. (1988). *Clues: Investigating solutions in brief therapy*. Ontario, Canada: Penguin Books.

DeDiego, A. C. (2016). A systemic perspective for working with same-sex parents. *Counseling Today*, *59*(4), 40–44.

DeFrietas, S. C., & Rinn, A. (2013). Academic achievement in first generation college students: The role of academic self-concept. *The Journal of Scholarship of Teaching and Learning*, *13*(1), 57–67.

DeGraff, A. N., O'Neal, C. W., & Mancini, J. A. (2016). The significance of military contexts and culture for understanding family well-being: Parent life satisfaction and adolescent outcomes. *Journal of Child and Family Studies*, *25*(10), 3022–3033. doi:10.100710826-016-0471-0

Delgado Bernal, D., Burciaga, R., & Flores Carmona, J. (2012). Chicana/Latina testimonios: Mapping the methodological, pedagogical, and political. *Equity & Excellence in Education*, *45*(3), 363–372. doi:10.1080/10665684.2012.698149

Dezelic, M., & Ghanoum, G. (2015). *Meaning-Centered Therapy Manual: Logotherapy & Existential Analysis Brief Therapy Protocol for Group and Individual Sessions: 8 Session Format*. New York: Palace Printing and Design.

DiAngelo, R. (2018). *White fragility: Why it's so hard for white people to talk about racism*. Boston, MA: Beacon Press.

Dickson, M., & Tennant, L. (2018). 'The accommodation I make is turning a blind eye': Faculty support for student mothers in higher education. *Studies in Continuing Education*, *40*(1), 76–97. doi:10.1080/0158037X.2017.1392296

Dinkmeyer, D. C., Dinkmeyer, D. C. Jr, & Sperry, L. (1987). *Adlerian counseling and psychotherapy* (2nd ed.). Columbus, OH: Merrill.

Dinkmeyer, D. C., & McKay, G. D. (1989). *The parent's handbook: Systematic training for effective parenting* (3rd ed.). Circle Pines, MN: American Guidance Service.

Dinkmeyer, D. C., McKay, G., & Dinkmeyer, D. Jr. (1980). *Systematic training for effective teaching (STET)*. Circle Pines, MN: American Guidance Service.

Dion, K. K., & Dion, K. L. (2002). Gender and cultural adaptation in immigrant families. *The Journal of Social Issues*, *57*(3), 511–521. doi:10.1111/0022-4537.00226

Dittmann, M. (2003). *Fighting ageism: Geropsychologists are striving to stop negative stereotypes and meet the growing mental health needs of older adults*. PsycEXTRA Dataset. doi:10.1037/e30112203-027

Dixon, C. G., Richard, M., & Rollins, C. W. (2003). Contemporary issues facing aging americans: Implications for rehabilitation and mental health counseling. *Journal of Rehabilitation*, *69*(2), 5–12.

Donahoo, S., & Caffe, R. A. (2010). A sense of home. The impact of church participation on African American college students. *Journal of Research on Christian Education*, *19*(1), 79–104. doi:10.1080/10656211003630471

Donnelly, K., Twenge, J. M., Clark, M. A., Shaikh, S. K., Beiler-May, A., & Carter, N. T. (2015). Attitudes toward women's work and family roles in the United States, 1976-2013. *Psychology of Women Quarterly*, *40*(1), 41–54. doi:10.1177/0361684315590774

Donovan, R. A., & West, L. M. (2015). Stress and mental health: Moderating role of the strong Black woman stereotype. *The Journal of Black Psychology*, *41*(4), 384–396. doi:10.1177/0095798414543014

Dooley, M., Dineen, T., Sarma, K., & Nolan, A. (2014). The psychological impact of infertility and fertility treatment on the male partner. *Human Fertility*, *17*(3), 203–209. doi:10.3109/14647273.2014.942390 PMID:25116275

Doucette, P. A. (2004). Walk and talk: An intervention for behaviorally challenged youths. *Adolescence San Diego*, *39*(154), 373. PMID:15563045

Douglass, S. C., & Dunn, R. E. (2002). Interpreting Islam in American schools. In H. Donnan (Ed.), *Interpreting Islam* (pp. 76–98). Thousand Oaks, CA: Sage. doi:10.4135/9781446217467.n5

Dreikurs, R., & Soltz, V. (1964). *Children: The challenge. New York, NY*. Hawthorn: Dutton.

Duffey, T., Haberstroh, S., & Trepal, H. (2009). A grounded theory of relational competencies and creativity in counseling. *Journal of Creativity in Mental Health*, *4*(2), 89–112. doi:10.1080/15401380902951911

Duffey, T., & Somody, C. (2011). The role of relational-cultural theory in mental health counseling. *Journal of Mental Health Counseling*, *33*(3), 223–242. doi:10.17744/mehc.33.3.c10410226u275647

Dunne, G. A. (2000). Opting into motherhood: Lesbians blurring the boundaries and transforming the meaning of parenthood and kinship. *Gender & Society*, *14*(1), 11–35. doi:10.1177/089124300014001003

Eckart, E. C., & Dufrene, R. L. (2015). Barriers to mental health counseling for soldiers. *Journal of Military and Government Counseling*, *3*(1), 40–55. Retrieved from http://acegonline.org/wp-content/uploads/2013/02/JMGC-Vol-3-Is-1.pdf

Eifert, G. H., & Forsyth, J. P. (2013). *Acceptance & commitment therapy for anxiety disorders: A practitioner's treatment guide to using mindfulness, acceptance, and values-based behavior change strategies*. Oakland, CA: New Harbinger Publications Inc.

Elsharnouby, T. H. (2016). Participation behavior among international students. *International Journal of Educational Management*, *30*(5), 679–697. doi:10.1108/IJEM-10-2014-0139

Eltaiba, N. (2014). Counseling with Muslim refugees: Building rapport. *Journal of Social Work Practice*, *28*(4), 397–403. doi:10.1080/02650533.2013.875523

Englar-Carlson, M. (2006). Masculine norms and the therapy process. In M. Englar-Carlson & M. A. Stevens (Eds.), *In the room with men: A casebook of therapeutic change*. Washington, DC: American Psychological Association. doi:10.1037/11411-002

Engström, H. A., Häggström-Nordin, E., Borneskog, C., & Almqvist, A. (2018). Mothers in same-sex relationships describe the process of forming a family as a stressful journey in a heteronormative world: A Swedish grounded theory study. *Maternal and Child Health Journal*, *22*(10), 1444–1450. doi:10.100710995-018-2525-y PMID:29740747

Erikson, C., & Abernethy, A. (2014). Integration in multicultural competence and diversity training: Engaging difference and grace. *Journal of Psychology and Theology*, *42*(2), 174–187. doi:10.1177/009164711404200205

Erikson, E. H. (1968). *Identity: Youth and crises*. New York, NY: Norton.

Erwin, T. (2007). Two moms and a baby: Counseling lesbian couples choosing motherhood. *Women & Therapy*, *30*(1/2), 99–149. doi:10.1300/J015v30n01_06

Esposito, J. L. (2010). *The future of Islam*. New York, NY: Oxford University Press.

Esposito, J. L. (2016). *Islam: The straight path* (5th ed.). New York, NY: Oxford University Press.

Esposito, J. L., & Mogahed, D. (2007). *Who really speaks for Islam? What a billion Muslims really think*. New York, NY: Gallup Press.

Evans, L., & Clay, C. (2018). Solidarity, double consciousness, and collective emotion work: Understanding negative black health outcomes resulting from systemic police terror. In *Inequality, crime, and health among african american males* (pp. 185–206). Bingley, UK: Emerald Publishing Limited. doi:10.1108/S0195-744920180000020009

Evans, S., & Noriega, P. (2011). Institutions of higher education marketing strategies in recruiting first generation African American students. *The Consortium Journal of Hospitality and Tourism*, *15*(2), 5–24.

Fairburn, C. G., Cooper, Z., & Shafran, R. (2003). Cognitive behavior therapy for eating disorders: A "transdiagnostic" theory and treatment. *Behaviour Research and Therapy*, *41*(5), 509–528. doi:10.1016/S0005-7967(02)00088-8 PMID:12711261

Farinde, A. A., & Lewis, C. W. (2012). The underrepresentation of African American female students in STEM fields: Implications for classroom teachers. *US-China Education Review*, *2*(4), 421–430.

Fernando, D. M. (2007). Existential theory and solution-focused strategies: Integration and application. *Journal of Mental Health Counseling*, *29*(3), 226–241. doi:10.17744/mehc.29.3.r01582660404v734

Fife, J. E., Bond, S., & Byars-Winston, A. (2011). Correlates and predictors of academic self efficacy among African American students. *Education*, *132*(1), 141–148.

Finkelstein, M., Wamsley, M., & Miranda, D. (2002). *What keeps children in foster care from succeeding in school: Views of early adolescents and the adults in their lives*. New York, NY: Vera Institute of Justice.

First Amendment California Supreme Court Holds that Free Exercise of Religion does not Give Fertility Doctors Right to Deny Treatment to Lesbians. North Coast Women's Care Medical Group, Inc. v. San Diego County Superior Court, 189 P.3d 959 (Cal. 2008). (2008). *Harvard Law Review*, *122*(2), 787–794. Retrieved from http://ezproxy.augusta.edu/login?url=https://search.ebscohost.com/login.aspx?direct=true&db=a9h&AN=35650955&site=ehost-live&scope=site

Flaherty, E. G., Thompson, R., Dubowitz, H., Harvey, E. M., English, D. J., Proctor, L. J., & Runyan, D. K. (2013). Adverse childhood experiences and child health in early adolescence. *JAMA Pediatrics*, *167*(7), 622–629. doi:10.1001/jamapediatrics.2013.22 PMID:23645114

Forbes-Mewett, H., & Sawyer, A. M. (2016). International students and mental health. *Journal of International Students*, *6*(3), 661–677. Retrieved from http://jistudents.org

Fr. A. Jarmus. (2018, December 6). The real difference between orthodoxy and the west [web log comment]. Retrieved from https://www.stnicholasonline.org/fr-andrews-blog/the-real-difference-between-orthodoxy-and-the-west

Frank, B. (1987). Hegemonic heterosexual masculinity. *Studies in Political Economy*, *24*(1), 159–170. doi:10.1080/19187033.1987.11675562

Frankl, V. (1946). *Man's Search for Meaning: An Introduction to Logotherapy*. New York: Simon & Schuster.

Frey, L. (2013). Relational-cultural therapy: Theory, research, adn application to counseling competencies. *Professional Psychology, Research and Practice*, *44*(3), 177–185. doi:10.1037/a0033121

Frey, L. L., Beesley, D., & Miller, M. (2006). Relational health, attachment, and psychological distress in college women and men. *Psychology of Women Quarterly*, *30*(3), 303–311. doi:10.1111/j.1471-6402.2006.00298.x

Frey, L. L., Tobin, J., & Beesley, D. (2004). Relational predictors of psychological distress in women and men presenting for university counseling center services. *Journal of College Counseling*, *7*(2), 129–139. doi:10.1002/j.2161-1882.2004.tb00244.x

Froerer, A. S., & Connie, E. E. (2016). Solution-building, the foundation of solution-focused brief therapy: A qualitative Delphi study. *Journal of Family Psychotherapy*, *27*(1), 20–34. doi:10.1080/08975353.2016.1136545

Frost, D. M., & Meyer, I. H. (2009). Internalized homophobia and relationship quality among lesbians, gay men, and bisexuals. *Journal of Counseling Psychology*, *56*(1), 97–109. doi:10.1037/a0012844 PMID:20047016

Frye, J. (2018). From Politics to Policy: Turning the Corner on Sexual Harassment. *Center for American Progress*. Retrieved from https://www.americanprogress.org/issues/women/news/2018/01/31/445669/politics-policy-turning-corner-sexual-harassment/

Fry, R. (2011). *Hispanic college enrollment spike, narrowing gaps with other groups*. Washington, DC: Pew Hispanic Center.

Fuehrlein, B. S., Mota, N., Arias, A. J., Trevisan, L. A., Kachadourian, L. K., Krystal, J. H., ... Pietrzak, R. H. (2016). The burden of alcohol use disorders in US military veterans: Results from the National Health and Resilience in Veterans Study. *Addiction (Abingdon, England)*, *111*(10), 1786–1794. doi:10.1111/add.13423 PMID:27061707

Galhardo, A., Cunha, M., Pinto-Gouveia, J., & Matos, M. (2013). The mediator role of emotional regulation processes on infertility-related stress. *Journal of Clinical Psychology in Medical Settings*, *20*(4), 497–507. doi:10.100710880-013-9370-3 PMID:23821009

Gates, T., Duffy, K., Moore, J., Howell, W., & McDonald, W. (2007). Alcohol screening instruments and psychiatric evaluation outcomes in military aviation personnel. *Aviation, Space, and Environmental Medicine*, *78*(1), 48–51. PMID:17225482

Gavin Williams, R. (2016). The role of school counselors in the career and college Readiness of foster care youth: An ecological systems theory approach. *Journal of Counselor Leadership and Advocacy*. doi:10.1080/2326716X.2015.1133335

Genero, P., Baker Miller, J., Surrey, J., & Baldwin, L. M. (1992). Measuring perceived mutuality in close relationships: Validation of the Mutual Psychological Development Questionnaire. *Journal of Family Psychology*, *6*(1), 36–48. doi:10.1037/0893-3200.6.1.36

Getrajdman, C., Lee, J. A., & Copperman, A. B. (2017). Co-IVF for same-sex female couples. *Seminars in Reproductive Medicine*, *35*(5), 415–419. doi:10.1055-0037-1605380 PMID:29073679

Gigliotti, D. (Producer), Chernin, P. (Producer), Topping, K. (Producer), Williams, P. (Producer), Mefli, T. & Melfi, T. (Director). (2016). *Hidden figures* [Motion Picture]. United States 20th Century Fox

Gilbert, D. (2002). *The American class structure in an age of growing inequality* (6th ed.). Belmont, CA: Wadsworth.

Gilford, T. T., & Reynolds, A. (2011). "My Mother's Keeper." The effects of parentification on Black female college students. *The Journal of Black Psychology*, *37*(1), 55–77. doi:10.1177/0095798410372624

Gilligan, C. (1982). *In a different voice: Psychological theory and women's development*. Cambridge, MA: Harvard University Press.

Gilligan, C., Rogers, A., & Tolman, D. (1991). *Women, girls, and psychotherapy: Reframing resistance*. Binghamton, NY: Haworth.

Gleeson, T. D., & Hemmer, P. A. (2014). Providing care to military personnel and their families: How we can all contribute. *Academic Medicine*, *89*(9), 1201–1203. doi:10.1097/ACM.0000000000000368 PMID:24979291

Gloria, A. M., Castellanos, J., Lopez, A. G., & Rosales, R. (2005). An examination of academic nonpersistence decisions of Latino undergraduates. *Hispanic Journal of Behavioral Sciences*, *27*(2), 202–223. doi:10.1177/0739986305275098

Gloria, A. M., Castellanos, J., Scull, N., & Villegas, F. J. (2009). Psychological coping and well-being of male Latino undergraduates: Sobreviviendo la universidad. *Hispanic Journal of Behavioral Sciences*, *31*(3), 317–339. doi:10.1177/0739986309336845

Gloria, A. M., & Rodriguez, E. R. (2000). Counseling Latino university students: Psychosocial issues for consideration. *Journal of Counseling and Development*, *78*(2), 145–154. doi:10.1002/j.1556-6676.2000.tb02572.x

Glover, R. J. (1998). Perspectives on aging: Issues affecting the latter part of the life cycle. *Educational Gerontology*, *24*(4), 325–331. doi:10.1080/0360127980240403

Goffman, F. (1963). *Stigma: Notes on the management of spoiled identity*. New York, NY: Simon and Schuster.

Goforth, A. N., Oka, E. R., Leong, F. T. L., & Denis, D. J. (2014). Acculturation, acculturative stress, religiosity and psychological adjustment among Muslim Arab American adolescents. *The Journal of Muslim Mental Health*, *8*(2), 3–19. doi:10.3998/jmmh.10381607.0008.202

Goforth, A. N., Pham, A. V., & Oka, E. R. (2015). Parent-child conflict, acculturation gap, acculturative stress, and behavior problems in Arab American adolescents. *Journal of Cross-Cultural Psychology*, *46*(6), 821–836. doi:10.1177/0022022115585140

Gofoth, A. N., Pham, A. V., Chun, H., Castro-Olivo, S. M., & Yosai, E. R. (2016). Association of acculturative stress, Islamic practices, and internalizing symptoms among Arab American adolescents. *School Psychology Quarterly*, *31*(2), 198–212. doi:10.1037pq0000135 PMID:27243243

Goldberg, A. B., Downing, J. B., & Richardson, H. B. (2009). The transition from infertility to adoption: Perceptions of lesbian and heterosexual couples. *Journal of Social and Personal Relationships*, *26*(6-7), 938–963. doi:10.1177/0265407509345652

Golombok, S., & Murray, C. (2006). Non-genetic and non-gestational parenthood: Consequences for parent-child relationships and the psychological well-being of mothers, fathers and children at age 3. *Human Reproduction (Oxford, England)*, *21*(7), 1918–1924. doi:10.1093/humrep/del039 PMID:16517564

Gonzales, P. M., Blanton, H., & Williams, K. J. (2002). The effects of stereotype threat and double-minority status on the test performance of Latino women. *Personality and Social Psychology Bulletin*, *28*(5), 659–670. doi:10.1177/0146167202288010

Graham, J. M., & Barnow, Z. B. (2013). Stress and social support in gay, lesbian, and heterosexual couples: Direct effects and buffering models. *Journal of Family Psychology*, *27*(4), 569–578. doi:10.1037/a0033420 PMID:23795604

Grant, L. E., & Cochrane, S. (2014). Acupuncture for the mental and emotional health of Women undergoing IVF treatment: A comprehensive review. *Australian Journal of Acupuncture & Chinese Medicine*, *9*(1), 5–12.

Greenberg, L. S., Watson, J. C., & Lietaer, G. (Eds.). (1998). *Handbook of experiential psychotherapy*. New York, NY: Guilford Press.

Greenwald, A., McGhee, D., & Schwartz, J. (1998). Measuring individual difference in implicit cognition: The Implicit Association Test. *Journal of Personality and Social Psychology*, *74*(6), 1464–1480. doi:10.1037/0022-3514.74.6.1464 PMID:9654756

Grier-Reed, T. (2013). The African American student network: Creating sanctuaries and counterspaces for coping with racial microaggressions in higher education settings. *The Journal of Black Psychology*, *39*(2), 169–184. doi:10.1177/0095798413478696

Guerney, L. F. (1997). *Filial therapy*. Hoboken, NJ: John Wiley & Sons.

Gulamhussein, Q., & Eaton, N. R. (2015). Hijab, religiosity, and psychological wellbeing of Muslim women in the United States. *The Journal of Muslim Mental Health*, *9*(2), 25–40. doi:10.3998/jmmh.10381607.0009.202

Gushue, G. V., & Carter, R. T. (2000). Remembering race: White racial identity attitudes and two aspects of social memory. *Journal of Counseling Psychology*, *47*(2), 199–210. doi:10.1037/0022-0167.47.2.199

Gushue, G. V., & Constantine, M. G. (2007). Color-blind racial attitudes and white racial identity attitudes in psychology trainees. *Professional Psychology, Research and Practice*, *38*(3), 321–328. doi:10.1037/0735-7028.38.3.321

Halbur, D. A., & Halbur, K. V. (2019). *Developing your theoretical orientation in counseling and psychotherapy* (4th ed.). Hoboken, NJ: Pearson Education.

Halbur, D., & Halbur, K. (2014). *Developing your theoretical orientation*. Boston, MA: Pearson.

Hall, L. (2008). *Counseling military families: What mental health professionals need to know*. New York, NY: Taylor & Francis Group, LLC.

Hamada, B. I. (2001). The Arab image in the minds of western image-makers. *The Journal of International Communication*, *7*(1), 7–35. doi:10.1080/13216597.2001.9751897

Hammer, T. R., Crethar, H. C., & Cannon, K. (2016). Convergence of identities through the lens of relational-cultural theory. *Journal of Creativity in Mental Health*, *11*(2), 126–141. doi:10.1080/15401383.2016.1181596

Haque, A., Tubbs, C. Y., Kahomodu-Fessler, E. P., & Brown, M. D. (2019). Microaggressions and Islamophobia: Experiences of Muslims across the United States and clinical implications. *Journal of Marital and Family Therapy*, *45*(1), 76–91. doi:10.1111/jmft.12339 PMID:29855055

Harris, J. R., & Wong, C. D. (2018). African American college students, the Black church, and counseling. *Journal of College Counseling*, *21*(1), 15–28. doi:10.1002/jocc.12084

Hartig, T., Mang, M., & Evans, G. W. (1991). Restorative effects of natural environment experiences. *Environment and Behavior*, *23*(1), 3–26. doi:10.1177/0013916591231001

Hasbach, P. H. (2012). Ecotherapy. In P. H. Kahn Jr & P. H. Hasbach (Eds.), *Ecopsychology: Science, totems, and the technological species* (pp. 115–139). Cambridge, MA: MIT Press.

Hayes, J. A., Youn, S. J., Castonguay, L. G., Locke, B. D., McAleavey, A. A., & Nordberg, S. (2011). Rates and predictors of counseling center use among college students of color. *Journal of College Counseling*, *14*(2), 105–116. doi:10.1002/j.2161-1882.2011.tb00266.x

Hayes, S. C., & Lillis, J. (2012). *Acceptance and commitment therapy*. Washington, DC: American Psychological Association.

Hayes, S. C., Strosahl, K. D., & Wilson, K. G. (1999). *Acceptance and commitment therapy: An experiential approach to behavior change*. New York, NY: The Guilford Press.

Hayman, B., & Wilkes, L. (2017). *De novo* families: Lesbian motherhood. *Journal of Homosexuality, 64*(5), 577–591. doi:10.1080/00918369.2016.1194119 PMID:27228787

Hearn, J. (2012). A multi-faceted power analysis of men's violence to known women: From hegemonic masculinity to the hegemony of men. *The Sociological Review, 60*(4), 589–610. doi:10.1111/j.1467-954X.2012.02125.x

Helms, J. E., Nicolas, G., & Green, C. E. (2010). Racism and ethnoviolence as trauma: Enhancing professional training. *Traumatology, 16*(4), 53–62. doi:10.1177/1534765610389595

Hendrickson, B., Rosen, D., & Aune, R. K. (2011). An analysis of friendship networks, social connectedness, homesickness, and satisfaction levels of international students. *International Journal of Intercultural Relations, 35*(3), 281–295. doi:10.1016/j.ijintrel.2010.08.001

Henfield, M. S., & Byrd, J. A. (2014). Recruiting and retaining gifted Black students in STEM majors: Implications for college counselors. In Gifted education: Current perspectives and issues. Emerald Group Publishing Limited.

Henry, B., Cormier, C., Hebert, E., Naquin, M., & Woods, R. (2018). Health and health care issues among upper-level college students and relationships to age, race, gender, and living arrangements. *College Student Journal, 52*(1), 7–20.

Herek, G. M., Gillis, J. R., & Cogan, J. C. (2009). Internalized stigma among sexual minority adults: Insights from a social psychological perspective. *Journal of Counseling Psychology, 56*(1), 32–43. doi:10.1037/a0014672

Hicks, J. F., Lenard, N., & Brendle, J. (2016). Utilizing filial therapy with deployed military families. *International Journal of Play Therapy, 25*(4), 210–216. doi:10.1037/pla0000032

Hindman, R. (n.d.). Integrating mindfulness into CBT. *The Beck Institute*. Retrieved from https://beckinstitute.org/integrating-mindfulness-cbt/

Hinton, D. E., Rivera, E. I., Hofmann, S. G., Barlow, D. H., & Otto, M. W. (2012). Adapting CBT for traumatized refugees and ethnic minority patients: Examples from culturally adapted CBT (CA-CBT). *Transcultural Psychiatry, 49*(2), 340–365. doi:10.1177/1363461512441595 PMID:22508639

Hipolito-Delgado, C. P., & Reinders-Saeman, R. (2017). What do allies do?: Providing culturally responsive counseling to communities of color. *Interamerican Journal of Psychology, 51*(2), 214–225.

Hohenshill, T. H., Amundson, N. E., & Niles, S. G. (2013). *Counseling around the world: An international handbook*. Alexandria, VA: American Counseling Association.

Holland, J. L. (1959). A theory of vocational choice. *Journal of Counseling Psychology*, *6*(1), 35–45. doi:10.1037/h0040767

Holman, Z. A. (2014). *So you call yourself a counselor? School counselor's impact on first-generation African American college students' post-secondary aspirations* (Doctoral dissertation). Retrieved from https://search-proquestcom. ezproxy.xula.edu/docview/ 1728305099/abstract/A3 297E78099F41F6PQ/1?accountid=40599

Hook, J. N., Davis, D. E., Owen, J., Worthington, E. L., & Utsey, S. O. (2013). Cultural humility: Measuring openness to culturally diverse clients. *Journal of Counseling Psychology*, *60*(3), 353–366. doi:10.1037/a0032595 PMID:23647387

Hopkins, J. J., Sorenson, A., & Taylor, V. (2013). Same-sex couples, families, and Marriage: Embracing and resisting heteronormativity. *Sociology Compass*, *7*(2), 97–110. doi:10.1111oc4.12016

Houlden, V., Weich, S., Porto de Albuquerque, J., Jarvis, S., & Rees, K. (2018). The relationship between greenspace and the mental wellbeing of adults: A systematic review. *PLoS One*, *13*(9), 1–35. doi:10.1371/journal.pone.0203000 PMID:30208073

Houshmand, S., Spanierman, L. B., & Tafarodi, R. W. (2014). Excluded and avoided: Racial microaggressions targeting Asian international students in Canada. *Cultural Diversity & Ethnic Minority Psychology*, *20*(3), 377–388. doi:10.1037/a0035404 PMID:25045949

Hsaio, C., Koren-Karie, N., Bailey, H., & Moran, G. (2015). It takes two to talk: Longitudinal associations among infant-mother attachment, maternal attachment representations, and mother-child emotion dialogues. *Attachment & Human Development*, *17*(1), 43–64. doi:10.1080/14616 734.2014.981671 PMID:25482104

Hudson, A. L. (2013). Career mentoring needs of youths in foster care: Voices for change. *Journal of Child and Adolescent Psychiatric Nursing*, *26*(2), 131–137. doi:10.1111/jcap.12032 PMID:23607825

Hurtado, S., & Carter, D. F. (1997). Effects of college transition and perceptions of the campus racial climate on Latino college students' sense of belonging. *Sociology of Education*, *70*(4), 324–345. Retrieved from http://www.jstor.org/stable/2673270. doi:10.2307/2673270

Hyun, J., Quinn, B., Madon, T., & Lustig, S. (2007). Mental health need, awareness, and use of counseling services among international graduate students. *Journal of American College Health*, *56*(2), 109–118. doi:10.3200/JACH.56.2.109-118 PMID:17967756

Ibrahim, F. A., & Dykeman, C. (2011). Counseling Muslim Americans: Cultural and spiritual assessments. *Journal of Counseling and Development*, *89*(4), 387–396. doi:10.1002/j.1556-6676.2011.tb02835.x

Ibrahim, F., & Heuer, J. (2016a). Application of social justice and cultural responsiveness strategies: Using cultural assessments in counseling and psychotherapy. In *Social justice counseling: Client-specific interventions* (pp. 169–237). New York, NY: Springer. doi:10.1007/978-3-319-18057-1_8

Ibrahim, F., & Heuer, J. (2016b). Worldview: Implications for culturally responsive and ethical practice. In *Social justice counseling: Client-specific interventions* (pp. 51–75). New York, NY: Springer. doi:10.1007/978-3-319-18057-1_3

Ijomanta, I. N., & Lasebikan, V. O. (2016). Lifetime and 12 months prevalence of alcohol use and alcohol use disorders among soldiers residing in a military community in Ibadan. *Substance Use & Misuse*, *51*(6), 722–732. doi:10.3109/10826084.2016.1153111 PMID:27070029

Institute of International Education. (2018). *Open doors: Report on international educational exchange.* Retrieved from http://www.iie.org/opendoors

Isenhart, C. E. (2005). Treating substance abuse in men. In G. E. Good & G. R. Brooks (Eds.), *The new handbook of psychotherapy and counseling with men.* San Francisco, CA: Jossey-Bass.

Ivey, A. E., D' Andrea, M. J., & Ivey, M. B. (2012). *Theories of counseling and psychotherapy: A multicultural perspective* (7th ed.). Thousand Oaks, CA: Sage.

Iwamoto, D. K., Corbin, W., Lejuez, C., & MacPherson, L. (2014). College men and alcohol use: Positive alcohol expectancies as a mediator between distinct masculine norms and alcohol use. *Psychology of Men & Masculinity*, *15*(1), 29–39. doi:10.1037/a0031594 PMID:25705133

Jackson, D. L. (2013). A balancing act: Impacting and initiating the success of African American female community college transfer students in STEM into the HBCU environment. *The Journal of Negro Education*, *82*(3), 255–271. doi:10.7709/jnegroeducation.82.3.0255

Jimenez, M. E., Wade, R. Jr, Schwartz-Soicher, O., Lin, Y., & Reichman, N. E. (2017). Adverse childhood experiences and ADHD diagnosis at age 9 years in a national urban sample. *Journal of the American Academy of Pediatrics*, *17*(4), 356–361. doi:10.1016/j.acap.2016.12.009 PMID:28003143

Johnson, A. G. (2018). *Privilege, power, and difference* (3rd ed.). Boston, MA: McGraw-Hill. doi:10.4324/9780429494802-12

Johnson, M. J., & Reynolds, A. L. (2018). Factors influencing academic success among African American college women: The impact of African American acculturation and religiosity. *The Journal of Black Psychology*, *44*(5), 403–421. doi:10.1177/0095798418777400

Johnson, W., Rosenstein, J. E., Buhrke, R. A., & Haldeman, D. C. (2013). After "don't ask don't tell:" Competent care of lesbian, gay and bisexual military personnel during the DoD policy transition. *Professional Psychology, Research and Practice*, *1*(1), 1–9. doi:10.1037/a0033051

Johns, R. D. (2016). Stories matter: Narrative themes of counselor educators' religious and spiritual competency. *Counseling and Values*, *62*(1), 72–89. doi:10.1002/cvj.12050

Jones, B. J. (2014). *Examining help-seeking attitudes in African American collegians: The role of minority student stress, out-group stress, out-group comfort, cultural congruity, and counselor racial preferences* (Doctoral dissertation). University of Texas-Austin. Retrieved from https://repositories.lib.utexas.edu/bitstream/handle/2152/26139/JONES-DISSERTATION-2014.pdf?sequence=1

Jordan, J. V., & Hartling, L. M. (2010). *The development of relational-cultural theory*. Jean Baker-Miller Training Institute. Retrieved from https://www.researchgate.net/publication/247836552_The_Development_of_Relational-Cultural_Theory

Jordan, J. V. (1997). *Women's growth in diversity*. New York: Guilford.

Jordan, J. V. (2009). *Relational-cultural therapy*. Washington, DC: American Psychological Association.

Jordan, J. V. (2010). *The power of connection: Recent developments in relational-cultural theory*. New York, NY: Routledge.

Jordan, J. V., & Hartling, L. M. (2002). New developments in relational cultural theory. In M. Ballou & L. S. Brown (Eds.), *Rethinking mental health and disorder* (pp. 48–70). New York, NY: Guilford Press.

Jung, M. (1998). *Chinese American family therapy: A new model for clinicians*. San Francisco, CA: Jossey-Bass.

Kabir, N. A. (2015). Muslim identity formation in the West: The case of Australian, British, and American Muslims. In D. Iner & S. Yucel (Eds.), *Muslim identity formation in religiously diverse societies* (pp. 105–126). Tyne, UK: Cambridge Scholars Publishing.

Kahaki, F., & Khosravi, M. (2014). A survey of the relationship between anxiety, stress, depression, and life satisfaction in fertile and infertile women. *Journal of Jahrom University of Medical Sciences*, *11*, 160–160.

Kananian, S., Ayoughi, S., Farugie, A., Hinton, D., & Stangier, U. (2017). Transdiagnostic culturally adapted CBT with Farsi-speaking refugees: A pilot study. *European Journal of Psychotraumatology*, *8*(2), 1–10. doi:10.1080/20008198.2017.1390362 PMID:29163870

Kaplan, S. (1995). The restorative benefits of nature: Toward an integrative framework. *Journal of Environmental Psychology*, *15*(3), 169–182. doi:10.1016/0272-4944(95)90001-2

Katz, J., Joiner, T. E. Jr, & Kwon, P. (2002). Membership in a devalued social group and emotional well-being: Developing a model of personal self-esteem, collective self-esteem, and group socialization. *Sex Roles*, *4*(9/10), 419–443. doi:10.1023/A:1021644225878

Kaufman, G. (1980). *Shame: The power of caring*. Cambridge, MA: Schenkman.

Kerker, B. D., Zhang, J., Nadeem, E., Stein, R. E., Hurlburt, M. S., Heneghan, A., ... McCue Horwitz, S. (2015). Adverse childhood experiences and mental health, chronic medical conditions, and development in young children. *Journal of the American Academy of Pediatrics*, *15*(5), 510–517. doi:10.1016/j.acap.2015.05.005 PMID:26183001

Keshishian, F., Brocavich, J. M., Boone, T., & Pal, S. (2010). Motivating factors influencing college students' choice of academic major. *American Journal of Pharmaceutical Education*, *74*(3), 1–7. doi:10.5688/aj740346 PMID:20498739

Kessler, S. J., Ashenden, D. J., Connell, R. W., & Dowsett, G. W. (1982). *Ockers and discomaniacs*. Sydney, Australia: Inner City Education Center.

Kim, B. S., & Lyons, H. Z. (2003). Experiential activities and multicultural counseling competence training. *Journal of Counseling and Development*, *81*(4), 400–408. doi:10.1002/j.1556-6678.2003.tb00266.x

King, B. (2015) *The shared experiences of counselors who practice in natural environments.* Retrieved from https://scholarworks.uno.edu/td/203

Kirk, C. M., Lewis, R. K., Nilsen, C., & Colvin, D. Q. (2013). Foster care and college: The educational aspirations and expectations of youth in the foster care system. *Youth & Society*, *45*(3), 307–323. doi:10.1177/0044118X11417734

Kirk, R., & Day, A. (2011). Increasing college access for youth aging out of foster care: Evaluation of a summer camp program for foster youth transitioning from high school to college. *Children and Youth Services Review*, *33*(7), 1173–1180. doi:10.1016/j.childyouth.2011.02.018

Kocet, M. M., & Herlihy, B. J. (2013). Addressing value-based conflicts within the counseling relationship: A decision-making model. *Journal of Counseling and Development*, *92*(2), 180–186. doi:10.1002/j.1556-6676.2014.00146.x

Koltko, M. E. (1991). The psychological foundations of the Mormon client in counseling and psychotherapy. *Journal of the Association of Mormon Counselors and Psychotherapists*, *17*(1), 1–26. Retrieved from https://scholarsarchive.byu.edu/irp/vol17/iss1/2/

Kottman, T. (1995). *Partners in play: An Adlerian approach to play therapy*. Alexandra, VA: American Counseling Association.

Kottman, T. (1999). Integrating the crucial Cs into Adlerian play therapy. *Journal of Individual Psychology*, *55*(3), 288–297.

Kottman, T. (2001). Adlerian play therapy. *International Journal of Play Therapy*, *10*(2), 1–12. doi:10.1037/h0089476

Kottman, T., Bryant, J., Alexander, J., & Kroger, S. (2009). Partners in the schools: Adlerian school counseling. In A. Vernon & T. Kottman (Eds.), *Counseling theories: Practical applications with children and adolescents in school settings* (pp. 47–83). Denver, CO: Love.

Kottman, T., & Warlick, J. (1989). Adlerian play therapy: Practical considerations. *Journal of Individual Psychology*, *45*(4), 433–446.

Krane, N. E. (2000). Four or five sessions and a cloud of dust: Old assumptions and new observations about career counseling. In S. D. Brown & R. W. Lent (Eds.), *Handbook of counseling psychology* (3rd ed.; pp. 740–766). New York, NY: Wiley.

Kress, V. E., Haiyasoso, M., Zoldan, C. A., Headley, J. A., & Trepal, H. (2018). The use of relational-cultural theory in counseling clients who have traumatic stress disorders. *Journal of Counseling and Development, 96*, 106-114. doi:10.1002/jcad.12182

Kress, V. E., Dixon, A. L., & Shannonhouse, L. R. (2018). Multicultural diagnosis and conceptualization. In D. G. Hays & B. T. Erford (Eds.), *Developing multicultural counseling competence: A systems Approach* (3rd ed.; pp. 558–590). New York, NY: Pearson.

Kropf, N., & Tandy, C. (1998). Narrative therapy with older clients: The use of a "meaning-making" approach. *Clinical Gerontologist*, *18*(4), 3–16. doi:10.1300/J018v18n04_02

Kubler-Ross, E. (2000). *On death and dying*. New York, NY: Macmillan.

Kugelmass, H. (2016). "Sorry I'm not accepting new patients" an audit study of access to mental health care. *Journal of Health and Social Behavior*, *57*(2), 168–183. doi:10.1177/0022146516647098 PMID:27251890

Kupers, T. A. (2005). Toxic masculinity as a barrier to mental health treatment in prison. *Journal of Clinical Psychology*, *61*(6), 713–724. doi:10.1002/jclp.20105 PMID:15732090

Landreth, G. (2012). *Play therapy: The art of the relationship* (3rd ed.). New York, NY: Routledge. doi:10.4324/9780203835159

Langer, N. (2004). Resiliency and spirituality: Foundations of strength perspective counseling with the elderly. *Educational Gerontology*, *30*(7), 611–617. doi:10.1080/03601270490467038

Larke, P., & Larke, A. (2009). Teaching diversity/multicultural education courses in the academy: Sharing the voices of six professors. *Research in Higher Education*, *3*, 1–8.

Layton, E., Hardy, S. A., & Dollahite, D. (2012). Religious exploration among highly religious American adolescents. *Identity*, *12*(2), 157–184. doi:10.1080/15283488.2012.668728

Leath, S. & Chavous, T. (2018). Black women's experiences of campus racial climate and stigma at predominantly white institutions: Insights from a comparative and within-group approach for STEM and non-STEM majors. *Journal of Negro Education*, *87*(2), 125-139. doi:10. 7709/jnegroeducation.87.2.0125

Leather, P., Pyrgas, M., Beale, D., & Lawrence, C. (1998). Windows in the workplace, sunlight, view, and occupational stress. *Journal of Environment and Behavior*, *30*(6), 739–762. doi:10.1177/001391659803000601

LeBlanc, M., & Ritchie, M. (1999). Predictors of play therapy outcomes. *International Journal of Play Therapy*, *8*(2), 19–34. doi:10.1037/h0089429

Lee, C. (2015). Social justice and counseling across cultures. In B. Helihy & G. Corey (Eds.), *ACA ethical standards casebook* (7th ed.; pp. 155–168). Alexandria, VA: American Counseling Association.

Lee, C. C., & Zalkalne, E. (2018). The culturally competent counselor as an agent of social justice. In C. C. Lee (Ed.), *Multicultural issues in counseling: New approaches to diversity* (5th ed.). Alexandria, VA: American Counseling Association.

Lee, J., & Rice, C. (2007). Welcome to America? International student perceptions of discrimination. *Higher Education*, *53*(3), 381–409. doi:10.100710734-005-4508-3

Legatum Institute. (2018). *The Legatum prosperity index 2018*. Retrieved from https://prosperitysite.s3-accelerate.amazonaws.com/2515/4321/8072/2018_Prosperity_Index.pdf

Lent, R. W., Brown, S. D., & Hackett, G. (2002). Social Cognitive Career Theory. In D. Brown (Ed.), *Career choice and development* (pp. 312–369). San Francisco, CA: Jossey-Bass.

Leon, R. A., & Chmiel, J. (2013). Counseling international students: Clients from around the world. *Journal of International Students*, *3*(2), 190–192. Retrieved from http://jistudents.org/

Lew, A., & Bettner, B. L. (1996). *A parent's guide to understanding and motivating children.* Connexions Press.

Liang, B., Tracy, A., Taylor, C. A., Williams, L. M., Jordan, J. V., & Baker Miller, J. (2002). The Relational Health Indices: A study of women's relationships. *Psychology of Women Quarterly*, *26*(1), 25–35. doi:10.1111/1471-6402.00040

Lim, J. W., Honey, A., DuToit, S., Chen, Y., & Mackenzie, L. (2016). Experiences of international students from Asian backgrounds studying occupational therapy in Australia. *Australian Occupational Therapy Journal*, *63*(5), 303–311. doi:10.1111/1440-1630.12307 PMID:27302157

Lindsey, R., Reed, S., Lyons, R., Hendricks, D., Mead, A., & Butler, K. L. (2011). Sources of stress among gender and classification for African American college students. *College Student Journal*, *45*(4), 749–757.

Lockett, A., W., Gasman, M., & Nguyen, T-H. (2018). Senior level administrators and HBCUs: The role of support for Black women's success in STEM. *Education Sciences, 8*(2), 1-12. doi:103390/educsci8020048

Loden, M., & Rosener, J. B. (1991). *Workforce America: Managing employee diversity as a vital resource*. New York, NY: McGraw-Hill Education.

Lopez, M. H., Taylor, P., Funk, C., & Gonzalez-Barrera, A. (2013). *On immigration policy, deportation relief seen as more important than citizenship.* Retrieved from http://www.pewhispanic.org/2013/12/19/on-immigration-policy-deportation-relief-seen-as-more-important-than-citizenship/

Loria, H., & Caughy, M. (2018). Prevalence of adverse childhood experiences in low-income Latino immigrant and nonimmigrant children. *The Journal of Pediatrics*, *192*, 209–216. doi:10.1016/j.jpeds.2017.09.056 PMID:29246345

Louma, J., Hayes, S. C., & Walser, R. (2017). *Learning ACT* (2nd ed.). Oakland, CA: New Harbinger Publications, Inc.

Louv, R. (2005). *Last child in the woods: Saving our children from nature-deficit disorder*. Chapel Hill, NC: Algonquin Books.

Lundberg, C. A., Schreiner, L. A., Hovaguimian, K., & Miller, S. S. (2007). First generation status and student race/ethnicity as distinct predictors of student involvement and -learning. *NASPA*, *44*(1), 57–83.

Lynch, K. D. (2008). Gender roles and the American academe: A case study of graduate student mothers. *Gender and Education*, *20*(6), 585–605. doi:10.1080/09540250802213099

Lyon, G. E. (1999). *Where I am from: Where poems come from*. Retrieved from https://www.sausd.us/cms/lib/CA01000471/Centricity/Domain/3043/I%20Am%20From%20Poem.pdf

Maas, J. J., Verheij, R. A., de Vries, S. S., Spreeuwenberg, P. P., Schellevis, F. G., & Groenewegen, P. P. (2009). Morbidity is related to a green living environment. *Journal of Epidemiology and Community Health*, *63*(12), 967–973. doi:10.1136/jech.2008.079038 PMID:19833605

Mahalik, J. R., Good, G. E., & Englar-Carlson, M. (2003). Masculinity scripts, presenting concerns, and help seeking: Implications for practice and training. *Professional Psychology, Research and Practice*, *34*(2), 123–131. doi:10.1037/0735-7028.34.2.123

Malchiodi, C. (2007). *The art therapy sourcebook*. New York: McGraw – Hill.

Malott, K. M., Schaefle, S., Paone, T. R., Cates, J., & Haizlip, B. (2019). Challenges and coping mechanisms of Whites committed to antiracism. *Journal of Counseling and Development*, *97*(1), 86–97. doi:10.1002/jcad.12238

Mappingyourfuture.org. (2017). *Guide to life after high School*. Retrieved from https://www.mappingyourfuture.org/guidetolife/

Markus, E., Weingarten, A., Duplessi, Y., & Jones, J. (2010). Lesbian couples seeking pregnancy with donor insemination. *Journal of Midwifery & Women's Health*, *55*(2), 124–132. doi:10.1016/j.jmwh.2009.09.014 PMID:20189131

Martinez, J. I., Gudiño, O. G., & Lau, A. S. (2013). Problem-specific racial/ethnic disparities in pathways from maltreatment exposure to specialty mental health service use for youth in child welfare. *Child Maltreatment*, *18*(2), 98–107. doi:10.1177/1077559513483549 PMID:23630401

Marx, H. A., & Moss, D. M. (2011). *My cultural awareness profile (MyCAP): A cultural awareness reflection tool for pre-service teachers*. Retrieved from http://www.nafsa.org/_/File/_/mycap_tool.pdf

Marzullo, A., & Libman, A. J. (2009). *Research overview: HAte crimes and violence against lesbian, gay, bisexual and transgender people*. Washington, DC: Human Rights Campaign Foundation. Retrieved from http://www.hrc.org/resources/entry/hate-crimes-and-violence-against-lgbt-people

Maslow, A. H. (1954). *Motivation and personality*. New York, NY: Harper & Row.

Mason, M. A., Goulden, M., & Frasch, K. (2009). Why graduate students reject the fast track. *Academe*, *95*(1), 11–16. Retrieved from https://www.aaup.org/article/why-graduate-students-reject-fast-track/#.XHdMcflKjIU

Masuda, A. (2014). *Mindfulness & Acceptance in multicultural competency: A contextual approach to sociocultural diversity in theory & practice*. Oakland, CA: New Harbinger Publications, Inc.

Masuda, A., Anderson, P. L., & Edmonds, J. (2012). Help-seeking attitudes, mental health stigma, and self-concealment among African American college students. *Journal of Black Studies*, *43*(7), 773–786. doi:10.1177/0021934712445806

Matthews, J. J., Barden, S. M., & Sherrell, R. S. (2018). Examining the relationships between multicultural counseling competence, multicultural self-efficacy, and ethnic identity development of practicing counselors. *Journal of Mental Health Counseling*, *40*(2), 129–141. doi:10.17744/mehc.40.2.03

Ma, Y., & Liu, Y. (2017). Entry and degree attainment in STEM: The intersection of gender and race/ethnicity. *Social Sciences*, *6*(3), 1–17. doi:10.3390osci6030089

McClure, J. W. (2007). International graduates' cross-cultural adjustment: Experiences, coping strategies, and suggested programmatic responses. *Teaching in Higher Education*, *12*(2), 199–217. doi:10.1080/13562510701191976

McConkie, B. (1966). *Mormon doctrine* (2nd ed.). Salt Lake City, UT: Bookcraft.

McGee, E., Bentley, L. (2017). The equity ethic: Black and Latinx college students reengineering their STEM careers towards justice. *American Journal of Education, 124*(1), 1-36. doi:10.1086/693954

McGee, E. (2018). Black genius, Asian fail: The detriment of stereotype lift and stereotype threat in high-achieving Asian and Black STEM students. *AERA Open*, *4*(4), 1–16. doi:10.1177/2332858418816658

McIntosh, P. (1989, July/August). White privilege: Unpacking the invisible knapsack. *Peace and Freedom,* 8-10.

McLaughlin, A. N., & Randolph, K. A. (2012). Development of school support scale for low-income mothers in college. *Research on Social Work Practice*, *22*(1), 68–76. doi:10.1177/1049731511415122

McNair, R., Dempsey, D., Wise, S., & Perlesz, A. (2002). Lesbian parenting: Issues, strengths,and challenges. *Family Matters (Melbourne, Vic.)*, *63*, 40–49.

McPherson, E. (2014). Informal in science, math, and engineering majors for African American female undergraduates. *Global Education Review*, *1*(4), 96–113.

Meany-Walen, K. K., Bratton, S., & Kottman, T. (2014). Effects of Adlerian play therapy on reducing students' disruptive behaviors. *Journal of Counseling and Development*, *92*(1), 47–56. doi:10.1002/j.1556-6676.2014.00129.x

Meany-Walen, K. K., Kottman, T., Bullis, Q., & Dillman Taylor, D. (2015). Adlerian play therapy with children with externalizing behaviors: Single case design. *Journal of Counseling and Development*, *93*, 294–428. doi:10.1002/jcad.12040

Mengesha, M., & Ward, E. C. (2012). Psychotherapy with African American women with depression: Is it okay to talk about their religious/spiritual beliefs? *Religions*, *3*(4), 19–26. doi:10.3390/rel3010019

Mereish, E. H., & Poteat, V. P. (2015). The conditions under which growth-fostering relationships promote resilience and alleviate psychological distress among sexual minorities: Applications of relational cultural theory. *Psychology of Sexual Orientation and Gender Diversity*, *2*(3), 339–344. doi:10.1037gd0000121 PMID:26380836

Mersky, J. P., Topitzes, J., & Reynolds, A. J. (2013). Impacts of adverse childhood experiences on health, mental health, and substance use in early adulthood: A cohort study of an urban, minority sample in the U.S. *Child Abuse & Neglect*, *37*(11), 917–925. doi:10.1016/j.chiabu.2013.07.011 PMID:23978575

Mesidor, J. K., & Sly, K. F. (2014). Mental help-seeking intentions among international and African American college students: An application of the theory of planner behavior. *Journal of International Students*, *4*(2), 137–149.

Meyer, E. G., Hall-Clark, B. N., Hamaoka, D., & Peterson, A. L. (2015). Assessment of military cultural competence: A pilot study. *Academic Psychiatry*, *39*(4), 382–388. doi:10.100740596-015-0328-7 PMID:26054708

Meyer, I. (2010). Identity, stress, and resilience in lesbians, gay men, and bisexuals of color. *The Counseling Psychologist*, *38*(3), 442–454. doi:10.1177/0011000009351601 PMID:24347674

Meyer, O. L., & Zane, N. (2013). The influence of race and ethnicity in clients' experiences of mental health treatment. *Journal of Community Psychology*, *41*(7), 884–901. doi:10.1002/jcop.21580 PMID:25400301

Miller, J. B. (1986). *What do we mean by relationships?* (Work in Progress No. 22). Wellesley, MA: Stone Center Working Paper Series.

Miller, J. B. (1976). *Toward a new psychology of women*. Boston: Beacon.

Miller, J. B., & Stiver, I. P. (1997). *The healing connection: How women form connections in therapy and in life*. Boston, MA: Beacon Press.

Miller, J. B., & Stiver, I. P. (1997). *The healing connection: How women form relationships in therapy and in life*. Boston: Beacon Press.

Minuchin, S. (1993). *Family healing: Strategies for hope and understanding*. New York, NY: The Free Press.

Mittal, M., & Wieling, E. (2006). Training experiences of international doctoral students in marriage and family therapy. *Journal of Marital and Family Therapy*, *32*(3), 369–383. doi:10.1111/j.1752-0606.2006.tb01613.x PMID:16933440

Moakler, M. W. Jr, & Kim, M. M. (2014). College major choice in STEM: Revisiting confidence and demographic factors. *The Career Development Quarterly*, *62*(2), 128–142. doi:10.1002/j.2161-0045.2014.00075.x

Morgan, A. (2000). *What is narrative therapy?: An easy-to-read introduction*. Adelaide, Australia: Dulwich Centre Publications.

Morrison, K. S., & Hopkins, R. (2019). Cultural identity, Africultural coping strategies, and depression as predictors of suicidal ideations and attempts amongst African American female college students. *The Journal of Black Psychology*, *45*(1), 3–25. doi:10.1177/0095798418813511

Morrison, M. O. (2009). Adlerian play therapy with a traumatized boy. *Journal of Individual Psychology*, *65*, 57–68.

Morton, T., & Parsons, E. D. (2018). #BlackGirlMagic: The identity conceptualization of Black women in undergraduate STEM education. *Science Education*, *102*(16), 1363–1393. doi:10.1002ce.21477

Murray-Garcia, J. L., Harrell, S., Garcia, J. A., Gizzi, E., & Simms-Mackey, P. (2014). Dialogue as a skill: Training a health professions workforce that can talk about race and racism. *The American Journal of Orthopsychiatry*, *84*(5), 590–596. doi:10.1037/ort0000026 PMID:25265221

Musu-Gullette, L., de Brey, C., McFarland, J., Hussar, W., Sonneberg, W., & Wilkinson-Flicker, S. (2017). *Status and trends in the education of racial and ethnic groups 2017 (NCES 2017-051)*. Washington, DC: U. S. Department of Education, National Center for Education Statistics. Retrieved from https://nces.ed.gov/pubs2017/2017051.pdf

Myers, J. (2007). Combating ageism: Advocacy for older persons. In C. C. Lee (Ed.), *Counseling for social justice* (2nd ed.; pp. 51–73). Alexandria, VA: American Counseling Association.

Myers, J. E., Sweeney, T. J., & Witmer, J. M. (2000). The wheel of wellness counseling for wellness: A holistic model for treatment planning. *Journal of Counseling and Development*, *78*(3), 251–266. doi:10.1002/j.1556-6676.2000.tb01906.x

Myers-Walls, J. A., Frias, L., Kyong-Ah, K., Meryl Ko, M. M., & Lu, T. (2011). Living life in two worlds: The stress of Asian international graduate student parents and spouses. *Journal of Comparative Family Studies*, *42*(4), 455–478. Retrieved from https://www.jstor.org/stable/41604463. doi:10.3138/jcfs.42.4.455

Nadal, K. L., Wong, Y., Issa, M., Meterko, V., Leon, J., & Wideman, M. (2011). Sexual orientation microaggressions: Processes and coping mechanisms for lesbian, gay, and bisexual individuals. *Journal of LGBT Issues in Counseling*, *5*(1), 21–46. doi:10.1080/15538605.2011.554606

Nassar-McMillan, S. C. (2010). Counseling Arab Americans. Boston, MA: Brooks-Cole: Cengage.

Nassar-McMillan, S. C., Al-Qimlass, A., & Gonzalez, L. M. (2018). Individuals and families of Arab descent. In D. G. Hays & B. T. Erford (Eds.), *Developing multicultural counseling competence: A systems approach* (pp. 87–104). New York, NY: Pearson.

National Council on Aging. (2018). *Healthy aging facts*. Retrieved from www.ncoa.org

National Foster Youth Institute. (2017). *51 Useful Aging Out of Foster Care Statistics*. Retrieved from, https://www.nfyi.org/51-useful-aging-out-of-foster-care-statistics-social-race-media/

National Science Board. (2016). *Science and engineering indicators* (NSB-2016-1). Arlington, VA: National Science Foundation. Retrieved from https://ww.nsf.gov/statistics/2016/nsb 20161/uploads/1/nsb20161.pdf

Nayar-Bhalerao, S. (2014). *Perceptions of international students in CACREP-accredited counseling programs* (Doctoral Dissertation). Retrieved from ProQuest Dissertations and Theses database. (UMI No. 3568184)

Nelsen, J. (2006). *Positive discipline* (Rev. ed.). New York: Ballantine Books.

Nelsen, J., Lott, L., & Glenn, S. (2013). *Positive discipline in the classroom: Developing mutual respect, cooperation, and responsibility in your classroom* (4th ed.). New York, NY: Three Rivers Press.

Neri, D. F., & Shappell, S. A. (1994). The effect of combat on the work/rest schedules and fatigue of naval aviators during Operations Desert Shield and Desert Storm. *Military Psychology*, *6*(3), 141–162. doi:10.120715327876mp0603_1

Neville, H. A., Worthington, R. L., & Spanierman, L. B. (2001). Race, power, and multicultural counseling psychology: Understanding White privilege and color-blind racial attitudes. In J. G. Ponterotto, J. M. Casas, L. A. Suzuki, & C. M. Alexander (Eds.), *Handbook of multicultural counseling* (pp. 257–288). Thousand Oaks, CA, US: Sage Publications, Inc.

Newcomb, M. E., & Mustanski, B. (2010). Internalized homophobia and internalizing mental health problems: A meta-analytic review. *Clinical Psychology Review*, *30*(8), 1019–10129. doi:10.1016/j.cpr.2010.07.003 PMID:20708315

Newhill, C. E., Safran, J. D., & Muran, J. C. (2000). *Negotiating the therapeutic alliance: A relational treatment guide*. New York, NY: Guilford Press.

Newman, K. (2017). *A look into older adults state of mind*. Retrieved from www.usnews.com

Ng, K. M. (2006). International students in CACREP accredited counseling programs. *Journal of Professional Counseling, Practice, Theory, & Research*, *34*(1-2), 20–32. doi:10.1080/15566382.2006.12033821

Ng, K. M., & Smith, S. D. (2009). Perceptions and experiences of international trainees in counseling and related programs. *International Journal for the Advancement of Counseling*, *31*(1), 57–70. doi:10.100710447-008-9068-7

North Coast Women's Care Medical Group, Inc. v. San Diego County Superior Court, 189 P.3d959 (Cal. 2008).

O'Brien, C., Keith, J., & Shoemaker, L. (2015). Don't tell: Military culture and male rape. *Psychological Services*, *12*(4), 357–365. doi:10.1037er0000049 PMID:26524277

O'Brien, L. T., Blodorn, A., Adams, G., Garcia, D. M., & Hammer, E. (2015). Ethnic variation in gender-STEM stereotypes and STEM participation: An intersectional approach. *Cultural Diversity & Ethnic Minority Psychology*, *21*(2), 169–180. doi:10.1037/a0037944 PMID:25244590

Oberst, U., & Stewart, A. (2003). *Adlerian psychotherapy: An advanced approach to individual psychology*. New York, NY: Brunner-Routledge.

Olshansky, E. (2003). A theoretical explanation for previously infertile mothers' vulnerability to depression. *Journal of Nursing Scholarship*, *35*(3), 263–268. doi:10.1111/j.1547-5069.2003.00263.x PMID:14562495

Orbe, M. P. (2004). Negotiating multiple identities within multiple frames: Ana analysis of first-generation college students. *Communication Education*, *53*(2), 131–149. doi:10.1080/03634520410001682401

Orbe, M. P. (2008). Theorizing multidimensional identity negotiation: Reflections on the lived experiences of first-generation college students. *New Directions for Child and Adolescent Development*, *120*(120), 81–95. doi:10.1002/cd.217 PMID:18521866

Otting, T. L., & Prosek, E. A. (2016). Integrating feminist therapy and expressive arts with adolescent clients. *Journal of Creativity in Mental Health*, *11*(1), 78–89. doi:10.1080/15401383.2015.1019167

Palmer, R. T., Arroyo, A., & Flowers, A. M. (2017). *The African American students' guide to STEM career*. Westport, CT: Greenwood.

Parent, M. C., Gobble, T. D., & Rochlen, A. (2018). Social media behavior, toxic masculinity and depression. *Psychology of Men & Masculinity*. doi:10.1037/men0000156

Parent, M. C., & Moradi, B. (2009). Confirmatory factor analysis of the Conformity to Masculine Norms Inventory-46. *Psychology of Men & Masculinity*, *12*, 339–353. doi:10.1037/a0021904

Parent, M. C., Moradi, B., Rummell, C. M., & Tokar, D. M. (2011). Evidence of construct distinctiveness for conformity to masculine norms. *Psychology of Men & Masculinity*, *12*(4), 354–367. http://dx.doi.0rg/10.1037/a0023837. doi:10.1037/a0023837

Parks-Yancy, R. (2012). Interaction into opportunities: Career management for low-income, first-generation African American college students. *Journal of College Student Development*, *53*(4), 510–523. doi:10.1353/csd.2012.0052

Pasco Fearon, R. M., & Belsky, J. (2011). Infant-mother attachment and the growth of externalizing problems across the primary- school years. *Journal of Child Psychology and Psychiatry, and Allied Disciplines*, *52*(7), 782–791. doi:10.1111/j.1469-7610.2010.02350.x PMID:21214546

Passel, J. S., & Cohn, D. (2008). U.S. population projections: 2005-2050. *Pew Research Center*. Retrieved from www.pewhispanic.org/2008/02/11/us-population-projections-2005-2050

Patterson, F. L., & Staton, A. R. (2009). Adult-acquired traumatic brain injury: Existential implications and clinical considerations. *Journal of Mental Health Counseling*, *31*(2), 149–163. doi:10.17744/mehc.31.2.1p42572p01435173

Pecora, P. J., Williams, J., Kessler, R. C., Hiripi, E., O'Brien, K., Emerson, J., & Torres, D. (2006). Assessing the educational achievements of adults who were formerly placed in family foster care. *Child & Family Social Work*, *11*(3), 220–231. doi:10.1111/j.1365-2206.2006.00429.x

Peterson, G. W., Sampson, J. P., Lenz, J. G., & Reardon, R. C. (2002). A cognitive information processing approach to career problem solving and decision making. In D. Brown & ... (Eds.), *Career choice and development* (pp. 312–369). San Francisco, CA: Jossey-Bass.

Petts, R. J., & Desmond, S. A. (2016). Adolescence and emerging adulthood. In D. Yamane (Ed.), *Handbook of religion and society* (pp. 241–262). New York, NY: Springer. doi:10.1007/978-3-319-31395-5_13

Pew Forum on Religious and Public Life. (2011, January 27). *The future of the global Muslim population: Projections for 2010-2030*. Retrieved from https://web.archive.org/web/20110202043556/http://pewforum.org/The-Future-of-the-Global-Muslim-Population.aspx

Pew Research Center. (2017a, July 26). *U.S. Muslims concerned about their place in society but continue to believe in the American dream*. Retrieved from http://www.pewforum.org/2017/07/26/findings-from-pew-research-centers-2017-survey-of-us-muslims/

Pew Research Center. (2017b, October 3). *Many countries favor specific religions, officially or unofficially*. Retrieved from http://www.pewforum.org/2017/10/03/many-countries-favor-specific-religions-officially-or-unofficially/

Phillips, D., & Lauterbach, D. (2017). American Muslim immigrant mental health: The role of racism and mental health stigma. *The Journal of Muslim Mental Health*, *11*(1), 39–56. doi:10.3998/jmmh.10381607.0011.103

Phinney, J. S., Horenczyk, G., Liebkind, K., & Vedder, P. (2001). Ethnic identity, immigration, and well-being: An interactional perspective. *The Journal of Social Issues*, *57*(3), 493–510. doi:10.1111/0022-4537.00225

Piel, M. H. (2018). Challenges in the Transition to Higher Education for Foster Care Youth. *New Directions for Community Colleges*, *2018*(181), 21–28. doi:10.1002/cc.20288

Pincus, S. H., House, R., Christenson, J., & Adler, L. E. (2007). *The emotional cycle of deployment*. St. Louis, MO: West Point Parents Club. Retrieved from http://www.west-point.org/parent/wppc-st_louis/Deployment/TheEmotionalCycleofDeployment.pdf

Pinder, P. J., & Blackwell, E. L. (2014). The "Black Girl Turn" in research on gender, race, and science education: Toward exploring and understanding the early experiences of Black females in science, a literature review. *Journal of African American Studies*, *18*(1), 63–71. doi:10.100712111-013-9255-4

Pistorello, J. (Ed.). (2013). *Mindfulness and acceptance for counseling sollege Students: Theory and practical applications for intervention, prevention, and outreach*. Oakland, CA: Context Press.

Pratt, I. S., Harwood, H. B., Cavazos, J. T., & Ditzfeld, C. P. (2017). Should I stay or should I go? Retention of first-generation college students. *Journal of College Student Retention*, 1–14. doi:10.1177/1521025117690868

Priester, P. E., Jones, J. E., Jackson-Bailey, C. M., Jana-Masri, A., Jordan, E. X., & Metz, A. J. (2008). An analysis of content and instructional strategies in multicultural counseling courses. *Journal of Multicultural Counseling and Development*, *36*(1), 29–39. doi:10.1002/j.2161-1912.2008.tb00067.x

Prieto-Welch, S. L. (2016). International student mental health. *New Directions for Student Services*, *2016*(156), 53–63. doi:10.1002s.20191

Prosek, E. A., Burgin, E. E., Atkins, K. M., Wehrman, J. D., Fenell, D. L., Carter, C., & Green, L. (2018). Competencies for counseling military populations. *Journal of Military and Government Counseling*, *6*(2), 87–98.

Prospero, M., & Vohra-Gupta, S. (2007). First generation college students: Motivation, integration, and academic achievement. *Community College Journal of Research and Practice*, *31*(12), 963–975. doi:10.1080/10668920600902051

Rai, G. S. (2002). Meeting the educational needs of international students: A perspective from US schools. *International Social Work*, *45*(1), 21–33. doi:10.1177/0020872802045001312

Rassool, H. G. (2016). *Islamic counselling: An introduction to theory and practice*. New York, NY: Routledge.

Ratts, M. J., Sing, A. A., Nassar-McMillan, S., Butler, S. K., & McCullough, J. R. (2015). *Multicultural and social justice counseling competencies*. Retrieved from http://www.counseling.org/knowledge-center/competencies

Ratts, M. J., Singh, A. A., Nassar-McMillan, S., & McCullough, J. R. (2015). *Multicultural and Social Justice Counseling Competencies*. Retrieved from http://www.counseling.org/knowledge-center/competencies

Ratts, M. J., Singh, A. A., Nassar-McMillan, S., Butler, S. K., & McCullough, J. R. (2015). *Multicultural and social justice competencies*. Retrieved from https://www.counseling.org/docs/default-source/competencies/multicultural-and-social-justice-counseling-competencies.pdf?sfvrsn=20

Ratts, M. J., Singh, A. A., Nassar-McMillan, S., Butler, S. K., & McCullough, J. R. (2015). *Multicultural and social justice counseling competencies*. Retrieved from http://www. counseling.org/docs/default-source/competencies/multicultural-and-social-justice-counselingcompetencies.pdf?sfvrsn=20

Ratts, M. J., Singh, A. A., Nassar-McMillan, S., Butler, S. K., & McCullough, J. R. (2015). *Multicultural and Social Justice Counseling Competencies*. Retrieved from https://www.counseling.org/docs/default-source/competencies/multicultural-and-social- justice-counseling-competencies.pdf?sfvrsn=20

Ratts, M. J., Singh, A. A., Nassar-McMillan, S., Butler, S.K., & McCullough, J.R. (2015). *Multicultural and social justice counseling competencies*. Retrieved from https://www.counseling.org/docs/default-source/competencies/multicultural-and-social-justice-counseling-competencies.pdf?sfvrsn=20

Ratts, M. J., & Pedersen, P. B. (2014). *Counseling for multiculturalism and social justice: Integration, theory, and application* (4th ed.). Alexandria, VA: American Counseling Association.

Ratts, M. J., Singh, A. A., Nassar-McMillan, S., Butler, S. K., & McCullough, J. R. (2015). Multicultural and social justice counseling competencies: Guidelines for the counseling profession. *Journal of Multicultural Counseling and Development*, *44*(1), 28–48. doi:10.1002/jmcd.12035

Ratts, M., Singh, A., Nassar-McMillan, S., Butler, K., & McCullough, J. (2016). *Multicultural and social justice counseling competencies*. Alexandria, VA: American Counseling Association.

Rausch, M. A., & Wikoff, H. D. (2017). Addressing concerns with lesbian couples experiencing fertility treatment: Using Relational Cultural Theory. *Journal of LGBT Issues in Counseling*, *11*(3), 142–155. doi:10.1080/15538605.2017.1346494

Ray, D. (2011). *Advanced play therapy: Essential conditions, knowledge, and skills for child practice*. New York, NY: Routledge. doi:10.4324/9780203837269

Redmond, S. A., Wilcox, S. L., Campbell, S., Kim, A., Finney, K., Barr, K., & Hassan, A. M. (2015). A brief introduction to the military workplace culture. *Journal of Prevention. Assessment & Rehabilitation*, *50*(1), 9–20. PMID:25547167

Reese, R. F., & Myers, J. E. (2012). EcoWellness: The missing factor in holistic wellness models. *Journal of Counseling and Development*, *90*(4), 400–406. doi:10.1002/j.1556-6676.2012.00050.x

Reid, L. M., & Dixon, A. L. (2012). The counseling supervision needs of international students in US institutions of higher education: A culturally-sensitive supervision model for counselor educators. *Journal for International Counselor Education*, *4*(1), 29–41. Retrieved from https://digitalscholarship.unlv.edu/cgi/viewcontent.cgi?article=1032&context=jice

Rendón Linares, L., & Muñoz, S. (2011). Revisiting validation theory: Theoretical foundations, applications, and extensions. *Enrollment Management Journal: Student Access, Finance, and Success in Higher Education*, *5*(2), 12–28.

Rendón, L. (1994). Validating culturally diverse students: Toward a new model of learning and student development. *Innovative Higher Education*, *19*(1), 33–51. doi:10.1007/BF01191156

Reyes-Rodriguez, M. L., Sala, M., Von Holle, A., Unikel, C., Bulik, C. M., Camara-Fuentes, L., & Suarez-Torres, A. (2011). A description of disordered eating behaviors in Latino males. *Journal of American College Health*, *59*(4), 266–272. doi:10.1080/07448481.2010.502205 PMID:21308586

Richardson, L. L. H., Hammer, T. R., & Chan, C. D. (2018, September). Relational-cultural theory: A social justice perspective of career development in the workplace. *Career Convergence*. Retrieved from https://www.ncda.org/aws/NCDA/pt/sd/news_article/185956/_PARENT/CC_layout_details/false

Richards, P. S., & Bergin, A. E. (2005). *A spiritual strategy for counseling and psychotherapy* (2nd ed.). Washington, DC: American Psychological Association. doi:10.1037/11214-000

Robb, C. (2006). *This changes everything: The relational revolution in psychology*. New York: Farrar, Straus & Giroux.

Rochlen, A. B., McKelley, R. A., Suizzo, M. A., & Scaringi, V. (2008). Predictors of relationship satisfaction, psychological well-being, and life satisfaction among stat-at-home fathers. *Psychology of Men & Masculinity*, *9*(1), 17–28. doi:10.1037/1524-9220.9.1.17

Rodriguez, A. L., Guido-DiBrito, F., Torres, V., & Talbot, D. (2000). Latina college students: Issues and challenges for the 21st century. *NASPA Journal*, *37*(3), 511–227. doi:10.2202/0027-6014.1111

Rogalin, C. L., & Brooks, J. E. (2018). Lesbians achieving pregnancy: The intersections of social location and the heteronormative medicalization of infertility. *Sociology Compass*, *12*(11), 1–11. doi:10.1111oc4.12637

Rogers, C. R. (1959). *A theory of therapy, personality, and interpersonal relationships: As developed in the client-centered framework* (Vol. 3). New York, NY: McGraw-Hill.

Rogers, C. R. (1977). *Carl Rogers on personal power*. New York, NY: Delacorte Press.

Rondini, A. (2012). "I thought I was so dumb…": Low-income first generation college students, inequities in academic preparation and reference group theory. In T. Hicks & A. Pitre (Eds.), *Research Studies in Higher Education: Educating Multicultural College Students* (pp. 161–187). Lanham, MD: University Press of America, Inc.

Rosa, K., & Mensah, F. M. (2016). Educational pathways of Black women physicists: Stories of experiencing and overcoming obstacles in life. *Physical Review Physics Education Research*, *12*(2), 1–15. doi:10.1103/PhysRevPhysEducRes.12.020113

Roscoe, L. J. (2009). Wellness: A review of theory and measurement for counselors. *Journal of Counseling and Development*, *87*(2), 216–226. doi:10.1002/j.1556-6678.2009.tb00570.x

Rosenberg, A., Groves, A. K., & Blankenship, K. M. (2017). Comparing Black and White drug offenders: Implications for racial disparities in criminal justice and reentry policy and programming. *Journal of Drug Issues*, *47*(1), 132–142. doi:10.1177/0022042616678614 PMID:28966392

Rostosky, S. S., Riggle, E. D. B., Horne, S. G., & Miller, A. D. (2009). Marriage amendments and psychological distress in lesbian, gay, and bisexual (LGB) adults. *Journal of Counseling Psychology*, *56*(1), 56–66. doi:10.1037/a0013609

Rotter, J. C., Horak, R. A. Jr, & Heidt, H. M. (1999). Incorporating children's drawings as early recollections in Adlerian psychotherapy. *Journal of Individual Psychology*, *55*, 316–327.

Russell, M. L., & Russell, J. A. (2015). Black American undergraduate women at a PWI: Switching majors in STEM. *Negro Educational Review*, *66*(1-4), 101–125.

Russo, T. J., & Fallon, M. A. (2015). Coping with stress: Supporting the needs of military families and their children. *Early Childhood Education Journal*, *43*(5), 407–416. doi:10.100710643-014-0665-2

Sacks, V., & Murphey, D. (2018). *The prevalence of adverse childhood experiences, nationally, by state, and by race or ethnicity*. Retrieved from https://www.childtrends.org/publications/prevalence-adverse-childhood-experiences-nationally-state-race-ethnicity

Sacks, V., Murphey, D., & Moore, K. (2014). *Adverse childhood experiences: National and state level prevalence* (Research Brief No. 2014-28). Retrieved from https://childtrends-ciw49tixgw5lbab.stackpathdns.com/wp-content/uploads/2014/07/Brief-adverse-childhood-experiences_FINAL.pdf

Saenz, V. B., Hurtado, S., Barrera, D., Wolf, D. S., & Yeung, F. P. (2007). *First in the family a profile of first-generation college students at four year institutions since 1971*. The Foundation for Independent Education. Retrieved from http://www.gseis.ucla.edu/heri/ PDFs/resSummary051807-Firstgen.pdf

Sakamoto, I. (2007). A critical examination of immigrant acculturation: Toward and anti-oppressive social work model with immigrant adults in pluralistic society. *British Journal of Social Work*, *37*(3), 515–535. doi:10.1093/bjsw/bcm024

Sandhu, D. S., & Asrabadi, B. R. (1994). Development of an acculturative stress scale for international students: Preliminary findings. *Psychological Reports*, *75*(1), 435–448. doi:10.2466/pr0.1994.75.1.435 PMID:7809315

Santiago, D. A., Calderón Galdeano, E., & Taylor, M. (2015). *Factbook 2015: The condition of Latinos in education*. Retrieved from http://www.nccpsafety.org/assets/files/library/ The_Condition_of_Latinos_in_Education.pdf

Schneider, K. J., & Krug, O. T. (2010). *Theories of psychotherapy series: Existential humanistic therapy*. Washington, DC: American Psychological Association.

Schreyer, R., Williams, D. R., Haggard, L., Easley, A. T., Passineau, J. F., & Driver, B. L. (1990). Episodic versus continued wilderness participation—implications for self-concept enhancement. In A. T. Easley, J. F. Passineau, & B. L. Driver (Eds.), The use of wilderness for personal growth, therapy, and education (General Technical Report RM-193, pp. 23–26). Fort Collins, CO: Rocky Mountain Forestand Range Experiment Station.

Segal, M. W., Smith, D. G., Segal, D. R., & Canuso, A. A. (2016). The role of leadership and peer behaviors in the performance and well-being of women in combat: Historical perspectives, unit integration, and family issues. *Military Medicine*, *181*(1S), 28–39. doi:10.7205/MILMED-D-15-00342 PMID:26741899

Seponski, D. M. (2016). A feminist-informed integration of emotionally focused and solution-focused therapies. *Journal of Family Psychotherapy*, *27*(4), 221–242. doi:10.1080/08975353.2016.1235430

Serres, N. S. (2017). Sexual harassment in the workplace in a #MeToo world. *Forbes*. Retrieved from https://www.forbes.com/sites/forbeshumanresourcescouncil/2017/12/20/sexual-harassment-in-the-workplace-in-a-metoo-world/#6ea3ae615a42

Shahid, N. N., Nelson, T., & Cardemil, E. V. (2018). Lift every voice: Exploring the stressors and coping mechanisms of Black college women attending predominantly white institutions. *The Journal of Black Psychology*, *44*(1), 3–24. doi:10.1177/0095798417732415

Sheperis, D., & Sheperis, C. (2015). *Clinical mental health counseling: Fundamentals of applied practice*. Upper Saddle River, NJ: Pearson.

Sherry, M., Thomas, P., & Chui, W. (2009). International students: A vulnerable student population. *Higher Education*, *60*(1), 33–46. doi:10.100710734-009-9284-z

Shetterly, M. L. (2016). *Hidden figures: The American dream and the untold story of the Black women mathematicians who helped with the space race* (1st ed.). New York, NY: William Morrow.

Sheu, H., & Fukuyama, M. A. (2007). Counseling international students from East Asia. In H. D. Singaravelu & M. Pope (Eds.), *A handbook for counseling international students in the United States* (pp. 173–193). Alexandria, VA: American Counseling Association.

Simpson, D., Bruckheimer, J., & Scott, T. (1986). *Top gun* [Motion picture]. United States of America: Paramount Pictures.

Singh, A. A., & Moss, L. (2016). Using relational-cultural theory in LGBTQQ counseling: Addressing heterosexism and enhancing relational competencies. *Journal of Counseling and Development*, *94*(4), 398–404. doi:10.1002/jcad.12098

Snow, M. S., Buckley, M. R., & Williams, S. C. (1999). Case study using Adlerian play therapy. *Journal of Individual Psychology*, *55*(3), 288–297.

Snyder, T. D., de Brey, C., & Dillow, S. A. (2016). *Digest of Education Statistics 2015 (NCES 2016-014)*. Washington, DC: National Center for Education Statistics, Institute of Education Sciences, U.S. Department of Education.

Softas-Nall, S., & Woody, W. D. (2017). The loss of human connection to nature: Revitalizing selfhood and meaning in life through the ideas of Rollo May. *Ecopsychology*, *9*(4), 241–252. doi:10.1089/eco.2017.0020

Soheilian, S., & Inman, A. G. (2009). Middle Eastern Americans: The effects of stigma on attitudes toward counseling. *The Journal of Muslim Mental Health*, *4*(2), 139–158. doi:10.1080/15564900903245766

Spanierman, L. B., & Smith, L. (2017). Roles and responsibilities of White allies: Implications for research, teaching, and practice. *The Counseling Psychologist*, *45*(5), 606–617. doi:10.1177/0011000017717712

Springer, P. R., Abbott, D. A., & Reisbig, A. M. (2009). Therapy with Muslim couples and families: Basic guidelines for effective practices. *The Family Journal*, *17*(3), 229–235. doi:10.1177/1066480709337798

Stephens, N. M., Fryberg, S. A., Markus, H. R., Johnson, C. S., & Covarrubias, R. (2012). Unseen disadvantage: How American universities' focus on independence undermines the academic performance of first-generation college students. *Journal of Personality and Social Psychology*, *102*(6), 1178–1197. doi:10.1037/a0027143 PMID:22390227

Stevens, P. W., & Smith, R. L. (2018). *Substance use counseling theory and practice*. New York, NY: Pearson.

Strom, T. Q., Gavian, M. E., Possis, E., Loughlin, J., Bui, T., Linardatos, E., ... Siegel, W. (2012). Cultural and ethical considerations when working with military personnel and veterans: A primer for VA training programs. *Training and Education in Professional Psychology*, *6*(2), 67–75. doi:10.1037/a0028275

Strong, T., & Pyle, N. R. (2009). Constructing a conversational "miracle": Examining the "miracle question" as it is used in therapeutic dialogue. *Journal of Constructivist Psychology*, *22*(4), 328–353. doi:10.1080/10720530903114001

Stuart, J., & Ward, C. (2011). A question of balance: Exploring the acculturation and adaptation of Muslim immigrant youth. *Psychological Intervention*, *20*(3), 255–267. doi:10.5093/in2011v20n3a3

Substance Abuse and Mental Health Services Administration. (2018). *National-level comparison of mental health estimates from The National Survey on Drug Use and Health (NSDUH) and other data sources*. Retrieved from https://www.samhsa.gov/data/sites/default/files/cbhsq-reports/NSDUHC2MentalHealthEst2018.pdf

Sue, D. W. (2010). *Microaggressions in everyday life: Race, gender, and sexual orientation*. Hoboken, NJ: John Wiley & Sons.

Sue, D. W., Ivey, A. E., & Pedersen, P. B. (1996). *A theory of multicultural counseling and therapy*. Pacific Grove, CA: Brooks Cole.

Sue, D. W., Rivera, D. P., Capodilupo, C. M., Lin, A. I., & Torino, G. C. (2010). Racial dialogues and White trainee fears: Implications for education and training. *Cultural Diversity & Ethnic Minority Psychology*, *16*(2), 206–214. doi:10.1037/a0016112 PMID:20438159

Sue, D. W., & Sue, D. (2016). *Counseling the culturally diverse: Theory and Practice* (7th ed.). Hoboken, NJ: Wiley.

Sue, D. W., Sue, D., Neville, H. A., & Smith, L. (2019). *Counseling the culturally diverse: Theory and practice* (8th ed.). Hoboken, NJ, US: John Wiley & Sons Inc.

Sue, D., Arredondo, P., & McDavis, R. (1992). Multicultural counseling competencies and standards: A call to the profession. *Journal of Multicultural Counseling and Development*, *70*(4), 477–486. doi:10.1002/j.1556-6676.1992.tb01642.x

Sue, D., Capodilupo, C., Torino, G., Bucceri, J., Holder, A., Nadal, K., & Esquilin, M. (2007). Racial microaggressions in everyday life: Implications for clinical practice. *The American Psychologist*, *62*(4), 271–286. doi:10.1037/0003-066X.62.4.271 PMID:17516773

Sumontha, J., Farr, R. H., & Patterson, C. J. (2016). Social support and coparenting among lesbian, gay, and heterosexual adoptive parents. *Journal of Family Psychology*, *30*(8), 987–996. doi:10.1037/fam0000253 PMID:27709970

Sung, S., Simpson, J. A., Griskevicius, V., Kuo, S. I., Schlomer, G. L., & Belsky, J. (2016). Secure infant-mother attachment buffers the effect of early-life stress on age of menarche. *Psychological Science*, *27*(5), 667–674. doi:10.1177/0956797616631958 PMID:26980153

Sy, M. (2018). A myth about unconditional self-acceptance [Web log post]. Retrieved from http://albertellis.org/a-myth-about-unconditional-self-acceptance/

Szymanski, D. M., Kashubeck-West, S., & Meyer, J. (2008). Internalized heterosexism: Measurement, psychosocial correlates, and research directions. *The Counseling Psychologist*, *36*(4), 525–574. doi:10.1177/0011000007309489

Tang, J. Y., Li, C., Rodger, R. F., & Ballou, M. (2016). Ethnic differences in the effectiveness of cognitive behavioral therapy combined with medication: Comparing Asian American and white psychiatric patients. *Asian Journal of Psychiatry*, *24*, 46–50. doi:10.1016/j.ajp.2016.08.012 PMID:27931905

Tatum, B. D. (1997). *Why are all the black kids sitting together in the cafeteria?* New York, NY: Basic Books.

Tello, A. M. (2015). *The psychosocial experiences of Latina first-generation college graduates who received financial and cultural capital support: A constructivist grounded theory* (Doctoral dissertation). Retrieved from ProQuest. (3702397)

Tello, A. M., & Lonn, M. R. (2017). The role of high school and college counselors supporting the psychosocial and emotional needs of Latinx first-generation college students. *The Professional Counselor*, *7*(4), 349–359. doi:10.15241/amt.7.4.349

Tervalon, M., & Murray-Garcia, J. (1998). Cultural humility versus cultural competence: A critical distinction in in defining physician training outcomes in multicultural education. *Journal of Health Care for the Poor and Underserved*, *9*(2), 117–125. doi:10.1353/hpu.2010.0233 PMID:10073197

The Association of Religion Data Archives. (2010). *County membership report: Bonneville county, Idaho.* Retrieved from http://www.thearda.com/rcms2010/r/c/16/rcms2010_16019_county_adh_2010.asp

The Book of Mormon . (1981). Salt Lake City, UT: The Church of Jesus Christ of Latter-Day Saints. (Original work published 1830)

The Church of Jesus Christ of Latter-Day Saints. (n.d.a). *About us*. Retrieved from https://www.mormon.org/about-us

The Church of Jesus Christ of Latter-Day Saints. (n.d.b). *Gospel principles*. Retrieved from https://www.lds.org/manual/gospel-principles/introduction?lang=eng

The Church of Jesus Christ of Latter-Day Saints. (n.d.c). *Scriptures*. Retrieved from https://www.lds.org/scriptures?lang=eng

The Church of Jesus Christ of Latter-Day Saints. (n.d.d). *Facts and statistics: United States*. Retrieved from: https://www.mormonnewsroom.org/facts-and-statistics/country/united-states

The Church of Jesus Christ of Latter-Day Saints. (n.d.e). *Prophets*. Retrieved from: https://www.lds.org/manual/true-to-the-faith/prophets?lang=eng

The Church of Jesus Christ of Latter-Day Saints. (n.d.f). *How the Church is organized*. Retrieved from: https://www.lds.org/topics/church-organization/how-the-church-is-organized?lang=eng&old=true

The Pell Institute. (2008). *Moving beyond access: College success for low-income first-generation students*. Retrieved from http://www.pellinstitute.org/downloads/publications-Moving_Beyond_Access_2008.pdf

Thompson, W. E., & Hickey, J. V. (2005). *Society in focus: An introduction to sociology* (5th ed.). Boston, MA: Allyn & Bacon.

Turner, M. J. (2016). Rational emotive behavior therapy, irrational and rational beliefs and the mental health of athletes. *Frontiers in Psychology*, *7*(1423), 1–16. doi:10.3389/fpsyg.2016.01423 PMID:27703441

Tym, C., McMillion, R., Barone, S., & Webster, J. (2004). *First generation college students: A literature review*. Austin, TX: Research and Analytical Services.

U.S. Census Bureau. (2017). *Income and poverty in the United States; 2016*. Report No. P60-259. Retrieved from https://www.census.gov/content/dam/Census/library/publications/2017/demo/P60-259.pdf

U.S. Census Bureau. (2019). *Quick facts*. Retrieved from https://www.census.gov/quickfacts/fact/table/US/RHI725217#RHI725217

U.S. Department of Education. (2018). *The Condition of Education*. Retrieved from https://nces.ed.gov/pubs2017/2017144.pdf

U.S. Department of Health and Human Services Administration for Children and Families. Children's Bureau. (2016). *The AFCARS report: Preliminary FY Estimates as of October 20, 2017*. US Department of Health and Human Services. Retrieved from https://www.acf.hhs.gov/sites/default/files/cb/afcarsreport24.pdf

U.S. Department of Health and Human Services. (2015). *Administration on aging: Aging statistics*. Retrieved from: http://www.aoa.acl.gov/Aging_Statistics/index.aspx

U.S. Immigration and Customs Enforcement. (2018a). *SEVIS by the numbers: Biannual report on international student trends.* Retrieved from https://www.ice.gov/doclib/sevis/pdf/byTheNumbersApr2018.pdf

U.S. Immigration and Customs Enforcement. (2018b). *Student and exchange visitor program.* Retrieved from https://www.ice.gov/sevis

Uchino, B. N. (2004). *Social support and physical health: Understanding the health consequences of relationships*. New Haven, CT: Yale University Press. doi:10.12987/yale/9780300102185.001.0001

UKCISA. (2004). Broadening our horizons: International students in UK universities and colleges. London: UKCISA.

United Press. (2011). *Foreign student numbers in U.S. hit record.* Retrieved from http://www.upi.com/ Top_News/US/2011/11/14/Foreign-student-numbers-in-US-hit-record/UPI-58861321323005/

United States Census. (2014). *Household characteristics of opposite-sex and same sex households ACS 2014.* Retrieved from: http://www.census.gov/acs/www

Unrau, Y. A., Font, S. A., & Rawls, G. (2012). Readiness for college engagement among students who have aged out of foster care. *Children and Youth Services Review*, *34*(1), 76–83. doi:10.1016/j.childyouth.2011.09.002

Valencia-Garcia, D., Simoni, J. M., Alegria, M., & Takeuchi, D. T. (2012). Social capital, acculturation, mental health, and perceived access to services among Mexican American women. *Journal of Consulting and Clinical Psychology*, *80*(2), 177–185. doi:10.1037/a0027207 PMID:22329824

Van Der Merwe, E., & Greeff, A. P. (2015). Infertility-related stress within the marital relationship. *International Journal of Sexual Health*, *27*(4), 522–531. doi:10.1080/19317611.2015.1067275

Vega, D., & Moore, J. L. III. (2012). African American and Latino first-generation students: Implications for teachers, school counselors, university officials, parents, and students. In T. Hicks & A. Pitre (Eds.), *Research studies in higher education: Educating multicultural college students* (pp. 3–25). Lanham, MD: University Press of America, Inc.

Velasquez, R. J., Gonzales, M., Butcher, J. N., Castillo-Canez, I., Apodaca, J. X., & Chavira, D. (1997). Use of the MMPI-2 with Chicanos: Strategies for counselors. *Journal of Multicultural Counseling and Development*, *25*(2), 107–120. doi:10.1002/j.2161-1912.1997.tb00321.x

Vélez, V. N. (2016). Organizing for change: Latinx im/migrant parents, school decision-making, and the racial politics of parent leadership in social reform. *Association of Mexican American Educators Journal*, *10*(3), 108–125.

von Borell de Araujo, B., Tureta, C., & von Borell de Araujo, D. (2015). How do working mothers negotiate the work-home interface? *Journal of Managerial Psychology*, *30*(5), 565–581. doi:10.1108/JMP-11-2013-0375

von Humbolt, S. V., & Leal, I. (2017). Older adults adjustment to aging: The impact of sense of coherence, subjective well-being and socio-demographic, lifestyle and health related factors. *European Psychiatry, 41*. doi:10.1016/j.eurpsy.2017.01.1134

Vonofakou, C., Hewstone, M., & Voci, A. (2007). Contact with outgroup friends as a predictor of meta-attitudinal strength and accessibility of attitudes toward gay men. *Journal of Personality and Social Psychology*, *92*(5), 804–820. doi:10.1037/0022-3514.92.5.804 PMID:17484606

Vontress, C. E. (1979). Cross-cultural counseling: An existential approach. *The Personnel and Guidance Journal*, *58*(2), 117–122. doi:10.1002/j.2164-4918.1979.tb00363.x

Vromans, L., Schweitzer, R. D., & Lowe, R. (2010). Narrative therapy for adults with major depressive disorder: Improved symptom and interpersonal outcomes. *Psychotherapy Research*, *21*(1), 4–15. doi:10.1080/10503301003591792 PMID:20306354

Wade, J. C., & Donis, E. (2007). Masculinity ideology, male identity and romantic relationship quality among heterosexual and gay men. *Sex Roles*, *57*(9-10), 775–786. doi:10.100711199-007-9303-4

Walker, M. (2008). Power and effectiveness: Envisioning an alternate paradigm. *Women & Therapy*, *31*(2-4), 129–144. doi:10.1080/02703140802146266

Walsh, W. M., & McGraw, J. A. (2002). *Essentials of family therapy: A structured summary of approaches* (2nd ed.). Denver, CO: Love Publishing.

Wang, C. D., & Castañeda-Sound, C. (2008). The role of generational status, self-esteem, academic self-efficacy, and perceived social support in college students' psychological well-being. *Journal of College Counseling*, *11*(2), 101–118. doi:10.1002/j.2161-1882.2008.tb00028.x

Ward, L., Siegel, M. J., & Davenport, Z. (2012). *First-generation college students: Understanding and improving the experience from recruitment to commencement*. San Francisco, CA: Joey-Bass.

Ward, L., Siegel, M. J., & Davenport, Z. (2012). *First-generation college students: Understanding the experience from recruitment to commencement*. San Francisco, CA: Jossey-Bass.

Warner, L. R. (2008). A best practices guide to intersectional approaches in psychological research. *Sex Roles*, *59*(5-6), 454–463. doi:10.100711199-008-9504-5

Warnick, J. (1995). *Listening with different ears: Counseling people over 60*. Ft. Bragg, CA: QED Press.

Warren, S. T., Lim, S. J., Nicholson, J., Ryalls, E. D., Cooley, S. C., Goodman, M., ... Kyles, L. (2012). The effect of participants' race and gender on perceptions of STEM and non-STEM images of women. *The International Journal of Science in Society*, *4*(3), 63–73. doi:10.18848/1836-6236/CGP/v04i03/59284

Watson-Singleton, N. M. (2017). Strong Black woman schema and psychological distress: The mediating role of perceived emotional support. *Journal of Black Psychology, 43*(8), 778-788. doi: 10.11770095798417732414

Wekhian, J. A. (2016). Acculturation process of Arab-Muslim immigrants in the United States. *Asian Culture and History*, *8*(1), 88–99. doi:10.5539/ach.v8n1p89

Wertsch, M. E. (1991). *Military brats: Legacies of childhood inside the fortress*. New York, NY: Harmony Books.

Whitaker, C., & Keith, D. V. (1982). Symbolic-experiential family therapy. In J. R. Neill & D. P. Kniskern (Eds.), *From psyche to system: The evolving Therapy of Carl Whitaker* (pp. 330–378). New York, NY: Guilford.

White, A. M., DeCuir-Guncy, J. T., & Kim, S. (2019). A mixed methods exploration of the relationship between the racial identity, science identity, science self-efficacy, and science achievement of African American students at HBCUs. *Contemporary Educational Psychology*, *57*, 54–71. doi:10.1016/j.cedpsych.2018.11.006

White, J., Flynt, M., & Draper, K. (1997). Kinder Therapy: Teachers as therapeutic agents. *International Journal of Play Therapy*, *6*(2), 33–49. doi:10.1037/h0089407

White, M. (2007). *Maps of narrative practice*. New York, NY: Norton.

Wilcove, G. L., Schwerin, M. J., & Kline, T. (2009). Quality of life in the US Navy: Impact on performance and career continuance. *Military Psychology*, *21*(4), 445–460. doi:10.1080/08995600903206362

Williams, R. G., Baker, S. B., & Williams-DeVane, C. R. (2018). Effects of customized Counseling Interventions on Career and College Readiness Self-Efficacy of Three Female Foster Care Youth. *The Professional Counselor*, *8*(2), 159–174. https://doi-org.ezproxy.nccu.edu/10.15241/rgw.8.2.159

Williams, S. L., Laduke, S. L., Klik, K. A., & Hutsell, D. W. (2016). A paradox of support seeking and support response among gays and lesbians. *Personal Relationships*, *23*(2), 296–310. doi:10.1111/pere.12127

Winkle-Wagner, R. (2010). College as life or death: The college choice and transition process of African American women. In T. L. Strayhorn & M. C. Terrell (Eds.), *The evolving challenges of Black college students: New insights for policy, practice, and research* (pp. 26–48). Sterling, VA: Stylus, Publishing.

Wintersteen, M. B., Mensinger, J. L., & Diamond, G. S. (2005). Do gender and racial differences between patient and therapist affect therapeutic alliance and treatment retention in adolescents? *Professional Psychology, Research and Practice*, *36*(4), 400–408. doi:10.1037/0735-7028.36.4.400

Woidneck, M. R., Pratt, K. M., & Gundy, J. M., Nelson, C. R., & Twohig, M. P. (2012). Exploring cultural competence in acceptance and commitment therapy outcomes. *Professional Psychology: Research and Practice, 43*, 227-233. doi:10/1037a0026235

Wood, K., Lambert, H., & Jewkes, R. (2007). Showing roughness in a beautiful way: Talk about love, coercion, and rape in South African youth sexual culture. *Medical Anthropology Quarterly*, *21*(3), 277–300. doi:10.1525/maq.2007.21.3.277 PMID:17937250

Woo, H., Jang, Y. J., & Henfield, M. S. (2015). International doctoral students in counselor education: Coping strategies in supervision training. *Journal of Multicultural Counseling and Development*, *43*(4), 288–304. doi:10.1002/jmcd.12022

Worden, J. (2018). *Grief counseling and grief: A handbook for the mental health practitioner*. New York, NY: Springer Publishing Company, LLC. doi:10.1891/9780826134752

Worden, W. (2008). *Grief counseling and grief therapy: A handbook for the mental health practitioner*. New York, NY: Springer. doi:10.1891/9780826101211

World Health Organization. (2002). *Active Aging: A policy framework*. Geneva, Switzerland: Author.

Yalom, I. (2009). *Staring at the sun: Overcoming the terror of death*. San Francisco, CA: Jossey Bass.

Yalom, I. D. (1980). *Existential psychotherapy*. New York: Basic Books.

Yoon, E., Change, C., Kim, S., Clawson, A., Clearly, S. E., Hansen, M., ... Gomes, A. M. (2013). A meta-analysis of acculturation/enculturation and mental health. *Journal of Counseling Psychology*, *60*(1), 15–30. doi:10.1037/a0030652 PMID:23163612

Yosso, T. J., Smith, W. A., Ceja, M., & Solórzano, D. G. (2009). Critical race theory, racial microaggressions, and campus racial climate for Latina/o undergraduates. *Harvard Educational Review*, *79*(4), 659–690. doi:10.17763/haer.79.4.m6867014157m7071

Young, J. L., Ero-Tolliver, I., Young, J. R., & Ford, D. Y. (2017). Maximizing opportunities to enroll in advanced high school science courses: Examining the scientific dispositions of Black girls. *Journal of Urban, Teaching, and Research*, *13*, 174–183.

Young, J. L., Young, J. R., & Ford, D. Y. (2017). Standing in the gaps: Examining the effects of early gifted education on Black girl achievement in STEM. *Journal of Advanced Academics*, *28*(4), 290–312. doi:10.1177/1932202X17730549

Zeiler, K., & Malmquist, A. (2014). Lesbian shared biological motherhood: The ethics of IVF with reception of oocytes from partner. *Medicine, Health Care, and Philosophy*, *17*(3), 347–355. doi:10.100711019-013-9538-5 PMID:24395218

Zinzow, H. M., Britt, T. W., Pury, C. S., Raymond, M., McFadden, A. C., & Burnette, C. M. (2013). Barriers and facilitators of mental health treatment seeking among active-duty army personnel. *Military Psychology*, *25*(5), 514–535. doi:10.1037/mil0000015

About the Contributors

Bonnie King, Ph.D., LPC, NCC, is an Assistant Professor at Midwestern State University in the Department of Counseling, Kinesiology, and Special Education. She works as a counselor in a small private practice in Dallas, Texas. Her research and teaching interests include international counseling, best practices for counseling LGBT and transgender client populations, and counseling in green space. Dr. King attended the Texas State University and University of New Orleans, and worked in an international school counseling role in Vietnam. She has counseling experience in school counseling, drug rehabilitation, private practice, and community mental health settings. Bonnie is currently the treasurer/secretary for the Texas Association of Lesbian, Gay, Bisexual and Transgender Issues in Counseling.

Tiffany Stewart is an Associate Professor at Midwestern State University. She has been involved in the counseling profession for over 15 years, in the areas of rehabilitation, community mental health, school, college, and private practice. Dr. Stewart is a Licensed Professional Counselor in Texas. She is currently a Regional Director for the Texas Counseling Association and holds professional memberships in the American Counseling Association (ACA), the Association for Counselor Education and Supervision (ACES), the Texas Counseling Association (TCA), and the Texas Association for Counselor Education and Supervision (TACES). She earned a bachelor's degree in Psychology from Southern University at New Orleans, a master's degree in Rehabilitation Counseling from Minnesota State University, Mankato, and a Ph.D. in Counselor Education and Supervision from the University of Akron. Her research interests include multicultural counseling, school counseling, urban education, advocacy, and counseling children. In her free time she enjoys reading, traveling, and exercising

* * *

Noreal Armstrong began her role at Montreat on June 1, 2016 as an Assistant Professor for the Adult and Graduate Studies Clinical Mental Health Counseling program. Within six months of her start date, Dr. Armstrong spearheaded the development of the Montreat College Counseling and Training Clinics for all three campuses. The clinic allows Montreat counseling students to provide free counseling to our local community members. She also assisted the department in its successful acquisition of CACREP accreditation in spring of 2018. Dr. Armstrong restructured the course offering format to a full-term semester and has shortened the CMHC program to two and half years while maintaining the integrity and rigor of the program. On June 1, 2018, Dr. Armstrong began serving as Department Chair for the Clinical Mental Health Program. During her nine years in the counseling profession Dr. Armstrong has worked in inpatient and outpatient settings, facilitated group, couple, and individual counseling, and supervised counseling interns. She is a licensed professional counselor supervisor, a national certified counselor, and a licensed chemical dependency counselor. Dr. Armstrong earned her Bachelor's in Psychology from Stephen F. Austin State University. She completed her Master's in Counseling Psychology from Texas A&M-Texarkana while teaching American Sign Language at Texas High School. Finally, Dr. Armstrong graduated from the University of Texas at San Antonio with her doctorate in Counselor Education and Supervision. Her dissertation was titled "A Phenomenological Study of the Lived Experience of Deaf Adults Participating in Alcoholics Anonymous in the United States." Dr. Armstrong has received service awards for her active participation in community, church, and school events. She the former Faculty Advisor for the Mu Chi Chapter of Chi Sigma Iota, an international counseling honor society. She has two published articles, a book chapter published, and has numerous presentations at local, state, regional, and national levels. Dr. Armstrong provides service to the counseling profession by being an active member in various ACA divisions and branches and enjoys fostering positive mentoring relationships.

Margaux H. Brown, PhD, LPC, NCC, is an Assistant Professor at Augusta University. She currently serves as the coordinator of the school counseling programs and is the faculty co-sponsor for Chi Sigma Iota. She holds a Ph.D. in Counseling from George Washington University, a Master's degree in Education and Human Development from GWU, and a Bachelor's degree in English from the College of William and Mary. Dr. Brown focuses her research on marginalized populations, school counseling, and counselor development. Her professional service includes national and state-level committees. Prior to joining the Counselor Education faculty at Augusta University, Dr. Brown served as faculty at GWU. Dr. Brown was a classroom teacher for five years and trained special education teachers to work with youth with emotional and behavioral disorders.

Szu-Yu Chen, Ph.D., a licensed professional counselor, national certified counselor, and registered play therapist. She earned her doctoral degree in counseling with a specialization in play therapy. She is an assistant professor of counseling department at Palo Alto University. She has worked with diverse populations in a variety of settings, including schools, community agencies, psychiatric hospital, and private practice. Her research interests include humanistic play therapy, family play therapy, school-based play therapy, and multicultural counseling and supervision.

Jeffrey K. Christensen, PhD, is an Assistant Professor at Lewis and Clark College, in Portland OR. He teaches Introduction to Assessment, Practical Skills for Counselors, and provides supervision to students in their practicum and internships. His research interests include student evaluation and remediation, survivors of suicide, and race and gender stereotypes depicted in video games.

Megan Clunan is an Assistant Professor within the Psychology and Human Services Department of Montreat College in Montreat, North Carolina. Dr. Clunan earned her BA from Florida State University in International Affairs. Dr. Clunan's graduate degrees were earned from the New Orleans Baptist Theological Seminary -- a MA in Marriage and Family Counseling, a Masters of Theology, and a PhD in Psychology and Counseling. Dr. Clunan is a Licensed Professional Counselor, a Licensed Mental Health Counselor and certified Supervisor for Mental Health Counseling and Marriage and Family Therapy interns pursuing licensure. She has extensive experience working with survivors of childhood sexual abuse trauma, at-risk youth, and issues related to marriage and family. She is certified in various evidence-based models, including Trauma Focused Cognitive Behavioral Therapy.

Kristen Dickens, Ph.D., NCC, ACS, is an Assistant Professor at Georgia Southern University in the Counselor Education Program. Her current research interests include multiple roles and relationships in counselor education, ethics and value conflicts, multicultural issues in counseling, and family systems work. Dr. Dickens has experience working in a variety of community mental health settings, including intensive outpatient facilities, university outpatient centers, inpatient treatment centers for eating disorders, and in-home counseling services.

Cort M. Dorn-Medeiros has been a full-time counselor educator since 2015 and currently serves as an Assistant Professor of Counseling Psychology in the Lewis & Clark College Graduate School of Education and Counseling in Portland, OR. Dr. Dorn-Medeiros' specialties include the assessment, diagnosis, and treatment of addictive disorders, substance use within LGBTQ+ populations, pedagogical strategies for teaching multicultural courses, and remediation and gatekeeping in counselor education.

Emeline C. Eckart is an Assistant Professor in the Department of Counseling at the University of Indianapolis. Prior to her career in counselor education she completed nine years of active duty service in the U.S. Navy as a helicopter pilot, four years as a flight instructor in the Navy Reserve component, and is currently a member of the Individual Ready Reserve force. As a clinical counselor she has worked in both the private and non-profit sector with a specialization in counselor supervision, and is currently a board member for the Indiana Counseling Association. Her research interests are on how female counselors and counselor educators manage work and family roles, professional advocacy, and the military population. She holds a BA from Marquette University, an MS from Capella University, and a Ph.D. in Counselor Education from University of New Orleans.

Chantel K. Gant is a licensed professional counselor board-approved supervisor, licensed addiction counselor, and national certified counselor. She is a doctoral student in the Counselor Education program at the University of New Orleans. She is the Associate Director of a college counseling center in her hometown of New Orleans. Chantel earned her master of education in professional counseling from the University of Georgia and bachelor of science in psychology from Xavier University of Louisiana. Chantel is a member of CSI, KDP, Psi Chi, ACA, LCA, AMCD, and ACCA. Her experiences include providing academic, mental health, and substance abuse counseling. She has presented at local workshops and summits, and a national conference. Chantel was one of the presenters for the virtual event SAMSHA BRSS for Recovery Live! Supporting Underrepresented College Student Populations Experiencing or At Risk of Serious Mental Illness or Substance Use Disorders.

John J. S. Harrichand, Ph.D., LPC, NCC, CCMHC, CCC is an Assistant Professor of Counselor Education at the College at Brockport State University of New York. He actively engages in program review, advocacy, mentorship, research, writing, and professional service, and frequently presents at local, state, regional, and national conferences. He publishes in the areas of counselor education leadership and burnout, group counseling, doctoral student research development in counselor education, emotional intelligence and counselor burnout, LGBTQ+ issues in counseling, professional and social justice advocacy, and international counseling students' education and retention. His teaching and research interests include counselor leadership and wellness, professional advocacy, multicultural counseling, counseling theories, diagnosis and treatment planning, emotional intelligence, resilience and post-traumatic growth, and addictions. His clinical experience encompasses working in community mental health and college and university counseling settings.

Justin Henderson is assistant professor in Professional Mental Health Counseling and faculty in the Department of Counseling Psychology at Lewis & Clark College in Portland, Oregon. Additionally, he is director of the Lewis & Clark Community Counseling Center, which is the training clinic for the Professional Mental Health Counseling, Professional Mental Health Counseling–specialization in Addictions, and Marriage, Couples, and Family Therapy programs. He is a licensed psychologist and a National Certified Counselor. He has clinical experience in a wide array of contexts including: university counseling centers, hospitals, inpatient and outpatient treatment facilities, schools, and residential treatment programs. He has a strong interest in supervision and training, having experience supervising both master's and doctoral students in counseling and psychology. He is a member of the American Counseling Association, Association for Counselor Education and Supervision, Counselors for Social Justice.

Elise Johns, Ph.D., LPC-S, NCC, is an Assistant Professor at Nicholls State University in the Department of Psychology, Counseling and Family Studies. She holds a doctorate in Counselor Education from the University of New Orleans and a master's in Counseling Psychology from Troy University. Dr. Johns has clinical experience in outpatient mental health treatment, grief counseling, crisis intervention, training clinics, and private practice. Dr. Johns has maintained a private practice in New Orleans for the past 5+ years. She is a Licensed Professional Counselor, a Licensed Professional Counselor Approved Supervisor and a National Certified Counselor. Dr. Johns' research and teaching interests include multicultural competencies, spirituality, and ethical competencies of clinicians working with terminally ill clients.

Krista E. Kirk, Ph.D., NCC is an Assistant Professor of Counselor Education at Liberty University. Through her identity as a counselor educator, she continually engages in advocacy and mentorship, while publishing in the areas of counselor educator development, gatekeeping, and social justice issues. In addition to being a professor, her previous clinical work has been in various settings including both the private and non-profit sector. She currently provides counseling services for a non-profit institution in Bronx, NY, with the mission of meeting the needs of this under-served population. Her research interests include identifying adaptive treatments for those with intellectual disabilities, mental illness stigma, and mental illness stigma in religious communities.

Ian Lertora is an assistant professor in Counselor Education at Texas Tech University in Lubbock, Texas. Ian has worked in various settings over the past 5 years that include trauma-focused play therapy, community counseling, college counseling, and career counseling. When working on colleges campuses Ian provided support for international student populations by providing transitional, academic, career, and mental health support. His areas of research are college student transitions, international student transitions, application of relational-cultural theory, and developing innovative and interactive teaching strategies for counselors and counselor educators.

Joy Maweu Mwendwa is an Assistant Professor in the Department of Counselor Education and Family Studies at Liberty University. She has worked in the counseling field for over 10 years at different capacities including serving as a counselor, counseling supervisor, and a counselor educator. Her work has been in varied settings such as in a college counseling center, in community mental health and in church settings, and internationally in Kenya, Tanzania, and Malawi. Her research interests are on qualitative and indigenous research methodology, the development of the profession of counseling internationally, multicultural competence and the supervisory relationship. She holds a Ph.D. in Counselor Education and Supervision from Old Dominion University.

Meredith A. Rausch, Ph.D., NCC, is an Assistant Professor at Augusta University. Her research focuses on underserved populations and mentorship.

Katie K. Sacco, M.Coun., LPC, NCC, is a first year PhD student in Counselor Education and Counseling at Idaho State University. She completed her masters of counseling in student affairs at Idaho State University in the spring of 2018. She has experience in career counseling as well as mental health counseling and is pursuing school counseling interests in the PhD program. She is a current professional member of ACA, MGCA, ICA, and ACES and was recently selected as an emerging leader for MGCA. Her current research interests focus heavily on military and veteran populations, LGBTQ+ populations, cultural intersectionality, and equine assisted counseling.

Brianne E. Scott, M.Coun., LPC, NCC, is a first year PhD student in the Counselor Education and Counseling program at Idaho State University. She is a current professional member of ACA, ACES, AMCD, and ALGBTIC and a past co-president of the Zeta Sigma Chi chapter of Chi Sigma Iota. In the summer of 2018, she completed her masters in Clinical Mental Health Counseling at Valparaiso University located in Valparaiso, Indiana. Her clinical experience includes working with adults and adolescents with substance use disorders in residential and outpatient settings. Her current research interests include cultural identity development, professional counseling program competencies, religion and spirituality, social justice and advocacy, and substance use populations.

Angelica M. Tello is an Assistant Professor in the Counseling Program at the University of Houston – Clear Lake. She received her Ph.D. in Counselor Education and Supervision from the University of Texas at San Antonio (UTSA). Dr. Tello also holds a Master's degree in Community Counseling from UTSA, is a Licensed Professor Counselor (LPC) in the state of Texas, and is credentialed as a National Certified Counselor (NCC). Her counseling experience includes working with college students at a public four-year institution and working in community agencies serving children and adolescents. Her primary focus has been working with students from underserved communities who have limited access to financial and academic resources. In 2015, Dr. Tello received ACA's Courtland C. Lee Multicultural Excellence Award for her commitment to providing counseling services to underserved clients. She also has been recognized as a 2013 NBCC Minority Fellow, a 2013 ACES Presidential Fellow, and a 2012 SACES Emerging Leader. Moreover, she has presented at counseling conferences on the state, regional, national, and international levels. Her presentations focus on topics related to multicultural counseling, diversity, and social justice. Dr. Tello's counseling and research interests include working with first-generation college students, bilingual counselor supervision, and Latinx counseling experiences.

Ari-Elle West, B.S., is currently seeking her Master's degree in Counselor Education with an emphasis in Clinical Mental Health Counseling. She is a counselor intern at East Central Regional Hospital and previously volunteered at a local sexual trauma center in Greenwood, South Carolina. She is passionate about advocacy for individuals with severe and persistent mental illness as well as underserved populations. Her research interests consist of attachment theory and suicide risk, prevention, and intervention. She has presented on attachment theory from early childhood to emerging adulthood at several regional conferences. She currently works as a Graduate Assistant for the Department of Advanced Studies and Innovation in the College of Education at Augusta University. In her free time, she enjoys spending time with her family. She anticipates pursuing doctoral studies in the future.

Haley D. Wikoff, Ph.D., LCPC, NCC, is an Assistant Professor at Western Illinois University. Her research interests focus on how counselors can engage with, and work to, create safe and inclusive environments for LGBTQ families and youth LGBTQ advocacy.

Regina Gavin Williams is a Clinical Assistant Professor in the Counselor Education program at North Carolina Central University She received her Ph.D. in Counseling and Counselor Education from North Carolina State University in 2016. Dr. Williams has worked in educational and community mental health settings, most recently working in student services within the NC State College of Education, and as a Licensed Professional Counselor primarily serving children and adolescents in the foster care system. Dr. Williams' research focuses on the career and college readiness and adult self-sufficiency of adolescents aging out of the foster care system, training therapeutic foster caregivers, and assisting adolescents with post-secondary education and career decision-making. She also focuses on enhancing the multicultural and social justice counseling competencies of counselors-in-training.

Index

L

M

N

O

P

Q

R

S

T

W

CPSIA information can be obtained
at www.ICGtesting.com
Printed in the USA
BVHW010806150420
577141BV00006BA/3

9 781799 800224